NOT JUST
TREES

NOT JUST TREES

The Legacy of a Douglas-fir Forest

Jane Claire Dirks-Edmunds
Foreword by Robert Michael Pyle

Washington State University Press
Pullman, Washington

Washington State University Press
P.O. Box 645910
Pullman, Washington 99164-5910
Phone: 800-354-7360   FAX: 509-335-8568
© 1999 by the Board of Regents of Washington State University
All rights reserved
First printing 1999

Printed and bound in the United States of America on pH neutral, acid-free paper. Reproduction or transmission of material contained in this publication in excess of that permitted by copyright law is prohibited without permission in writing from the publisher.

Cover photograph ©1998 John Warden/Alaska Stock Images

Library of Congress Cataloging-in-Publication Data

Dirks-Edmunds, Jane Claire.
    Not just trees : the legacy of a Douglas-fir forest / Jane Claire Dirks-Edmunds : with a foreword by Robert Michael Pyle.
       p.   cm.
    Includes bibliographical references (p.   ) and index.
    ISBN 0-87422-169-2 (cloth). —ISBN 0-87422-170-6 (pbk.)
      1. Forest ecology—Oregon—Saddle Bag Mountain Region.
    2. Douglas fir—Ecology—Oregon—Saddle Bag Mountain Region.
    3. Dirks-Edmunds, Jane Claire.   4. Saddle Bag Mountain (Or.)
    I. Title.
    QH105.07D57   1999   98-46721
    577.3'09795—dc21   CIP

To my mentors:
James Arthur Macnab, who unlocked the door
and
Victor Ernest Shelford, who unveiled the treasures within

Victor Ernest Shelford, 1877-1968   James Arthur Macnab, 1899-1985

Ballad of a Crayfish

I walked the creek on Sunday week
and heard a crayfish moan
and saw it rest a shriveled claw
upon a greenish stone.

"What sorrow lies behind your eyes
to cause this weary tone?"
"The poisons spread on fields above
where farms were once unknown

defile the bed where shellfish fed
and I am left alone
to crawl about this once sweet stream
from which all joy has flown."

"Then why not seek a forest creek
untamed and overgrown?"
"Death's spray is on the forest too;
there is no untouched zone."

The current, murmuring, concurred,
and with a whispered groan
the crayfish turned its belly up
and rolled down past the stone.

Ross Yates, 1998

Contents

Part IV: Essence of the Forest

Foreword

by Robert Michael Pyle

Y EARS AGO, when I was working as Northwest Land Steward for The
Nature Conservancy, I became interested in the Oregon giant earthworm. This remarkable animal may exceed sixty centimeters in length and
was known to occur only in certain rich, deep soils in the Willamette Valley.
In hopes of locating a colony that might be manageable, I made contact with
Dorothy McKey-Fender and her son Bill Fender, the recognized authorities
on western earthworms. Nothing much came of the project, and the continued existence of this amazing organism is still in question. But during my
interviews with Mrs. McKey-Fender, I learned of one of the most notable
ecological studies ever undertaken in the Pacific Northwest when she presented me with a 1958 paper that bore an intriguing title: "Biotic Aspection
in the Coast Range Mountains of Northwestern Oregon."

The idea of the paper, and the years of research that led to it (chiefly
1932-1938), was to characterize everything that could be learned about the
animals, plants, physical setting, elements, and their interaction with one
another and the seasons—the whole *oecos*. There was no precedent for such
work in the Northwest, and precious little of it was being done twenty years
later, as the age of specialization advanced. I was very attracted by the
premise, and though the tools were simple, the paper was fascinating. I always intended to try to learn more about that pioneering exercise in systems
ecology, and the man who organized the study and wrote the paper, James
Macnab. But time went by, I moved abroad, and when I later returned to the
Coast Ranges to live, the "Aspection" had retreated to a box and an occasional tickle in the back of my mind.

Another twenty years on, before Professor Macnab and his aspection
came back to me abruptly and delightfully when Keith Petersen of WSU

Press asked me to read a manuscript awaiting publication. The name of the author, Jane Claire Dirks-Edmunds, seemed familiar to me, and should have—I had received a letter from her just months before about a common concern. Now, here before me was the opportunity to read how this classic field study was conceived and carried out, by whom, and what was learned. And, just as compelling, as it happened, to get to know a gifted scientist-teacher and writer who worked alongside Macnab, and eventually carried his work much further herself.

Jane Claire Dirks began working with Professor Macnab, whom she always called Prof, when she was an undergraduate at Linfield College. She became the chief assistant for his studies in the field and the lab, the project's primary cheerleader, and in time, Prof's stand-in. Ultimately, years later, she replicated many of the original investigations in order to plot the changes that time and forestry had wrought. I read her manuscript with pleasure and eagerness, finding it warm and companionable, a bit like looking over the shoulders of those involved in those frequent forest treks to Saddleback Mountain. I came to know the field team, to anticipate Macnab's "Profisms," and to marvel at the challenges of plying a complex landscape for its ecological secrets—especially at a time when examples of comparable work, and resources for the undertaking, were few.

The Macnab Aspection appealed to me especially because of its wonderful name. ASPECTION: a view all about. Or, as Macnab defined it, "the seasonal rhythm of the presence and activities of conspicuous organisms within a community." It is what all naturalists hope for: to see a place from all sides, in all weathers. It is something we never achieve and always aspire toward. Most people I know have a special place, an island or a mountain, a vacant lot or a field or perhaps a forest that is more to them than the sum of its parts—even if anyone could ever count all the parts. But the opportunity, vision, and dedication to find out just what makes a place tick are as rare as the love of place is common. That a habitat as magnificent and little known as this old-growth forest became that special place for Professor Macnab and his team of students, followers, and woodsprites is our good luck, and a grace note in the history of American ecological research.

Place-portraits of such breadth and depth have seldom been attempted. I think of the Monks Wood National Nature Reserve in England, the Rocky Mountain Biological Laboratory in Colorado, the Yale Forest in Connecticut, and the H.C. Andrews Forest of Oregon State University, among the few I know. This Saddleback Mountain exploration was one of the first ecological omnibus studies in the West. Prof's people had the dedication and the curiosity, they built the skills and the tools, and they took the initiative to do it—to slog steep, muddy, snowy, buggy, and especially rainy trails far uphill, over and over again, to see what they could find—and that's what this book is about.

In *Not Just Trees*, we learn of the trees, of course, that made up the vast old-growth forests of the Oregon Coast Range. But we also read of the rest of the threads of the green fabric, from lichens to trilliums, and the animals, vertebrate and invertebrate, that make this special site their home. The effort that goes into collecting and identifying the plants, the small mammals, and the aerial, ground, and soil insects, is prodigious. The methods were learned or made up as they went along, like almost everything that happened on that charmed mountain.

As an account of a great field study, the book is invaluable. But I enjoyed it as much for the stories of the people who felt this work was important: Prof, working on his doctorate and the first really synthetic Northwest eco-portrait; Jane Claire, his student, field and lab assistant, and friend of the family, who would go off to graduate school to study under a great ecologist, Victor E. Shelford. She returned with her doctorate to assume responsibility as primary investigator; and a cast of other students, friends, and co-conspirators including Dorothy McKey and Kenny Fender, who would marry. In later years, Dorothy became an earthworm authority, while Kenny pursued entomology. (The much-reported Fender's Blue butterfly, once thought to be extinct but recently rediscovered and now the object of energetic conservation measures, was named for him.) Their adventures afield make an engaging narrative.

The sheer physical effort involved in these field studies, the many miles walked over rough terrain and back, the equipment carried, the repetitive tasks once they got there, the vicissitudes of Prof and the weather, all might have discouraged a lesser set of collaborators. That they not only carried on, but looked forward to each visit as a privilege, must have assured Macnab that he had the right crew. In particular, Jane Claire's persistence in carrying on even after Prof, even after logging, then after "salvage," is a saga of faith, hope, and fidelity that we seldom see in science today.

In fact, such studies are not done much today. The painstaking documentation of a single site through a sustained effort by a small team is passé, having been supplanted by huge group campaigns of specialists with no one even trying to integrate the whole into an "aspection" that a person could come close to grasping. In part, this is because the generalist, in academia, is dead or in hiding; in part, because contemporary tools are more complex and subtle, the statistical side of science all the more paramount, and the job simply bigger, as we come to understand just how complex the world can be.

Perhaps it was naive of Professor Macnab to imagine that he and his acolytes could truly case out the land. If so, it was a naiveté that permitted a fresh, innovative approach to a challenge that might have seemed all too daunting given more sophistication up front. Callow or not, the notion of an "aspection" ultimately produced one of the great generalist looks at an American landscape.

And it was an elegiac look, of course. A place such as Saddleback was indeed much more than trees. With its accreted knowledge, it should have become a national monument, a biosphere reserve, a cherished baseline for every other Coast Range forest that used to be. That it did not work out that way is a tragedy. It makes me all the more grateful that Jane Claire Dirks-Edmunds has given us this extraordinary portrait of a love affair with one particular place. It is the sort of a place that few of us will ever know, or ever even have the chance to know. How lucky we are that this intrepid band of friends and proto-ecologists saw it for us, and saw it and saw it, and that its loving scribe has told us in elegant, enjoyable, compelling, and ultimately heartbreaking terms, just what was vouchsafed to them by these lost woods.

Dr. Jane Claire Dirks-Edmunds became one of the major ecologists of her time, having apprenticed on Saddleback Mountain. How badly we need, once again, the whole view that she brought to the forest, and brings to us in this magical book. How grateful I am that she has brought Macnab's Aspection to life.

Prologue

*N*OT *JUST TREES* HAS BEEN, for me, a sixty-five year journey, often over paths of varied and unclear destination. The prelude to that journey began in the autumn of 1924 when I, as a sensitive twelve-year-old, newly transplanted from the Kansas plains, fell in love with the massive lichen-draped druids of Northwestern Washington. Before that, I had never seen, or even imagined, trees so huge, forests so fascinating.

Fate, a curve in the path, or whatever, removed me within a year from those venerable forests of Washington to the less verdant oak- and conifer-cloaked hills in the Umpqua Valley of Oregon where I attended Roseburg High School and worked for two years in a bank before enrolling at Linfield College.

That journey of unperceived destination, an enduring romance with an ancient forest, led to the writing of this book. It began on a field trip December 30, 1933, midway through my sophomore year at Linfield College in Oregon's Willamette Valley.

After that December day when I hiked through miles and miles of ancient forest on Saddleback Mountain in Oregon's Coast Range, I became an acolyte of that pristine forest, impelled by its every mood. Thus captivated, I was privileged to assist Professor James A. Macnab (Prof to us, his helpers) for three and a half years in his study of that forest community, a path that led me to graduate school.

During my final year in graduate school our ancient forest was destroyed by logging. Though grieved by that loss, I felt impelled to learn what would next occur.

Aspiration to keep an eye on the research site, plus a need for employment, lured me back to Linfield, to a job as assistant to the registrar and part-time instructor in biology.

That path was full of detours and road blocks. Nevertheless, it did permit me to visit the research site and to learn that, within two years of logging, weeds carpeted the ground which had been the forest's floor and, in eight more years, a mixture of brush and seedling conifers replaced those weeds.

Could it be, I wondered, that the tattered shreds of that ancient forest, like the ashes of the phoenix of mythology, are giving rise to a new forest?

I longed to make a detailed study of that special place but my teaching load was too demanding, my salary too meager. Nineteen years passed. A grant from the National Science Foundation finally activated my dream.

After three and a half years of data-gathering from a now thriving young forest, I was eager to tell the story of our ancient forest and its off-spring. Again, impediments blocked the way, but I kept on organizing data, and hoping.

In 1974 John Boling retired from his position as chair of the Biology Department at Linfield. We had worked together for years—first as student helpers under Prof in the 1930s and later as the Biology Department faculty. I decided to retire, too. New faculty members were taking over. Besides, my husband Ray—now a semi-invalid—needed more of my time. Perhaps I can write my story now, I thought. But, no, that path was not yet open.

In 1983 Ray died. I moved into a retirement home. The path now seemed clear. I began writing.

When the spotted owl controversy arose in the late 1980s, I made a temporary detour from the book to write op-eds to newspapers and letters to our politicians. Though my story of the forest was far from finished, I wanted my voice heard regarding this issue.

Finally, a decade later, the book, *Not Just Trees*, emerged.

I have relied on my memory for much of the anecdotal material used in the telling of this story. Fortunately, however, I have had Professor Macnab's field notes to keep me on track with dates, persons, and other factual details.

Hundreds of individuals have been involved, in one way or another, in the many years and varied phases of the Saddleback Mountain research and in the development of this book. I am grateful to all of them.

More than seventy systematists helped in Professor Macnab's research and an additional fifty in mine. These specialists gave of their time and ex-pertise in identifying the horde of little beasties we collected: the insects, spi-ders, slugs, snails, and other invertebrates, as well as the birds, mammals, and plants. Without their gifts of time and knowledge our forest's biota would be almost nameless.

Approximately one hundred student assistants, friends, acquaintances, curiosity seekers, and professionals participated in Prof's five years of field and lab work, and another half-hundred or so aided in my research that followed. Facets of information gathered by those people have "fleshed out the bones" of this story of the forest. At the same time the forest experience was pivotal to the lives of some participants.

During the five years of Prof's study, three couples met and were drawn together by the aura of that ancient forest. On December 1, 1935 Dorothy McKey and Kenneth Fender became acquainted on this, the first of many trips together.

Two years later, when Prof was winding down his field research and much of the work was being done at the college, Frances Westall and Howard Daniels met in the research lab where Frances was working. She had often run across Howard's name in the field notes and was eager to meet him. They soon discovered that they shared many interests in addition to the Saddleback research.

Milton Ray Edmunds and I met on April 20, 1935, a misty-moisty day with brief sunshine and light showers. Since Ray had studied forestry at Oregon State College, Prof had invited him that day to see the forest and take pictures. Prof stayed at Boyer cabin, leaving John Boling and me to introduce Ray to the research area and do some photography. In the weeks that followed, it became evident that our guest had been impressed as much with the young woman assistant he met that day as he had been with the forest.

Friendship, courtship, and, eventually, marriage followed each of these encounters: Dorothy and Kenny with a June 5, 1937 wedding; Frances and Howard on July 5, 1939; Ray and I on August 11, 1944.

Anecdotes involving the Fenders and the Danielses occur throughout *Not Just Trees*. However, the book does not tell that Kenny's fascination with "bugs" and tennis perhaps even more than his responsibility for a home and family, drew him away from college before he earned a degree. He became a rural mail carrier. Nevertheless, in 1951, Linfield granted him an honorary M.S. in recognition of his status as an internationally known specialist on Cantharidae, the soldier beetles.

I have lost contact with many of Prof's devoted helpers, but several, in addition to John Boling and me, became academicians: Dorothy McKey-Fender, besides raising a family of four and acquiring international recognition as an earthworm specialist, was a research associate at Portland State University; Frances Daniels supervised the Linfield general biology lab for several years; and Minnie Heseman Percival, Archie Strong, and Russel Hugg taught high school.

Arnold Soderwall, with a Ph.D. in endocrinology from Brown University, had a long stint of teaching and research at the University of Oregon. Mark Nickerson, Ph.D. and M.D., became Professor of Pharmacology and Therapeutics at Canada's McGill University and chairman of the department. Jim Henry was a lab technician before retiring to his ranch home in Kaysville, Utah. Eunice Boone Farschon became a homemaker and a librarian; James Kilen a public works engineer; and Bob Peck a radiological technician.

Special recognition is due Arthur Fairhill, one of Prof's most dedicated volunteers, who for several years trudged to and from the research station week after week, helping in any phase of the work where needed. He loved plants and served Linfield as caretaker of grounds and buildings until his untimely death.

In as much as Howard Daniels provided most of the photos of the ancient forest, besides aiding in the surveying of Prof's study area, it was natural that he and Frances became mainstays in my follow-up NSF study.

A corps of students assisted in the field, lab, or both during the years of the young forest research. Several wrote senior theses based upon data from the project, while five students—Bill Good, John Kerr, Dorwin Lovell, Nancy Myron Nunley, and Nick Simpson—did noteworthy personal studies referred to in the book.

Following graduation from Linfield, Bill Good attained a doctorate at the University of Wyoming and found his niche as a research specialist for the Western Agricultural Research Center at Montana State University. He says his work is "studying plants, the insects that feed on them, and the parasites of those insects"—work very similar to projects he did on Saddleback Mountain.

John Kerr reports from Shelter Island, New York, "I have been teaching life science and biology in the seventh and eighth grades for sixteen years. Over 2,000 students have heard about you, the Saddleback research area and my own research [the role of insects in decomposition of a fetal pig]. Each student does a research project. Many choose ecology."

Dorwin Lovell, one of my principal helpers in the field, produced a well-detailed senior thesis, "Ecology of the Soil Microfauna," using data tabulated from many soil samples. Now retired after thirty-three years of teaching in both public and private schools at Coos Bay, Oregon, he says, "Early on it was fun talking about 'bio-ecology' with students and fellow teachers. It was a new term to them and many [found the study] fascinating. I used my research paper and [information from the original study] in my classes. Students were always amazed at the number of animals in a small section of the earth. I was pleased to open up this world of ecology to them."

Nancy Myron Nunley put her inquiring mind to work on project after project while helping with the field research. After learning details of the life history of bronze flea beetles, she tackled the mindboggling task of identifying mushrooms and other fungal growths. Now a registered nurse, Nancy is enjoying a career as Public Health Manager for Yamhill County, Oregon. She is still fascinated with nature.

Nick Simpson, now a successful dentist at Waldport, Oregon, while doing a bird study in the young forest on Saddleback had a face to face encounter with a cougar. Nick reports, "We were in Denver recently and the museum had a cougar in the same position I remember from my experience. Still scared me....I am able to enjoy the environment to the fullest due to my education."

I am grateful for the interest in the research these and all my student helpers displayed and the contributions they made to the forest's story. That phase of the Saddleback Mountain research was supported by National Science Foundation grant G-8779.

My gratitude is extended also to the following individuals who helped in special ways.

Members of Linfield's Computer Science Department for the initial printing of *Not Just Trees* while in manuscript form, and Nancy Cook for proofreading that initial printing.

Grant Stockton for hours spent in solving computer puzzles.

Librarians Nancy Hori, National Park Service, who located a rare reference, and Lynn K. Chmelir, Linfield College, for her helpful, prompt, and cheerful responses.

Carl Zimmer, senior editor, *Discover Magazine*, for supplying references on mycorrhizal tree interactions by Suzanne Simard.

Dr. E.P. Odum for use of his photos. Frances Daniels for use of Howard's photos. Dorothy McKey-Fender and uncredited photofolk, for use of photos.

Dr. James K. Agee, Professor of Forest Ecology, University of Washington and Dr. Robert Michael Pyle, author, who reviewed the manuscript, caught errors, and made many helpful suggestions and encouraging comments. And a special thanks to Dr. Pyle for contributing the foreword.

Dr. Jane Lubchenco, Distinguished Professor of Zoology, Oregon State University; Dr. Anne Ehrlich, Senior Research Associate, Stanford University; Martha Bell Brookes, Forestry Sciences Lab, OSU; Dr. Ann Brodie,

Animal Sciences, OSU; Erica Prince, Counselor, Linfield College; Tom Booth, OSU Press, and many others who encouraged me to persevere even when the outcome seemed dubious.

My nephew, Jack Dirks, for his interest and contagious enthusiasm, his help in contacting publishers, and the vignettes he has supplied.

My sister, Myrtle Hartley, who has quietly bolstered me during the dozen years I have been working on the book, serving as a critic for many passages and patiently and uncomplainingly doing countless small chores to free me for more time with my writing.

I owe a tremendous debt of gratitude to five persons who changed mere opportunity into reality in the shaping and publishing of this story.

My mentor, James A. Macnab, who introduced me to the forest.

My beloved husband, Ray Edmunds, who chauffeured and accompanied me to Saddleback Mountain for most of the visits in the nineteen years from the time the ancient forest was logged until the NSF study of the young forest began. He also helped in that research as his health permitted. Without Ray's interest, his encouragement, and his unrelenting support, those visits to the young forest would not have occurred, the NSF research would never have been done, and *Not Just Trees* would not have been written.

Dorothy McKey-Fender has struggled along with me throughout the entire production of this volume. She has edited chapters, provided the story of native earthworms, named unfamiliar plants, supplied names and habits for countless insects, recalled "Profisms" and anecdotes, and many a time has clarified fine points of grammar. Her help has been only a phone call away! If I had not had Dorothy's help and encouragement I would have given up long ago.

Lyle Hubbard, Ph.D., now a retired professor from the University of Alaska at Juneau, and also one of my students from years gone by, has been my pillar of encouragement and help during the last several years. Lyle expresses regret that he graduated before my NSF research project and has only seen the present clearcut shambles of forest on Saddleback Mountain, neither the ancient forest nor even the thriving young growth. Lyle bolstered me when faced with a major revision of *Not Just Trees*, led me through the maze of confusion that resulted from changing computer systems, critiqued passages of text, compiled glossaries, and aided in countless other ways.

Keith Petersen, my editor at WSU Press, encouraging and helpful from my first contact, has been approachable and flexible. He has clarified and constrained my sometimes excessively wordy and erratic prose with gentle good humor. The successful completion of this project owes a great deal to the efforts of Keith and other members of the WSU Press staff.

I owe so much to so many. "Thank you" seems inadequate, but I *am* most grateful.

Sadly, Professor Macnab and many of his helpers, including Kenny Fender, John Boling, Howard Daniels, and my husband, Ray, are no longer living. In many ways *Not Just Trees* is a tribute to each of them.

I have waited long to tell this story of the forest.

The old-growth forest in the 1930s.

Part I

Babes in the Woods

Babes in the Woods

My dear, do you know, how a long time ago,
Two poor little babes, whose names I don't know
Were stolen away on a bright summer's day
And left in the woods, I've heard people say.

They sobbed and they sighed and they bitterly cried,
And the poor little babes, they lay down and died.

And when they were dead, the robins so red
Gathered strawberry leaves and over them spread.
And all the day long, they sang them this song
"Poor babes in the woods, poor babes in the woods."
-Author unknown

In the days of this research we were truly babes in the woods. Ecology was a new field of study without guide books and with very few examples.

*This little song from my childhood has a long history. According to I. Opie and P. Opie (*The Oxford Book of Children's Verse, *Oxford University Press, 1973, and* The Oxford Book of Narrative Verse, *Oxford University Press, 1983), it first appeared under the title* The Babes in the Wood *in 1595 as a twenty-verse narrative poem by an anonymous author. The Opies found it again, anonymously written, c. 1800 in four verses akin to the ones I learned in the early 1900s. Where that version came from no one seems to know.*

WASHINGTON

Pacific Ocean

Astoria

Seaside

Clatsop

Columbia

St. Helens

Vancouver

Garibaldi

Washington

Forest Grove

Portland

Tillamook

Tillamook

Tualatin

Yamhill

Newberg

McMinnville

Willamette River

Clackamas

Boyer

Grand Ronde

Lincoln City Otis

Saddleback Mtn.

99W

Salem

Marion

Polk

101

Newport

Lincoln

Albany

Corvallis

Linn

Benton

Willamette River

OREGON

Lane

Statute Miles

40   20   10   0

Kilometers

20   10   5   0

NORTH

Chapter One
Forest, a Living Being

Before us in the fading light stretched a great expanse of ancient forest northwesterly to Haystack Rock twenty miles distant at Pacific City on the ocean, north fifteen miles to Mt. Hebo, the highest peak in that part of the Oregon Coast Range, and eastward beyond ten-mile-distant Grand Ronde, past Valley Junction and Willamina to farmland in the Yamhill Valley. On that day, December 30, 1933, the only visible breaks in all that expanse were tiny clusters of buildings that formed the towns. Forest even hid the Salmon River Highway as it wound through the pass below.

We had scrambled from the trail nearby to reach this promontory near the top of 3,200-foot Saddleback Mountain and now stood in awed silence, hearing only the sighing of wind-stirred trees.

Finally, our leader, my college biology professor James A. Macnab, declared, "That forest extends northward far beyond Mt. Hebo, across the state of Washington, through British Columbia, into southeastern Alaska. In back of us it goes south all the way to San Francisco Bay, a great band of ancient trees—Douglas-firs, hemlocks, spruces, cedars, true firs, and redwoods. It's a *living being*, sheltering and sustaining a vast array of unknown animals and plants."

He paused, then added, "That's why we're here. That forest draws me like a magnet. I must uncover its secrets."

Reluctantly, as the last light slipped away, we left the viewpoint to retrace our steps down the mountain. Ahead lay an arduous hike of more than five miles.

Long before daylight that December morning, we had left Linfield College in McMinnville with Professor Macnab to visit his research site in the coniferous forest of the Coast Range. Prof, as we affectionately called him, was a bit of a Pied Piper—his infectious enthusiasm for this research made it easy to enlist others in the project. Arthur Fairhill, the custodian of buildings and grounds at Linfield; Minnie Heseman, a recent graduate teaching in a nearby high school; James Kilen, Prof's research assistant; and Howard Daniels, Kilen's friend and amateur photographer, all had accompanied Prof on other trips. For me this was a new venture.

I knew from field trips in Prof's geology class the year before that this snappy-eyed, red-headed Scotsman with the "cookie duster" mustache was energetic and could lead one on a merry chase. Now, as a sophomore majoring in biology, I was eager to learn more about his research. However, I was not fully prepared for the experiences of that day.

Leaving McMinnville, we followed the Salmon River Highway (now State Highway 18) westward toward the mountains, passing through Sheridan, Willamina, Valley Junction, and Grand Ronde before arriving at Boyer, barely over the line into Tillamook County.

The name Boyer commemorated the site of an overnight hostelry and toll gate run by John and Julia Boyer from 1908 to 1920, situated at the entrance to a toll road leading to the coast. Julia had died, but John and his son Mervin and his family still lived in this tiny valley where the Little Nestucca River has its source.

After parking his car near Mervin's home, a multipurpose log building serving also as service station and store on the recently opened highway, Prof visited briefly with Mervin. Then we began our hike, following the highway for about a mile before we entered the forest trail which led to the top of Saddleback Mountain.

Taking the lead in order to record signs of animal activity—including even the number of spider webs stretched across the trail since his visit the week before—Prof guided us over varied terrain.

At first we followed brief stretches of "corduroy" remnants of the old Salmon River toll road, littered with twigs, boughs, and trunks of trees blown down by a recent violent windstorm. Then after crossing the alder and fern-fringed channel of Little Salmon River and ascending a short, steep grade, we passed over Summit Prairie, a nearly flat plateau where lone Douglas-firs stood like giant sentinels above scattered alders and vine maples, clumps of hazelnuts, and an undergrowth of salal and ferns.

Beyond Summit Prairie the trail wound through ever-changing vistas of primeval forest. Ancient Douglas-firs and hemlocks, bearded with moss and lichens, dimmed the light and hushed our conversation. Waist-high sword fern banked both sides of the trail and extended among the trees. Here

and there groups of shiny green salal and Oregon grape stood out in contrast
to the rougher textured ferns, while branchlets of young hemlocks made lacy
patterns against the trunks of trees. Spindly red huckleberry shrubs, leafless
at this season, went almost unnoticed. A mat of mosses undulated over the
ground and covered decaying logs and fallen limbs. Sometimes an unobtru-
sive yew tree kept company with vine maples or hazelbrush and occasionally,
in moist places, we caught glimpses of the flat sprays of cedar boughs.

The grade was gentle, and at first mostly downward toward Salmon
River, but our travel was difficult because trees felled by the recent storm often blocked the trail. Though we managed to climb over or crawl under
some of the mammoth logs, many times we had to scout out a detour
through jumbles of fallen trunks, shattered tops, and tangled brush.

I was fascinated. Though I had been in forest many times since moving to the Northwest from the plains of Kansas as a twelve-year-old, I had
never seen so intimately anything like this endless display of huge conifers.
It was another world, silent and eerie.

Salmon River was a wide, swiftly-racing torrent. A substantial foot log
bridged the main channel. I approached this crossing with dismay, for I was
frightened by bodies of water and even more terrified at having to walk a log
across a stream. However, since the others proceeded without hesitation, I
concealed my anguish and slowly made my way. Getting over the remaining
narrow part of the river wasn't easy—it involved leaping across on a series of
boulders most of which were surrounded by rushing water and some of
which were even slightly submerged.

Beyond the river lay another nearly level area of massive trees before we
began the final, steady ascent to the research area. As we climbed, we saw
noble firs for the first time—huge trees, as large as the biggest Douglas-firs.
And there were more wind-thrown trees and snags toppled by that latest
storm, a total of fifty-three between the highway and the research site.

Roughly halfway up the mountain, a little less than a mile beyond the
river, at an elevation of about 1,500 feet, we reached a terrace of sorts. Leaving the main trail, we walked westward along the ridge 100 yards or so to the
research station, using logs as much as possible to keep our route hidden
from curious passers-by.

There was little to identify the area as a place of research. A crude lean-
to made of shakes salvaged from a nearby abandoned cabin served as a storage place for a supply of dry fuel and a few research materials. Naturally, it
was known as the "fire shelter." Barely six feet high at the side which opened
toward the fire, this shelter was too small for more than one or two to use as
a refuge from the elements.

The day was mild for December but cloudy and cool with temperature in the low forties. Since our clothes had become damp from a misty rain and the continual drip under the trees, someone started a fire as soon as we reached the station. While we relaxed by the fire eating our lunches, I reveled in the beauty of the setting.

All about us, deeply-grooved trunks of Douglas-firs, four to six feet in diameter and bare of branches for at least 100 feet, towered skyward like columns in a vast temple. Details of the trees' wide-spreading crowns were lost in the dark green canopy high above. Hemlocks, smoother of bark, stately and straight of trunk, reached up at least 150 feet into the lower branches of the firs. A short distance in front of us, an equally large smooth-barked noble fir added its branches to the canopy of green.

Young hemlocks seemed to be everywhere. Lacey-twigged infant trees graced the base of nearly every large fir or hemlock. Saplings, several inches in diameter, often stood alone hiding their tops among the lower branches of the parent trees, while a short distance up the ridge, "teenaged" hemlocks about fifteen feet tall clustered so closely that nothing but a sparse cover of moss survived beneath them.

Recently-fallen logs formed convenient pathways through scattered patches of sword fern, salal, and Oregon grape, while older logs, moss-covered and disintegrating, supported rows of young hemlocks or clusters of huckleberry and salal. The straight, stiff stems of red huckleberry bushes could be seen here and there, and Prof said that many kinds of flowering herbs would appear in the more open areas in spring and summer.

A sound coming up from the slope below attracted our attention. Looking closely, we saw a woodpecker hammering away on a snag—a large dead tree, topless from some winter storm and now pockmarked with holes made by birds as they searched for insects. Other snags in various stages of decay dotted the area, some mere stubs of crumbling wood.

A mat of mosses spread over the ground, the logs, the bases of tree trunks, and the upper surfaces of fallen limbs—everywhere except in the densest shade under the young hemlocks. Beneath the mosses, needles, decaying duff, and humus cushioned the ground for at least another two inches.

While we sat near the fire shelter chatting as we ate our lunches, someone asked Prof how he had happened to select this location for his research. "I hiked all over this mountain last year," he said. "Nearly every weekend I was out here, searching for a site typical of the Coast Range forest, either alone or with Leo Isaac or someone else from the Forest Service, or with Mervin Boyer.

"Mervin and I, especially, put in countless hours. He knows the old trails and where the early settlers' cabins had been. Finally, in February, I chose this place. It doesn't look like it has been affected by human settlement and it's a long way from the highway. I hope it's far enough from the main trail that it won't be disturbed by anyone going to the top of the mountain."

Hearing Prof's story and drinking in the beauty of the place had me almost mesmerized. Finally I asked, "Prof, do you have any idea how long it's taken for this place to get like this? How old these huge trees are?"

"The trees are somewhere between 250 and 300 years old," he responded. "Apparently in the mid-1600s, a great fire swept over this part of the mountain, destroying all but a few scattered trees. Those trees provided seed for this forest. If the fire was not intense, young fir trees may have begun growing immediately. However, if the fire was severe, burning all the organic matter out of the soil and leaving the area exposed to erosion, many years may have passed before the forest became reestablished.

"Over there across the ravine," he said, pointing toward the northwest, "there has been a more recent fire. Those trees are noticeably smaller and are only 50 to 100 years old. The Tillamook fire last August destroyed a lot of trees like these and studies have shown that similar burns, probably caused by lightning, have long been occurring in these forests. Periodic fires, landslides, or other natural calamitous events, such as the windstorm which toppled so many trees across our trail, have been essential for the survival of Douglas-firs. Though they are long-lived, they cannot live indefinitely, nor can young firs grow in the dense shades the ancient trees produce. Many changes take place in the forest while the fir trees grow to maturity. It also took eons of time and inconceivable numbers of plants, animals, and microorganisms to prepare the way for this magnificent forest."

I had learned about the evolution of life the year before in Prof's geology class, but for some reason I had not thought of the forest in that way.

Soon our time of rest and relaxation ended. Howard had begun taking candid photographs of everyone while we rested and now Minnie and Fairhill each picked up a net and set out to catch any insects or spiders they could find. Rising from his seat under the fire shelter, Prof said, "Come along, Jane Claire, Kilen and I are going to check the instruments and I'll tell you about them and the research."

Prof led the way for about 300 feet from the fire shelter along a large log to a place where the terrace sloped off toward the west. Talking as he walked, the Professor explained, "In this study I'm going to include the plants and all of the animals—not just birds and mammals but anything else we can find, including insects and all the creepy-crawlies. I'm particularly interested in earthworms.

"But that isn't all. This study is to be a complete ecological picture of this forest community, and to do that it must include the physical environment. Weather affects plant and animal activities. Together, weather and the activities of living things determine the seasons. That is why instruments are so important and why they must be read regularly, year-round, no matter how miserable the weather. At this time of year, when there isn't a great deal of plant or animal activity, checking these instruments is the most important thing we do."

Ahead I could see two small box-like shelters, painted green, a couple of galvanized metal cylinders, each about a foot high, and a metal device about eighteen inches high that remotely resembled a miniature windmill except that its four arms rotated horizontally instead of vertically.

"I put the instruments here on this slope where they'll be out of sight from the fire shelter in case some stranger discovers the research site. Besides, here they won't be affected by activities around the fire.

"Now this," he said, indicating the mock windmill, "is an anemometer or wind gauge. These cups at the tips of the arms catch the wind, rotating the wheel on its axis. As the wheel moves, the gauge on the axis records in miles whatever wind has blown through here between our weekly visits."

Moving on, we reached one of the two cylinders. "These are rain gauges. This one is where it will catch the drip from the trees and the other one is under a break in the canopy. That way I can learn what effect trees have on precipitation as well as what the total rainfall is." The gauges looked to me like oversized food cans with funnels for lids.

Moving into a patch of scattered salal, he continued, "Now over here are atmometers. When they work, they measure evaporation. They're crude and full of problems, but they're the only thing we have. This one needs attention. Kilen and I'll have to take care of it." I could see they were just jars of water with cuplike tops of clay.

"That shelter where Kilen is houses a clock-driven hygrothermograph," Prof said, pointing toward one of the boxes at the top of the slope. "It records changes in temperature and humidity on a paper chart. There is a thermometer inside the shelter that registers the highest and lowest temperatures at that level between our visits. We call that kind of thermometer a Maxi-Min.

"In that other shelter, a little farther down the hill, is a double thermograph. It's also clock-driven. One of its two thermometers records the temperature inside the shelter and the other records temperature a few feet away at the end of a cable beneath moss and soil.

"I have another Maxi-Min thermometer fastened to one of the trees which support the little platform in that cluster of small hemlocks up the slope from the fire shelter. It gives a comparable temperature record for fifteen feet above the ground. That's all the instruments I have at present, but I hope to get a ladder built up one of these hemlocks. Then we can have instruments 80 or 100 feet above the ground."

"These instruments must have cost a lot. Did the college buy them for you?" I asked.

"At first I had only a Maxi-Min thermometer. Then the college bought a few things, but the most expensive instruments, especially the recording ones, are on loan from either the Forest Service or the University of Nebraska."

"How did you get all these things up here?

"Kilen and various other helpers and I have packed them from the highway on our backs, an instrument or a shelter at a time. Since the shelters were made of panels, they were broken down and then reassembled after we got them here. Whenever an instrument needs repair or has to be returned to its owner, we have to pack it back down to the highway. It's an ongoing thing.

"Now, maybe you'd like to see what Minnie and Fairhill are doing. I've got to get Kilen to help fix that atmometer."

Minnie and Fairhill had put their nets aside and were searching for creatures which might be found living in and around a well-decayed log and an old rotten stump. That seemed to offer an opportunity for learning, so I joined them.

In the decaying wood we discovered a tiny salamander with a yellow stripe down its back, several small snails, a couple of beetles, a red mite, a centipede, many tiny white spiders, a false scorpion, fifteen thread-thin white worms, and about thirty tiny yellowish insects which Minnie said were springtails. We had no hint as to why any of them were there. I don't recall that we even commented about that "why." It seemed we were just collecting stuff for Prof.

About mid-afternoon Prof suggested that we hike up the mountain to learn how much damage the storm had done there. Initially, the trail meandered gently across the remainder of the terrace but, as the mountain became steeper, it zigzagged and crossed several small streams. Douglas-firs decreased in size as we climbed higher and, finally, medium-size noble firs replaced them entirely. Not far from our destination, a little stream crossed the trail near the base of a steep, rocky outcrop dotted with rhododendrons. There, Minnie declared that she was too tired to go any farther and Fairhill volunteered to make a fire and stay with her while the rest of us went on to the viewpoint.

At the saddle between the peaks of the mountain—the "Notch" as we called it—we left the trail for a brief, steep climb toward the west to the viewpoint. Even the largest trees at this 3,000-foot elevation were much smaller than those at the station, and most of them were younger. I was intrigued and charmed by the stiffly formal young noble firs. Hemlocks were common, and there were a few western red cedars. Dusk was settling inside the forest before we emerged at the viewpoint.

When we stepped back into the forest a few minutes later, after our distant view across the valley, trees blotted out even the faint light from the sky, engulfing us in darkness so intense it seemed we could reach out and touch it. Prof Macnab, apparently having eyes in his feet and being familiar with the trail, moved on to join the ones who had stayed down the trail, leaving Howard and Kilen to fend for themselves—and **me**.

We groped our way in the blackness aided only by the slender beam of a flashlight Howard had brought with him. I didn't know then that an experienced woodsman seldom uses a flashlight, preferring to depend upon light from the stars and the sensitivity of his feet to find his way in the night. Sometimes that light helped us to stay on the trail or to find it again when we were forced off by a fallen tree. At other times it confused us by distorting shadows and restricting our range of vision.

The trail should have been quite passable, but the recent storm had changed that. There were sixteen new downed trees between the station and the viewpoint. Those, added to the fifty-three between the highway and the station, made a never-ending series of obstructions. Coping with those wind-thrown trees in the dark terrified me. We clambered over many of them and crawled under others. But sometimes we had to feel our way along a fallen tree on uncertain footing away from the trail until we could get over, under, or around the obstruction. Then we had to relocate the trail.

I nearly panicked when we came to the river. I hadn't bargained for this nighttime crossing. *Why,* I asked myself, *had I thought this kind of outing would be fun?* There was no other way to get home. I had no choice. I had to give it a try. With the young man ahead holding the light and the other behind offering reassurance, I jumped cautiously from one boulder to the next, across the first narrow strip of swift water. Then, ever so slowly, we inched along the log spanning the main channel. Crossing the river was the most frightening part, but the whole trip from the lookout to the highway was a nightmare.

Arriving at the highway revived my spirits though I was physically exhausted and one of my hips ached. With my first step on the hard pavement I realized that the heel was missing from one of the leather boots I had borrowed from sister Dorothy. I hoped, since she was on her honeymoon, she wouldn't be too angry with her kid sister. Anyhow, I was too tired to worry about it. I still had a mile to go to reach the car. Thankfully, the way was on pavement, downhill, and with no obstructions.

The dawn of New Year's Eve was near when we got back to McMinnville. What a day it had been. Weary as I was, I had become captivated by that ancient forest. And I, a timid soul—not at all the rough and ready tomboy type—had survived the challenges of that grueling day.

Yet, when I finally fell asleep, I could not have guessed that on that December day I had discovered the focus for my life.

Chapter Two

Spring Comes to the Forest

THE ACHES AND PAINS of my first trip soon vanished and the hardships faded from memory. The lure of that forest haunted me.

When I returned in mid-February, wrens warbled by the trailside, buds on trees and shrubs were swelling, the trail had a freshly-plowed appearance from the tunneling of small mammals, and insect activity indicated a quickening of the pulse of life. On each later visit I saw new evidences of the forest's miraculous awakening from dormancy to the abundance of spring. I was hooked. I had to go back.

Now it was May 6, 1934, my eighth trip. When we reached Boyer at 7 a.m. I wondered what new venture awaited us.

As we hiked up the highway to the trail head we were a motley group strung out behind Prof. Since the weather was cool and unpredictable and a shower might occur almost without warning, we each had on our most waterproof clothing. Prof, Fairhill, Kilen, and Howard wore typical logger's garb—heavy "tin" pants and coats of canvas, topped by an old felt hat. Such luxury was not for students working their way through college or even former students living on a shoestring. Minnie, still in her first year of teaching, wore a tan jacket and brown whipcord riding breeches, topped with a multicolor knitted beret. I sported a navy blue sweater, brown whipcord breeches, and a much-worn red suede hat, while John Boling brought up the rear in a green Mackinaw, tan corduroy pants, and white stocking cap. As one of Prof's student assistants, John carried a packboard loaded with tools. No one had any of the many kinds of light rain gear in use today. It did not come into being until the Age of Plastics, following World War II.

We must have created quite a spectacle as we wound along through the woods—clambering over or crawling under the logs across the trail. It's too bad there was no one to see us. Prof brushed aside spider webs, counting and recording them along with mole, mouse, and shrew burrows and such creatures as slugs, snails, and orange-and-black millipedes. The presence of large black ground beetles, which we later learned to call *Scaphinotus,* "the snaileater," clearly indicated that spring had arrived.

Eyes and ears alert, we did little talking as we hiked along. The air was fresh with the indescribable fragrance of spring. The day overflowed with life. Winter wrens, chickadees, nuthatches, and other birds we could not yet identify warbled and sang—advertising their territories or calling mates. A blue grouse exploded from a tree near its dusting area beside the old toll road, and a black-capped, yellow-bodied Wilson's warbler chattered in the bushes near Little Salmon River.

And the plants! Yellow violets grew in profusion. Salmonberries and thimbleberries, in full leaf, were heavy with bloom and even bore a few ripe berries. Alder trees displayed new green finery.

On Summit Prairie, interlocked fronds of head-high bracken fern formed nearly impenetrable barriers, while three-feet-high younger stems, straight and slender, still held their fronds in tightly coiled fiddle necks. At trailside in the deeper woods, green Lilliputian sentinels stood guard above the moss carpet, each one a soon-to-open heart-shaped main leaf of a lily-of-the-valley sheathing a spike of tiny white flowers. Sprays of false Solomon's seal overhung the lilies-of-the-valley, and Clintonia blossoms dotted the ground like dime-sized white stars where the carpet of moss was thin.

Here and there, graceful panicles of purple bleeding heart nodded among their delicately dissected leaves, but the lovely white trilliums which had been plentiful a few weeks earlier had all disappeared. Only a few, now pink with age, remained.

Every clump of sword fern had in its center a ring of fiddle necks, fuzzy unfurled fronds only a few inches tall, like brownish-green gnomes standing at prayer with bowed heads.

The conifers, too, showed new growth. Boughs of hemlocks were etched in palest green, and in openings young Douglas-firs bore soft green paint brushes at the tips of their branches.

Near some of the larger trees, dainty white blossoms peeked out from beneath the three-lobed leaves of wood sorrel, and all along the way candy-striped spring beauty flowers sprinkled the forest floor.

Impressed by this profusion of new life, Prof exclaimed, "Do you know, I believe spring is fully a month earlier this year than last."

As we moved deeper into the forest, we heard the eerily-plaintive whistle of varied thrushes, which we called Alaska robins.

Then—thrill of the day for me—a large black and white bird, flitting through the woods, called out a ringing "cuk, cuk, cuk" as it alighted on a dead snag. It did a long rolling drum as it began working on the side of the snag. Maneuvering around, I could see that the slender bird was about the length of a large crow. It had a black back and bright red crest.

"What is it, Prof?" I whispered.

"Oh, that's a pileated woodpecker," he said, bracing one foot on a convenient log and making an improvised desk of his thigh in order to jot something in his notebook. "Let's watch it a bit. It's the largest woodpecker in the west."

Soon we saw chips flying from the place where the woodpecker hammered. John said, "I'll bet some of those chips are three inches long."

"No doubt of it. These birds are noted for the big holes they make. Whenever you see a large oblong opening in an old snag, you can be sure there's a 'cock of the woods' not far away."

"What's it looking for?" Minnie asked.

"It's probably hunting carpenter ants," Prof responded. "Those big black ants seem to be the main food of pileated woodpeckers." Then, as he straightened up and tucked his notebook under his arm, he added, "Now, we'd better get on our way."

"Minnie, what are these?" Fairhill called, pointing to a patch of sprawling plants with dark green, heart-shaped leaves in a damp shady spot near the turn-off from the main trail to the research area. Checking to see what the plants might be, Minnie exclaimed, "Oh, aren't they lovely? The flowers are brownish-purple and look as soft as velvet. What are they, Prof?"

"Try crushing a leaf," Prof suggested.

"Why, they must be wild ginger!" she exclaimed. "I've never seen the plant before."

The three-cornered little flowers, nestled between two heart-shaped leaves, reminded me of pictures I had seen of Medieval tricorn fool's caps. Each corner was drawn out into a long backward curling point.

After we arrived at the station, a comforting fire soon blazed beside the shelter. We rested there a bit while Prof recorded data. Then, as he closed his notebook, the Professor gazed into the canopy saying, "You've all heard me talk about wanting to study the tree canopy. I've dreamed and schemed but I can't come up with anything except building a ladder into one of these trees. Today we'll start that project." Rising to his feet, he looked around, appraising the situation. Then, pointing toward one of the larger hemlocks slightly in back of the fire shelter, he said, "We'll use that hemlock over there. It's centrally located and reaches up to the lower limbs of the Douglas-firs.

"We'll cut small trees outside the research area for the rungs. I'll show you where to get them. When the ladder is finished, I want to have a platform built on the tree's first branches. The platform can serve as a base from which to study birds and collect insects, and we can put weather instruments on it. We'll get shakes from the Hood Craven cabin for the platform.

"Even with a platform up there we won't be able to do all that I'd like. It's too stationary. I'd like to learn what's going on at all levels of the canopy and in different areas. We need sky hooks!"

As construction began, the man on the tree trunk needed both hands free and he also had to have some means of clinging to the tree which was about thirty inches in diameter. For this, Prof had borrowed a high-climber's safety belt. Taking turns, John or Kilen strapped the harness around the tree and around his hips, inched the safety belt upward, stepped onto a rung, and then inched the belt up some more until he was in position to fasten the next rung. Howard and Fairhill, preferring to keep their feet on the ground, carried supplies.

Building that ladder was no simple task. A deep notch had to be cut through the bark of the tree into the wood beneath for each rung of the ladder. Then, at fifteen-inch intervals the entire distance from the ground to those first branches high above, a four-foot length of pole as big around as a man's wrist was fastened securely into place with six-inch spikes. The hemlock selected was small compared with the Douglas-firs around it, and only about half their height. Even at that, it was about 150 feet tall, as high as a small skyscraper of twelve to fifteen stories. Its lowest branches were more than eighty feet above the ground.

The men used a rope tied to one of the limbs to hoist materials. The platform built at that lofty height was barely large enough to seat two people comfortably.

After giving instructions, helping the men get young trees for the first rungs, and watching the work get under way, Prof left construction of the ladder to his helpers and devoted his time to learning more about spring in the forest community. I'm sure he stepped out of the project with reluctance, for he would never be able to climb that ladder or see the insects and birds in the tree tops.

At the age of sixteen, while crawling through a fence on a hunting trip, he had accidentally discharged a shotgun blast into his right arm, a tragedy that almost cost his life and caused his right hand and arm to be shriveled and nearly useless. Prof never referred to his crippled arm as a disability or treated it as a handicap. He did with his left hand everything that he would have done with his right, and whenever the task couldn't be done with one hand alone, he assisted with his crippled hand or his teeth. Since he demanded much of himself, Prof also demanded much of his students. He never mollycoddled us but taught us independence and self reliance—sometimes, we thought, a bit too abruptly, like my experience in returning to the car on that first trip.

Soon a swarm of tiny black fungus gnats emerging from an old log attracted his attention. Months earlier, adult gnats had laid eggs inside the moist well-rotted remains of that log, ensuring survival of the species through the winter. Now each little gnat took a half-hour to shed its pupal skin, which it then left with other skins clustered around openings in the log. Some of the newly-emerged insects immediately became tidbits for orb weavers and large brown ground spiders. Others dispersed. In an hour and a half the last tiny gnat had emerged.

Net in hand, Minnie began collecting insects that hovered around the fragrant yellow Oregon grape blossoms and the flowers of various herbs. She, too, was gathering information about the new season.

I did what I had learned to do on earlier trips—sorted through a sample of forest litter and soil. Prof wanted to learn what he could about all the creatures of this forest, in all seasons. He suspected that those in this layer were vital to the life of the forest. As a result, on almost every trip the year-round, we searched through rotten wood or a mixture of soil and wood, or through litter and duff seeking whatever we could find.

My procedure, unsophisticated and amateurish, consisted of counting and identifying as accurately as I could all the bugs I discovered in a two-square-foot area of moss, litter, and surface soil: tedious, boring, back-breaking, and eye-straining, but important.

That task finished, I joined Minnie on the steep bank below the fire shelter where she studied insects on the flower cluster of a five-foot-high devil's club plant.

"Watch out," she warned as I approached. "Those long yellow stickers on the veins of the plant's leaves and woody stalk are poisonous. If you touch any of them, you'll learn in a hurry why this plant's called 'devil's club.'"

Small insects—gnats, rove beetles, and flies—almost covered the tiny greenish flowerets. Among them were four or five little wasplike insects which appeared to be parasitizing the pollen-eating insects. While we watched that activity, a stonefly from the streamlet below alighted on one of the plant's large fanshaped leaves.

The gurgling and splashing of the swift little stream (the source of our cold drinking water) drew us downward. Beside the stream, in the shelter of an old log, we discovered three little tailed frogs—my introduction to woodland amphibians. These frogs, known as *Ascaphus truei,* live only in the forests of western North America and are called tailed frogs because adult males have a copulatory appendage resembling a tail.

The frogs were active little animals, between one and two inches long, flat-bodied and toadlike with rather rough skin. Their colors varied. The females were reddish-brown and smaller than the green or greenish-brown male.

We also discovered a three-and-one-half-inch long salamander on the moss near the creek. Its body was reddish, and it had a pale yellow streak in the middle of its back. Later we learned that it was called a woodland salamander. It is one of the lungless salamanders, which live their entire life on land, never going to water.

Two to three inches of rain had fallen the previous week, making the woods damp and cool, an ideal place for these little amphibians.

Hazy clouds hung over the mountain. The sun shone only occasionally. A breeze made a fire welcome. We were not slaves chained to our tasks. All of us enjoyed periods of relaxation and conversation around that comforting blaze.

The men worked until twilight, but the project of building that ladder was too ambitious to be completed in one day. So, once again we returned to the car in darkness.

Singing seemed to shorten the miles as the car rolled along on the way home. I remember feeling that "Joshua Fit the Battle of Jericho" and other old songs which rang out in John's clear tenor, supplemented by Prof's baritone, made a perfect ending for a day filled with some of the wealth of information Saddleback Mountain held in store.

This research was opening a whole new world to me. What surprises might the next trip bring?

Chapter Three

Lost Prairie

THE PROMISE OF A BRIGHT new day lighted the eastern sky as Prof, Minnie, and I headed for Saddleback Mountain one morning in mid-June. I had been looking forward to this trip all week. The college year had ended and I would soon be returning to Roseburg for a summer's job at the bank where I had worked before coming to Linfield. Concerns about the future weighed heavily on my mind. I wanted to stay in college and continue with the research, but I had to finance my way. I had no reserve. Though this was only the end of my sophomore year I had already borrowed on my life insurance policy. My summer's earnings would not go far toward another year's expenses. My future was uncertain at best. This could be my last trip to Saddleback. I hoped it would be something special.

Prof's voice brought me back to earth. "When we get our work done today I want to do some exploring."

"Oh, good!" Minnie exclaimed. "Where'll we go?"

"We'll hunt for Lost Prairie. I've wanted to find it again for a long time," Prof explained as he drove along. "Lost Prairie's a large basin a little way down on the south side of Saddleback Mountain. I suspect it was gouged out as a glacial cirque, and when the ice melted a small lake remained. Over the years, the area became filled with a sphagnum bog which forms the headwaters of Salmon River. As the newborn stream meanders about, draining water from the bog, it goes through a strip of forest and makes its way to the notch between the two humps that form the saddle of the mountain. Then it passes through the notch and plunges down the mountain."

"Isn't there a trail to the Prairie?" Minnie asked.

"No, not all the way. I've only been there twice. I was scouting around with other people and we came in from a different direction each time. I think both times we probably stumbled onto the basin more or less by chance."

"What's Lost Prairie like, Prof?" I asked.

"The basin's so high on the mountain that it accumulates a good deal of snow every winter. As a result, much of it is full of potholes and hummocks, a typical old sphagnum bog. However, part of the area is fairly dry. I've been told that several families who had timber claims near the top of the mountain built their cabins close together on Lost Prairie. We'll be looking for that settlement."

"If there isn't a trail from Boyer to Lost Prairie," Minnie asked, "how did those people get their supplies?"

"There are a number of ways to get there. Supplies may have been taken in from Grand Ronde on the east, or from Rose Lodge on the west, or even from the south.

"Back in about 1910, when that whole region in the Coast Range was opened for timber claims, a lot of people swarmed into the area. Within a mile of the research station there are five or six small clearings where cabins and barns were built and I've seen many others when I've been hiking. They even built a road on the north side of the mountain for hauling freight to those cabins. It ran all the way from Boyer to the Hood Craven cabin site about a half-mile beyond the station. We follow remnants of that abandoned road every time we use the trail up the mountain.

"A few years later, about 1912, the big logging companies came in and bought those timber claims. Pocketing their tidy profits, the former owners moved out practically overnight. Some even left furniture and provisions in their cabins and sheds full of firewood.

"Then the timber companies sent in crews to destroy the buildings. Very few escaped. The trails and roads soon became blocked by fallen trees and brush. All of this discouraged travel in the region and soon the wilderness reasserted itself.

"In the heyday of the timber claims there was an official post office in the Boyer home, and Mervin was postmaster. About once a week, for the convenience of those who lived on that part of the mountain, Mervin put all of the mail for those families in a saddlebag and carried it on horseback some four miles to a cache dubbed 'Post Office' near the top of the mountain. As a result, some old-timers still refer to the mountain as 'Saddlebag.'

"Well, here we are at Boyer," Prof said as he drove off the highway to park his car in the usual spot near the Boyers' log building. "You girls can go on ahead if you want to. I'm going to see if Mervin can tell me how to get to Lost Prairie. I'll catch up with you later."

With the prospect of adventure before me, I soon forgot my worries. Minnie was a good companion, observing and cheerful. We hiked along to the accompaniment of bird songs—an occasional breezy *toe whee* from a rufous-sided towhee, the bright, warbled notes of a yellow warbler, or a long, eerie, quavering whistle of a varied thrush, or—most frequently of all—the infectiously buoyant, rich, silver-threaded song of a winter wren.

We savored the tangy odor of resin from young fir boughs warming in the summer sun, drew deep draughts of fresh mountain air, and feasted our eyes on all the bright new shades of green around us.

We discovered that all the logs which previously barricaded the trail to Salmon River had been cut, making the way amazingly easy. We guessed a timber company crew or perhaps the state forest service had done the work as a fire protection measure.

As we approached the river, a bright-eyed weasel suddenly poked her head from among the plants at the side of the trail. We watched, frozen in place. She looked around nervously before advancing into the trail far enough for us to see all eight and one-half inches of her cinnamon-brown body. Her throat was creamy white; an inch of black tipped her short tail.

Then, wonder of wonders, a baby weasel appeared at the mother's side. In a minute or two, the mother grasped her baby by the nape of its neck and the two disappeared into the brush. Later we learned that they were long-tailed weasels, which are quite often seen in the daytime and are avid hunters of mice and other small game.

Beyond Salmon River, luscious, large, blue huckleberries tempted us to loiter. However, our snack time proved to be very brief, for Prof caught up with us there.

"Cut it short, you two," he teased. "No more playing around. We have work to do. Remember, we're going for a hike as soon as we take care of the weather instruments and do a little collecting."

At about two o'clock we began our odyssey. We followed the trail for a quarter mile or so and passed the fallen remains of Hood Craven cabin in its small clearing beside one of the mountain streams. Many handsplit cedar boards still remained, though the site already had supplied boards for the fire shelter and the platforms built at both the low and high levels in the hemlock trees.

After crossing the stream, we left the trail to use a route defined only in Prof's mind, so far as I could tell. Now and then he pointed out dim marks on trees which he said were blazes to indicate a trail. Up and up we climbed through the forest. Several times we entered small cleared areas nearly reclaimed by the encroaching forest. In the center of each were the crumbling and moss-grown but unmistakable timbers of small cabins—mute evidence of a bygone era.

Finally we passed over one of the humps of Saddleback Mountain and began our descent down the south slope. At this elevation hemlocks and noble firs formed a shorter and more sparse forest than did the trees at the station.

At about four o'clock, we abruptly came upon the infant Salmon River flowing ever-so-slowly through deep, grass-bordered, tree-shaded pools at the edge of the forest. Crossing the stream on a footlog, we emerged into a bowl-shaped opening of several acres. We had reached our destination, Lost Prairie.

The ground, covered with small grassy hummocks, seemed dry enough for us to walk on and was fairly well drained. Farther out in the prairie we found pothole remnants of the old glacial lake which, Prof told us, were too deep to have been plumbed. Yet they were so small that it was hard to realize they were ever part of a lake. The prairie was a mass of lush grasses and myriads of subalpine flowers. Cougar, bear, and deer sign seemed to be everywhere.

Far out from the trees, we found the object of Prof's search—gray-white boards of three cabins flattened to the ground and bleached by the sun of many summers—skeletal remnants of a vanished community. We hunted for bits of old newspapers or other evidence as to who might have lived there, or when, but the decaying timbers revealed nothing. Prof said he had heard that some McMinnville people had profited from sales of timber claims in the Coast Range. *Was it possible*, we wondered, *that anyone we knew had lived in one of these places? What had life here been like?* We wished the boards could speak.

Sphagnum moss trailed over the boards and crept up on the remnants of a fence at the fringe of the settlement. Sphagnum grows out into old lakes, forming mats, turning lakes into bogs. Such bogs ultimately fill with peat—the dead and decomposing lower layers of the moss. In this bog remnant, sphagnum was well on its way toward removing all evidences of human habitation.

We sat quietly for a long while, thinking and enjoying the peace, silence, and beauty of the setting. In front of us the late afternoon sun highlighted a spectacular scene: a perfect amphitheater surrounded by forest-clad mountains. To the north and east the grass- and moss-grown bottom of the prairie bowl rose gently into a white rim of shaley rock. On the crest of the bank a tangle of large rhododendrons displayed cluster after cluster of rose-colored blossoms. Behind them the coniferous forest formed a backdrop of deep green, interrupted here and there by the stark white of a dead snag.

Had the timber claim holders who lived here reveled in the splendor of this setting? Did they ever wonder how this amphitheater was formed? Surely money was not their only reward for the time spent here.

When we finally rose to return to the research station and home, we looked back toward the west where we had entered the prairie. There, grazing peacefully in the lengthening shadows, was a large black-tailed buck.

We could see fog drifting in from the Pacific Ocean when we climbed to the viewpoint on our homeward journey.

"That fog reminds me of my first encounter with Lost Prairie," Prof commented. "It was one of those unsettled days in the fall of the year when clouds can come and go, but sometimes stay—and you find yourself in the middle.

"We broke out of the forest at the north end of the prairie just above the shale bank where the rhododendron tangle is its worst. The rhododendrons there are really old, matted down by snows of many winters and terribly contorted. It was almost impossible to get through them.

"Suddenly, we were surrounded by a vapor cloud—with fog swirling and eddying all around us, alternately concealing and revealing shapes and figures. It was an eerie, other-worldly feeling as though we had been transported in time and space. We felt like we might be on the moors of Britain and the hound of the Baskervilles could be upon us at any moment.

"After a time the fog lifted enough for us to scout around a bit. We found remains of one old cabin nearly matted over by sphagnum which also festooned scattered bits of picket fence.

"Not far from that cabin site the prairie was full of potholes and typical bog plants, much wetter than most of what we saw today.

"The mood was entirely different that day."

By the time we returned to the car we had hiked between fifteen and twenty miles and visited seven cabin sites.

Memories of that day would sustain me, I knew, until September—when I hoped to be back for more research adventures.

Boyer Service Station. Here the car was parked and the group going to the research station took the forest trail. John Boyer on the left; Professor Macnab on the right.

Chapter Four

Indian Summer

I N SEPTEMBER I RETURNED to the campus eager to get back into my studies and the research. But when I arrived at the campus, I learned I could not have the half-tuition assistantship I had been promised unless I ate at the college commons. I could not afford that. I planned to have my meals with my recently married sister and her husband and do typing for a professor to pay for sleeping quarters with other coeds in his home. After petitioning and much waiting, I was granted permission to have the assistantship if I worked for my meals in my sister's home. With those arrangements added to what I had made during the summer, I thought I could get through the year financially.

The last Saturday of the month I was once again on the way to my beloved forest. The foothills of the Coast Range were a riot of brown, green, purple, red, scarlet, gold, and yellow. My spirits soared at the display. Summer was over. We were in the Indian Summer phase of early autumn. Light showers earlier in the month had dampened the woods and ushered in a new season.

The warm sunny days and cool star-capped nights had beguiled Prof, Minnie, Bernice Farrens, and me into planning a weekend of camping on Boyer Flat. This would be Bernice's first trip. She was not a biology major, but a senior whose interest in biology had been sparked the year before by one of Prof's classes.

We arrived early in the morning at the rustic campsite under tall fir trees. Its only amenities were a couple of rough picnic tables and an old cookstove on a rock base but, equipped with pots and pans, assorted food items, and blankets, comforters, and pillows rolled up in ticking or tarps, we were prepared to rough it. That's what camping was in those days. Such things as air mattresses and snug sleeping bags became common only after World War II.

While Prof visited with the Boyers, we girls began our hike to the research station. The day was warm and smoky, with a slight breeze.

Minnie, the experienced one of our trio, recorded information, while Bernice and I helped with the counting. Prof had recorded no spider webs the week before but we found nearly 100 new webs hung across the trail—evidence that the baby spiders hatched this year were beginning to fend for themselves, Prof told us later. Moles or mice had pushed up many fresh burrows in our pathway. Giant green slugs, snails, and large black ground beetles, which we hadn't recorded for some time, had renewed their activity. Mosquitoes, too, were busy. Whenever we stopped to rest they zeroed in for a feast unless the breeze hit us.

We caught glimpses of wrens hunting insects in the brush beside the trail, noted a pair of brown creepers probing the crevices in the bark of a tree, and heard chickadees, Steller's jays, and varied thrushes as we hiked along. Near Salmon River, a grouse flew up, and as we approached the station we heard a woodpecker hammering on an old snag. We saw a band-tailed pigeon below the station, but most of the summer-nesting birds were gone, and many of the flowers of spring now bore seeds.

The highlight of our day came as we began climbing the last steep section of trail below the station. We were moving along quietly when a sudden crashing in the timber to our left froze us in our tracks. Wide-eyed and startled we stared at one another.

"Wha-a-t's that?" Bernice stammered.

"It's a bear," Minnie whispered, "a big black one. See it over there running through the bushes?"

As the bear kept on its course away from us, downhill through the brush, my goose prickles began to subside, and I ventured, "Maybe it's as scared as we are. It doesn't act like it's going to come back and attack us."

Finally the bear bounded onto a large log, paused, and looked back toward us, as though seeking assurance that we were not pursuing it. Then, evidently satisfied, it ambled away out of sight.

None of us had ever seen a bear anywhere, except in a zoo. That sleek, black creature looked ominously large to us. It probably weighed between 200 and 400 pounds.

We searched the area thoroughly for bear "sign." Heavy scratches on logs, piles of dung of various ages, and several trails through the brush told us that the bear had been around for a while. We discovered an old snag about twenty-five feet from the trail with a litter of woody fibrous cells scattered at its base. High above, we could see that a wasp nest had been torn up.

We gave the bear credit for that project and decided it may have been working on it when surprised.

When Prof caught up with us at the station we were still so excited that we all talked at once, trying to give our version of the encounter. Eventually we quieted down enough for Prof to say, "I don't think we need to be afraid of these bears, though they can be dangerous if cornered or if a person gets between a mother and her cubs. Mervin Boyer tells me they're fairly common. We'll probably see more of them if we're alert."

The Indian Summer evening was mellow and pleasant when we returned to Boyer Flat after a busy day at the station, collecting insects from shrubs, decaying wood, and forest floor. We talked and sang far into the night around our campfire before finally settling down to sleep on the ground, snugly wrapped in our blankets. Stars in the canopy above never seemed brighter or nearer than they did that night.

Since this was hunting season, Prof set out at daybreak, rifle in hand, in search of a nice buck. In those days of meager salaries, a supply of venison was a welcome addition to any family larder. Besides, though the hunt might be unsuccessful, it was a good way for Prof to become more familiar with the area.

After a day of reading and contemplation, we girls put our books away and packed everything into the car in preparation for leaving. Still, Prof had not returned. Minnie, who often sparked our activity, said, "I'm tired of sitting here waiting for Prof, why don't we visit Grandfather Boyer? He tells interesting stories about the early days in this area."

John Boyer, a man of medium stature and build, bespectacled and graying, greeted us cordially at the door of his two-story frame house on the west side of the little bowl-like valley. Learning that we were interested in hearing about the old Salmon River toll road, he showed us the place between his house and the present highway where its locked gate had once stood.

Then he said, "Now come on into the house and I'll tell you more about it."

After seating us in the living room, he began his story. "Long before the white man came into this country, groups of Indians regularly passed through here on their way to fish or to gather shellfish at the coast. They camped at certain places along the way where arrowheads and other artifacts can be found even now. You may know about some of those camps out in the valley.

"Somewhere around the middle of the last century white settlers started to use the route, then known as the Old Elk Creek trail. As far as we know, James Quick was the first white man to bring his family this way. He settled in the Tillamook area in 1852. Other pioneers soon followed. I've also heard that in the summer of 1837, the Methodist missionaries Jason Lee and Cyrus Shepard took their brides over this trail on a trip to the coast from their mission station on the Willamette near Wheatland."

"I'm not sure I would have liked that kind of honeymoon," Bernice commented.

John Boyer smiled, continuing, "After Indians were moved onto the Grand Ronde and Siletz reservations in 1856, the military used the trail in patrolling the area and in traveling between the two reservations. Little was done to improve the trail until about 1864 when Yamhill, Polk, and Tillamook counties got together and made it into a toll road. Even then, it wasn't much better. When we came here in 1908 it was still impassable in the winter. And so, after our family got settled, I told the officials I would work on the trail if the toll gate could be here by our place and we could have a share of the tolls for my work.

"I did my best to keep the road up for year-round use, but it was an impossible job. In the wintertime the mud kept getting deeper and deeper. The streams were always overflowing and washing out the logs I cut and laid crosswise for the stretches of corduroy road. I cut and placed tons of those logs, but it was just too much. During those years our home was used as a way station for travelers who wanted to spend the night. My wife took care of that. Julia's gone now, but for years she tended the gate, prepared and served meals, and made travelers welcome when they stopped here on their journeys to or from the coast. After 12 years of it, I gave up. That was in 1920."

The stories John could tell seemed endless. Many guests had spent the night in his home. An engraved stone slab at the side of the highway now serves as a historic reminder of the Boyer way station.

Though John Boyer had given up on trying to maintain a road to the coast, the need for such a route increased as more cars came into use. Building the coast highway (now US 101) in 1925 gave impetus to the Salmon River cutoff and on July 19, 1930, Oregon State Highway 18 was officially opened. According to highway department statistics, fifty-three vehicles passed over the roadway on Sunday, October 14, 1928, about two years before it was officially completed. But three years after completion, on August 13, 1933, another Sunday, the count was 2,545 vehicles. If the road had not been built, Prof would not have been able to scout Saddleback for a research site.

John Boyer often spoke of his love for this ancient forest. Though logging had not yet affected the area very much, he could see the day coming when the giant trees along the highway would all be gone unless steps were taken to save them. When the Van Duzer Forest Corridor came into being, Prof often said that it should have been named "Boyer Corridor" because it had been John Boyer's dream. Instead, it bears the name of Henry B. Van Duzer, a lumberman who was chairman of the state highway commission at the time the highway was built.

The Salmon River Highway has a reputation as a spectacularly beautiful scenic route to the coast. But many changes have been made. *The* (Salem, Oregon) *Statesman Journal* of August 11, 1989 commented on one of these changes: "Fir trees, some as old as 250 years, have been cut in the Van Duzer Corridor to make room for the addition of a...$2.9 million, 10,000-foot-long passing lane in the west section of the corridor....About 150,000 board feet of lumber, worth $130,000, was harvested in the operation."

Now, in 1998, this scenic corridor's existence is being threatened once more by agitation to enhance traffic flow to and from the coast resulting from an increase in Willamette Valley population, casino development, and coastal tourist attractions.

Indian summer weather lingered, as it often does, and in mid-October, six of us enjoyed another research-hunting-camping venture on Boyer Flat.

That Saturday, after completing research activities at the station, we went to the top of the mountain and added our names to the list of members of the "Damn Fool's Club" on our make-shift monument at the viewpoint. Then, as usual, in pitch-blackness, we stumbled and groped our way down the mountain with only the beam of a tiny pen flashlight to guide all six of us. Prof's notes about that return trip merely record, "Deer and owl scared up. Possibly cat heard on top." We reached our campground at midnight.

In keeping with the practice at that time, Mervin Boyer had been burning brush and old logs in the recently cut area on the hillside above the east side of the flat. Prof replenished the fire of one of the smoldering logs near an old skid road, and we four girls spread our bedrolls beside that welcome source of heat. Prof and Archie Strong camped beside another fireplace nearby.

On Sunday the other girls and I stayed at camp, talked, and studied while Prof and Archie hunted. It was a gloriously beautiful day, very warm in the afternoon. Toward evening a breeze sprang up, rekindling the fires on the hillside. Before we left that night the hill was a blaze of flames—an awesome spectacle that recalled the Tillamook burn holocaust which had destroyed thousands of acres of virgin forest in August the year before. None of us had seen that fire, but smoke from it had darkened the sky for miles all around and, at first, great quantities of charred needles were carried out to sea, to be washed back onto the beaches by the tides. Later, after the wind changed, similar needles were blown far inland. This October night there was slight danger of Mervin's fires getting out of hand because the woods were damp and the humidity high.

That was the evening we christened Prof's car "Shasta," for sh'asta have oil, sh'asta have gas, sh'asta have water, sh'asta have her windshield cleaned, and **finally** sh'asta go home!

As had become our custom, we sang all the way back to McMinnville.

Chapter Five

The Rains Came

O UR GLORIOUS INDIAN SUMMER ended suddenly the next weekend. Friday, October 18, was warm and sunny. A light film of clouds, signaling an approaching storm, may have drifted in late in the day. If there were such a warning, we didn't know what it meant. Intending to camp for two nights on Boyer flat, Prof, Bernice, and I headed for the mountain late that evening, but, having no weather service to alert us about an approaching storm, we were dismayed when we ran into heavy rain before we arrived at Boyer. At that time of year sudden weather changes are not unusual in northwestern Oregon. Storms, moving in from the ocean where weather is made, reach the Coast Range long before their approach is evident in the Willamette Valley.

All was dark at Boyer. The family had retired. Camping on the flat in this storm was out of the question, and the log cabin Mervin had started to build for Prof's use was little more than a dream, so we sneaked into the Boyer home and settled down for the night—girls on the couch in the dining room and Prof on the floor in the room used as a store.

Before Mervin and his family awoke in the morning we slipped out and, loading our bedding into the car, drove up the highway to a little-used road near the starting point of the Saddleback trail. There Prof parked the car and departed in the downpour at 8:30 for the research station, leaving Bernice and me to wait out the day in the car. About noon the storm let up somewhat, but by mid-afternoon when Prof returned, rain had begun falling again. Hungry, cold, and miserable we returned to McMinnville. Camping was over for that year.

The next week, one storm followed another. Rain poured down almost constantly, day after day, for the entire week. Finally, a clearing trend began and Prof, Ed Ross, and I set out for the mountain Sunday morning, grateful for the break.

When we arrived at Boyer, I cried out, "Look at that! Those two big firs are down right across the stove and tables where we camped two weeks ago. And the campground is **flooded**. I can hardly believe it!"

As he guided the car into the usual parking spot, Prof said, "I knew it was raining a lot during the week, but I didn't expect to see this. The whole flat is under water."

Later, Mervin Boyer showed us a barrel in which he had been collecting water since the fall rains began. Curious as to how much the barrel contained, Prof measured and, to his surprise, found fourteen inches. We didn't realize fully what that meant until we checked the rain gauges at the station, each of which had a capacity of 7½ inches. They were both level full and obviously had run over. So we had no way of knowing precisely how much rain had fallen, but that barrel at Boyer gave us a clue.

According to our record of the amount of rain collected since the first showers began in September, only 3⅓ inches had fallen until this rainy period began. That meant there must have been almost eleven inches during the storms of the past eight days. We marveled that the forest floor had been able to absorb so much water. The river was not especially high.

It was noon when we left Boyer for the station. The morning had been sunny, the day mild and pleasant. Mole and mouse burrows practically covered the trail in several places, and we saw all sorts of the usual autumnal creatures as we hiked along, including great numbers of large black ground beetles and big green slugs, a yellow-bellied brown salamander (now known as the rough-skinned newt), and four of the little tailed frogs. We heard or saw chipmunks, wrens, and a varied thrush. Of especial interest were the tracks of a bobcat and several sets of deer tracks.

At the station we had little time for anything but attending to the weather instruments because Prof wanted to get back to the river to look for salmon. He had not seen any when we crossed the river on the way to the station although silver salmon (coho) make the run to their spawning grounds right after the first heavy fall rain. He wondered whether the run was already over.

When we reached the river, we could see a few fish. Prof said, "Let's work our way upstream a bit here to see what we can find."

Struggling through the brush along the river bank, we finally came to an open place where coarse gravel formed a bar at the side of the stream. There in the shallow water flowing around the boulders and over the gravel lay scores of salmon, their greenish-brown backs no longer silvery and shiny but dull and drab. Streaks of red still brightened their sides and heads, but patches of white fungus blotched their bodies where the colorful scales had been battered away by rocks as the fish fought their way upstream against the current. Jaws of the males, elongated and distorted, were out of proportion to the rest of their heads. Fishermen often call such males "alligator jawed" because of their grotesque appearance.

In these spawning grounds fish sixteen to eighteen inches or more in length and weighing around six pounds, had given their all that the species might endure. Their eggs, deposited and fertilized here in the finer gravels between scattered boulders, would soon hatch. Young fingerling salmon, nourished by the diverse life in this mountain stream enriched by the bodies of the spawning parents, would be large enough by spring to seek the ocean. There they would continue feeding until maturity.

Two years later, lured back to the shore by some long-remembered chemical stimulus, those fish would seek out the stream of their birth and, as the first heavy rain flushed it out, join the multitude of other returning silvers in an ancient cycle that is part of the heritage of the forest.

The rainy season was right on target. This was October 28.

Though the forest in Washington's Olympic Peninsula is the one often referred to as "the rainforest," actually, the coniferous forest of the entire Pacific Northwest, from Alaska to northern California and from the ocean to the crest of the Cascades, is temperate rainforest. In this part of Oregon deluges in mid-October often usher in the rainy season which extends to mid-March or the first of April, with November and January usually being the wettest months. During the five years of Prof's study the average annual rainfall at the research station was nearly ninety inches, almost all of which fell between September and April.

In that year of 1934, northwest Oregon deserved its reputation for wetness. Week after week the rain poured down. To be sure, there were sunny periods, and there were even rain-free research days, but on far too many weekends violent storms with torrential rain zeroed in on our Saturday or Sunday trips. Logic would dictate that such storms be distributed equally throughout the week, but storms, it seems, have their own patterns and do not follow logic.

An exceptional amount of the wet stuff came down that October and November. By the end of December, our record showed that almost fifty inches had fallen, nearly fifteen inches more than the average for those three months during the five years of Prof's study.

I enjoyed being out in a storm for an hour or so. To me it was exhilarating. But that year, on the trips to Saddleback I was often wet and cold all day long. Pants were my chief concern. Jackets could be managed—a firm wool fabric did fairly well except in the heaviest rains. But my legs were forever drenched as they brushed against waterladen ferns and shrubs along the trail. Cotton pants were all I owned. Even if women's wool slacks had been available then, I couldn't have afforded them. Undergarments, too, were a problem. The best I could do was cotton flannel pajamas—warm when dry but with an atrocious affinity for moisture, becoming clammy and clinging tightly to my legs whenever they were wet.

I began experimenting. Men's overalls seemed the most utilitarian garment available. But, like cotton pants, overalls also drank up water—immediately siphoning it from nearby bushes. Something had to be done.

I tried lining the legs of overalls with oilcloth. That helped fend off some of the moisture but stiffened the legs and made hiking difficult, especially uphill, and before long the oilcloth cracked and peeled, losing any water-repelling properties it had offered.

Then I melted paraffin and soaked the fronts of the overall legs with it. That helped some, but it, too, stiffened the fabric and soon cracked and flaked away—leaving me again at the mercy of the elements. Nothing I contrived helped much. The not-yet-invented nylon outer garb and thermal underwear were long overdue.

Nor did I have adequate footwear. On rainy days my leather hiking boots became wet and sloppy even after a generous application of neats'-foot oil the night before. My feet were always cold.

Rain is but one of the forms that precipitation takes. It occurs also as fog, snow, sleet, or hail. Fog—the gentlest of these—may be only mildly dampening, or the droplets of vapor can be so close together that the effect is almost like being immersed.

On the morning of December 15 as we climbed to the station, serpentine masses of fog filled the lower valleys, and light tongues of vapor extended upward along the lower flanks of the mountain. It soaked us through.

When we reached the station at 9:30, we were above the fog. The sun was bright, warm and beautiful. But fog soon began enveloping us. As the vapor crept upward, the sun's rays, coming from the south at a low angle over the top of the mountain, pierced the fog in long shafts between the boughs of the trees—some shafts broad, others mere slivers—all of them together forming a superbly lovely sunburst. It was a spectacular, unforgettable scene.

Moments later the sun vanished, wiped out by the vapor shroud which rose from the valley.

The next week, Prof, Bob Rieder, and I left McMinnville at six o'clock in the morning in wind and pouring rain. Bob was a Linfield student who knew much about insects and had helped Prof on many trips. He had grown up in McMinnville and in spite of accidental loss of his right hand was an excellent tennis player. He also wielded a wicked insect net.

When we arrived at Boyer, the flat was flooded again and rain poured down. While waiting for the rain to slacken, Prof settled down in the car for a nap. With his heavy administrative and teaching schedule, he was often in need of rest. At about ten o'clock when the rain and wind finally let up a little, we started for the station.

Little Salmon River was far too deep for us to cross at the usual place, forcing us to leave the trail and find another log before we could continue.

At Salmon River, we found a raging torrent with water half way up on the sides of the crossing log and racing wildly around both ends. Prof said the river was the highest he had ever seen it. Using that customary crossing was out of the question. Rain had finally saturated the forest floor; there was nothing for it to do but run off.

Fighting our way upstream through the underbrush fringing the river, we came to a much smaller log which Prof said he had used the year before when the river was at flood stage. The channel here was narrower so this log spanned the entire stream. But the water was also wilder and deeper.

I had always been so fearful of water that I had never walked a log across any stream until I got into this research. Watching that roiled and muddy torrent rushing by made me quake. How could I, with all my phobias and fears, cross that wild river? However, I was even more scared to stay alone in the forest. I had no choice but to go with the men who seemed so sure of themselves.

They cut a vine maple for the three of us to hold onto as we inched our way across—two men, each of them with only one good arm, with a very scared girl sandwiched between. The log trembled and shook as the current surged and tore at it. There would have been no hope of rescue from that wild river if one of us had slipped.

Fortunately we made a safe crossing and eventually arrived at the station. Starting a fire proved more tedious than usual. All the wood, even the kindling, was damp and balked at burning. Cold and wet, soaked to the skin, with rain still dripping down on me, eyes and nostrils filled with smoke till my head was splitting, hungry but too uncomfortable to eat, I was thoroughly miserable—but after I had time to rest and recoup, crazy enough to go back for more! The rain stopped in the afternoon and I dried out enough to help with the research.

Prof recorded seeing tiny whiteflies on salal leaves and a few crane flies and fungus gnats flying about. On cool, wet days such as this, few flying insects were active, and so, as usual in addition to helping take care of the weather instruments, I spent my time sorting through humus and soil samples while Bob searched for beetles, salamanders, spiders, or whatever he could find in decaying wood.

We did not see any of the large black, banjo-shaped beetles that had been common along the trail since the first fall rains began. Evidently, their season of activity had passed.

There were differences in birds, too. We saw a dozen or so red-breasted nuthatches on the hemlock trees at the station and, in mid-afternoon, noted a flock of crossbills flying high overhead through the tops of the trees, in addition to the half-dozen chestnut-backed chickadees and winter wrens we had seen along the trail and a grouse that we flushed out of a tree in a swampy area below the station.

On our way back to the car Prof estimated that Salmon River had fallen a foot, making it possible for us to cross at the usual place, even though it was still somewhat hazardous. A gorgeous moonrise above the trees at Boyer made a lovely, peaceful ending for a harrowing day.

The end of December came and with it Christmas vacation. As we made plans for the final trip of 1934, Prof said, "Let's have a housewarming. For two years, ever since I started the research, I've wanted a place where we could stay overnight. The cabin Mervin has been building at Boyer is finally ready for use and we should celebrate. Dr. Mayfield wants to go with us. Being from the Midwest, he's been eager to study the geology of the mountain and I suspect both Howard and Minnie would like to go, too. We'll plan to stay two nights."

As usual it was late when the five of us arrived at Boyer on Saturday the 29th, but we were in good spirits. We had fun carrying our luggage the 100 yards or so from the car to the cabin through a light snowfall.

The one-room building was rustic and primitive, with unfinished log walls, a hand-crafted door of rough lumber, and three small windows. A plank counter, a few benches, and a huge old cast-iron kitchen range were the only furnishings. There was no plumbing. We carried water in buckets from the service station at the highway. Our "bathroom" was a private spot outside with no seat and no roof overhead. Our beds were bedrolls—assemblages of pillows, blankets, and comforters, wrapped in canvas—spread on the bare, cold, and drafty floor. We had brought pots and pans for cooking and eating and used candles for light. Nearly impossible to heat, the cabin supplied only a camping place, sheltered from the elements. We had little sleep that night.

Our activities for this initial overnight use of the cabin suffered severely from lack of organization. Sunday morning it was eleven o'clock before we finished KP duty and started our hike up the highway toward the trail to the station.

Entering the forest, we found a fantasyland created by the first snow of winter. Lingering on tree boughs and lightly covering the ground, the snow sparkled in the sunlight and formed delicate and interesting patterns. The air was fresh—the usual forest odors lay buried beneath the blanket of white, which also muted sounds.

Snow is like a book for those who can read the language. Tracks indicated that snowshoe hares and timber rabbits had been active on top of the snow, and irregular burrows heaved up from beneath revealed that moles or mice had been busy underneath.

Mixed flocks of chickadees and tiny kinglets flitted through branches of the smaller hemlocks, intriguing us with their soft calls. Winter wrens busied themselves beside the trail. On Summit Prairie a couple of nuthatches *yank, yanked* from an old snag and we caught sight of the black crested heads and deep-blue wings and tails of Steller's jays as they flew through the trees, uttering low-pitched raucous squawks. A solitary varied thrush alighted on a tree near Salmon River, and at the water's edge a slate-colored water ouzel, or dipper, flitted and bobbed. A little way below the station we heard the high-pitched, metallic *peek*, of a hairy woodpecker, and after we arrived at the station, two flocks of crossbills *chip, chip, chipped* as they flew through the crowns of the Douglas-firs high above.

Nearly three inches of snow covered the ground at the station. With air temperature hovering near the freezing point, the low-angled winter sunlight reaching us there on the north side of the mountain gave little comfort. We needed the warmth of a fire to keep us from chilling as we rested from our climb.

As clouds began moving in everyone took part in completing the day's tasks. Prof had discovered that one of the atmometers was taking in water. While he, with his one good hand, and I struggled with that tedious, finger-chilling problem—involving glass tubing, glass jar reservoir, and icy water—Minnie completed reading the instruments and Howard and Dr. Mayfield set some cheese-baited mouse traps to be left out overnight. A shower of hail inspired a hasty retreat to our quarters down the mountain.

Monday, after a leisurely morning in the cabin, Prof suggested that we close out the year by going to the top of the mountain. While his primary purpose, supposedly, was to observe animal activities and snow conditions at the higher elevations, the proposal implied adventure.

The sun was already below the rim of the mountain and wintertime mid-afternoon dusk was settling before we left the station. We located and retrieved traps set out the day before, with a catch of one lone deer mouse.

At first walking through the shallow snow was easy. Skylight reflected from the snowy surface lighted our way and we could see more rabbit tracks and also some deer tracks. However, the light soon dimmed so much that we could no longer identify tracks, the snow deepened, and we became aware of a hard surface crust.

By the time we were halfway to the notch, the snow depth had increased to a foot, and Prof, Dr. Mayfield, and Howard began taking turns breaking trail. At each step the leader's foot broke through the crust and sank ten to twelve inches into the soft snow beneath. We stepped carefully into the holes, hoping with each step that hitting the sharp edge of the crust wouldn't bruise or cut our legs.

The snow at the notch must have been well over three feet deep. I remember seeing only the tips of small noble firs above the snow at trail side. It became obvious that we would not be able to reach the viewpoint. All of us were tired and soaked from the hips down. We finally realized that we would be in a serious predicament if one of us were injured or collapsed from exhaustion there, five miles or more from the highway. Though reluctant, we gave up our objective and turned back. Despite our physical discomfort we had been enjoying the adventure.

At 10:30, weary and wet, we reached the cabin.

After welcoming the New Year, we packed our belongings into the car for our homeward journey and arrived in McMinnville at three o'clock in the morning of January 1, 1935. All agreed that our New Year's Eve celebration had been unique.

Chapter Six

Trial by Fire

JANUARY 1935 WAS COLD with many light snowfalls in the mountains. On the first Saturday, ten inches of newly fallen snow covered two inches of old snow at the station, and the thermometer stood at 36°F, a bone-chilling temperature for one not moving about actively.

The next Saturday when we arrived at Boyer, huge wet snowflakes were falling and clinging to everything. They adorned shrubs and boughs of trees with fluffy whiteness and covered bare areas of ground with a two-inch-deep carpet, transforming the forest into another world, a place of mystical beauty.

By the third week really cold weather had arrived. The air temperature at the station was only 24°F and one of the thermometers recorded a minimum of 18° for the preceding week. Tracks of deer, snowshoe hares, mice, and winter wrens decorated the fresh snow and in one spot a feather-and-claw pattern told the story of an owl catching a mouse.

On those cold snowy days we learned that a few species of hardy insects, such as fungus gnats, may be found on hemlock boughs or flying about under small hemlock trees even when the temperature is in the thirties, and we saw large green stink bugs resting on hemlock boughs loaded with snow. But when the temperature dropped into the twenties the few insects we found were dormant.

We also took samples of humus and duff in an attempt to learn whatever we could about where and how insects manage to live through the winter.

The last Saturday in January I could not go to the mountain. Final exams would begin on Monday, I still had reports to complete, and I was moving into the Macnab home that weekend. I had been living with some other girls in the home of Professor Mahaffey where I did typing to pay for my room.

I had been typing for Prof ever since my freshman year and I now knew enough about his research to be of real help. The move to the Macnab home would enable me to concentrate my free time on Prof's work instead of dividing it between two professors. In return, the Macnabs would give me both board and room.

The Macnab home, a two-story frame dwelling situated near the campus at the edge of town, was small and unpretentious, much like the homes of other faculty members. However, Mrs. Macnab's baby grand piano made their home special, an exception to the house's generally modest furnishings.

The Professor and Mrs. Macnab had met in Albany, Oregon, at Albany College (now Lewis and Clark College of Portland) when handsome, young James Arthur Macnab was a biology student, and talented and charming Mamie Irene Lenhart, nearly ten years his senior, held the positions of Dean of Women and instructor in music. (The Professor was known to say he had fallen in love with Mamie because she was a beautiful *older woman*, not because she was a beautiful *young* woman.) Mamie was a slender, lithe, and willowy brunette, slightly shorter than James. Their romance culminated in a wedding in Lincoln, Nebraska—Mamie's hometown—on the Fourth of July following James's graduation.

According to Mamie, a city girl from the Nebraska flatland, honeymooning at a fire lookout on the top of a mountain in a remote area of the Umpqua National Forest provided a more adventurous summer than she had expected. She enjoyed the serenity and beauty of the forest, but for her that summer was a nightmare she would never forget. Cooped up in that glass-sided room atop the lookout, she felt she had the privacy of a goldfish in its bowl. Descending and ascending the ladder to fetch water from the spring or go to their privy was treacherous, and she was certain that those dark woods were full of bears, cougars, and maybe even wolves.

Not so for James. He loved every bit of it. As a youth growing up in the small community of Roseburg, Oregon, he enjoyed nature and the out-of-doors. Forests held an especial fascination for him. He had spent his early childhood in forestless North Dakota where he was born, the son of parents of Scottish ancestry and staunch Presbyterianism. (His father was a Presbyterian minister.) James had even dreamed of one day becoming a forest ranger, but that dream was shattered when he was sixteen by a hunting accident which nearly took his life and left his right arm permanently crippled.

James received a master's degree in biology from the University of Nebraska. In 1924 when their first child, James Lester, was an infant, the Macnabs moved to Linfield, a struggling, poorly financed Baptist college of some 200 students. Few of the faculty members had more than a bachelor's degree. The new biology professor soon learned that Linfield had little in the way of a biology curriculum. But, like leaven in bread dough, this energetic young Scotsman began changing things. For the dedicated students he was an exciting teacher who rewarded them with friendship and personal interest in their life goals. The department grew in stature and enrollment, and he soon had students going on to graduate school and gaining Ph.D. degrees. Quite naturally, then, in the 1930s the Professor began considering the continuation of his own education toward that higher degree.

Mrs. Macnab kept up her musical expertise after the family moved to McMinnville by giving both voice and piano lessons to supplement the family income and occasionally sang soprano solos at community functions or at Presbyterian Church services.

I knew "Mrs. Mack" fairly well before I moved into their home, for she was patroness in the local sorority I joined as a freshman. I had stayed in their home one Thanksgiving vacation and had also been a "sitter" on other occasions for their three children: eleven-year-old James Lester, "Jimmie"; six-year-old Adelia, "Dee"; and three-year-old Colin.

The weekend after finals that January, Prof was ill. He asked me to take responsibility for the field work. John and Fairhill would help, he said, and Mrs. Macnab would drive us to Boyer. With his excessive burden of teaching, administrative duties, research, and family responsibilities, Prof had been pushing himself to the breaking point. Now the flu had caught up with him.

Prof's assignment came as a jolt. Neither John nor I had ever had charge of a research trip. Feeling overwhelmed by the responsibility, I departed for the campus to contact the men and prepare for the trip.

Before daylight the next morning we headed westward toward Boyer and Saddleback Mountain. Dropping us off at the trailhead, Mrs. Macnab drove back to Boyer to await our return, and Fairhill, John, and I began our trek up the mountain.

Frost covered the ground. Only a trace of rain had fallen the week before, leaving the air invigorating and dry. I led the way in order to count and record spider webs before they were brushed aside and to note anything else in the trail which should be recorded. For the past five weeks there had been very few spider webs but today seventy-five hung across the trail.

Soon Fairhill, a keen observer of plants, asked, "Have you noticed the new pale green fringe at the tips of hemlock branches?" And, as we neared Little Salmon River, he drew attention to the purpling of catkins on alders and swelling buds on other trees. All these things were clear evidences, on this early February day, that temperatures were warming and life was awakening from winter's dormancy.

Many birds shared the forest with us—some familiar and recognizable, others new and unknown. A *pick* sounded from the woods on our left. We glimpsed a black-and-white speckled bird before it flew away into the forest. It must have been a downy or hairy woodpecker. Some barely perceptible sound or a movement caught our attention as four Oregon jays glided like ghosts from tree to tree. Drawn by unfamiliar sounds, these gray birds, often called camp robbers, obviously were curious about our presence.

We heard or saw numerous winter wrens, a flock of "chipping birds"— later identified as crossbills—and several mixed flocks of chickadees, kinglets, and brown creepers. Great numbers of birds seemed to be on the move.

As we neared the abrupt rise to Summit Prairie, John exclaimed, "Listen to that twittering. I can see a bunch of birds around the alder trees over there."

"We'd better see if we can identify them," I said, detouring from the trail. As we hurried along, Fairhill commented, "They're always on the move, flying back and forth from one tree to another and they seem to be feeding on alder catkins."

"Some of them are in the tops of those Douglas-firs," John added, "feeding on cones there, too."

After a while I asked Fairhill how many he thought there were. He had been going from one tree to another watching the birds.

"I'd say about 200," he replied, adding, "Have you noticed how they fly, moving up and down, a lot like ocean waves or someone doing a breast stroke?"

"Yes, that's distinctive. They're not like anything I've seen before."

John joined us and working together we concluded that the birds were four to five inches long, with slender, gray-brown bodies and notched tails. There was a bit of yellow in their wings and tails and we could see they had dark streaks on their sides though they were lighter underneath.

"I guess we'd better go on now," I said, closing the notebook in which I'd been jotting the description, "but I sure hope Prof will know what these birds are."

"You two go ahead. I'll stay and watch a while longer," John said. "Maybe I can collect one of the birds or see something else that will help with their identification."

Fairhill and I moved on but stopped at the edge of Summit Prairie to investigate a group of freshly-dug holes. "Mountain beaver burrows," he said. "I understand they are found in places like this." Later we learned he was right.

It was cold in the forest. High clouds drifting eastward from the ocean increased the chill and made the pale wintertime light even dimmer among the huge old trees.

Twice we heard Steller's jays, and, as we neared the station, the croak of a raven flying high overhead.

Putting his pack aside as soon as we reached the station, Fairhill began removing the boards at the front of the fire shelter in preparation for making a fire while I jotted down a few more notes.

Shivering, while waiting for the fire to get underway, I thought, *If only these clouds would clear away, it might warm up a little.*

Soon, with the fire burning briskly, Fairhill left to gather fuel for the remainder of the day while I finished the trail notes and warmed myself briefly. Then I set out to check the research instruments.

Kneeling, I removed the door from the first shelter. In it was a hygrothermograph, an instrument for furnishing an accurate, continuous recording of relative humidity and air temperature. Servicing it required concentration and care. The humidity element was a six-inch long band of extremely fine human hair which we moistened every week by gently stroking distilled water onto it with a camel's hair brush. We had discovered that my hair could be used to replace broken hairs. Tiny barrels on the delicate recording pens needed to be filled each week with a special purple ink. Too much ink caused splattering; too little, no tracing. Charts required careful positioning on the cylinder and above all, we must **never** forget to wind the cylinder clock!

Absorbed in my task, I heard *tsick-adee-dee* and glanced up to see a couple of chestnut-backed chickadees working nearby in a small hemlock tree. I paused to enjoy these perky little birds with their dark brown caps and bibs, white cheek patches, and chestnut sides and backs.

Then a high, thin note drew my attention to a large Douglas-fir near the chickadees where a tiny brown creeper busily searched for a meal. I watched in fascination. That mite of a bird, less than six inches long from tip of bill to tip of tail, seemed even smaller than it was. It worked jerkily upward along a spiral path, with its tail levered against the tree for support as it probed bark crevices with its curved bill. I was so absorbed in birdwatching that I didn't hear Fairhill as he came up behind me from his wood gathering.

"What do you see?" he asked.

"I've been watching a brown creeper. It's disappeared on the other side of a tree, but I think it'll be back again in a minute. See, there it is, now."

"It's sure little," Fairhill commented, "and doesn't seem a bit afraid."

Quietly watching, we heard the call of another creeper.

Then Fairhill said, "I think I've gathered enough wood to last a while. What should I do now?"

"All I've done so far is take care of the hygrothermograph. I'll tackle the atmometers next. You might start with the double thermograph and proceed from there." I knew he was competent to do this as he took care of some weather instruments on the college campus.

"Okay, I'll go to work," he responded, moving downhill toward the double thermograph shelter. Soon he moved on to the two rain gauges. Only 0.01 inch of rain had fallen the preceding week.

He then went to the anemometer, or wind gauge, perched on a slight rise nearby. The day's reading was 820 miles—an average of a little more than five miles an hour for the entire week—slightly more than the week before but normal for the time of year.

Meanwhile, I struggled with the atmometers. I always dreaded taking care of these primitive contraptions for measuring evaporation. However, they were the only method available, so we did our best to obtain usable data with them. In this instrument the evaporation unit is a porous clay cup attached by glass tubing to a jar containing water. As water is lost to the atmosphere by evaporation, more is drawn up from the reservoir.

The trick in taking care of one of these instruments was to remove from the glass jar the clay cup, the stopper through which the tubing passed, and the glass tubing, *as a unit*. Then pour in water to replace what was lost, measuring it as it was poured. And *then* replace the whole mechanism without getting air bubbles into the system. Other problems occurred too, like broken tubing, frozen glass reservoirs, cracked clay cups, or growth of green algae.

I was fighting air bubbles when Fairhill came by after finishing with the other instruments. "You look cold and miserable," he commented. "I'll check the thermometers at the low hemlock platform so you can go back to the fire when you get through here."

"I *am* cold. And I *am* miserable. And I *thank* you. I'll be glad to get back to the fire." Even though the sun had come out while I was busy with the instruments, the sky was hazy and the temperature a chilly 44°F.

"Here are the figures for this week," Fairhill reported as he rejoined me at the fire shelter. "What do you make of them?"

"Well, let's see. It looks like last week there in the hemlocks the highest temperature was 3½ degrees warmer and the lowest was 1½ degrees colder than here at shrub level. Right now it is ½ degree warmer there at that higher level. Not much difference."

A few minutes later John arrived. "You timed that just right," Fairhill teased. "We have all the instruments checked and are ready to eat lunch."

"I knew it was lunch time," John said. "My stomach told me that. But I watched those birds in the alders for a long while trying to find out what they were. They were too fidgety though—always on the go. I couldn't see anything new to help identify them. I did see two more Oregon jays—one at the edge of Summit Prairie, the other a little way this side of Salmon River."

It was noon. We were hungry. Alert to see or hear any bird that came into the vicinity, we took time out to relax around the fire and eat. I had never before had a sandwich of ripe banana on whole wheat bread, but the one in my lunch was delicious. Later I learned this was a Macnab regular.

After lunch the men began work on a humus and duff sample.

Net in hand, I set out in pursuit of whatever creatures might be flying. Wielding one of the gauze "butterfly nets" may sound—or even look—simple. Live insects, however, are unpredictable and can be extremely elusive—flying higher, lower, faster, slower, dodging to right or left, soaring to heights or dropping out of sight into the vegetation. The chase can be frustrating and futile while appearing hilarious. Fortunately for me, few insects were on the wing. I caught some craneflies, fungus gnats, and tiny midges.

At 1:30 I halted my pursuit of insects to begin a series of photometer readings, a technique with which I had become familiar in plant physiology class. I placed a small, opened, pocket-watch case on the log supporting the fire shelter. Inside this primitive light meter, or photometer, was a piece of sensitive photographic paper covered with a close-fitting metallic disc, shaped like a pie from which a wedge-shaped piece had been removed. If the photometer case were left open, the paper in the wedge-shaped space would be exposed to light and become darker in proportion to the light intensity. After a timed interval the disc could be rotated to expose a new area. I made a series of four exposures during the next two hours. Later the paper would be developed at the lab.

Since light regulates many life activities, it is an important factor in the forest environment. As light passes downward from the crown to the forest floor, it is filtered by each of the many layers. As a result its intensity is decreased tremendously by the time it reaches the ferns, shrubs, herbs, and mosses. Even on a clear summer day direct shafts of sunlight rarely reach the forest floor. When they do, it is fleeting.

In winter, light is reduced even more. Since the sun is not directly overhead but far to the south, its rays come at a low angle. Further, for all but a few hours during the short winter days the top of the mountain shaded this forest community on its north slope. Add to normal winter-time conditions the filtering effect of haze covering the sky, as it did this February day, and light intensity falls even lower.

We wanted to get accurate measurements of light intensity under different conditions and in all seasons. We knew this photometer was inadequate, but it was the best thing we had, so I made readings with it week after week whenever weather permitted. Ultimately, we did get some useful information from these records.

As the men finished their sample of humus and soil, we heard band-tailed pigeons overhead and glimpsed them slipping through the tops of trees.

John jumped up, exclaiming, "I'm going up to the high hemlock platform. Maybe I can get a better look at those pigeons and see if anything else is going on up there."

He climbed the eighty-three-foot ladder to the tiny platform among the lower branches of the forest canopy. There he stayed for the next hour and a half.

After watching birds a while—first, a hairy woodpecker as it chipped at a snag down the slope from the fire shelter and then a pair of ravens as they moved through the forest canopy—I joined Fairhill to work on two more samples of duff.

Sitting by the fire, sifting through the litter in pans on our laps, we counted, recorded, and preserved the tiny creatures large enough for us to see. Though from different types of locations—one in an open area, two under ferns and other kinds of plants—the three samples apparently had similar forms of life, although the number of individuals varied from seventeen to forty-six.

As I placed identifying labels in the vials of specimens we had collected, Fairhill said, "I'll do one more sample before we leave for home. Where shall I take it?"

Pointing up the slope, I directed, "Oh, up there in that little salal patch. With the others we've done, that should make a good variety for the day."

Suddenly, feelings of misgiving swept over me. Here I was trying to supervise this research. I wasn't the **boss** but I was having to play that role. Fairhill had been with Prof on many more trips than I had, and I—half his age—was telling **him** what to do.

After stoking the fire, Fairhill began working on his sample of litter. Soon he grumbled, "I can't see a blessed thing in this dirt."

"The light is poor and it's getting late," I suggested. "Maybe it's too dark for you to see the little creatures."

"No. I just don't think there's anything here." But he continued his search.

At about four o'clock, John came down from his lookout in the tree tops. "What was it like being in a crow's nest for an hour and a half?" Fairhill asked.

"It was sort of cramped, so I got up now and then and stretched. But it was interesting. I watched birds come and go, and some insects were flying around. I think they were Diptera, but they were too far away for me to get a good look. Wished for wings—then I could have caught some."

Conscious of my task as a recorder, I asked, "What birds did you see?"

"Soon after I got up there a mixed flock of about thirty-five golden-crowned kinglets, creepers, and chickadees began working through the tree tops. I got a good look at the kinglets. They hopped from twig to twig at the tips of branches, flicking their wings all the time as they searched for food."

"I've never seen a kinglet up close," Fairhill interrupted. "What do they look like?"

"They're very small and have olive-gray backs but are lighter underneath. I could see a bright orange-yellow patch on the heads of some of them so I'm sure they were golden-crowned kinglets, not the ruby-crowns.

"One flock flew away but another showed up in a little while. Some of the birds stayed around for an hour and seemed quite sociable."

Fairhill stood up abruptly, dumping the soil sample he had been sorting, and proclaimed in disgust, "If there's anything in there, I can't find it. It all looks like dirt to me. I give up."

I began packing our gear while John put out the fire and Fairhill replaced boards covering the front of the fire shelter.

Soon we were trudging down the trail homeward bound. I thought, *It's been quite a day. We gave it our best. I hope Prof is satisfied with what we did. And I do hope he will be back next week.*

Prof wasn't back on the job the next week. He hadn't fully recovered from the flu and was burdened with completing grade reports for the first semester while getting the second semester's classes under way.

During the depressed economy of the 1930s, the road to survival was precarious for all small independent institutions of higher education. Linfield College was no exception. To entice a larger enrollment, the administration had introduced innovative curricular changes. One of these was a lecture and laboratory biology orientation course.

For Prof this meant writing an entirely new syllabus and then—with untrained assistants—teaching the new course to eighty students for the first half-semester, followed by a second group of eighty students for the second half-semester. This, with his regular courses, made a teaching load of eighteen hours. He also had committee meetings to attend, supplies to order, and all sorts of other departmental administrative detail to attend to.

Even without his research, that was a nearly impossible undertaking. Prof's health suffered. It now appeared that his research would suffer as well unless John and I could continue taking care of the field work.

As a senior biology major, John was in the midst of an extremely busy year. He was president of the student body, "house parent" for a group of young men living in the upper floors of Pioneer Hall (the only men's dorm on the campus at the time), and an assistant in biology—in addition to carrying a full schedule of courses. Though he could ill afford to take the time for the research trips, he was dedicated and willing. Professor and student had developed a bond of genuine friendship.

So once again, John and I accepted the challenge. For this second trip we had no helper, though Mrs. Macnab again served as chauffeur.

John was a good companion, kindly, good-natured, a willing worker. As far as I could determine, his only fault was that he was already firmly committed to another girl. His friendship offered no chance for romance. At Boyer the weather was crisply cool and frosty.

Animal activities along the trail were similar to those of the week before.

Again the unknown birds were in the alder trees at the edge of Summit Prairie. This week they seemed even more restless and less intent on feeding. Hoping to identify them, we spent much time watching, but to no avail— they still remained a mystery.

Caring for the instruments at the station proceeded smoothly until we reached the atmometers. The porous clay cup (the evaporating unit) of one was cracked. We had to take the whole apparatus apart and start from scratch assembling a workable unit. With the temperature only 38°F that was a finger-chilling, temper-testing undertaking. We not only had to fill narrow glass tubing with water without getting any air bubbles into the system, but at one point we had to insert that cantankerous, unmanageable liquid—mercury—into the tubing. It was a task to try the temper of a saint. I was grateful that even-tempered John was working with me.

Conveniently for us the day was too cold for many insects to be active. The only ones we saw were a few craneflies and fungus gnats and other small dipterans.

However, new red leaf buds on huckleberry bushes indicated to me that spring was not far away. I thought, *What if spring is early this year? John and I don't know all the signs to look for. Prof just has to get back soon to supervise this work.*

In spite of my uneasiness, Prof seemed satisfied with what we had accomplished when we reported to him later.

Another weekend arrived with our mentor still too bogged down with college work to return to his research.

That Saturday Kenny Fender went with John and me. He had been a "bugologist" from the age of five when he started chasing butterflies with a homemade net. During his childhood and youth Kenny had caught, displayed, and identified an impressive collection of these colorful beauties, but he had now transferred his interest to other insects and was well on his way toward becoming an authority on beetles. He had assisted on many of the early trips and was presently helping to organize the collection taken back to Linfield. John and I welcomed his presence.

Prof had issued an ultimatum—on this trip we **must** collect one of the "mystery" birds we had seen feeding on alder catkins and Douglas-fir cones. He said it was necessary for us to know what they were since they had been present in great numbers two weeks in succession.

At that time birds of the whole western part of the United States were only sketchily known. There wasn't any kind of field guide for western birds. We had two or three other bird books, but nothing adequate. Gabrielson and Jewett's *Birds of Oregon*, the first comprehensive book on Oregon birds, did not appear until 1940.

Studies such as ours were the main source of accurate information about the range and distribution of a species. So it was essential to collect birds for identification. Sensitivities were different then and a "bird in hand" was the only acceptable means of identification. After being identified by a recognized authority, carefully prepared skins of the birds would be placed in the college's museum.

At least 300 of the unknown birds were feeding on alders in the valley of the Little Salmon River, but they were so continually on the move that it took John two hours to shoot one. With the bird in hand, Kenny exclaimed, "Why, this is a pine siskin!" Obviously he knew birds, as well as bugs.

Later when I read about these birds, I learned that they are wanderers in the winter and may occur in flocks of thousands. One book stated that their name *siskin* comes from a Danish or Swedish word meaning "chirper."

Time spent in collecting the siskin curtailed our activities at the station, but with Kenny's help we collected insects and made soil samples as well as servicing the instruments.

Prof seemed to think we had done well, but I felt uneasy. Subtle little things told me that winter's grip was loosening and that spring, with all its exuberance of life, was not far away. Birds had seemed more active than usual. We had seen a song sparrow, and I had heard three unidentified "trillers" warbling till I thought their throats must ache. Moles or voles had been busy tunneling beneath the soil. We had found some earthworms and caught new insects.

For all our willingness, we lacked experience. We knew few of the animals and not all of the plants. But the fourth weekend in February came and Prof was still overly burdened by college responsibilities. Once again he asked John and me to do the field study. There were only the two of us this time. John drove the Macnabs' car out to Boyer.

On our way to the station I discovered that the exuberant songsters of the week before were our ever-present little friends, the winter wrens. We heard them at intervals all along the trail, twenty or more in all, and I saw five clearly. One was perched on a low brush warbling and trilling to advertise his private territory.

Though there had been dense fog, ice, and heavy white frost at McMinnville, the sun was bright at the station. But it was too cold for comfort. By mid-afternoon the temperature had barely risen to 37^{0}F and we were surrounded by new patches of icy snow even though nearly four inches of rain had fallen during the preceding week.

In that chilly setting, we again had the dubious pleasure of assembling a new atmometer. The clay cup of one was cracked. We assumed it had frozen.

Caring for weather instruments, making photometer readings, doing routine collections, and recording observations gave us a busy, full day.

Though to us the weather didn't feel very springlike, we found new leaves on an elderberry bush, buds bursting on salmonberry, huckleberry, and vine maple plants, and new growth beginning on Oregon grape and salal. Fully developed leaves graced some small cascara trees, and we were surprised to find a few Johnny-jump-ups and wood sorrel plants peeking through the soil along the trail.

A large swarm of tiny insects dancing in the sun near Salmon River, many midges, craneflies, and gnats also indicated that winter's dormancy was ending.

When will Prof be able to return to the mountain? I wondered in desperation. *How much longer can John and I, who know so little about it, do the work without the research being seriously handicapped?*

For six weeks I had to manage the field work, with a single exception—March 2 when Prof was along.

On March 22 the Professor was finally back on the job. During the rest of the semester he supervised the field activities except on an occasional day when the pressure of college work became too great and someone else had to take charge. Usually I was that person. I was becoming more familiar with the plants and animals—particularly the ultra-important insects. As I gained confidence, bearing responsibility for the field work gradually ceased to worry me. Its challenges became ever more alluring.

Prof (last in line) and crew hike the Salmon River Highway to the trailhead, 1930s.

Chapter Seven

To Skin a Hummingbird

"WHAT DO I DO NOW, PROF?" I asked in despair as I stared at the blob of flesh and feathers lying on the table in front of me—all that remained of a pretty little golden-crowned kinglet.

"The book says, 'The skin should be worked carefully over the head, being pushed from the back of the head with the thumb- and fingernails.'"

"But, Prof," I wailed, "how am I to work **this** tissue-paper skin of **this** matchstick neck over **that** head? It's **impossible**."

"Well, the book says to 'work it slowly from all points, gradually stretching the skin until it slips over the widest part of the skull.'"

"I wish the author were doing this," I grumbled, "not me."

Armed with nothing more than a guide book and a few essential items, Professor Macnab and I were trying to make a "museum specimen" out of the skin of a kinglet that we had collected the day before on Saddleback. We had already struggled with the task for about two hours, but the job had to be completed today or we would lose the specimen. To me it seemed hopeless.

I had never even *seen* a study skin. How could I prepare one from this tiny bird only 3½ inches long from tip of bill to tip of tail, its body barely an inch? My hands seemed huge and hopelessly clumsy by comparison with that mite of a bird. Even measuring it had been tricky. I questioned whether my hands, untrained for fine dissection, could make the first incision through the delicate skin without penetrating the abdominal cavity. They couldn't. I cut too deep.

From then on, fluids kept oozing out and I had to wipe them up with cotton or blot them with cornmeal to keep feathers from clinging to the flesh. Detaching legs, wings, and tail, and cleaning away the flesh had been nerve-wracking and time-consuming. And now I was faced with skinning the head.

I was ready to quit, but Prof was determined that we should follow the instructions all the way through. "A poor specimen is better than none," he insisted. And so, with him standing over me, breathing down my neck, supervising every step of the way, we persevered.

Prof read on, "As the back of the head comes through, there is seen on each side the membranous tube of skin running into the aperture of the ear. These bits of ear skin may be pulled from their hollows by grasping them between the nails of thumb and forefinger, or with the forceps."

I worked the ear skin loose.

He continued, "A little farther on the eyeballs appear under their transparent membrane which connects the eyelids with the eyeball. Cut through this membrane carefully but be sure not to cut the eyelid. A cut eyelid can never be properly mended."

"That's a happy thought," I groaned.

The reading went on, "Pry the eyeballs out of their sockets with the handle of a scalpel or with large forceps, but avoid breaking the eyeballs, as the juice is almost sure to run out through the eyelids and gum up the feathers of the head and neck."

"I don't want that to happen. This poor bird's feathers are too gummed up already. I don't want any more gunk on it." So saying, I managed to work the eyeballs out without breaking them.

Much later, I finally completed skinning the bird.

Then followed treating the skin with preservative, stuffing the tiny body cavity with cotton, sewing up the incision, and even attaching an identifying label to the miserable-looking specimen. (As a finishing touch, I carefully swaddled it in a small sheet of cotton, and—my own idea—after winding it snugly with several strands of thread, tied it up, secure from prying eyes.)

Why had Prof insisted that I prepare this specimen? Because he needed to know the kinds of birds that lived in the Saddleback forest community. This was 1935. Having no field guide, he had started collecting the birds he could not identify. Since these specimens had to be kept, he wanted me to learn the technique of preparing skins as museum specimens.

The only way we could collect a bird was to shoot it. Nearly all songbirds are so tiny that the finest caliber bullets and shotgun shot are huge by comparison. Even .22 shot can blow them to bits. As a result, most of the birds we collected at first were badly damaged. Much later in the research Prof bought a small-gauge shotgun and the smallest ammunition made, called dust shot. That gave me a new job reloading the shells. Dust shot worked fairly well, but even it damaged really small birds when they were killed at close range.

In the meantime we took the birds as they came, and some came in nearly hopeless condition. However, we did the best we could with them regardless. As scientific specimens they were important, and the Professor kept insisting, "A poor specimen is better than none."

Even with the bird in hand we were unsure of the species of some of the ones we acquired. We took those to Stanley G. Jewett, Sr., regional biologist of the U.S. Bureau of Biological Survey in Portland, for his identification.

Both the book and Mr. Jewett recommended that we make the study skins as soon as possible after killing the birds. So we assembled a skinning kit we carried with us on our weekly trips. I used that kit in preparing a study skin of the pine siskin John Boling collected in mid-February. Personally, I don't recommend field-preparation, especially on a cold, damp day. Seated on the ground in front of a sometimes-smoky fire, my lap my only table, scalpel, scissors, and other gear spread about within reach, I became cramped, chilled, and crabby after an hour or so. In spite of those handicaps, while no beauty prize winner, the siskin turned out better than the kinglet.

Frankly, those first study skins looked awful. Prof said, "They could be better." To give me some encouragement, he took me to Portland to talk with Mr. Jewett and to see the hundreds of attractive specimens he had made during his many years of field work. Stanley Jewett was kindly, interested in my plight, and suggested things I could do to improve my work. I came away inspired and thinking that perhaps I, too, could make attractive study skins.

I soon learned that with proper care at the time of collection, birds did not have to be skinned in the field. I could do a much better job in the laboratory. Mr. Jewett said that slightly overstuffing the bird's breast greatly enhanced appearance. Before I tried that even my reasonably neat specimens looked undernourished and flat-chested. Afterwards, my bird skins gradually improved.

These skins were not intended to be examples of taxidermy for display, but were prepared so that they would take up a minimum of space when stored in museum cases for future reference. The skinned and stuffed bird was expected to be a neat-appearing creature, lying on its back with its underside exposed, head laid back, wings carefully folded close to the sides (on the back rather than down the chest), the feet primly crossed and fastened together by an identifying label, the feathers all smoothly in place.

Owls, many woodpeckers, and some other birds required special treatment.

When I skinned my first woodpecker, I was fascinated to discover why these birds are able to probe deeply into holes. I found that the bird had two slender bony roots or "horns" encased in muscle and extending backward, one from each side of its tongue. These delicate structures curved upward around the base of the skull, ran forward over the forehead, and were attached close to the nostrils. This apparatus makes the woodpecker tongue highly extensible. In life, the fleshy tongue is barb-tipped and coated with sticky saliva which helps the bird catch insects and larvae.

The eyes of owls are stiffened with bony plates and are forward-looking. It is impossible to keep the natural facial appearance if the eyeballs are taken out. So we removed the fluid from the eyeballs and filled the sockets between the eyelids and the emptied eyeballs with cotton. Then we stuffed the owl's head so that its eyes would look forward.

The first owl I worked with was a slate gray California pygmy owl, not quite seven inches long. His bill and feet were greenish-yellow and he was white underneath. His coloring provided a near perfect camouflage against the wood tones of the forest. When sitting quietly these little fellows are seldom seen by human eyes even though they are often abroad in daytime. Probably this one would have gone unnoticed had not the scolding cries of small birds attracted attention to him. He was grasping a kinglet tightly in his claws when he was shot.

The most offensive skinning project I ever tackled was a screech owl that Prof collected in mid-July 1936 when I was working in Eugene. Prof packaged the bird for shipping and Mrs. Mack rushed it to the post office while he telephoned me that the bird was on its way. But it didn't arrive for nearly a week. The owl sat in the hot post office for an entire weekend before being sent out. Unrefrigerated for that long during the heat of midsummer, the specimen had badly decomposed by the time it reached me. My family thought I was going beyond the call of duty when I set up a card table outdoors and began working on the putrid creature. Though breezes carried away some of the odor, before I was through I had lost my appetite.

We collected many birds during the spring of 1937, the final year of Prof's research. I didn't have time to prepare skins as fast as the birds accumulated so we placed most of them in the Macnabs' cold storage locker until summer.

After school was out I began doing one or two study skins nearly every day. The frozen birds were more difficult to work with than fresh specimens, but I managed to make presentable skins. By August I had nearly completed the task. Since I had now made about forty study skins and was fairly good at the procedure, I thought I was ready for what I knew would be my greatest challenge—preparing a hummingbird skin.

As I worked, slowly and carefully, I discovered that the hummingbird's tiny skull had crescent-shaped roots extending up from the base of the tongue, making it highly protrusible like the tongues of woodpeckers and enabling the bird to feed upon nectar deep in the heart of flowers.

Everything went well. I produced a colorful, near-perfect little museum specimen. I fastened the identifying label to the tiny feet, picked up the scissors to snip through the excess thread, and **cut off the tip of one wing**. I didn't cry. I just sat there. Numb. Devastated. There wasn't a **thing** I could do.

One of my most memorable associations with birds was the day I collected a crossbill.

For the entire span of Prof's research we had been tantalized by birds that often passed in flocks through the tops of the Douglas-firs high above us, *chip, chip, chipping* as they worked from tree to tree. We thought they must be feeding. Since we could never see them well enough for identification, we simply recorded them as "chipping birds" for the characteristic sounds they made. We desperately needed to learn what they were.

In the last summer of Prof's field work we saw birds on the forest floor that we felt certain were some of the chipping birds. Prof issued a specific assignment to the young assistant who carried the shotgun, "Get one of those birds!" But the season passed and we were still empty handed.

The next year when I returned to the research station on July 19 to gather more material for my own research, several of the birds came down to the ground and began feeding near us in the station area. They didn't seem particularly flighty or afraid. This opportunity was crucial. We mustn't fail. I couldn't trust it to anyone else. Seizing the gun, I fired point blank at the nearest bird. Luck was with me. I had never fired a shotgun before—nor have I fired one since—but I killed the bird and, wonder of wonders, it was in usable condition though I was so close to it that I still marvel that I didn't blow it to bits. Its skin rests as a museum specimen in the Linfield College collection, a demure female red crossbill. Later that day, the young student assistant collected a male, making a pair for the museum collection.

Red crossbills, which are about the size of a sparrow, are found throughout the coniferous forests of the Northern Hemisphere. Here in the West they wander irregularly. Their scientific name is derived from their distinctive bill. It is *Loxia*, "crossed," *curvirostra*, "curved bill."

Mature male crossbills have brick-red bodies and even brighter rumps. Their wings are dusky and their tails dark. Females lack the red color. Their bodies are buff-yellow, their wings dark, and their tail dusky. Young males resemble the females or may be more orange with touches of scarlet on their crowns, breasts, and rumps.

Their slender bills, curved at the tip and crossed like the blades of scissors, are highly adapted for tearing cones open to get at the seeds. When a flock moves through the crowns of the trees, they are said to act much like small parrots as they dangle from the branches, working on cones. They also eat the tender green buds of conifers, seeds of several kinds of deciduous trees, and many insects. When these birds come to the ground it is usually to feed on the seeds of fallen cones or on insects.

Before I finished helping with Prof's field work, I had produced more than fifty study skins of birds—woodpeckers, pygmy owls, robins, varied thrushes, warblers, flycatchers, pine siskins, kinglets, a wren, a water ouzel, a screech owl, a hummingbird, and several other species. For me, preparing those specimens was one of the more exacting and challenging phases of the Saddleback Mountain research. It was also a technique that I used many times later in graduate school and in teaching.

Chapter Eight
Babes in the Woods

B Y THE SUMMER OF 1935, it became very clear that Prof and his helpers were pioneers in this new science of ecology. We had collected a great mass of specimens, but didn't know what most of them were, or how to proceed from there. Prof gleaned whatever "how to" information he could from the research of others, but few studies such as his had been done in America (or anywhere for that matter) and none in Northwest forests. Questions and challenges arose constantly. With no textbooks on ecology or ecological research and no field guides for this region, we were literally babes in the woods. We had to work out our own techniques and procedures.

Professor Macnab had taken a course on marine life given by Dr. Victor E. Shelford in the summer of 1925 at the Puget Sound Biological Station at Friday Harbor, Washington. There he learned about ecology (or oecology), a field of study only recently introduced into this country from Europe. As suggested by its name—*oikos,* for house or home and *logos,* for science—ecology is a division of biology which deals with organisms "at home" in their natural surroundings. This meant that an ecologist should know, as nearly as possible, *all* the plants and *all* the animals (from birds and mammals to insects, mites, fungi, and bacteria) which make up the community of life being studied. That's why we had collected so much stuff.

The ecological approach to biology fascinated the Professor. He loved the forest. Quite naturally then, when in the early '30s he decided to continue his own education toward a Ph.D. degree, he chose an ecological study of the Douglas-fir forest of the Oregon Coast Range which was almost unexplored biologically.

At that time ecology was being offered only by some of the larger universities. Dr. Shelford at the University of Illinois was regarded as the father of animal ecology in this country and Dr. Irving H. Blake, who had been one of Shelford's students and was now at the University of Nebraska where Prof had obtained his master's degree, became Prof's mentor.

Now, as we began the third year of this research, we faced the challenge of what to do with the mass of insects and other creatures we had collected and stored in vials, pill boxes, or cellophane envelopes. Whom could we get to identify them? They were useless without identification. Prof made inquiries and I wrote to my entomologist brother Charles at the University of Maine for advice.

Most of the people who knew these creatures well enough to name them—*systematists*, they're called—were overworked and underpaid government employees or college professors who identified material in their free time because of a special interest. I wrote to anyone we heard about who might help us and before the study ended we involved seventy-two systematists.

But first, the mass of material had to be sorted. Most of the little creatures were insects, though some were other kinds of invertebrates. Kenny Fender had been working on the collection since early spring. His knowledge of butterflies and beetles gave him a head start with insects. I began working with him and though I didn't really fancy these critters, it was a task Prof gave me to do, so I learned.

None of us, including Prof, had taken even an elementary course in entomology, the study of insects. We learned the hard way—by using reference books, of which we had precious few, and by scrutinizing specimens with a hand lens. At that time we didn't have even a primitive dissecting microscope and the marvelous scopes in general use today hadn't been developed. Later, the college did purchase a simple Bausch and Lomb dissecting scope for the biology department. We thought it was wonderful.

By midsummer we had struggled through the accumulation of bodies, wings, and dislocated legs, and placed the intact specimens in cellophane envelopes. Prof reported to Dr. Blake, "The collection...is now in first-class condition" and ready for obtaining identifications.

Then came the fateful blow. For insects to be identified, Dr. Blake explained, they had to be freshly-collected, pinned specimens. Ours were in envelopes. Most of the sorting effort had been wasted, two years of collecting down the drain.

In response to this challenge, we set up an entirely new system so that all collections would be comparable. We always used the same size collecting nets, made the same number of sweeps, and transferred our catch to a small container which we carried to the lab where a student sorted the critters, counted them, and recorded a brief description of each. At this time, I was usually the one who did this.

We preserved spiders and other soft-bodied creatures in vials of alcohol or formalin to prevent them from shriveling, and we pinned most of the insects, a tricky task. Kenny was expert at this. I soon learned!

Large insects, such as bees, flies, and most beetles, could have a special insect pin stuck through their thorax, while smaller and more delicate insects, such as mosquitoes, had to be cemented to the tips of lightweight cardboard triangles with clear nail polish. The triangles were then mounted on the pins.

Next, tiny handprinted labels were arranged on the pin, making sure that the locale, the date, and the kind of collection (herbs, shrubs, duff, or whatever) were all included. Each precious specimen was then securely (we hoped) positioned in a box of related insects, far enough apart that they would not brush against one another when shipped to a systematist. If the insects touched or became dislodged, they were usually gone goslings.

Today insects are stored in standardized wooden boxes lined with styrofoam, but we created our containers out of cigar boxes or anything we could find that was sturdy and of the right dimensions and lined them with corrugated cardboard. Butterflies, moths, dragonflies, and grasshoppers required special handling. Before being pinned and labeled, they were placed on drying boards to display their wings.

A year or so later we began using a beating square for collecting from conifer boughs. This new contraption was a yard of lightweight canvas, hemmed at the edges, with the corners turned in to form pockets into which the ends of the two crossed sticks which supported the square were inserted. This crossed-sticks frame was fastened together with a wing nut, making the assemblage collapsible. Creatures dislodged from the trees were picked up with a small bulb aspirator.

Our work never ceased. Field trips came each week and as much as possible each week's collection was cared for as it came in. However, in the months of greatest insect activity, there was nearly always a backlog of sorting waiting to be done.

I shall never forget the hours and hours we labored to sort dipterans— flies and gnats. Saddleback was loaded with dipterans, so it was urgent for us to get them named. But to do that we had to segregate them into families, of which there seemed no end. It was easy enough to recognize that they were Diptera, two-winged insects, but determining families was something else.

In Comstock's *Manual for the Study of Insects*, the book we used, the section on recognition of dipterous families is labeled, "For advanced students." We certainly weren't advanced students when we began this work, but we tackled the task anyhow.

Diptera come in many forms and sizes and are intriguing insects with beautiful and interesting details. Their thin, membranous, or gauzy wings are usually naked or covered with microscopic hairs, but those of mosquitoes are scaly. Many, for example mosquitoes, crane flies, and fungus gnats, are gauzy-winged but a whole legion of "fly-like" dipterons have other kinds of wings.

Details of the head, or shape and size of the body, are distinctive for some Diptera, but for gnatlike ones it became clear that we would also have to learn variations in the form of the wings and patterns of wing venation.

The wings of some were long and narrow, those of others short and more rounded. Tiny veins were crowded and much-branched on some wings. These vaguely resembled the pattern of highways near a city, while others had few veins that were nearly parallel in arrangement and with almost no interconnections, like freeways in wide open spaces. Some patterns were so similar that they required extremely careful study. Learning the names of veins and keeping the patterns in mind was a truly phenomenal undertaking. Even Prof became frustrated as he struggled along with us.

As though that challenge were not enough, another problem we had is that life cycles of insects are complex. Frequently a young insect bears no likeness to its parent. To cope with this, we had to understand the different insect life cycles.

Kenny knew something about them, for he had raised adult butterflies from their chrysalises, and Prof was also aware of the general pattern within the different groups of insects. But for me and most of the other helpers, this was an entirely new subject.

Most insects lay eggs, in keeping with the habits of nearly all animals except mammals, and the eggs then develop outside the female's body. Newborn human beings and the young of familiar animals look much like their parents and need only growth to complete development. Insects are different. The creature which emerges from an insect egg may have one of three forms.

Newly hatched springtails and other primitive insects are small-scale replicas of the parents, just as human babies are. Unlike human babies, though, these immature insects grow to adult size by periodically splitting their too-tight skin and crawling out of it, protected by a new larger skin which has formed inside the old one. From the time they leave the egg until death, they change little except to grow larger and, like all other arthropods, including crabs and shrimp, they can grow only by shedding their armorlike outer covering, a process known as *molting*.

Grasshoppers, aphids, spittlebugs, stink bugs, and some other insects have the second growth pattern. The creatures emerging from these eggs are called *nymphs*. Though nymphs lack wings, they usually have the same feeding habits as their parents and resemble them in many other ways. Wings appear after a series of molts and the young gradually turn into full-fledged adults.

The early naturalists who gave insects these names were students of classic Greek and Latin, so they chose names from mythology. In both Greek and Roman mythology nymphs were nature goddesses—beautiful maidens living in rivers, mountains, trees, and meadows.

For the nymphs of aquatic insects they used the even more imaginative term *naiads*. Naiads in mythology were the lovely nymphs that lived in and gave life to springs, fountains, rivers, and lakes. Naiads breathe by gills, look much different from their parents, and usually prey upon smaller organisms that live near them in the water. After several molts they crack their shell-like skins for the last time and emerge as air-breathing, winged adults. The nymphs of dragonflies, mayflies, and stoneflies are naiads.

In the third type of development, a very different-looking creature, a *larva*, emerges from the parental egg. Larva, Latin for "ghost" or "specter," is akin to the Latin word for guardian spirits—the deified ancestors who watched over and protected the households of their descendants. It is amazing that those early naturalists were able to recognize in the bizarre forms of maggots, grubs, and caterpillars the blueprints for flies, beetles, and butterflies! That was centuries before our modern-day understanding of genes and genetics.

A larva does not resemble its parents in any way. It has no trace of wings and often its body is soft and thin skinned. Many larvae and adults live in totally different environments and follow different ways of life. We found larvae in rotten wood, in the humus beneath the mosses, on herbs and shrubs, and on hemlock boughs.

Some moth caterpillars have been given special names. For instance, larvae in the moth family Geometridae are commonly known as *inchworms* or *measuring worms*, for they move along by grasping with small leglike projections on the end of the body while stretching the rest forward. Then, holding with the true legs, they hump their backs to bring up their rear. This looping motion gave rise to the additional name of *looper*. We found many looper larvae and used that name for them during our study.

When a larva is fully grown, it stops feeding and becomes what is called a *pupa*, Latin for "doll" or "baby," an appropriate term since pupae are often encased in a silky or fibrous cocoon spun by the larva and, wrapped in this way, resemble an infant in blankets. I have read that the term pupa was proposed by Linnaeus because he thought the pupal stage looked so much like an Indian papoose.

Originally the term *chrysalis*, "golden," was reserved for the golden-colored pupal stage of certain butterflies, but we used it for the parchment-like case of any butterfly, a common practice among today's entomologists.

Most pupae are quiet and seem lifeless, so this is often referred to as a "resting stage"—a very misleading term, for the pupal stage is a time of tremendous biological activity during which the insect's entire body is rebuilt. When that is completed, the insect sheds its pupal skin and emerges as an adult.

Larvae go through remarkable changes in becoming adults—changes that transform a caterpillar into a butterfly, a grub into a beetle, or a maggot into a fly.

About 90 percent of all known insect species—butterflies, moths, beetles, flies, ants, bees, wasps, and some others—have this kind of life cycle, known as *complete metamorphosis*. They develop from an egg into a larva, transform into a pupa, and finally emerge as an adult. They are true masters of the art of change.

As we discovered, deviations occur within these complex cycles. An insect's life usually begins with a fertilized egg, but without fertilization of the eggs aphids may produce a long series of females, a method known as *parthenogenesis*. Blow flies and a few other kinds of insects do not lay their eggs. Their eggs begin developing inside the female and larvae emerge to the outside world.

We discovered that we were faced with a forest full of unsolved mysteries. Since the lives of insects are so complex, how could we find out what the adult insect looked like and what its role in the forest would be when we started with a fat grub feeding on a salal leaf, an inch-long maggot squirming in the humus of the forest floor, or a looper larva descending to the ground by a weblike thread from a hemlock twig high above? We had to try to learn such things if we were to understand the interactions in this forest community.

Solving these mysteries demanded ingenuity and creativity. Prof knew of no guidelines or special equipment for this work, but when something has not been done before, the pioneer improvises. Prof assembled the materials he thought might do the trick: clay flower pots, string, cellophane sacks (there was no nylon mesh then nor today's assortment of plastics), and some fine-mesh copper screen, and began trying to raise larvae. Soon several helpers joined in the project.

We enclosed larvae feeding on shrubs in cellophane sacks tied to the branch where they were found. Ones from the soil we returned to the soil in flower pots filled with duff and covered with a sheet of cellophane after placing a piece of copper screen in the bottom to keep the larva from escaping.

We had lots of problems. Larvae which feed on shrubs often go into the soil to pupate. When sacked up, they had no way of reaching the ground. If they were placed in pots on the ground, their food supply could not be kept fresh and the contents of pots dried out because cellophane did not let in the rain. And, as if that were not enough, cellophane often split, letting the larva escape. In spite of all the problems, we did get some exciting and valuable results.

At that time a casual observer walking through the forest could have noticed blotchy dime-sized patches resembling white tissue paper or splashes of thinned paint on the upper surfaces of the leaves of some salal plants. They weren't present on all of the plants, but were often conspicuous on some. Tiny blotches appeared in early October and grew to full size by late April or the first of May in the following year. That sharp-eyed observer, like Prof, might have wondered what caused these spots.

On one of our July trips, the Professor surprised Mabel Fowler, the college nurse, and me by saying. "I want you girls to help today with a special project. We'll check for leaf miner damage on salal leaves."

"For goodness sake," Mabel exclaimed, "what kind of critters mine salal leaves?"

"They're the larva of an insect," Prof explained as we moved toward a patch of salal. "I don't know for sure what kind of insect is involved, but I suspect it's a tiny moth. They're called leaf miners because they eat out the soft cells near the upper surface of the leaf—the food-making factory for the plant. Presumably the female insect deposits her egg on the surface of the leaf. Then after the egg hatches, the larva might chew its way inside.

However," Prof continued, his voice lifting into its professorial tone, "more likely the larva gets in through one of the tiny porelike openings which control the passage of air and water vapor into and out of the leaf.

"See this little squiggly area?" He pointed to a tiny pattern in a salal leaf. "That's where a larva began its feeding. As it grew and fed more, the serpentine channels became larger. Now look at these round areas. They were made later. You'll observe that many of them are clear and about the size of a dime. Some even larger. Here the larva has eaten all of the soft cells, leaving nothing on the top of the leaf but the paper-like epidermal layer. These spots are conspicuous enough to be seen easily.

"We'll start with this plant we've been looking at and count all the infected leaves in a square meter. You girls can count and I'll record."

"Oh, goody gumdrop!" Mabel retorted as we went to work.

We examined the plants in six groups and found 200 infected leaves in an area about three feet wide by twenty feet long. The number varied from thirteen to sixty-three in a square meter.

Then Prof said, "Let's do one more sample and open the spots on the leaves to see what we can learn."

The first few had nothing in the mined areas. Suddenly Mabel exclaimed, "Look, here's a tiny, flat cocoon. What do you suppose it is, Prof?"

"I think that's the pupa of the leaf miner. The larvae are flat little critters, so I suspect their pupae are flat, too."

Soon I found an even smaller cylindrical cocoon fastened at one end by a slender thread. "Look at this one, Prof. It's different. What do you think it is?"

"That must be the cocoon of a parasite, probably a small wasp," Prof answered. "Such parasites are nature's way of keeping the leaf miners under control. Almost every species of insect has something of the kind. You've heard, haven't you:

> Big fleas have little fleas
> Upon their backs to bite 'em,
> And little fleas have lesser fleas
> And so on, ad infinitum!

We laughed.

Prof summarized, "We've opened thirty-five infected leaves. In thirteen of them apparently the larvae died, as we found nothing else. In eight there were flat cocoons of leaf miner pupae. Nine had cylindrical cocoons of the parasite, and we found both kinds of cocoons in five. The abundance of mined leaves suggests to me that we may have a problem with this insect. However, from the number of cylindrical cocoons we found, I think the parasite is gaining control.

"We should have counted the bright green uninfected leaves to learn the ratio between mined and unmined ones in our sample plots, but we don't have time left to do it today."

"That was fun," Mabel declared. "Mother Nature does take care of things, doesn't she?"

In August small moths emerged from salal leaves which Prof had sacked up in May and June. Some of the moths were light golden brown, others gray. They were identified for us by a systematist as *Cameraria gaultheriella*, a name derived from *Gaultheria shallon*, their host plant, salal. We called these little moths salal leaf miners. By early October, other larvae Prof had sacked in May and June had developed into adults. Those moths had mated and laid eggs from which larvae had emerged and were now beginning to eat holes in leaves. The cycle had run complete.

We unveiled another facet to the salal leaf-miner story. Four tiny wasp-like parasitic Hymenoptera known as chalcids emerged from black pupa cases we found in some of the leaves which contained dead salal leaf miner larvae. The wasps were pretty little things with greenish heads and dark red eyes. Their bodies, about two millimeters long and very slender, were mostly black but had a bronzy metallic luster. We were told that these chalcids were new to science and, like so many of the insects we found, were undescribed. But this kind of wasp was keeping the leaf-mining moth population under control.

We gathered much valuable information from the salal leaf miner project, but, unfortunately, we did not have the "manpower" to do many studies involving so much detail.

The "fat brown salal larva" was another interesting project. Every year in April we noticed tiny light brown grubs with dark heads eating tender salal shoots. They cut off new leaves and ruined new buds. They weren't everywhere, only in certain patches of salal. The grubs kept growing and got larger and fatter. Finally we caged some of the largest grubs in a couple of clay pots and gave them fresh salal leaves. They soon changed into quiet pupae. Then in late September we found a dark leaf beetle ten millimeters long in one of the pots and another appeared in early October. Kenny recognized these beetles as *Timarcha intricata* (for which there is no common name). Since most adult leaf beetles feed on leaves, we assumed that this one might also be a leaf eater.

Sometimes our sleuthing paid off quickly. Curious about what a cylindrical, inch-long brownish-tan larva I found while sorting through a soil sample might be, I potted it in May. By late August it had transformed into a robust black click beetle about an inch long which we immediately recognized as *Hemicrepidius morio* (no common name) a beetle we often saw during the warmer months resting on vanilla leaf and some other lower herbs. While we have no exact information about the role of this species, we do know that the larvae of click beetles, which are generally known as wireworms, are often highly injurious to the roots of plants.

We also raised a small carrion beetle from a larva we found feeding on fungus. It was a species in the genus *Choleva* and, naturally, since it was new to science and had never been described, it had no common name.*

One final project produced some interesting results and also tells something about how poorly forest insects are known. We raised two tiny beetles from the Family Cephaloidae, a little-known family of beetles. The larvae of both species were removed from decomposing wood. The first, a tan beetle of a kind Prof had seen eating pollen on devil's club flowers, pupated in a white cocoon I found in June just below the outer layer of a rotting log and the adult, identified as *Cephaloon pacificum*, emerged in early July. A closely related beetle identified as *Cephaloon bicolor*, pale with dark markings—as its name suggests—also emerged in July. It came from a pupa developed by a small white, transparent larva Minnie had discovered in November, "eating passageways in half-dry rotten wood." These are slender little beetles with a peculiarly narrow head and neck and bodies that taper at both ends. (Neither one has a common name.) Later, we caught some of these beetles from shrubs but we did not discover anything more about their habits. The trifle we learned about these two beetles seemed to be more than others had ever learned about that entire family. Without question, the forest still has an abundance of unsolved mysteries.

---

*Checking through Prof's catalog of invertebrates found at the station, I discovered more than thirty species of new-to-science insects, in addition to three kinds of soil mites, four false scorpions, one species of tiny white earthworm, and an *unnamed genus* of our "giant" earthworms. Five of the species that were named bore the designation "macnabi" in recognition of having been found during Prof's research. Many, many insects were incompletely named. Doubtless, a significant number of them were also new to science.

Summer of 1935 proved to be the middle point in Prof's five-year field study on Saddleback. When he began the research he had no idea how long the project would last. From the very first, he had planned to take a leave of absence from Linfield to complete the requirements for his doctorate at the University of Nebraska, where he hoped an instructorship would become available. However, year after year went by without an opening.

Even before Prof selected the research site, he had been cautioned by Forest Service men and various entomologists that what he proposed to do was "enough for ten men for ten years," and Dr. Blake repeatedly urged him to restrict his work and organize his material. But, as the years passed, Prof became fascinated by what the forest offered and was drawn more deeply into the research.

He was overworked and frustrated at being forced to carry an unbearably heavy teaching and administrative load with no apparent appreciation of the high quality of his teaching, almost no financial aid for his research, and no recognition of the significance of the research nor credit for it as part of his academic load. His health, as well as the research, suffered from the constant stress. But James Macnab, naturalist and perfectionist, recognizing the weaknesses in his research, carried on.

Professor Macnab was a born teacher—happiest when working with a student, or students, in the laboratory or in the field, learning something that was new to him, or helping whomever was with him to learn something new. He knew how to involve students and inspire them to do more than they dreamed they could. He also loved to explore—not only the natural world but also his own capabilities—and he loved challenges. He challenged students to stretch themselves, to do the impossible, just as he challenged himself.

Helpers came and went. More than 100 individuals, students and others, made that grueling trip to the station, once, twice, or more. Many were only curiosity seekers. Eighteen or twenty students went at least five times, and other volunteers—such as Minnie Heseman, who had been one of Prof's students, Arthur Fairhill, and Howard Daniels—contributed much genuine service. Some biology majors were paid assistants who worked for a semester, or a year, but a few of us stayed on and on.

There is no way to evaluate the impact that this research had on the lives of those of us who shared in it. Every person who visited the research station had a unique opportunity to see research at work. It was a wonderful learning process, the real thing, not just something we read about.

Though Prof regarded release of responsibility into the hands of students as a weakness in his research, that student participation proved to be one of the strengths of his teaching. Several of us, whose first glimpse of research took place on Saddleback Mountain, were inspired to devote our lives to scientific study.

Chapter Nine

A Better Way

THE LAST WEEKEND OF JULY we stayed overnight at Boyer cabin. "Sody," Arnold Soderwall, a senior biology major, had come from Portland with his girlfriend, Alice (who later became his wife). Fairhill and I rounded out the crew. As always, our departure was frustratingly delayed and it was late in the evening before we left McMinnville. When we arrived at Boyer, rain poured down until midnight.

In the morning, as we prepared to hike up the mountain, Prof said, "Last Sunday evening when we were hiking back to Boyer, a car coming from the coast almost hit Jane Claire. So today, instead of following the highway, we'll go to the upper end of the meadow and scout out a route through the woods connecting with the trail up the mountain. I've been thinking for some time that we need a better way from Boyer to the main trail. Traffic along the highway is just too heavy and fast for us to go that way safely any longer."

With that explanation, he put on his coat and hat and, stuffing his notebook into a pocket, said, "Now let's get going."

Falling in line behind Prof, we traversed Boyer flat, zigzagging around clumps of grass and sedges like a family of geese following its leader. Through the meadow we trudged, toward the forest at the upper end, crossing on our way the meandering streamlet that gives rise to the Little Nestucca River.

Now, at 9:30 a.m., the sun was warm and pleasant and the sky clear, with no hint of the deluge that had greeted our arrival the night before. That changed abruptly as we entered the brush-grown forest edge, for every tree or bush we touched dumped its burden of moisture on us, quickly soaking our clothing through to the skin. As the men forged ahead through the mixture of waterladen vegetation, fighting their way up the steep hillside, Alice and I struggled along behind, grateful that they had already knocked much of the water off the plants.

I don't think this was the kind of outing Alice had expected. She had come with Sody for his introductory trip as field research assistant replacing John Boling who had graduated in June. She probably had something more like a picnic in mind. **This** was no picnic. The climb, far from easy for me, must have been horrendous for Alice. Polio in her childhood had caused one leg to be shorter than the other, resulting in a limp. In spite of that disability, I don't recall hearing a word of complaint from her.

At the top of the ridge, Prof led us into traces of an old wagon road used during the 1910-1915 timber claim period. Still distinct in places, it made a good trail for us to follow as it wound along this watershed between the Little Nestucca and Little Salmon rivers.

A forest of mature Douglas-firs and hemlocks crowned the ridge. Banks of sword ferns and clumps of Oregon grape flourished and a deep carpet of mosses covered old logs and cushioned our way. Shrubs and herbs accented the top of the ridge and young hemlocks fringed our path.

Soon we descended to the Little Salmon River, which separated this ridge from the one which held the trail to the top of the mountain. There we found a pair of fir logs which, arranged in tandem, spanned the stream. The logs were frighteningly high above the ground, and we had to step down from the first one to reach the second, but we inched our way along them rather than fight through the tangle of berry canes, shrubs, and small trees that bordered the river.

Luckily, on the far side of the stream, the end of the second spanning log lay close to the old wagon road ascending the slope to the trail above. The road here was deeply eroded and confined within earth walls six to eight feet high and a log that had fallen across the road partially blocked our way through this channel. After crawling under the log, we continued up the road, the sides of which were overgrown with the tallest salal plants I had ever seen. They must have been at least six feet high and, growing out from both banks toward the middle of the road where there was more light, their branches intertwined to form a tunnel through which we worked our way.

Emerging from this maze onto the eastern border of Summit Prairie, we soon found the main trail up the mountain. From that point on, the day was typical and filled with routine research activities. When evening came, we followed the old familiar trail down to the highway and back to Boyer rather than trying to retrace our morning route.

The next week Bob Rieder and Dorothy McKey were along. Prof planned to hunt for an easier approach from Boyer flat to the wagon road than the steep brushy one we had used the week before. He drove directly to the trailhead on the highway and let Dorothy and me out so we could go on to the station while he and Bob returned to Boyer to work on the trail.

This was Dorothy's first trip. A born naturalist who had been learning the names and habits of plants and all sorts of living creatures from a very early age, she was now a college sophomore planning to major in biology. Hoping to discover potential research assistants, Prof had recently started carefully observing new students and had decided that Dorothy was worthy of cultivation.

The morning was pleasant but partly cloudy and cool, every bush newly washed and heavy with rain from a recent shower. The freshness heightened all our senses. Colors seemed brighter, sounds sharper, and the myriad odors more distinctly fragrant, acrid, or earthy. We delighted in our surroundings.

Our gaiety subsided abruptly as our legs and feet became drenched with the moisture from bushes along the trail. Like a sponge, Dorothy's corduroy pants siphoned moisture from every bush she passed and her feet sloshed about in the lightweight sandals she wore—the only shoes she owned in that period of depression. She was miserable long before we reached the station. My pants, damp but not soaked, evidently had not been as thirsty as hers, and my feet, inside well-oiled hiking boots, were comparatively dry.

As a rule, August was hot and dry, but this time when we reached the station I quickly uncovered the reserve fuel and kindled a fire while Dorothy removed her soggy pants, wrung out of them all the water she could, and suspended them over the fire to dry. The short dress she wore as a top to her outfit kept her modest enough, but she created an unforgettable scene as she stood barefooted and barelegged, dangling her pants from a stick over the fire as though toasting them for lunch, her sandals perched at the fire's edge to dry.

By the time the men arrived in mid-afternoon Dorothy was reclothed and quite presentable but we laughed and kidded about the show they had missed.

Dorothy and I had taken care of all the instruments except the ones in the high hemlock. Bob, undaunted—with his one good hand and other strong arm—climbed into the treetop perch to care for them and collect insects. Dorothy, curious about life at the eighty-five foot level, followed him up the tree. In all the years of the research, she was the only girl daring enough to make that climb.

We were busy at the station until dusk. Then, once again we returned to Boyer by way of the highway.

Two weeks later, August 15, Prof drove to the beginning of the trail where he, Dorothy, and I got out and Mrs. Macnab took the car back to Boyer.

We had a busy, full day and didn't leave the station until after dark. It was a warm night with a nearly full moon. Shafts of light from that August moon streamed through the crowns of the forest trees forming bright patches which contrasted sharply with the blackness of the shadows. To Prof and me, who were accustomed to finding our way in darkness relieved only by light reflected from the sky, the contrasting patterns were totally unfamiliar and confusing. As we hiked down the mountain, we were soon stepping over moonbeams that we thought were logs and tripping on small logs we had mistaken for shafts of moonlight. We laughed a lot at our antics—and nursed our barked shins.

The night was so bright and pleasant that we must have become a bit moonstruck. Anyhow, when we reached the edge of Summit Prairie, Prof said, "How about going out over the new route? I'm sure I can find the way."

"Oh, that would be fun," Dorothy and I responded. "Let's do it!"

"We may have a little trouble locating where the new trail comes in," Prof warned. "I'll scout to the left here. You girls move slowly and carefully to the right. That old road to Little Salmon is in here somewhere, but it's well hidden by the salal."

With that, he continued along the trail, leaving us in a patch of shrubbery with nothing but a mosaic of light and shadow to aid in our search for the new trail. I took the lead as we moved forward, cautiously.

Suddenly I was lying head downward in the salal tunnel struggling to get free from the tangle into which I had fallen.

"Jane Claire, I've lost you. Where are you?" Dorothy's wail came to me, muffled and distraught.

"I'm down here. Can't you see my feet? They're waving to you," I called, giggling at the absurdity of my position.

"Yes, I see your feet now, but what happened?"

"I guess I've found the trail the hard way. Wait till I get myself upright. You don't need to follow my example."

I had fallen into the deeply eroded, salal-overgrown route for which we were searching.

Prof rejoined us and we moved on, slowly. How we found our way across the log bridge at Little Salmon River and on through the forest, I'll never know, though Prof's light blue shirt reflecting starlight or moonlight whenever he passed through a break in the trees did serve as a lead light. I had been over that route only once, and Dorothy not at all, but Prof had a remarkable sense of direction and memory for detail.

Somehow we inched our way along, stepping over moonbeams and tripping on logs all the way back to Boyer and an understandably perturbed Mrs. Macnab. It was nearly midnight. She was used to her husband being late, but not like this. She knew some catastrophe must have overtaken us. Someone must have broken a leg, or we'd had an encounter with a cougar, or we were hopelessly lost in the forest.

It was nearly two-thirty in the morning when we finally got back to McMinnville. Dorothy's parents were fit to be tied. Their daughter had never, no never, stayed out like this before. Worried and angry, it's a wonder that her father ever permitted her to go to the mountain again. But, relieved that all were safe and unharmed, he forgave Prof for keeping her out so late. Eventually Dorothy became one of Prof's most valued helpers.

On September 13, Sody and Bob Rieder "cut the trail" to the top of the ridge under Prof's supervision. The new trail then became our regular route of access to the station. Not only was it free from highway hazards and noise, it was also somewhat shorter.

The crew at the fire shelter on a winter day. The author is on the left; Prof is on the right.

Chapter Ten

Troubled Seasons

The last week of October 1935 began ominously. For several days a brisk north wind dried the air and sent oak leaves scurrying across the campus. Snow fell unseasonably early during the night of Tuesday, October 29. More snow came on Wednesday, and the bitter north wind continued into Friday.

We had special plans for this Halloween weekend. Prompted by urging from Sody and me, our philosophy professor, Dr. Tom Tuttle, was going with us to Boyer cabin. He had accepted Prof's invitation before there was any hint of this sudden change from Indian summer into winter.

As so often happened, Prof was not ready on Friday until long after the time agreed upon for our departure. After a full day at the college, he had to shop for groceries for the family and split a supply of kindling and firewood for this weekend of unanticipated, exceptionally cold weather.

Finally we were on our way. Arriving at Boyer at eleven-thirty, chilled from the long ride in an unheated car, we were greeted by a damp cabin, frigid as an icebox. In spite of our discomfort, we gradually relaxed and became engrossed in conversation as we huddled around the old kitchen range, listening to a crackling fire. We reluctantly retired to our pads of bedding on the cold, hard floor, at three o'clock in the morning of November 2.

When we left the cabin at eleven o'clock that morning, snow sparkled like millions of tiny diamonds under the cloudless blue sky and crunched and squeaked beneath our feet as an icy wind hastened us toward the forest at the south end of the flat. Inside the forest, the trees quieted the wind and helped hold the earth's warmth, providing some relief.

The fresh snow held a graphic record of recent animal activity. Chipmunks and snowshoe hares had been busy in areas all along the trail. Bobcats had left tracks in several places. Deer had been active, and above Little Salmon River on Summit Prairie we traced the route of a cougar to a large log where the tracks disappeared. We thought the cougar must have jumped up onto that log.

No mouse tracks were apparent in the lightly crusted shallow snow along the first part of the trail though we had seen their burrows in many places in that area the week before. However, mouse tracks were plentiful in the deeper, less compact snow between Salmon River and the station.

In the entire distance to the station we saw only two spider webs, though more than 100 webs had been draped across the trail the week before. The bodies of several dead spiders lay on the snow. We saw no snails, slugs, or beetles. There were almost no insects. Even birds were quieter and less abundant than usual. All these things gave mute evidence of winter's precipitous arrival. We were impressed.

Dr. Tuttle, from the plains of Texas, had never seen anything like this spectacular forest. He was a scholar, a rather portly one, and made no pretense of being an outdoorsman. He had difficulty with much of the trail and didn't relish walking the snow-covered logs that served as our bridges across the rivers. He was a good sport, but was obviously relieved whenever we slowed our pace for any reason or paused to identify tracks. Of course, both Sody and I, being students in his history of philosophy class, were only too willing to assist him whenever we could.

On the north flank of Saddleback Mountain the snow was deeper and contained more moisture. Falling in huge flakes, it had clung to needles, boughs, ferns, and shrubs, transforming the evergreen forest into a place of exceptional beauty. We were glad Dr. Tuttle could share this beauty with us, for he had seen snow rarely and never in such a setting.

The depth of snow increased to almost three inches before we reached the station. It was cold there, only 28°F. So Sody, Prof, and I all pitched in to do our bit, and we were soon able to relax in comparative comfort around a cheery fire. After lunch, Sody and I began checking the weather instruments, leaving Prof and Dr. Tuttle by the fire, where Prof recorded data and rested while the two of them visited. Prof said he had a sore throat and admitted that he was not feeling well. Though we hurried, it was almost four-thirty and getting dusky when Sody and I finished with the instruments. We immediately prepared to return to the cabin. Sody added Prof's heavy coat to the backpack of research materials he was carrying so that Prof would not become overheated in his return to the cabin. True to form, the Professor promptly disappeared down the trail, leaving Sody and me to help the newcomer.

Our progress was slower than usual for Dr. Tuttle was not only middle-aged and portly but also nearsighted and had difficulty finding his way in the dimness of the unfamiliar forest. On a clear night such as this one, a surprising amount of starlight is reflected from snow, even in a forest. For Sody and me, though the light was not bright, it was adequate, but for Dr. Tuttle it was far too dim.

Eventually we arrived at the edge of Boyer flat and found a thoroughly chilled Professor waiting for his coat. He had started across the windy flat to the cabin but the cold hit him severely, forcing him to seek refuge among the trees. Now, even with the protection of his coat, his teeth chattered and he shivered uncontrollably. Clearly, Prof was a very sick man.

Shocked, we hurried to the cabin, packed our belongings quickly and headed home with Sody at the wheel. Prof had never before permitted a student to drive his car when he was along. It had been a bitter-sweet outing—certainly not the kind we had planned. This was no occasion for rest and fun.

The next day Prof lay in bed with a high fever and an acute case of tonsillitis, the beginning of a rapidly developing sequence of critical illnesses.

Monday, I received word that one of my sisters had died unexpectedly. I left immediately for Roseburg to attend her funeral and spend a few days with my family.

Responsibility for the field work fell on Sody the weekend I was away. Though he had made few trips to the station, he managed well. Minnie and Kilen went along to help.

When I returned to McMinnville Prof was still ill. He now had severe sinusitis.

The following Sunday, November 17, a cold, fog-enshrouded day, Sody and I made the research trip. The fog hanging in the treetops hid the sun and darkened the forest and the damp cold chilled us to the bone. I was depressed by my sister's death, and both Sody and I were worried about Prof. We accomplished all essential tasks but it was a dismal experience.

On November 22, Prof was taken to the hospital for treatment of a mastoid abscess. His illness had progressed from acute tonsillitis, through acute sinusitis, to this infection. In that era before the development of antibiotics the doctor feared that Prof might have to have mastoid surgery, a precarious procedure in which part of the mastoid bone behind the ear is chipped away.

Before leaving for the hospital, the Professor had to get some long-overdue material into the mail. So, though I was not feeling well and had a fever, I got out of my bed in my unheated room and did the necessary typing. Three days later lumps behind my ears warned that I had mumps, which I had picked up, unknowingly, on my trip to Roseburg. That illness kept me bedfast for two weeks.

By the time I was on my feet, Prof had recovered from the mastoid infection, without surgery, but now had mumps.

Coping with an infectious disease such as mumps in a hospital was an intolerable situation in those days, and so, though Prof was still a bed patient, he was ousted. He became critically ill with his temperature soaring to 104.5°F and the doctor called in a nurse to care for him.

During all this, Sody took responsibility for the field work, missing only one day. Kenny and Dorothy and several other people helped on some days, but during Christmas vacation he made the trip entirely by himself. In January I was well enough to begin helping again. But Prof did not return to the field until March.

Chaos prevailed in the Biology Department. Prof was the only biologist on the college faculty. So faithful, dependable Sody added the burden of botany—the beginning biology course—to field research, classwork, and his duties as student body president. He worked doggedly to keep that botany class going even though he had taken only a single semester in the subject. The eight or ten of us students in more advanced courses struggled along the best we could, without instruction.

As soon as he was well enough, about mid-January, Prof returned to the campus, rescuing Sody and the botany students and completed that course by the end of the semester. Advanced courses, however, were either canceled, postponed until summer, or finished during the second semester along with other courses scheduled for that time.

Most of that 1935-36 college year was a nightmare for the Macnab family (where there was even more sickness), the biology students, Prof's other research helpers, and me.

On February 1, Prof resumed a full program of work at the college and also began driving to Boyer, taking those who would do the field work to the trail head and going back to the cabin to rest or work without interruption.

For me, the one redeeming feature of the year was the field research. Weakened by the mumps, I was trying to do too much too soon and it became apparent that I would have to spend a fifth year at Linfield. I looked forward to the weekly data-gathering trips to the mountain. They helped to lift my spirits and restore my health.

All that year the weather seemed caught up in a stress-producing syndrome of its own. Winter had come early and stayed late. In spring it seesawed back and forth from mild to cold, from dry to wet, retarding the early part of spring and dragging out the season. Then warm rains, followed by a few very pleasant days, ended spring and initiated summer. But rains began again, slowing development so much that summer ended later than usual.

Commencement Day arrived, a day of rejoicing for classmates and friends. But I wasn't graduating.

Summer came. The year of troubled seasons had ended.

Prof at rest.

Chapter Eleven
Ellis Barn

I PLANNED TO SPEND the summer of 1936 helping Prof with the Saddleback research, but in mid-June I learned of an office job open in Eugene. It would pay real money, not just provide room and meals like the Macnabs could do, so Prof told me to take the job.

I was a reasonably good stenographer, but that office was noisy, the work tedious and boring, and I had nothing in common with the other girls. I longed to be back in my beloved forest.

At last the summer ended and I returned to McMinnville. The day was warm and humid. Clouds built up in the afternoon and by evening rain began falling. What a surprise. It was only September 1st. Rains seldom began that early.

After supper I was busy preparing lunches for the next day's trip to Saddleback when Prof stomped into the kitchen carrying his hiking boots under his good arm and a can of neat's-foot oil in his hand, ready to begin the weekly wet-weather ritual of boot-greasing.

"Better oil your boots, too, Jinkler," he grumbled. "The woods'll be soaking wet tomorrow."

"Okay. I'll do that as soon as I finish the sandwiches," I said, as I lathered peanut butter onto the bread I had laid out.

Without further comment, which was unusual for him, Prof put a few drops of oil on his boots, rubbed it in, and added more oil, repeating the process many times, apparently concentrating on what he was doing. Finally, he blurted, "You know we won't have use of the cabin."

"No! What's happened?"

"Hadn't I told you? Boyer sold it this summer."

"That's a pretty kettle of fish. What're we going to do? We can't trap without a place to stay overnight." Then, jabbing at the bread with my knife as though it had caused our predicament, I added, "We can't set out traps unless we can check them the next day."

Prof studied a boot, as though searching for an answer, before saying, "Maybe we'll be lucky and have good weather after this rainy spell. There's almost always a couple weeks of Indian summer. We'll make day trips until then."

"But what good'll Indian summer do if we don't have a place to stay?" I insisted, waving the knife wildly.

Pouring more oil on his boot and rubbing it in before answering, Prof looked up with a mischievous twinkle in his eyes and said, "Well, we could camp at the Hood Craven cabin site. It's only four miles from the highway. Of course we'd have to pack in everything." He continued to rub, giving me a chance to think before he asked, "Do you think you could make it?"

Mulling over Prof's question while finishing the sandwiches, I finally answered, "I think I could all right, but I don't know who I can get to go with me. Dorothy McKey can't go. She's down with rheumatic fever. There aren't many girls around who would enjoy that kind of outing, and I'd be kicked out of college if we didn't have some other girl along as a chaperone."

"Well, you think about it and see what you can do," Prof said, putting his shoes aside and getting up to leave the room. "I have to go over to the college to pick up the surveying equipment. Want to check some elevations tomorrow. When we get that all done, we can start a map of the station."

With that he left. Lost in thought, I finished preparing the lunches. *Who could I get to go along?*

The rain stopped during the night, but the next morning the bushes were still very wet all along the way to the station. We could see where water had been running down the trail. With a partly overcast sky, the day was chilly enough that we were happy to be active, not only to keep warm but also to ward off mosquitoes that swarmed about us, biting viciously.

The next week was drier and cooler. We noticed frost at Boyer flat, and Mervin Boyer reported that there had also been frost there the night before. This, like the rain on September 1st, was exceptionally early. Again, it was a busy day for those who made the trip, with mosquitoes less numerous, but no less vicious.

The third weekend of September was cloudless but hazy with smoke in the air from slash-burning. Rain had fallen since the last trip, dampening the premises and bringing out more mosquitoes. The milder temperature made them more active. Hordes of at least three kinds of blood-suckers bedeviled us all day. Prof noted in his journal, "Two to six at one time, very vicious, bite persistently." Yellowjackets also were numerous and irritating, but many insects that had been common a few weeks earlier were no longer around. All of these changes indicated that autumn was progressing toward winter.

At last, when the final week of September came, Prof said the weather looked stable enough for us to risk an overnight trip. Enlisting Mark Nickerson and Georgia Jones, we assembled a stack of gear—food, pots and pans, traps, bait, and bedrolls of whatever we could find (none of it light-weight or well insulated), plus the regular research equipment—and set out for the mountain, arriving at Boyer about ten o'clock that night to **begin** the hike to our campsite.

Mark, Prof's new field assistant, a sophomore, had been initiated into the research the preceding week. This was to be Georgia's first and only over-night trip. She was my special friend. Together we had struggled through Prof's courses the year before. As a senior she was an assistant in the biology department, but she was not an outdoor person. She planned to become a nurse and embarked on this venture solely out of friendship for me.

Trudging up the mountain in the dark, loaded with all that gear—climbing over, crawling under, and walking around logs, crossing the high log bridge over Little Salmon, and jumping from rock to rock across Salmon River—was a grueling five-hour experience. In daylight we could have made it in two. Finally at three o'clock Saturday morning, we collapsed in a small clearing beside a murmuring mountain stream, with a starry dome over our heads and sentinels of the forest guarding us.

Perhaps I had become callous after nearly three years of coping with Prof's field research methods and his ideas of fun, but I have no clear recol-lections of that trip. I do remember that Georgia had difficulty navigating the trail but she was good natured about her difficulties and often used her favorite expression, "Oh, Elmer!"

I remember carrying heavy, bulky bedrolls **sometime** and struggling over and under logs that barricaded our way, but I don't know whether those memories are from **that** trip or from some similar one. Many nightmare ex-periences are telescoped in my memory.

I don't recall ever feeling driven to perform these feats of endurance. Rather, Prof cajoled us to stretch ourselves—to do a bit more than we thought we were capable of doing. We were young and energetic. After all, if he, a dozen years our senior, could do these things in spite of his crippled arm (to which he never referred), we **should** be able to as well.

All too soon we awakened to broad daylight and the stark reality of our surroundings. We were camped beside the much weathered, handsplit shake remnants of a tumble-down cabin near where the trail to the mountaintop crossed Hood Craven Creek. Mice, bats, and woodrats called that disheveled mass of boards home. We could only guess what other creatures might live there. For the next thirty-six hours it would be our home, too, since it—the former Hood Craven cabin—was conveniently close to the research station.

Revitalized by a makeshift breakfast, we began collecting insects in the clearing and set out mouse traps in likely spots around the cabin debris before moving on toward the research station in mid-afternoon, setting more traps and some snares near mountain beaver burrows along the way.

It was a sunny, dry, warm day with the temperature near 70° F. Hard gusts of dry wind from the northeast blew through the tree tops all day long.

After servicing the instruments, we used the rest of the day observing insects, spiders, birds, and any other creatures we could find. Prof concentrated on two marked square meter plots of salal which he had often studied. Mark collected any insects he could reach from the high hemlock platform and, with Georgia, searched through a sample of rotten wood. All of us did some random collecting of insects. I spent most of my time supervising Georgia and Mark, caring for the collections, and recording information gleaned by all of us.

After another night of camping under the stars, we picked up the twenty traps which we had set out. We had three deer mice and, unfortunately, one little brown winter wren. Though the wren was badly damaged and most of its tail feathers were missing, Prof's ultimatum, "A poor specimen is better than none," prevailed and I prepared its skin for the collection.

Then Georgia and I turned our attention to the mice, which we skinned and stuffed as museum specimens, a procedure basically like that of making bird study skins. The main differences are that for mammals the skull, which is often used in identification, must be removed and saved and replaced by a "skull" of cotton inserted in its place. The tail vertebrae also have to be slipped out of the skin and replaced by a wire covered with a thin layer of cotton, always a tricky operation and sometimes well-nigh impossible. Then, on cork or cardboard, the finished specimen is neatly pinned to dry—belly down, feet close to the sides, and tail straight out between the hind feet.

From the very first, mammal study skins had been easier for me to make than bird skins. I had prepared a dozen or so and knew that these mice shouldn't be very difficult or time-consuming. One of them, however, was badly damaged by black ground beetles. I worked with that one and prepared another mouse while Georgia received her initiation into the art of making a museum specimen. By the time we had finished it was getting dark and the men had assembled our gear. Soon, loaded like so many pack animals, we were on our long trek back to the highway and Prof's old Hudson car.

In the weeks that followed, the weather was remarkably pleasant, permitting such activities as surveying, camping, and searching for a possible overnight shelter, in addition to the routine research work.

On one stay at the Hood Craven site, Prof and Mark had a midnight visitor—a bushy-tailed woodrat that came out from the cabin wreckage and moved about actively, apparently unafraid. Its body was about a foot long and its bottlebrush tail added another foot to its length. By flashlight it appeared to be bluish-black with a dark head and black tail, white beneath its chin and at the base of its whiskers. Woodrats are much more attractive than their cousin, the common Norway rat.

October was passing. We had been favored by weeks of pleasant Indian Summer weather with much sunshine after the first rains in early September. This could not go on forever. Winter was almost here. Prof knew all too well that rains or snow would come soon. An overnight shelter must be found, but where?

After talking with Mervin Boyer and others who knew the area, he assigned student helpers who were good woodsmen to search for a possible shelter on the old timber claims.

I do not remember, and the records do not tell precisely when, or by whom, the place was discovered, though I think it was Jim Henry who found it. At any rate, on November 14, after completing work at the station, we hurried up the mountain to inspect a place which someone had found.

With Jim and Mark acting as guides we followed the trail for a half mile or so before crossing a small stream into territory unfamiliar to Prof and me. Closely paralleling the stream on our left, we ascended ever higher through the ancient trees. Finally, at an elevation about 1,000 feet above the station, we emerged from the forest into a picturesque setting. On the right stood a small barn partially surrounded by extremely high gooseberry bushes. The tall, narrow building was sturdily made of poles and cedar shakes and had two horse stalls and a place for hay.

On the left, near the stream which skirted the clearing, were the timbers of a cabin, nearly flattened by the ravages of time and the snows of many winters. Beside the cabin's wreckage, a woodshed survived, filled with neatly stacked old-growth fir wood, fairly pleading to be used. That treasure of fuel, supporting the roof, had kept the shed intact.

It was an idyllic spot—the ancient forest cradling the little clearing and its buildings. Fascinated, we searched for evidence of the former occupants. Tattered remnants of newspapers covering the cabin walls told us little. We looked for a date on them, but found none. Somewhere we did find the name "Ellis."

With a stream nearby for water, a winter's supply of split, dry wood, a building with four walls, a floor, and an intact roof overhead—a snug shelter for any kind of weather—what more could we ask? Of course it was a strenuous, backbreaking distance from the highway, and some kind of stove would have to be packed in, but those were trivial matters. At last we had an overnight shelter—Ellis Barn.

By the time we stepped from the clearing into the forest after our inspection, it was pitch-dark. We had been so intent on examining the premises that we had become oblivious to the passage of time. We had no light, and there was no track for us to follow. We knew we must stay close to the stream on our right and that we must cross it before we could reach the trail.

After a short descent we crossed the stream but did not find the trail. We had miscalculated the distance to the crossing place and, unknowingly, had gone too far downstream. Slowly we moved ever farther down the mountain, searching for the trail.

After much floundering in the dark forest, Prof put his pack on the ground saying, "This has gone on too long. Jane Claire, you stay here with the packs while Mark and Jim and I look for pitch. We've got to have a light to find our way out of here."

Soon someone located an old Douglas-fir log and split off a piece loaded with resinous, sticky pitch. Prof lighted it with one of the matches he always carried for starting the fires at the station. Even with that light, though, we had trouble getting our bearings. However, aided by the torch, Prof's familiarity with the mountain eventually paid off, and he located the trail. Then, pretty well exhausted, we made our way to the highway and the car.

Our return to McMinnville that night was late indeed. It was three o'clock in the morning when we arrived at the campus!

During the remaining months of the research, Ellis Barn became a weekend haven. Our group first used it on New Year's Day 1937. On that day Mark Nickerson and Jim Henry hiked in carrying on their backs a small airtight heating stove, staple supplies, their bedding, and traps for mice and other small mammals.

Jim, though only a college freshman, had hiked and trapped in the woods and mountains since childhood. He was now an experienced woodsman, who had joined our research group in the fall. He knew the tracks of many forest animals and on that day identified those of mice, rabbits, bobcats, and cougar in the fresh snow between the highway and the barn.

After a night in the barn, the young men set out for the top of the mountain to see what new information the snow might reveal. Besides the usual mouse and rabbit tracks, they found many deer tracks and fresh scars on some alder trees where a buck had rubbed his antlers to free them from the "velvet," the no longer functional layer of soft furry skin that had nourished the antlers during their development. Near the notch, they found fresh raccoon tracks in a hemlock thicket and saw a place where a large cougar had rested on its haunches after coming up the ridge from a lower part of the mountain. Returning to the barn, they checked the traps they had set the day before and put out a few more.

At about 9:30 that evening, Prof, his son Jimmie, Twila (Mrs. Macnab's cousin and my current roommate), and I joined the young men at the barn. We had left McMinnville late that afternoon and, loaded with bedding and other supplies, had labored up the mountain in the dark. As we passed the research station, we heard the deep *whoo! whoo! whoo! whoo!* of two great horned owls, and farther on, Prof noted bobcat tracks in the light snow just below the barn.

We had a great time in our rustic, stable shelter, clustered around the little heater, swapping yarns and singing by candlelight. Twila had a lovely soprano voice. Prof and Jim vied with one another in their storytelling, and, Jim, who enjoyed teasing, bedeviled Twila constantly about her Texan drawl. She was from Muleshoe, Texas.

Eventually, we settled down to rest—Twila and I wrapped in our blankets in the first horse stall and the men in their stall at the far side of the building.

The next morning after breakfast we gathered up the traps and our bedding and started home, going as far as the research station. There, we checked the weather instruments and made notes on bird and mammal activity and the few insects that were around.

Our catch for that trip consisted of six more deer mice and two new animals. One of the new ones looked like a small meadow mouse. However, Mr. Jewett said it was a redbacked vole, few of which had been caught in Oregon. Our other find was a spotted skunk, a pretty little creature. Her silky black coat had a collage of white spots and narrow white stripes, and her black tail was tipped with white. Though the skunk wasn't odoriferous, we insisted that Jim, who had caught her, must walk down the mountain at a discreet distance behind the rest of us with his prize dangling from the end of a pole.

The next day, grateful that the cold weather had changed our procedure, I skinned and stuffed the animals in the comfort of the laboratory. I had no difficulty avoiding the skunk's scent glands and made an attractive museum specimen which is still on display at Linfield College.

Snow continued to fall off and on during January and into February, providing excellent opportunities for us to study tracks and gain an idea about the relative numbers of mammals on the mountain.

February 6 turned out to be an especially interesting day. Since Prof owned no camera, he had asked a college student who was an amateur photographer to come with us and use the college's camera for a series of pictures. Up to that time, a few pictures by Howard Daniels and some taken by Ray Edmunds in April 1935 were the only ones we had of research activities.

Because photography is such a popular hobby now it seems strange that we did not have more pictures. In 1937 money was available only for necessities; hobbies were not commonplace. The Eastman Brownie Kodak was around in fair numbers but pictures obtained with it were not of high quality. The Leica, the first successful 35mm handheld camera, was very expensive, and the Kodachrome color slide process was a recent invention.

On that February day snow clung to every log, rock, and twig, transforming the forest into a place of exceptional beauty. Old stumps became giant toadstools, logs were huge brownie bars with white icing, and young hemlock boughs resembled delicate lace.

Prof led us through this wonderland at a leisurely pace, making frequent pauses to interpret the story revealed by tracks, to listen to birdcalls in the snow-muffled stillness, or to record on film the beauty of our surroundings. After a four-hour trek, we arrived at the research station. Under a six-inch blanket of snow, it, too, had an otherworldly appearance.

Continuing snowstorms during the following weeks worried Prof. He was concerned about conditions at Ellis Barn.

We inveigled Eunice Boone and June Whitman, two new biology majors, to go along on February 13 for an overnight stay. Loaded with the essential heavy bedrolls, we began the venture at 1:30 in the afternoon. Most of the snow had disappeared from the vegetation at the lower elevations but some lingered on the ground and the temperature was below freezing. It was dusk when we arrived at the barn. There we found three feet of snow covering everything in the clearing.

As soon as a fire in the little heating stove had warmed us and taken the chill from the place, the girls and I spread our blankets on the floor of the ladies' stall and began preparing an evening meal.

Suddenly, we heard an ominous groaning overhead. Then the roof timbers began creaking, and in no time at all they fairly shrieked.

"Mark, grab a shovel and come help," Prof yelled as he rushed out the door.

Somehow the men reached the top of the barn and began frantically shoveling snow off the overburdened roof.

Light had been so dim at the time of our arrival that Prof had failed to notice the depth of snow on the old roof. As heat from the stove worked up through the split shake roof, some of the snow had melted and, sliding downward, had increased the weight in a low area that was now threatening to collapse.

Soon the roof was safe, the excitement over, and we got back to more normal activities. Eventually we retired. For a time all was peace and quiet. But our sleep was fitful. The other girls and I had put all our covers together, hoping in that way to have a more comfortable bed than we would have by sleeping separately. Our scheme didn't work. The girl in the center was too hot. Those on the outside, often only half covered, were cold.

Besides that, a bushy-tailed woodrat that had built a nest on the timbers overhead disturbed everyone with its antics. For a creature of its size, it made an amazing amount of noise. It would gallop across the floor like a horse. Then, stopping briefly, drum a slow *tap, tap, tap* with one of its hind feet before again racing off to investigate, and rattle, a utensil in our kitchen area. Then it would romp through the cabin again, dragging a piece of wood, or it would tap, or rattle. This went on and on. We might have found such behavior entertaining had we not wanted to sleep.

We survived the night but didn't get much sleep. We spent most of that Sunday relaxing. Prof often used research trips for a bit of rest, away from the constant pressures and demands of the campus and responsibilities of home.

When we left the barn at about two o'clock for our trip back to the car, the temperature had risen slightly. It was now above freezing and snow and ice were beginning to fall from the crowns of the taller trees. We found only four inches of snow on the ground at the station.

The next Saturday Prof, Jim Henry, Twila, and I packed in again for my final wintertime overnight stay at the barn. It was a miserable day with snow underfoot, a steady drizzle falling, and a temperature of only 38° F with a light wind increasing the chill factor. Our blankets got damp though they were wrapped in oilcloth. And again that night the woodrat disturbed us with its antics!

There was a sequel to the woodrat story. In October 1937 after I had left Linfield and was far away in graduate school, Prof, Jim Henry, Frances Westall, and Mrs. Macnab spent a night at Ellis Barn.

That night Prof had Jim set a trap to catch the woodrat. This is the story as told by Jim:

"I found a newly-made nest on top of some extra shakes laid on the crossbraces near the gable of the roof. As I was a trapper, I wrapped the jaws of a steel trap with cloth so as not to break the animal's leg and set it in the nest above, tying it to one of the crosspoles by a long string.

"At about three in the morning the rat came to his nest, sprang the trap, and fell the length of the string with his tail dangling in the faces of the girls sleeping in one of the horse stalls below.

"As Prof and I were sleeping in the other horse stall, we awakened to the squealing of a packrat and the screams of the girls.

"I could not have planned it better except that I had to get up in my longhandles and capture the whiskered hairy-tailed, beady-eyed packrat. I put him in a ten-pound lard pail with a snap lid that I punched holes in so the rat could breathe on the way back to the laboratory."

Somehow, I can't imagine Mrs. Mack being on that trip! But Prof's notes read, "J.H. [Jim Henry], F.W. [Frances Westall], & Mamie." (There was no other Mamie.) Mamie Macnab did not like such outings and, as far as I know, she was *never* on any of the other trips. When she drove the car to take any of us out to the mountain, she always spent the day with Mrs. Boyer. The explanation for her being along on this trip must be that Prof had special work for Frances to do and persuaded Mamie to go along since, in those days, the college forbade girls to go on any overnight event with a member (or members) of the opposite sex unless accompanied by another female.

The college had no facilities for keeping animals in captivity. That being the case, someone, perhaps it was Jim, took charge of that woodrat and kept it alive as best he could at the Macnab home. It died a couple of months later—presumably of malnutrition. Its pelt then joined the collection of skins of small mammals in the biology department museum.

So ends the saga of Ellis Barn and "Bushy," the night visitor.

Chapter Twelve

Saddleback? Saddlebag? Saddle Bag? Saddle? Where Are We?

O UR MOUNTAIN SITUATED in the northeast corner of Lincoln County has often been confused with Saddle Mountain, the well-known peak in Clatsop County, near Astoria. Our mountain has been called many names. We chose Saddleback, the name in use at the time of Prof's study. (The official United States Board on Geographic Names designation is Saddle Bag Mountain.)

Prof needed a map. Today, finding almost any kind of map is no big deal. There are road maps, Forest Service maps, recreational area maps, aerial maps, and even contour maps made from aerial photography. In the 1930s, at the time of this research, it was a different matter. Prof could find no map for Saddleback Mountain.

A map was the only way the study area could be located accurately or visualized. Obviously, the area had been surveyed and a grid of townships and sections established before timber claims were recorded, but those surveyors did not make maps. That wasn't their kind of work. Though there are early topographical maps for some parts of the state, Prof found none for this area. There wasn't even a Forest Service map, let alone a map showing the tiny spot on the ridge where Prof undertook research.

For countless hours Prof had hiked all over the area, either with men familiar with the region, or alone, guided only by a sketch in his hand or by a map in his head fashioned out of conversation with someone. After he selected the site for his research he kept on expanding his knowledge of the mountain through additional hikes and, in so doing, located a section corner near the site.

That determined Scotsman decided that he would not let the fact that no map of the area had ever been made stop him. He would make his own.

Beginning in the spring of 1935 and equipped only with his tenacious spirit and the simplest of tools—none of the sophisticated and cumbersome instruments that surveyors use today—Prof went about this task like a pro. He had a pocket compass, a hand level, an aneroid barometer, a notebook, and pencil—all of which he could carry in his pockets—a surveyor's staff and chain, a handful of rags for markers, and some loyal assistants.

He started at the section corner, its location precisely recorded by surveyors. By checking repeatedly with the aneroid barometer, he soon affirmed that the elevation there was 1,520 feet. The work progressed at snail's pace. We spent a few hours on it whenever we could find time and the weather permitted.

From the section corner southwest of the station, we worked our way eastward along the section line, down through the undergrowth and across the creek bottom, then upward south of the station to the ridge the trail followed on its way to the top of the mountain. Beyond the trail we continued eastward down a gradual slope toward Hood Craven Creek, then up slightly, to cross a broad hump before the final plunge into the narrow channel of Buck's Creek, a total distance of some 750 meters—close to one-half mile.

To accomplish this Prof sighted through his compass to keep us on course, due east. In this way he guided one of us as we tied white rag "flags" to shrubs to mark the position of the line. Then we used the surveyor's chain (sixty-six feet long) for measuring, ever so slowly—leveling the chain (or a part of it) as we went down a decline or up a rise in order to keep our horizontal distance as accurate as possible.

We used the first 700 meters we laid out along the section line as the base for a grid of hectares. ("Hectare" is Greek for an area 100 x 100 meters, or 2.47 acres, roughly two football fields side by side.)

The plotting of hectares was really tricky because, to be accurate, they needed to be laid out horizontally on all four sides. To do that kind of work, leveling of the surveyor's chain was absolutely essential. Portions of the chain had to be adjusted carefully up or down, foot by foot (or meter by meter), as we climbed steep ridges or descended into the stream-cut gullies. (This eternal problem of converting from feet to meters was a real pain. It's a problem that continues to plague ecologists today.)

Starting at the section corner, Prof plotted seven hectares toward the east, then moving north 100 meters, he plotted another seven toward the west, then a third tier, from west to east. The research station was in this tier—the rain gauges, anemometer, and original instrument shelters in the southeast quarter of Hectare 16; the fire shelter, hemlock ladder tree, other instruments, and area of greatest activity in Hectare 17. The final tier of hectares lay below the station, to the north.

Then the real challenge began—the plotting of contour lines. These are lines that connect points of equal elevation above sea level. On professional maps they are used to show the height and shape of ridges and mountains, the positions of streams and depths of the gullies or canyons through which streams flow, and other features. By studying a carefully made contour map a person can form a mental picture of a mountain, such as Saddleback, or a research site such as Prof's.

On the small map he was making, Prof wanted to create such a picture. He wanted to show the position of the research site on the ridge, its relation to the nearby streams, and the way Hectares 17 and 16 dipped down into the gully at their northeast and northwest corners and tended to level off as the ridgetop was reached. Since the elevation of the section corner was 1,520 feet, he knew that the research site was about halfway up the north flank of that 3,200 foot mountain.

Determining contours proved to be the most time-consuming task of all. We began again at the section corner where we now knew the elevation and worked down into the gullies and up and across the ridges, with Prof using a hand level to sight through and a surveyor's staff marked in one-foot intervals and held by an assistant to sight to. Inching along in this manner, he plotted a series of lines at twenty-five-foot intervals, vertically, that outlined the contours of the terrain in a block of twelve hectares, including the two that held the station and the surrounding area where we did most of the research. With much checking and rechecking, he reckoned the elevation of the station to average between 1,425 and 1,450 feet above sea level and its distance to be roughly 1,200 to 1,500 feet from the section corner.

Weeks stretched into months. The surveying went on and on, extending through November of 1936 and involving at least thirty partial days in both 1935 and 1936.

Sometime during the winter of 1936—the field notes do not say exactly when—we divided Hectare 17 into an imaginary grid of twenty-five squares, each twenty meters on a side. It was only after we had laid out that grid that I could sketch with any accuracy the positions of trees, logs, and other details surrounding the fire shelter.

On January 24, 1937 I began a sketch of the research area. That doesn't sound very impressive, but it was the final stage of one of the most important projects of the research, one that had involved countless hours and many helpers for nearly two years. We had finished the necessary surveying in November. Then for two months rain and snow kept me from starting this sketch. Now, though my fingers were nearly numb from the cold, I simply must begin showing what was where—I couldn't let a little thing like freezing fingers stop me!

Eventually I included all of Hectare 17—the mature trees, the Douglas-firs, noble firs, and hemlocks; the groves of uneven-sized young hemlocks; the large and small logs; the rotten snags; the patches of sword fern, salal, Oregon grape, and huckleberry; the meanderings of our trails; the fire shelter and the instrument shelters; and the same sort of details in the portion of Hectare 16 where there were instruments.

While I did this work I developed a sense of intimacy with the towering giants of this forest. They became individualized. I soon knew the precise location of the two magnificent noble firs and most of the seventy-five deeply furrowed Douglas-firs in Hectare 17. The eighty smoother-barked large hemlocks were less distinctive. With the exception of the hemlock ladder tree, they lacked personality. Their locations did not become fixed in my mind, nor did hardly any of the 530 young hemlocks, three to perhaps seventy-five or eighty feet high, huddled in dense clusters of anonymity.

This project was fun and challenging, but I was interrupted so often by other responsibilities and bad weather that I did not complete the main features of the sketch until the end of May, and I did not add the patches of herbs until even later in the summer.

The map which resulted has proved to be invaluable. It showed the fire shelter, where the instruments were, the location of each of the large trees, the trails, and all other important features. As I, an untrained amateur, filled in those details, I had no inkling of how important that sketch would be.

In 1941 I used that sketch in my doctoral thesis and even later it formed the basis for the professionally drafted map Prof used in the published portion of his doctoral thesis. Then after the area was torn up by logging, this same map made possible the relocation of the research site. In addition, time after time over the years, a copy on film has been projected and, supplemented by pictures of the area, has helped to tell the Saddleback story.

But, I'm getting ahead of my story.

When contour maps of the Coast Range (based on aerial photography) finally became available in 1942—five years after Prof finished his field work—it took four of those maps put together (Euchre Mountain, Valsetz, Spirit Mountain, and Nestucca Bay) to get a picture of the mountain.

Saddleback is big, its circumference being about twelve miles at the 1,500-foot level, the elevation of the upper part of the research station.

Viewed from the air the mountain is fascinating. As a student hiking step-by-step over forest trail, my feet fettered to the earth, I had no idea of Saddleback's size or charm. I never realized that it had three peaks, not just the two which form the saddle where the notch is, and that the highest of the three, with an elevation of 3,359 feet, lies southwest of Lost Prairie, not between that basin and the station.

Salmon River is an important stream. It has long been a fisherman's paradise. Shortly after leaving its birthplace in Lost Prairie, the river makes its way east a short distance before swinging abruptly toward the north to plunge down the mountain past the research area to an elevation of about 800 feet. It then swings west, creating a wide semicircle around the north side of the mountain. In that journey, the river forms more than three-fourths of a circle. It then flows more or less directly toward the ocean.

The station, the downward plunge of Salmon River, and most of the other places associated with the research were in the Spirit Mountain Quadrangle, as were the segment of Salmon River Highway over which we hiked and the Boyers' homes and Boyer Flat—the little meadow-like valley where the log cabin was situated and through which meanders the headwaters of the Little Nestucca River.

On August 21, 1938, between my first and second years of graduate school, we finally measured the trail from the station to Boyer, a project that Prof had wanted to do for years.

That day, for what we thought would be the grand finale of the field work on Saddleback Mountain, six of us, including Prof, made the trip. Measuring the trail took a lot of time because we tried to achieve a surveyor's measurement. As we ascended or descended a grade we adjusted for changes in elevation by leveling portions of our 100-foot chain a bit at a time, as Prof had done at the station. Our figures are not in linear miles but in what we were told were called "ranger miles," the way distances are usually given on maps showing trails in mountains.

In ranger miles it was only 3.6 miles from Boyer to the station by way of the highway and 3.24 miles by the route we took in the latter part of the study, not the five miles or more that experienced hikers had assumed. Those ranger miles were a great deal shorter than the actual distance covered. The "ups" and "downs" which we adjusted out of our measurements would have lengthened the mileage materially if they had been included. That extra distance doesn't show on any map, but we walked it on every trip.

Oregon (Red) Salamander and eggs.

Chapter Thirteen

Even Fairy Tales End

A LIGHT WIND WHISPERED through the treetops. Cool breezes ruffled my hair. Lost in thought, I sat with my back braced against a huge old fir, gazing into branches towering skyward, layer upon layer. Insects hovered over sweet-scented vanilla leaf plants nearby or buzzed softly as they crowded upon the fragrant, bright yellow Oregon grape. Leaving my companions near the center of the research site a short time before, I had set out, net in hand, to catch insects. This sunny spot had lured me to pause for a quiet time of thinking.

I had graduated from Linfield the day before. All my hopes, dreams, and plans hinged upon further study in ecology, but I had no money for graduate school and there was no way for me to continue my education without an assistantship.

In February I had applied to the University of Illinois. If I received an appointment there, I would be a student of Dr. Victor E. Shelford, under whom Prof wanted me to get my training. However, to avoid gambling everything on one bet, I had also applied at the University of Nebraska, where I would work under Dr. Blake, Prof's mentor.

It's June now, I mused, *nearly four months have passed. Why haven't I heard from someone?*

I recalled the warning received from my brother Charles, an entomologist at the University of Maine: "You will be very fortunate if you can be placed as an assistant while working for your degree....You must realize that you will be passed up time after time because you are a woman. Many administrators will under no circumstances consider the application of a woman."

Certainly that was not a very hopeful prospect for me. However, Dr. Shelford had written Prof, "Send me a good student, either male or female. Their sex isn't important."

For months I had been working my tail off in one capacity or another. I did Prof's secretarial work and was his laboratory assistant in plant physiology. Each week I took an active part in the research trips, never-endingly sorted, recorded, and classified insects as they were brought in, and made study skins from the birds and mammals we collected or supervised students who wanted to learn the technique. I had worked up data and designed a form on which rainfall records could be compared, week by week, over the years of the research, and had prepared a paper on the birds of Saddleback Mountain and another on our experiences in trying to raise baby Oregon salamanders. I presented these papers at the Willamette Valley Student Science Conference in April 1937 in Portland.

The salamander project was interesting and unique but rather sad. On April 25, 1936, Kenny found two reddish-brown, female Oregon (or red) salamanders (*Ensatina eschscholtzii*) in decaying wood beneath the bark of old hemlock logs. The females were nearly four inches long and had their bodies wrapped around a cluster of ten or twelve whitish eggs, each about a quarter inch in diameter. These females had large eyes and walked with their heads held well above the ground, a characteristic shown by no other kind of salamander in this region.

These were plethodont amphibians, as were also our little yellow or red-striped woodland salamanders (*Plethodon vehiculus*). Plethodonts, so named because of their numerous teeth, were unique to us, for they have neither lungs nor gills—their entire moist skin acts as a respiratory surface. They lay their eggs in rotten wood or some other moist place, not in water as most salamanders do, and the entire larval stage takes place inside the egg membrane from which the young salamander emerges as a minute replica of the adult.

We placed one of the females with her eggs in rotten wood in a medium-sized flower pot with a piece of wire gauze in the bottom and a sheet of cellophane tied over the top and then partially buried this "cage" in a shady spot. We checked it each week, replacing the wood with fresh material. During the summer the cellophane split and the mother escaped.

We replenished the pot and covered it with fresh cellophane, hoping that the eggs would hatch. On September 10 we discovered several babies, but only five survived the trip to the college. They grew slowly. When about two weeks old they were noticeably darker than the adults, very slender and about three-fourths of an inch long. They were highly irritable, lashing their tiny bodies about pitifully whenever disturbed. Although we tried to keep their home comfortably moist and adequately supplied with minute

creatures, our efforts were futile. The last baby salamander died by the end
of the year. Perhaps they needed the presence of a mother, for I have read
that the mothers of plethodont salamanders usually stay with the eggs until
the babies emerge, sometimes even longer.

For at least a year Dr. Blake had insisted that Prof had more information
than he could possibly use and urged him to begin organizing data and end
the field work. But Prof, determined and tenacious, needing to be certain
that nothing essential had been overlooked—there was so much more he
wanted to get done—kept right on with the field work. (Besides, the trips
were fun!)

During recent months, an uneasy awareness had warned us that the
forest on Saddleback Mountain was not indestructible. Logging beside the
highway between Boyer and the trail, unfamiliar boot tracks along the trail,
survey marks on trees—ever nearer the station—all added to the sense of
urgency. Finally, Prof decided this would be his last year of field work.

With the arrival of summer vacation, the tempo and intensity of the
research increased. Everything went into overdrive since this was to be Prof's
final year.

When Mark Nickerson left to work elsewhere for the summer, and Jim
Henry got a job with a logging company in the woods nearby (but came to
help whenever he could), Prof enlisted new helpers. Frances Daniels, Eunice
Boone, and Enid Emery, who had completed their junior years as biology
majors, became assistants, and Bob Peck, "BP," a recent high school graduate, joined the group nearly every week, partially filling the void caused by
the absence of Mark and Jim.

The pace of work accelerated in both lab and field. Usually we devoted
only one day a week to field work, but activities in the lab went on for five,
or sometimes six days. Caring for insects and other creatures collected in the
field absorbed many hours in the lab. Fresh material could be more readily
identified than preserved stuff and nothing important must be overlooked.
I was busy much of the time writing letters to prospective systematists, box-
ing specimens for shipment, or tabulating data.

We collected everything more intensively than ever before: birds—a
pileated woodpecker, a junco, an Oregon jay, a Steller's jay, a pair of chestnut-backed chickadees, a ruby-crowned kinglet, a lutescent warbler, a
hummingbird, a golden-crowned sparrow—twenty birds in all; mammals—
deer mice, shrews, a snowshoe hare, wood rats, a spotted skunk, a bat,

mountain beavers, and redbacked voles; amphibians—tailed frogs and several kinds of salamanders; and thousands of insects, spiders, and other sorts of invertebrates.

We introduced new techniques and refined old ones in an attempt to determine more accurately the relative numbers of different kinds of insects and other creatures. Curiosity seekers, hearing about the research, continued to join us occasionally, but they usually found the outings so strenuous that they never came back. We regulars delighted in the camaraderie, the interplay, the challenge of the research, and the beauty of our surroundings.

Each time offered something different. There might be a new person in the group, or there could be a new "Profism," such as, to someone very tired, "Why don't you just sit down and rest your hands and face?" Or, when we'd solved some especially difficult problem, "Two heads are better than one, even when one is a cabbage head." He was full of such sayings and he delighted in playing pranks, telling jokes, and teasing.

Sometimes we found a new plant, saw or heard a new bird, observed a new bug, glimpsed a new sight, or heard some whole new symphony of nature. Though I was in my fourth year of helping, I enjoyed every trip and felt cheated whenever I missed one.

On July 25, I heard from the University of Nebraska. I could have a job there as a graduate assistant in the zoology department. Then, on July 29 a telegram came assuring me of an assistantship at Illinois.

If roughing it in the wilds can be called a vacation, the research team, consisting of Prof, Frances, Enid, B.P., and me, had two four-day working vacations at Ellis Barn that summer. The first one was during the week before I heard from the University of Nebraska, the other a month later. We worked hard and accomplished a lot, but we also had fun during those days in July and August.

Mammal trapping was, supposedly, the primary purpose of the ventures. We had so little information about the mice, shrews, moles, and other small furred creatures of this forest that Prof wanted to try again to increase our knowledge. During the long uninterrupted days, while he concentrated on the trapping, the rest of us had time to observe and collect a tremendous number of insects. Our work schedules were not burdensome. We had much free time.

Our meals suffered from lack of variety. Several kinds of berries were still around. However, they were scattered and few to a bush. One morning I announced, "I'll make a cobbler this evening if you guys gather the berries for it."

"Great. Will do," they agreed.

When we returned to our shelter after the day of work at the station, the others brought forth their offering of fruits. One had small red huckleberries, by far the most plentiful fruit available. Another had a cupful of plump, juicy, blue huckleberries from a lone bush found beside a stream. The third presented a mixture of salal berries and Oregon grapes. Someone had found a few ripe salmonberries. It seemed a weird combination of fruits but we were hungry, and hunger has few scruples.

I liked challenges. With a minimum of utensils and a stove that had no oven, meal preparation was always a challenge. This one was especially so. Since we had only one kettle with a tight lid, preparation of the berry dessert had to wait until we had eaten our chowder.

Setting the berries aside, I concocted the chowder. First I fried a bit of bacon. Next I added potatoes, onions, and water, and put the combination on the stove to stew. Then I opened a can of salmon—to be added, with some canned milk—when the vegetables were tender.

The chowder disappeared as if by magic—licked up to the last spoonful. Soon the freshly washed kettle held a temptingly aromatic mixture of simmering berries. After blending a bit of sugar and some milk into a cup or so of pancake mix, I dropped balls of the dough into the bubbling berry sauce, popped on the lid, and shortly we were feasting.

"Mmm-good. Delicious. Best I ever tasted," chimed the chorus.

"What shall we call it?" someone asked.

"Why, *squawberry dumplings*, of course," came the answer.

One evening after our meal, Prof suggested that we hike up to the viewpoint. "It won't take long," he said, "since we're already halfway there from the station, and we'll go directly up from here. None of you have ever been up that way."

So up we went. The climb through the first part of the forest was steep, but about halfway to the mountaintop we reached a semilevel area. Suddenly, we were in a different world. Shafts of sunlight, slanting through the forest at a low angle from the west, lighted up an unbroken expanse of golden-brown columns, clothed in strange blocky-patterned bark, like tile or a scaly snakeskin, soaring straight and limbless to an over-arching canopy high above. In all directions as far as one could see, the tree trunks glowed, illumined by rays from the setting sun as though lighted from within. A cushion of long brown needles carpeted the forest floor. All was hushed at this vesper hour. This place of enchantment was a grove of mature white pine.

Time has not erased the memory of that first encounter with a pine forest. For me it was more than a physical experience. It had a spiritual quality.

Years later, while seeking information as to the exact location of this stand of pine, my husband Ray and I were told, most emphatically, by a graduate student at Oregon State University, *"There is no pine in the Coast Range!"*

Though Ray never saw those trees, he knew the species had to be somewhere in the vicinity. As early as the 1920s when he was engaged in white pine blister rust control work for the United States government, he had found the aecial (intermediate) stage of the rust's life cycle on currant bushes along the coast. Again, on his first trip to Saddleback in 1935, he had noted black currant bushes heavily infected with this disease at the place where we crossed Salmon River. Both of us knew that *there had been white pine on Saddleback Mountain!*

Our trapping was very successful. In July we caught a mountain beaver and a Trowbridge shrew. The record for August was only slightly better. On August 15, Jim set out traps in anticipation of some of us being in the area the next day to check them. We didn't get there until August 23. Then, during the four days we stayed at Ellis Barn, Prof set more traps and left some of them for Jim to pick up on August 29.

In that two-week period we caught eleven deer mice and two red-backed voles. One of the voles was a pregnant female with four small embryos. Though they were beetle-chewed and fly-blown, we were delighted to have the voles, especially the pregnant female. Mr. Jewett, who had identified the one we caught earlier, now urged us to work up a paper for the *Journal of Mammalogy* because so little was known about these creatures.

Prof had also collected a little big-eared bat that he found sleeping under old roof shakes at the Hood Craven cabin site. This bat was really tiny—its total length less than 4 inches and its buffy-brown body barely 2¼ inches long. Black, leather-like wing and tail membranes encircled its entire body except for its head, and its ears—from which it got its name—were longer, larger, and wider than those of most bats of the region. Little big-eared bats are found only at the edges of dense forest where they take refuge under the loose bark of trees or in similar niches. Prof had often seen them flying at dusk, busily plucking insects out of the air.

(My first close look at a bat was when I made a museum specimen of one caught in a building at Linfield. Studying and measuring the unusual body of that tiny mammal, feeling its soft fur, and examining its peculiar wing and tail membranes intrigued me in a way that has never left. While in graduate school, I watched, spellbound, as a captive mother bat fed and cared for her young. Later, at a scientific meeting in Philadelphia, I was privileged to hear the exciting report given by the two young graduate students who were the first to learn that bats use echo location in finding insects and avoiding objects. Bats continue to fascinate me.)

On September 9, two trips after our August stay at Ellis Barn, I visited the research station for the last time as one of Prof's helpers. Nothing particularly noteworthy happened that day. We did the usual things, made the usual observations and collections.

My feelings were mixed. I knew I might never return to the research area. I was eager to go on with my education and yet apprehensive about the future. I knew that the forest might be logged. I was reluctant to leave this familiar place—this venerable forest which had taught me so much.

This was a place of mystery, and yet a place of harmony. I sensed that all the bits of information I had gleaned in four years—though now as scrambled as the color-chips in a kaleidoscope—must somehow fit together in a beautiful mosaic if only I could find the key. Subconsciously, an understanding of ecological rhythm was forming in my mind.

Soon I would leave for Illinois to begin a new chapter in my life. Whether I ever returned, whatever happened, I knew this forest would be there forever—even if only in my memory.

Part II

Evolution of an Ecologist

THE LAKE IS TO THE NATURALIST a chapter out of the history of a primeval time....It forms a little world within itself—a microcosm within which all the elemental forces are at work and the play of life goes on in full, but on so small a scale as to bring it easily within the mental grasp.

Nowhere can one see more clearly illustrated what may be called the sensibility of such an organic complex, expressed by the fact that whatever affects any species belonging to it, must have its influence of some sort upon the whole assemblage.

>   —Stephen A. Forbes, Chief,
>   State of Illinois Natural History Survey
>   Paper read February 25, 1887
>   to the Peoria Scientific Association

This is excerpted from Forbes's "The Lake as a Microcosm" (Illinois Natural History Survey Bulletin, 15(1925; 9): 537-550) *which was required reading for ecology students taught by Professor V.E. Shelford at the University of Illinois.*

The author at the University of Illinois, 1940.

Chapter Fourteen
Evolution of an Ecologist

F OUR DAYS AFTER THAT last visit to the ancient forest, I was on the *City of Portland*, Union Pacific Railway's new streamliner, bound for gradu-ate school. Scheduled to arrive in Chicago exactly thirty-nine hours and forty-five minutes after leaving Portland, that train was the fastest means of transportation between the two cities in those days before airliners.

Sody and Alice met me in Chicago. He was working toward a master's degree in embryology at the University of Illinois and had come to Chicago to visit Alice, who had found a job there. After a full day of sightseeing, Sody and I took an Illinois Central train to Champaign, arriving there at 2 a.m.

The following days were crammed with registration, getting ac-quainted with campus life, finding a place to live, and all the things involved with adjustment to life in new surroundings.

Originally the entire university campus had been inside the town of Urbana, but as the school grew it spilled over into nearby Champaign on the west. Now, in 1937, only a narrow street separated the two communities, with the major portion of the university still in Urbana, but many new buildings in Champaign.

The Natural History Building, where I would be assisting and attend-ing many classes, was a rambling, wooden building with creaky floors. It was near the north end of the campus in Urbana, and only a few blocks from the more recently built Vivarium, Dr. Shelford's stronghold, in Champaign.

The Vivarium stood by itself, surrounded by a high iron fence to keep its grounds undisturbed and natural. Genetics research laid claim to the first floor and some of the space in the greenhouse-like live room attached to the back of the building, but the Vivarium was really the realm of ecologists. Dr. Shelford's office, the office of his associate Dr. Kendeigh, a classroom, an experimental laboratory, the seminar room with its cubicles for graduate students, the storeroom, and even the attic were all part of the ecological domain—as were also the controlled environment rooms in the greenhouse-like building in back and outdoor research space. Here, and in natural areas near and far, I would learn to be an ecologist.

My assisting assignment the first semester was in zoology I, where for two hours, twice a week, I worked with about thirty-five students in one of several lab sections in a class of 350. In addition I put in four to five hours every week grading papers, preparing exams, and attending assistants' meetings. Second semester the assignment changed to a similar routine for zoo. II, comparative vertebrate anatomy.

As I watched the hordes of students streaming from building to building across the campus quadrangle, I thought of some anthills I had seen, and breathed a prayer of gratitude that I had done my undergraduate studies at tiny Linfield College, where both faculty and students called me by name, where I was not lost in anonymity and identified only by a number, and where I, an undergraduate, had been part of a team doing real-life research. Though I appreciated what the university could offer me as a graduate student, I knew that undergraduate study at one of the Big Ten schools would not have been right for me.

My new home was in Urbana about a half-mile north of the campus. By simply moving a few pieces of furniture and installing a small gas range, the owners had created, in two upstairs rooms, an apartment for four female graduate students. It was typical middle class America of the day and not unlike what I was accustomed to. It was also the usual kind of quarters available to graduate students at that time.

In the entire zoology department there were only three other female graduate students in a flock of males. Most of the graduate students had a master's degree when they came to the university. Seemingly I was an exception since I didn't have one.

I was eager to meet Dr. Shelford and work out my course of study and yet, at the same time, I was hesitant. He was one of the pioneers in ecology and considered to be the father of animal ecology. To me he was an object of veneration.

Much to my surprise, Dr. Shelford was not the extrovert I had expected but a rather reticent man of medium stature, sixty years of age, reserved and quiet. Even so, I was too shy and too much in awe of him to be completely at ease.

Dr. Shelford suggested that I work directly toward a doctorate, waiving the master's degree, because in his estimation, a student wasted time when doing research for a year or two to earn a master's degree and then had to begin new research for the doctorate. He wanted me to use the knowledge I had gained from the Douglas-fir forest. He thought Professor Macnab might let me use data from Saddleback, supplemented with information I would add during the next summer. Then I could compare the Douglas-fir forest with a deciduous forest near the university.

Dr. Shelford's introductory course was required of all the university's majors in zoology and all graduate students in that department. I was soon being steeped in ecology with Dr. Shelford's course in animal ecology plus a unit of research from him, vertebrate ecology from Dr. Kendeigh, and plant geography of North America by a professor in the botany department.

Dr. Shelford was low key as a lecturer, but he had personal experience to draw upon. The concepts and principles he taught were hammered home by field trips. Lacking television, movies, or even color slides, he opened new worlds to us when he introduced the African grasslands, the Australian outback, the jungles of South America, and other little-known ecological communities with the only tools at his disposal—his enthusiasm and black and white lantern slides.

A master organizer, his class included a rigorous schedule of field trips—one somewhere every Saturday or weekend until severe winter weather set in. Then, for a few weeks, laboratory experiments might take the place of trips until field work began again in the spring.

Our field studies included sites recovering from the devastation of strip mining, places showing the stages of succession in tamarack bogs and lake shore dunes, and forests in the beech-maple biome, as well as other interesting natural areas. But for me, the never-to-be-forgotten study was our five-day visit to Reelfoot Lake, Tennessee, in April 1938.

Reelfoot Lake was formed in 1811-12 by a series of earthquake-caused upheavals which dropped a meandering portion of the Mississippi River several feet, filling it with water, severing it from the river's mainstem, and leaving it a relatively shallow oxbow lake, fourteen miles long and four-and-a-half miles wide, fringed by cypress swamps.

It was a new world, sunny, balmy, and warm. I had never seen anything even remotely resembling this assortment of semitropical trees. The cypresses, with their branches bearing long, trailing strands of "Spanish moss" and their strange "knees" projecting out of the water, engraved in my mind an indelible image. The calls of herons and egrets in nearby rookeries, the symphonies of bird song, the chirps of insects and croaks of frogs, and the fragrances—the blended scents from flower, vine, and tree—all signaled the full-blown arrival of another spring, a season vastly different from the first touch of spring we had left in Illinois. (In spite of all that, I was always un-easy about the possibility of encountering a cottonmouth moccasin.)

These field trips expanded my horizons and stretched my imagination. Two things were always emphasized, the numbers of individual plants or animals in a unit area and what the animals were doing.

Each graduate student was responsible for specific equipment and for carrying out the work related to it. We kept notes according to prescribed form and turned them in promptly after each trip. I learned to organize ma-terial and analyze field data—all invaluable training.

We traveled by buses. Detailed schedules were available and posted in advance. Though his rules were strict and unvarying, they were also reason-able and for the good of all.

The students of Dr. S. Charles Kendeigh often took part in these trips. Tall, soft-spoken, and dignified, Dr. Kendeigh was precise and meticulous. He and Dr. Shelford worked well together, both being highly organized and demanding much from their students. I learned a great deal about birds, mammals, and other vertebrates from Dr. Kendeigh's classes.

An important facet of our study was the Ecology Club. The idea for such a seminar had begun in 1917 when students started meeting with Dr. Shelford to discuss ecological literature and research. Now the club's pro-gram included guest speakers and reports by students as well as reviews of current ecological literature. When I was scheduled to speak, I told about the Saddleback Mountain research and showed the few black and white prints I had.

One crisp day in mid-October, Dr. Shelford whizzed me in his big Buick out to the village of White Heath about twenty miles west of Champaign to introduce me to the forest community he had selected for my research. (He liked to drive fast but was a good driver. Dilly-dallying was never for him.) The site was a privately owned woodlot of some eleven acres near the Sangamon River, about a mile north of White Heath. Fenced and protected from grazing and browsing by livestock, it boasted several kinds of oaks, some elms, black walnuts, and shagbark hickories, about two feet in diameter and seventy to seventy-five feet tall. Larger hickories, which had dominated the forest area, had been harvested many years before. "This woodlot," Dr. Shelford said, "is a very small remnant of the oak-hickory for-ests that were once common in Illinois, but it is representative. It is one of few wooded areas still accessible for study."

To make my studies I rode the electric interurban train to White Heath whenever some friend did not take me to the woodlot. Although I had to hike about a mile in Champaign to catch the interurban and another mile from it to the woods, this didn't really seem to be much after my years on the Saddleback study.

Frost had touched the trees with scarlet and gold when I made my first solo visit to the woodlot. Acorns had fallen, and leaves were coming down in showers. Shrubs were nearly bare and white snakeroot was the only herb left in abundance, its leaves curled and seeds flying.

With the forest at such a low level of activity, it was easy for me to establish a routine. A brief time to describe the weather, count birds, record evidences of mammals, make a series of sweeps over herbs and another over shrubs, take a humus and soil sample, and I could be on my way. Usually I visited the forest every second week.

When colorful fall gave way to winter's bleakness, even the snakeroot withered. Trees and shrubs stood stark and bare. Insects died or sought refuge in the mantle of leaves covering the ground. Sweepnet collections were no longer needed. But soil samples were with me always. These I gathered faithfully, taking each back to the lab to be sorted carefully. Often the days were bitterly cold with snow or ice covering the frozen ground and a chill wind whistling through the leafless trees.

The tempo of my research changed with the surge of plant and animal activity that came in the spring. To have more time for observing and recording, I began using the interurban regularly, sometimes going out at 8:00 in the morning and staying until evening.

About the middle of March the first tender shoots of herbs appeared and tiny leaves of shrubs began unfolding. A few insects became active. Spring was on its way. One week later, I heard a mourning dove, found the delicate blossoms of spring beauty plants, and saw a few Mourning Cloak butterflies. Tarnished plant bugs, flea beetles, leafhoppers, lacewings, and chinch bugs on herbs and shrubs indicated that the upward migration of insects from the ground layers had begun.

One day in early April, I was surprised to find more than 100 robins in the woodland. Then I realized that these birds would normally have been feeding on the floodplain of the nearby Sangamon River, but it was covered with water, forcing the birds to seek higher ground. By the tenth of April, blue violets, Dutchman's breeches, and toothwort were blooming, and butterflies were everywhere. That day, twenty species of insects were active on the herbs and I found sixteen in the shrub layer. In a mere two weeks in that month of April, the stark grove had transformed into an oasis of vibrant life. The forest floor became covered with herbs, rank of growth and full of bloom—wake robins, spring beauties, Dutchman's breeches, toothwort, phlox, wild geraniums, Jack-in-the-pulpit, and violets, both yellow and blue. Buds of the late blooming May apple and false Solomon's seal were swollen and turgid.

Above the carpet of herbs, leaves were unfolding on low-growing shrubs. Next above them, young elms—performing the role of taller shrubs—were in full leaf, while in the canopy high above, leaflets on hickory trees were opening and buds on oaks were swelling. Stratification of plants in the woodlot was obvious.

With this abundance of plant life supplying food, insects were everywhere. And with the resurgence of insect life, birds had arrived to stake out nesting territories. Their songs filled the air. Rich, whistled songs of Carolina wrens, a soft trill from a Myrtle warbler high in a tree top, or a robin's caroling alerted me to the return of migrant summer-nesting birds, while such permanent residents as the cardinal, titmouse, hairy woodpecker, and blue jay also advertised their presence. One day in May at the height of the spring migration I noted twenty-three species of birds.

While many of the plants, birds, mammals, and other creatures here were new to me, I found help—from people and from books. This was not an unexplored world like the coniferous forest of the Northwest.

On my visit of June 9, I discovered that the maturity of summer had begun to replace the exuberance of spring. Early herbs were forming fruits. Jewelweed, a plant of the summer season already in bud, was shoulder high in open places and vigorous plants averaged three feet in height throughout the woods. Giant ragweed, that plague for hay fever sufferers, was as tall as the jewelweed.

Birds moved about silently, attending to nesting activities. Click beetles, weevils, flea beetles, tumbling flower-beetles, leafhoppers, ants, fungus gnats, crane flies, snipe flies, other flies of assorted sizes, moths, microlepidoptera, tiny parasitic wasps, immature plant bugs, and spiders were active on herbs and shrubs. A large species of cranefly was particularly conspicuous as it flew about, and mosquitoes were biting viciously—an all too obvious sign that summer in Illinois is a damp, humid season. These mosquitoes were larger than *Aedes*, the little tree-hole mosquitoes that plagued us so frequently on Saddleback, but they were equally noxious.

This was to be my last trip to the woods until autumn. A friend would fill in for me during my absence. I was leaving in a few days to spend the summer in Oregon.

It had been a good year for me. I had become a better ecologist. I had passed both my French and German exams, had learned much, and made good grades in my courses—though not all "A's."

At 11:15 the night of June 11, 1938 aboard the Great Northern Railway's *Empire Builder*, I began my journey westward from Chicago to arrive in Portland some fifty-eight hours later.

The summer overflowed with activity. I needed to do some collecting on Saddleback and to make a study of marine plankton for graduate school credit, a requirement of the zoology department.

My plans were greatly complicated by staying with the Macnabs. Prof was scheduled to set out with his family about the first of September on a two-year leave of absence to complete courses for his doctorate at the University of Nebraska. This meant that the research collection must be whipped into shape and specimens sent to specialists for identification during that one brief summer while fulfilling my own obligations and helping the Macnab family prepare for their move.

Organizing the research collection and data was a monumental undertaking. Three or four students helped, but Prof expected me to supervise them and take responsibility for the collection while he attended to academic and personal matters. Since I would be using some of the data in my thesis I had a special interest in this effort.

For two days I checked through correspondence to find names and addresses of systematists who would identify material. Then we began preparing specimens for shipment.

Pinned insects are more brittle and fragile than eggshells and must be packed with extreme care. Spiders, worms, and other creatures preserved in liquid in glass vials also require special treatment to assure that corks do not come out or vials break. We learned that the only safe procedure was to double pack every shipment—carefully cradling the box containing the collection in a nest of excelsior or crumpled newspaper inside a larger, sturdy, corrugated cardboard box.

I have no idea how many boxes we packed and shipped, but we began in June and were still mailing boxes in September. A cover letter had to accompany every shipment. I wrote the letters, but other assistants helped with the detailed list of contents enclosed in each box.

Once we had organized that procedure, we began planning my projects. According to agreement with the University of Illinois, Prof supervised my plankton study to which we devoted much of our time for six weeks. He helped plan the project, provided transportation, and collected some of the material for me to study and identify.

Even while I worked on the plankton project, I was never completely free from responsibility for the Saddleback research, for there were letters to write, boxes to prepare for shipment, and data to tabulate.

There was also my personal study on Saddleback. Two student helpers and I visited the research site on June 24 and again on July 19, making the usual careful observations and collections, which, as always before, I cared for in the lab.

And it was hot in McMinnville—up to 107°, with ten consecutive days above 100°—new records for the area and a terrible summer for forest fires, with 250 reported in Oregon on July 18 alone.

August 21 was the grand finale for the field work on Saddleback Mountain. Prof went along to do some final checking of surveying data and to supervise measuring the trail on the way out. We packed up the rain gauges, thermometers, and other equipment used during the summer, and took them with us back to the college.

From the trail measurements made on this trip we concluded that the distance from Boyer to the station was not quite four ranger miles, much less than it was in linear distance, the distance we actually walked.

The deadlines for Prof's departure and my return to Illinois were fast approaching. Though it was near the end of August, there was still much to be done: birds to be skinned and stuffed, specimens sorted, boxes packed, lists compiled, letters written, and files moved from the Macnab home to the lab since their house would be rented while they were away. Activity quickened to a frantic pace. Prof was busy with academic affairs; the students and I with the research stuff; and Mrs. Macnab with household needs and the children. She was especially concerned about little Colin who had begun having epileptic seizures a few years before. Finally, at 8:20 on the morning of September 5, with their car loaded to the gunwales, the Macnabs began their journey across the mountains and plains to Lincoln, Nebraska.

The student helpers and I prepared the last of the bird skins, packed and mailed the last boxes of insects, and cleaned the lab. I wound up my plankton study, and after a few days with members of my family in the Puget Sound area, boarded the *Empire Builder* for my second year at the University of Illinois. I soon settled into a routine of the essential stuff of graduate school—classes, research, assisting, and caring for the necessities of daily living.

I spent Christmas vacation with the Macnab family at Lincoln, Nebraska, grading papers for Prof and updating details of our Saddleback research.

The summer of 1939 I remained in Illinois, studying my oak-hickory forest plot and preparing media and cultures for an advanced class in genetics. The weather was hot, the humidity nearly unbearable. My hands and arms stuck to the desk whenever I tried to write, and perspiration dropped from my face onto the desk as I sorted through soil samples from my research. Nights were insufferable—hot, sticky, and plagued with thunderstorms. The summer seemed endless.

A particularly trying academic year followed. First semester, I had the usual schedule of classes and research plus an exceptionally heavy assisting schedule with larger than normal groups of students and an instructor who gave little help or supervision.

During Christmas vacation that year I attended the Ecological Society meeting of the American Association for the Advancement of Science (AAAS) at Columbus, Ohio. A vivid picture from that experience stands out in my mind—one of throngs of starlings huddled on windowsills in the heart of the city, seeking a bit of warmth on bitterly cold winter nights. Starlings, those sometimes noxious, shiny black birds brought to this country in the late 1800s, were new to me. They had not yet invaded Oregon.

Final exams followed my return to the university. My last one was a particularly harrowing experience. Since I was scheduled to check in at the Champaign hospital for major surgery by midmorning immediately following the exam, I was given an oral in embryology, an early morning special dispensation by Dr. Shumway, head of embryology work and one of the three full professors in the zoology department. I barely knew him. He gave the lectures for the course but let others supervise lab work. He later commented to my roommate, the teaching assistant for the lab I was in, that I "seemed rather nervous."

Who wouldn't be nervous? The prospect of surgery was scary. I had never before been a patient in a hospital except for a night or two when I was ten years old and had a broken leg. Now, here I was, alone, and thousands of miles from home and family. Severe abdominal pain had plagued me off and on since late summer and my doctor, a very kind and sympathetic man, urged me to have surgery before my condition became critical. He was certain that my appendix was involved but feared the problem was even more complicated. He was right. I had ovarian cysts as well as an inflamed appendix.

My assisting load for the spring semester was lightened somewhat. I needed that adjustment for convalescence. Still, during that period, in addition to my research and classes, I took the last of the zoology department's three required day-long, exacting and exhausting, written qualifying exams and also had the oral preliminary exam for my thesis.

Somehow that spring I also managed to wedge in among those more vital activities the preparation of a report on the redbacked vole—the mouselike rodent we had caught on Saddleback. The American Society of Mammalogists accepted the paper for presentation at its meeting to be held in Denver in June.

As soon as I finished my year's work at the university I started westward by bus. Enroute, I spent a few days at Lincoln, Nebraska, putting finishing touches on the vole paper and working with Prof on Saddleback research. Then it was on to Denver for presentation of the paper.

I was one scared kid—traveling alone, staying in an unfamiliar city where I didn't know anyone, scheduled to speak to a group of total strangers. I missed the support of friends.

The meeting was in Denver's new Museum of Natural History. The quiet beauty of that place somehow made me feel more at ease. As people assembled, men far outnumbered women. I saw no one I recognized though some were widely known mammalogists. As my place on the program approached, in near panic I thought, *What am I doing here? Why did I let Prof persuade me to give this paper?* The appointed time came. Suddenly the ordeal was over. I received no great accolade of applause, but I hadn't expected one. Apparently I had done all right.

At the end of that session, Kenneth Gordon, a youngish zoology professor from Oregon State College (now OSU), introduced himself. He had given a fascinating motion picture presentation on the natural history and behavior of Oregon mammals, featuring golden-mantled ground squirrels and chipmunks in the Cascades. I felt at ease with him—he was someone from home. Gordon was a herpetologist as well as mammalogist, and the next year, when he was helping me untangle the names of our salamanders on Saddleback, he wrote, "I hope you can get back out in the West. There are so many problems that can be worked on, and so much fine country to work in."

After the pause at Denver I traveled by bus to the West Coast where I planned to use July as a time of rest and relaxation at my parents' home on Arlington Heights near Everett, Washington. However, even there I could not completely abandon ecological pursuits. Using small snap traps, I added some western mammals to the collection of museum specimens begun with my study of the oak-hickory woodlot, and also caught some for an ecologist student friend back at the university. Most of all he wanted a live sewellel (mountain beaver), which are found only in the Northwest.

Sewellels are hard to trap and extremely difficult to keep alive in captivity according to all reports I've read. Anyhow, though I did manage to catch a sewellel, it died enroute to Illinois. I had done everything I could think of to insure the creature's survival, but the trip was long and at that time trains were not air conditioned. Also, its food may not have been suitable or adequate, or it may have died of inactivity, thirst, or even of stress.

The summer sped along. In late July, I journeyed to McMinnville. There I learned from Dorothy and Kenny Fender, who had now been married for several years, that the research site had been logged. They had made that discovery on June 22 while climbing the mountain to complete a plant record of the area. They could not find the research site.

Heartsick at this news, I went with them to try to relocate the station. The destruction began far down the mountain. Using a logging road which seemed to replace our former trail, we climbed to what we felt was the proper elevation. We were surrounded by a jumble of felled trees, graveled roads, and crisscrossed logs, extending from the research area across the terrace to the last steep climb toward the top of the mountain. Where was the station?

Utter havoc lay all around. Where regal fir trees had formed a shaded sanctuary, the sun now beat upon the prostrate trunks and shattered crowns of the forest monarchs. A few survivors of the slaughter stood isolated and forlorn, with fragmented branches, battered and broken by their falling companions. The larger hemlocks—worthless from the loggers' point of view—were tattered or topless snags. Smaller trees lay crushed beneath huge logs lying at close intervals all over the area. Tips of branches of surviving trees were yellowed as though scorched by fire. The air was parched and pungent with the odor of sunbaked pitch. Ferns, shrubs, herbs, and moss carpet lay mashed under logs or hidden beneath the tangle of broken boughs.

This was a foreign land, a place totally unfamiliar to us. Our beautiful, quiet forest was nothing but a memory.

We worked our way laboriously over logs and through the broken tree tops, searching for some familiar object. Insects we had never before encountered assailed our senses. Grasshoppers, more properly called red-legged locusts, leapt from beneath our feet, snapping their wings as they moved from place to place. Wood-boring buprestids and sap-feeding longhorned beetles were reveling en masse in this bounty of fallen timber. Thistle-feeding painted lady butterflies and a common garden pest, the spotted cucumber beetle, had invaded the area. The air was far too dry for mosquitoes, which normally plagued us at this time of year. Everything was discolored and withered under the unrelieved summer sun.

Finally, we found relics from those happier days: a remnant of the hemlock ladder tree—broken off some twenty to twenty-five feet above the ground; boards from the fire shelter and the low hemlock platform; and a hole where a soil sample had been taken by the counting chamber (a cylinder of stout aluminum thirty-five centimeters—about fourteen inches—in diameter) one of our later methods for taking large soil samples of known volume.

The fire shelter tree, a huge Douglas-fir which towered above that activity center, was one of the few firs left standing.

As yet, no logs had been removed, but a donkey engine that would pull them out was set up beside a spar tree at a loading site perhaps 500 feet below the station. Apparently the loggers were about ready to begin bucking up the lots and hauling them away.

We were a dejected, heartbroken trio as we retraced our way down the mountain. The destruction of that ancient forest had been like the death of a special friend. I had shared intimately in the life of the forest and it had nurtured my spirit. My first reaction was, *I never want to go there again.* But I did go back within the next few days with Ray Edmunds, whom I had met on a trip to the research station several years before. Ray was a graduate in forestry at Oregon State College and was much interested in Prof's research. He took pictures and helped me with some trapping of small mammals.

Unlike the clearcutting done today, that initial logging was somewhat selective. Some of the ancient firs were spared, perhaps as seed trees, or they may have been overmature and thus not considered worth taking, or too large for the equipment in use. We do not know which it was but the ones left did serve as seed trees. Loggers did not fall large hemlocks, but falling trees had broken their tops and stripped away many of their branches.

Patches of salal, Oregon grape, red huckleberry, and sword fern remained intact, as well as small plots of herbs and mosses. Old logs, snags, and stumps were scattered over the terrace. The duff and soil of the forest floor were not badly disturbed though they were covered by much woody debris from the logging and compacted in places. All the essentials for natural reforestation seemed to be present.

That devastation planted the germ of an idea in my mind. Dr. Shelford had shown us examples of succession. Forests do regenerate after catastrophes such as logging. *Did I dare to dream of doing further study on Saddleback? Sad as the loss of that forest was, might it be offering me a challenge, a chance to turn a misfortune into an opportunity?* With that in mind, I returned to Illinois for my final year of graduate study.

I had now completed all requirements for my degree except my thesis and the final oral exam. Though I still had duties as a graduate assistant, they were not heavy in comparison with the work of earlier years. I was assigned to help Dr. Shelford who was now officially chair of the zoology department.

This final year at the university I concentrated on preparing my thesis. I had completed my field work in the oak-hickory woodlot the preceding spring. Now I set to work organizing the specimens I had collected and sent them away for identification with the hope that reports from systematists and data I needed from Saddleback would all arrive in time for me to work up a respectable comparison of the two forest communities. Identifications for my Illinois study trickled in slowly, and getting the information I needed from Prof took time, patience, and many letters.

At Christmas break, a carload of us graduate students decided to drive 700 miles to Philadelphia where I was to give a report on my research at the meeting of the Ecological Society division of the AAAS. Though we left Urbana-Champaign early, darkness overtook us long before we reached Philadelphia but, joy of joys, a section of the Pennsylvania Turnpike, the first toll highway in the United States, had just opened. We whizzed along over it, grateful at not being slowed by small towns and crossroads.

That Philadelphia meeting was my first experience speaking before such a venerable group of ecologists. Naturally, I was scared. But I had slides telling much of the story and a "cheering section" of Illini friends to bolster me. Also, my brother Charles had come down from Maine to visit and hear my paper. Though it was nothing phenomenal, the paper was well received, and Charles was impressed with my research.

Two papers presented at that AAAS meeting stand out in my memory. One was by the two young men who discovered the use of sound by bats in guiding their flights. The other told about the need by female mosquitoes for a blood meal to make their eggs viable.

Back at the university, I struggled to find a theme, a thesis, for my research. Early ecological studies of natural communities were, almost without exception, purely descriptive because little research had been done on the behavior of animals, and what *had* been done was usually on a single species. I wanted my thesis to be more than that. I hoped to deal somehow with the dynamics of the two forest communities. But I had had little time for such observation, and the roles of individual species in these forests were much like so many pieces of a huge jigsaw puzzle. No one really understood how they fitted together.

Superficially, the two forests appeared to be quite different. One was dominated by trees that shed their leaves in winter, while in the other the trees remained green the year round. In the oak-hickory forest, summer was the wet season; in the coniferous forest, summers were dry and heavy rains came in the wintertime. Temperatures also were different. In the deciduous forest winters were colder and summers hotter and far more humid than they were in the coniferous forest. The animals, too, were different. Not one animal species that I found was present in both forests.

Yet, in many ways the communities were similar. In both, the trees reduced light intensity, intercepted rainfall, and modified temperature, humidity, and wind velocity; plants enriched the soil; animals dug, fragmented, and mixed soil, enhanced it with their excrement, and finally died, adding their bodies to the soil complex. In both forests, many sorts of animals fed on a wide variety of plant parts, and there were predators, parasites, and scavengers in both.

Further, even though different kinds of plants and animals lived in them, the basic activities going on in the two forest communities were more alike than different. The *dynamics* were the same. I called the species that had similar roles *ecological equivalents*. Before long, the term *ecological niche* was being used to refer to the specific role of an organism. My pioneer work was one of many studies that finally led to the *ecosystem concept* widely accepted today.

When my thesis finally reached Dr. Shelford's standards, the deadline was near for its acceptance, or rejection (heaven forbid), by the Graduate School. After it passed that grueling ordeal of letter-perfect typing and precise formatting, I distributed copies to the five professors on my committee in preparation for my final oral examination scheduled for a few days later.

That examination went smoothly, except for a few questions by Dr. Shumway, who had the reputation for making students squirm. However, I knew what I had written and defended the ideas I had expressed.

In June, at the Seventieth Commencement of the University of Illinois, I received my Ph.D. Now I was a jobless female zoologist/ecologist headed west.

Chapter Fifteen

Hiatus

WHEN I RETURNED TO MCMINNVILLE in the summer of 1941, I found that Prof, as usual, was snowed under with work. He had returned from Nebraska the previous fall and now faced a deadline for getting his data organized and his thesis written. Dorothy McKey, now McKey-Fender, was his assistant. She and Kenny, both of whom had been fascinated with "bugs" since childhood, had fallen in love almost immediately after they met while helping with Prof's field work and had now been married nearly four years.

At this time Dorothy was struggling to condense and make sense out of the overwhelming mound of weather data Prof had amassed. In that pre-computer day, she was plodding along without even an adding machine, doing all the calculations by hand until I showed her how to operate an old Monroe calculator Prof had obtained from somewhere.

That summer Ray Edmunds and I made a series of visits to Saddleback Mountain to do some more trapping and to record the changes occurring as a result of logging. These outings did much to promote our friendship. By this time the shock of seeing that treasured sanctuary so ravaged had eased and I was eager to learn how nature would restore the forest. Those trips were full of surprises. Ray took pictures and I kept notes on plants, animals, and human activity. Plants deserved (and received) most of our attention because, as in most terrestrial ecosystems, they were the dominant species which shaped the environment for all living things.

I received an offer to work as a laboratory technician at the University of Illinois, but I turned it down. I did not want to spend my life in a laboratory. At registration time that fall, while at Arlington visiting with my parents, I was invited to return to McMinnville to work at Linfield as assistant to the registrar and instructor in biology. I accepted that job because it gave me a chance to work with Professor Macnab and return to the Saddleback research.

Two years passed. I was given increasing responsibility in administrative affairs but little time for teaching. Then in November 1943, without a hint of warning, I received a request from a young man whom I had known as a graduate student at Illinois, requesting that I apply for his position as chair of the biology department at Whitworth College in Spokane, Washington. He was leaving in January to join the Army Specialist Training Program to become a medical doctor. His departure would leave the biology department at Whitworth unstaffed. This was the kind of position I had been hoping for.

However, I hesitated at accepting. Linfield needed time to find a replacement for me in the office, and I was still deeply committed to the ecological work on Saddleback and to helping Prof as he strove to complete his doctoral thesis. While teaching a full course load he had to complete his thesis by spring and be ready to go back to Nebraska in May to take his final doctoral examination. That was crucial.

After sifting through a large amount of data with Dorothy's help, Prof had finally settled on a thesis involving the plant, animal, and physical indicators of seasonal changes, which ecologists call *aspection.* Now it was imperative that all essential material be carefully scrutinized and organized in such a way that he could use it in writing the thesis.

With Dorothy in charge, she, Kenny, and I—a team of Prof's former students—worked at a hectic pace toward accomplishing that task. Dorothy was there most of the day. Kenny, who was employed by the postal service, and I joined her in the evening. We often worked far into the night. Prof came whenever he could. When he began writing, Dorothy or I would type what he had written, often making changes, for Prof tended to be wordy and rambling. Frequently he'd change back into his original wording. We'd try to make the writing more concise. He'd ramble. And so it went.

A replacement was found for me at Linfield, and after much urging by the president of Whitworth, I accepted their offer and started teaching there in March 1944, at the beginning of the spring term. To make this change, I expected to resign from Linfield but instead was granted status as a Ph.D. instructor in biology "On Leave."

I was happy teaching at Whitworth. Though the work was rigorous and I had new courses to work up, I enjoyed the students and found a greater warmth among faculty and staff than I had experienced before.

Prof summed up his research and received his Ph.D. from the University of Nebraska in May 1944. He then returned to his teaching position at Linfield.

The following August, in a quiet ceremony without any pomp or circumstance and with only the necessary witnesses, Milton Ray Edmunds and I were married. We had been acquainted for nine years. Ray was a World War I veteran with a medical discharge—a graduate in forestry interested in forest ecology, and a kindly gentleman devoted to both me and my research. However, he was a bachelor, seventeen years my senior, whose health had been undermined by frequent illness, and his roots were firmly planted in McMinnville. Our marriage was a surprise to almost everyone we knew.

When I went back to Whitworth that fall, I returned to chaos. With a new dining facility nearing completion, the biology department had been removed from the meager space it had claimed in one dormitory and deposited helter-skelter where the dining facility had been in the basement of another dormitory.

In response to war needs, Whitworth had joined with one of the Spokane hospitals in adopting a Cadet Nurse Corps program. This doubled or tripled enrollment in biology, called for changes in the curriculum, and made it necessary for the college to hire another staff member, a young woman, who would teach botany and microbiology.

In the process of creating necessary classrooms and laboratories, sawing and hammering in the departmental quarters went on for months. I recall trying to write on a blackboard on one side of a wall while a carpenter hammered on the other. And no one knew where anything was!

I was under constant stress. At the end of the fall term, I was hospitalized for a low fever, back pain, and other symptoms that the doctor could not diagnose. He said, "When we don't know what else to call it, we call it flu," and sent me home to McMinnville to recover. That put me on leave from Whitworth for the winter term.

When I returned to Whitworth for the spring term, I visited a dentist to have my teeth cleaned. He observed that my gums were inflamed and ordered x-rays. My teeth were sound but he said there was a pus pocket around every tooth and with that amount of infection, it was a wonder I was not crippled with arthritis.

Extractions began almost immediately. But the teeth did not come out easily. "With that amount of infection," the dentist said, "they should have been ready to fall out. Instead, they pulled like telephone poles."

In spite of pain, swelling, and facial discoloration, my teaching responsibilities continued. Somehow, I finished the term. Faculty and staff friends were most supportive. Mother came over from Arlington at the end of the school year to care for me while the extractions were completed. The dentist said that I should wait six months before getting dentures after all that infection and disturbance to the bones in my jaws.

To my horror, I realized **I was to be a toothless old hag for six months!** I wouldn't be able to teach that summer or even in the beginning of the fall term.

There seemed no alternative but for me to resign from my position as chair of the biology department at Whitworth, much as I regretted having to do so. I returned to McMinnville and spent a quiet summer regaining my health and adjusting to married life.

Ray's home, now ours, was his much-prized possession: the only home he had ever owned, though he had lived in many houses. It was a plain two-story frame house, built in 1882 (at least that's what a date on the fireplace mantel implied). It was shaded by seven stately white oaks and three large walnut trees and was surrounded by stretches of lawn, scattered fruit trees, shrubs, and flowers. A vegetable garden thrived near the rear end of the lot.

Moreover, that property **had a history**! Ray first saw the place in the early 1900s when he was a small child visiting his grandparents. He felt drawn to it—the big white house, the trees, and the **red barn** where the garden now thrived. "Some day," he declared, to the amusement of his relatives, "I'm going to **own** that place!"

This was the Handley house, built by Charles Handley, a former British sea captain. Born in England, he and his wife met and married in Tasmania. A dozen years later they moved to Oregon, where, as a means of livelihood, Captain Handley became one of the early surveyors in Yamhill County. Eventually the Handleys bought 3H acres on the west side of South Baker Street, north of the old McMinnville Hospital, and built three houses there. Our home, the last of the three, was the final home for Captain Handley, his wife Sarah and an unmarried daughter, Elizabeth, who had been the first teacher in District 40 to hold a teaching certificate. Now that it had become his home, Ray treasured the place for itself, its history, and his early memories of it.

This was also the first unrented home I had lived in. My parents were tenant farmers who moved frequently, always seeking a better locale for their large family, of which I was the youngest child. Though Ray and I shared many interests, our life-styles were different. I lived by schedule; his days were unscheduled. And this house was **full** of Ray's things. He had lived here nearly ten years with his keepsakes. I had to make many adjustments. However, I, too, learned to cherish the place.

Linfield had neither a teaching nor administrative position for me either that fall or the next spring, due to the low wartime enrollment. Still, my name remained in the college catalogue as Assistant Professor, Ph.D. "on leave." (The "powers that be" deemed it important for my name to be there since it was still the only name of a female Ph.D. on the college faculty.)

Being otherwise unemployed, I now had time to refine my thesis, which was published in the July 1946, issue of *Ecological Monographs.* Then in June 1946, Professor Macnab, disillusioned with the existing administration at Linfield, resigned and took a position as chairman of the biology and geology department at Lower Columbia Junior College in Longview, Washington. In 1950, he moved to Portland. He became chairman of the biology department at Portland State College in 1953 and remained there until he retired in 1969.

With Prof's departure, an era ended. In his twenty-two years he had been instrumental in transforming Linfield from a small, unknown parochial school into an institution recognized for excellence in science, according to Robert H. Knapp and H.B. Goodrich, who add in their 1952 book, *The Origins of American Scientists:*

> The Biology Department of Linfield is one of the most interesting science departments reviewed in this study. Its brilliant achievement from 1928 to 1939 appears to be attributable almost solely to the unusual talent of its one faculty member and chairman, J.A. Macnab...who, operating under considerable handicap, still achieved a very remarkable record for his department and for the institution....One important factor was his devotion to research, in which his students participated regularly....The morale of the department [was] particularly keen...deriving from his tremendous scientific sincerity, his professional competence, and his keen interest in his more promising students.

John Boling, with whom I had worked as a student, became chairman of the biology department. Linfield's enrollment zoomed that fall as veterans from World War II swarmed to college to take advantage of the "GI Bill," which provided them the opportunity to get an education. This influx was too great for John to handle alone, so I was called back from "leave" that fall to teach an upper division class.

But I couldn't forget Saddleback Mountain. It haunted me.

Professor Macnab, my mentor, the person who had introduced me to ecology and to that beloved forest, was gone. But I felt compelled to find out what was happening where we had done our research. Breaks between trips were unavoidable, but for the next several years Ray and I visited the site in late summer or fall, always taking pictures and making notes about the community of life developing there. No one, as far as I could learn, had ever studied a young forest that developed, after logging, at the precise locale where an ancient forest had been. I **had** to do that. But how could I without experienced helpers and financial assistance?

Gradually, year after year the number of classes assigned to me increased until the fall of 1950 when John was unable to teach, because of a mysterious, long-lasting illness. I then taught his class in general biology, and, from then on, essentially all of the courses required for biology majors. Although I had been advanced to Associate Professor in 1948, I was still listed in 1950 as a part-time faculty member without full pay.

Eight more years passed and 1958 arrived. It was now nearly twenty years since the research site was logged and a quarter century since Prof began his research. In that interval ecology had become much more sophisticated. Studies of plant and animal communities were no longer in vogue, and when they were undertaken it was usually by teams of ecologists, each of whom was a specialist in the study of such things as mushrooms, mosses, flowering plants, insects, birds, or mammals. These scientists followed new procedures and used expensive, complicated equipment. To think that one lone zoologist/ecologist could tackle this task was audacious, especially since I was not a specialist in any phase of the work.

Hoping to enlist some specialized help, I tried to spark interest in the project at Oregon State University but encountered no enthusiasm there. I was disappointed but couldn't give up the dream I had held from the time the area was logged.

Although I lacked sophisticated equipment and experienced scientists, I could still pattern the study after Prof's research. By paralleling that study I could compare the life of the young forest with that of the ancient one. I was determined to learn all that I could about that young forest.

Encouraged by members of the recently organized Linfield Research Institute (LRI), in January 1959 I applied to the National Science Foundation (NSF) for a grant. Having that financial help would make it possible for me to gain more complete information about this stage of forest development.

On May 25, I received notice that the NSF had funded my proposal. That was cause for celebration! Still there was much to be done before the field work could begin. I had to give and grade final exams and turn in the grades to complete the academic year. In addition, setting up a research program with LRI involved much detail. That nitty-gritty took the entire month of June. I chose the Fourth of July for starting the field research at Saddleback.

Part III

Phoenix

IN EGYPTIAN MYTHOLOGY, [the Phoenix] is a bird of great beauty, said to live for 500 or 600 years in the Arabian Desert and then consume itself by fire, rising from its ashes young and beautiful to live through another cycle.

-The Reader's Digest Great Encyclopedic Dictionary

View from the fire shelter, August 1940.

Chapter Sixteen

Out of the Ashes

I OBSERVED SIGNIFICANT CHANGES at the research area in the two decades following the holocaust of 1940, which Kenny had graphically portrayed in a letter to Prof on June 23 of that year, the day after he, Dorothy, and Bob Peck had discovered that the site had been logged:

> Hitler at his worst couldn't have raised more havoc. Your quiet, beautiful "woods" is nothing but a happy memory. The place we visited is a total stranger to us. All three of us stood there and cursed, we had to to keep from bawling.
>
> I reckon this hit me about as hard as it could anybody but you and J C D. I was the first one that went with you in search of your desired location. It was on one of these trips that I first met my wife. [Actually, they met on a trip several years later, not on one of these scouting trips.] And now to me falls the duty of writing FINIS. I have a vague idea of how this is going to make you feel. I hope you will never go up there and see the Hell that has been raised.

Prof's response to Kenny dated July 5 was equally touching:

> Your last letter was a tragedy....I could see that the devastation wrought on our old station had affected you deeply. My wife wanted to know what was the matter with me when I got home that night and so I handed her the letter, which she said explained my attitude. It certainly is a pity but it does bring home the fact that in this life the only permanent things are our memories. Everything else is doomed to change....I presume that my emotions would have been stirred more deeply had it occurred while I was still making my trips or still there at Linfield....However, it seems to me that this misfortune may be changed into a wonderful opportunity by using it properly.
>
> I only wish that the work which I did had been better done, but that will serve as a fine means of comparison of conditions in their natural state with those which are brought about by destruction of the forests.

I was visiting with my parents in Washington at the time Dorothy and Kenny discovered the logging and did not learn the sad news until I went to McMinnville in late July. That was when the three of us returned to Saddleback and relocated the research station. Though crushed by what I saw I soon realized, as Prof had, that this "misfortune" offered unique opportunities for further study.

Spurred by these thoughts, Dorothy, Kenny and I revisited the site in early August and recorded data similar to our earlier research. Ray and I also made trips at that time, trapping small mammals and taking pictures.

Then, after I finished graduate school, Ray and I began the first of a series of more inclusive trips to the site. On our initial visit in 1941, I was surprised at how barren the place looked. When we were there the year before none of the logs, which were so prominent, had been removed. Now they had all been snaked out and hauled away. We could find no sign of the fire shelter. The ground where its boards had lain was charred and black. Much of the rest of the slope had been burned, too. We wondered what had happened.

Though the burning may have been done by the owners, a procedure essentially required in those times due to liability laws, we were told that a thunderstorm had passed across the mountain shortly after the choice logs had been removed. It looked as though a bolt of lightning had struck the mammoth Douglas-fir in the northwest corner of the hectare, setting that tree on fire, and from that lowest point the fire had swept upward through much of the study area. It was so intense along the west side all the way to the southwest corner of the hectare that it burned through needles, cones, and tinder-dry debris down to the mineral soil and charred logs, stumps, and the bases of ancient trees. Where the fire fanned out into the middle of the research site, it destroyed the boards of the fire shelter and the residue from logging as well as burning low plants and the duff and litter of the forest floor. However, the east fringe of the research hectare was burned only lightly and some small patches of vegetation escaped entirely. In all, that fire had heavily burned or at least touched about two-thirds of the study site.

Where the deepest burning had been we found only a few tiny seedlings and some very small moss plants. But, in unburned or lightly burned places where the original ground cover had been rather sparse or where it had been disturbed by the logging activities, a few plants of wood groundsel and fireweed had come in among the original forest herbs and shrubs.

Tender herbs, such as vanilla leaf and even sword ferns, were yellowed from the increased exposure and dryness, but all species that were present before logging had survived the year.

Through field trips with Dr. Shelford I had learned that even after disturbances as devastating as this, forests and other plant communities are capable of eventually returning to a state somewhat similar to their previous successional status through a series of stages during which assemblages of plants gradually replace one another, a process known as plant succession. Still I was amazed at how rapidly the community of life changed as one group of plants followed another. Ray, with camera in hand, made a pictorial record of these changes.

In 1942, the second year after logging, unfamiliar plants crowded the place—plants referred to as "weeds" because they do not normally occur in the mature forest. A dense cover of wood groundsel (*Senecio sylvaticus*) had shot up to three or four feet wherever the fire had passed. With its many small, pale flowers that go to seed almost immediately, this plant thrives briefly on logged and burned-over forest land. It dominated the burned parts.

Scattered among the groundsel were some showy spikes of fireweed with dainty rose-colored blossoms; pearly everlasting plants with clusters of tiny, egg-shaped white flowers; and a few foot-high thicket lotus (*Lotus aboriginus*) plants, heavy with pink blossoms and clustered seedpods. Dandelion-like plants of gosmore (*Hypochaeris radicata*), a common lawn pest, bloomed nearby, and an eight-inch Douglas-fir seedling peeked out from among the weeds.

Clouds of seeds from wood groundsel, fireweed, and gosmore drifted in the breeze and, falling to the earth, made bare ground look as though there had been a light snowfall.

A few seedling red elderberry bushes and young canes of thimbleberry had appeared as other newcomers, but clearly, a weed stage of succession held sway.

Transition from a weed to a weed-brush stage began as early as the third year and continued for about five years. Initially, dense patches of eighteen-inch thicket lotus replaced the wood groundsel that had dominated the heavily burned areas, and Oregon grape plants began growing under the lotus. Several small willows and a wild rose joined the elderberries and thimbleberries. Three-foot tall bracken ferns flourished in the open, and a group of salmonberry plants sprang up at the base of the hemlock ladder remnant. The eight-inch Douglas-fir we had noted the year before had grown more than a foot during the year, and was now nearly two feet tall. Also, many other young firs were large enough to be noticed. Fireweed, pearly everlasting, and grasses were still present.

Over the next several years we watched brushy plants, such as ocean spray, alders, thimbleberries, and salmonberries come in, crowd out, and replace most of the "weed" herbs.

Seven years after logging, willows and alders, some as much as fifteen feet tall, topped everything but the original trees that were still there. Many young Douglas-firs were almost ten feet high, and young hemlocks were nearly as tall. A picture taken by Ray shows me nearly hidden in the middle of a mixture of brush, young conifers, bracken, and persisting herbs that had sprung up in the burned-over area between the hemlock ladder and fire-shelter trees. Wherever logging had not disturbed the ground cover, salal thrived, red huckleberry bushes formed dense patches, and the little hemlocks present before logging made a spurt in growth. Clearly, the young forest was passing from the weed-brush stage into a brush and seedling conifer stage of succession.

In the winter of 1947-48 a mighty storm roared in from the coast, uprooting trees as it swept a diagonal path across the terrace from the southwest corner of the hectare toward the northeast. Like dominos, many of the forest giants took others with them as they fell. Trunks of once magnificent trees lay prostrate, awaiting the recycling services of beetles, carpenter ants, termites, and fungi. The fire-shelter tree and most of the other ancient firs were victims of that storm. Craters signaled where the mammoths had stood and immense jumbles of roots packed with soil walled the downwind side of these cavities.

From that time, the fire-shelter tree crater, the crater of its neighbor to the east, and the decaying snag of the hemlock ladder tree became our major points of reference whenever we visited the research site.

Ten years after logging, a brush and seedling conifer stage was well established. Elderberry bushes, clusters of ocean spray, salmonberry canes, and generous numbers of blackberry brambles enriched the mixture of plants. Willows and alders were about twenty feet high and a bitter cherry was nearly fifteen feet.

The ancient firs had done a good task of producing seeds. Their seedlings grew rapidly, after a few years during which root systems became established, some as much as forty inches in a year, and as Ray would say, were now "thick as hair on a dog's back." Many of these young firs were now more than ten feet tall and overshadowed the herbs and shrubs. Young hemlocks were equally thick and almost as tall, but smaller in diameter. Conifer saplings now formed a dense and conspicuous cover over much of the hectare. Bracken fern, fireweed, and patches of thicket lotus were common, pearly everlasting plants were scattered, and salal, Oregon grape, and red huckleberry plants thrived in the more open areas. Shade tolerant species such as sword fern, deer fern, and wood sorrel that had persisted from the original forest became more plentiful.

On that trip in 1950 Ray said, "This rank growth of young trees reminds me of an experience I had many years ago when I was a forestry student at OAC. A famous forester, a professor from Germany, was with us on one of our annual field trips during which we visited logging operations, tracts of ancient forest, and sites that were undergoing natural reforestation following logging. The German professor was amazed at what he saw. He had never been in a region like this where reforestation occurred naturally. All the forests in Germany, such as their famous Black Forest, have been planted. Finally, overcome by the sight, he said in his strong accent, 'You are ferry vortunate here. Vere de loggers go und spit de tobacco juice, dere de trees, dey come oop, und vere de loggers go und don't spit de tobacco juice, dere de trees, dey come oop, too!'" Ray was full of such vignettes from his earlier years.

Moving about through these thickets was nearly impossible. Trees were so close together on the upper part of the logging road that we could no longer use it as our route to the station. Instead we came in by way of the spar tree below, using the trunk of a fallen fir for most of the steep climb up the mountainside.

In the summer of 1954 we discovered that the logging road had been reopened all the way to the research site. Loggers with chain saws had felled the few remaining firs and bucked up any sound logs they could find. They took sections from several trees which had blown over during the winter storm six years before. They also cut into the trunk of the fallen fire-shelter tree but did not remove any of it. We wondered why. A few years later we found a huge pile of sawdust lying beneath that log, evidence that carpenter ants were busy inside.

Using caterpillar tractors, the workers had dragged logs to the nearby logging road, loaded them onto trucks, and hauled them down the mountain to mills. They left unmarketable logs where they lay or pushed them aside, often in tight groups and, frequently, with some of them stacked on top of others. Sawdust, chips, splinters, and great slabs of bark, knocked from the logs, smothered parts of the forest floor. Wherever "cats" had moved they crushed young trees and other plants and compacted ground. This activity reopened a wide strip from north to south just east of the center of the hectare. At its south end the space merged with other openings near the eastern boundary. This "salvage logging" had made access to the station much easier than it had been for several years.

In 1957 I returned to the research site with a group of students. We counted trees and tabulated the relative numbers of Douglas-firs, hemlocks, and noble firs. We also tagged and numbered many of them and measured their diameters for future reference, we hoped. This young forest had become impressive. I longed to study it in detail, to compare it with the ancient forest from which it had emerged. That opportunity came with the NSF research grant.

Chapter Seventeen
A New Eden?

THE FOURTH OF JULY, 1959, dawned beautifully—cloudless and sunny without a hint of rain, and pleasantly warm—an ideal day for an outing. I'd been dreaming for almost twenty years of the time when I could systematically study this young forest which had sprung up where a previously studied ancient forest had been—something no one had ever done. Now the day for beginning was here.

In this research there was no such thing as a typical day. Even the days that were most similar varied. Each was unique. From weekly field days covering a period of three years under the NSF grant and a few widely spaced ones thereafter, this picture of the developing young forest emerged.

Midmorning on that July Fourth, 1959, Howard and Frances Daniels and their daughter Wanda arrived at my home with copious lunches, binoculars, collecting gear, surveying equipment, eggbeater psychrometer, and soil thermometer tucked into the trunk of their car (the only weather instruments we had at that time, though I had ordered others).

My little Puli dog Timidity and I joined them. Ray was recuperating from a long siege of flu and had to miss this special day for which he too had been waiting. Soon we were on our way to Saddleback Mountain.

Frances, Howard, and Ray would be my primary helpers in this work, while students would come and go. Frances (who, like me, had helped with Prof's research)—as my part-time graduate assistant—would be my chief helper, both in the field and in the lab. Howard, who had also helped with Prof's study and was now a professional surveyor, would help in relocating boundaries of the station and in reconstructing a map of the area. He would also do other tasks as the weather and his job in the county surveyor's office permitted. Both Howard and Frances, avid birders, were interested in plants and insects, as well. Ray, my devoted companion, would be my constant encourager and helper in untold ways.

As we traveled westward toward the mountains, we reveled in the beauty of the countryside and the many rich tones displayed by the trees now in their full summer verdure. Just beyond Grand Ronde, we stopped to pick up a key for the Murphy Road gate at the home of the Crown Zellerbach woods foreman. That road, built many years earlier by the Murphy brothers, would be our route of access to the research area. It led from the summit of the Salmon River Highway (State Highway 18) into the Murphys' forest property on the north side of Saddleback Mountain.

There was now no other way to reach the research area. Logging during the late '30s and early '40s had destroyed the trail we used for Prof's study. The Boyer locale was no longer recognizable, the buildings all gone. A clump of English laurel marked the place where Mervin Boyer's log building had been, and a really alert person whizzing by on the highway could see on the south side of the road a historic marker memorializing the Boyer Toll Gate.

Down Murphy Road, four miles southwestward from the highway, we crossed a log bridge over Salmon River and, turning westward to the right, followed a less traveled road for a mile to an unnamed branch of the Salmon River below the research site. Howard parked in that shady place and we listened to the music of flowing water while we ate our lunch before starting our trek to the station.

From the bridge, at an elevation of 1,035 feet, a logging road—to us "the trail"—led to the research station on a terrace at 1,400 to 1,500 feet. About every 100 feet of its gradual ascent the trail changed somewhat, enabling convenient subdivision. Halfway to our destination, the trail divided, with the fork on the left—the "high road"—leading directly up the mountain, and the one on the right—the "low road"—proceeding almost straight ahead, skirting the north face of the mountain in a very gentle climb, westward to the noble fir spar tree which stood some 400 or 500 feet below the station.

At the junction, Howard and Frances, who were carrying surveying equipment as well as a barometer for use in calculating elevations, turned to the left, the slightly shorter way, while Wanda, Timidity, and I continued on the low road toward the spar tree. From there, a short, steep climb took us to the north boundary of the research site just east of the former fire shelter. For much of that climb instead of fighting undergrowth and fallen limbs and logs we used the trunk of a windthrown fir, the "walk-up" log.

When we had all arrived at the station we began looking for a suitable place from which to carry on our study. The fire shelter site, the center for

Prof's study, was no longer suitable. It was now a saucer-like depression, a crater formed when the severe winter storm of 1948 had uprooted so many trees. Besides, a dense growth of young trees now thrived in that area. We needed a place in the open.

Moving into the space which salvage logging had cleared of trees and logs, we finally decided upon a relatively level spot a short distance inside the south border. With two mammoth logs, one on top of the other, as a backdrop, young conifers framing the sides, and a view across the valley to Mt. Hebo in the far distance, this airy, open space became the hub from which our activities radiated for the duration of the project. Now in mid-afternoon, the day was still lovely with a blue sky, no visible clouds, and a light wind from the southwest keeping the air comfortably cool. We enjoyed this pleasant setting and marveled at the beauty of the distant view.

Before us, a lane wound downhill, snaking around young trees, logs, and upturned roots, to the north edge of the hectare. There, the ground dropped away steeply. Below us, perhaps 500 feet away, we could see the noble fir spar tree used twenty years earlier in removing logs. Long cables attached near the top of the spar tree's straight, 100-foot column were used in "yarding" logs: dragging them to the loading area—the "landing"—to be hauled away.

To us everything seemed so foreign that we wondered how it could be the place where we had spent many happy hours only a little more than twenty years earlier. Nothing was at all familiar except the slope of the land and even that seemed steeper with all the ancient trees gone. Now, instead of Douglas-firs towering overhead, topless hemlocks and barkless snags stuck up above the dense groves of young conifers that covered about three-fourths of the hectare.

The fallen giants of the forest, marking the path of that gale which had felled them in 1947-48, prevented us from moving about freely. Many, rejected during the salvaging operations, now formed barricades, pushed side by side or stacked one on top of another. Most of those showed little sign of decay, but snags and older logs were crumbling. Some logs we had used as part of our trail at the time of Prof's study lay nearly buried beneath the debris from logging. All of these provided reservoirs of biodiversity saved from the original forest.

Wherever we looked, we saw young Douglas-firs, no longer saplings but well on their way toward becoming sturdy trees. Twenty to thirty feet tall and four inches in diameter four feet above the ground (diameter at breast height—dbh), the firs now competed for light with the willows and alders which had been their nurse-crop when they were seedlings, as well as with the slower-growing, shade tolerant hemlocks which outnumbered them two to one. Seedlings of both conifer species had sprung up so close together that their limbs now interlocked in the thickets. A few stiffly formal, bluish-green noble firs grew at the fringes of the thickets or in the open, some only a few feet high. Few plants, even mosses, had been able to survive in the dense shade of the groves, and the ground there was covered with needles and dead twigs.

Some of the craterlike spaces and the small openings which had persisted since the site was logged were choked with salal and wispy huckleberry stalks. The fire shelter tree crater and the crater just east of it were larger and different. Surrounded by some of the largest young firs, they were near the edge of the steep north slope where only filtered sunlight reached the ground. Mosses, ferns, starflowers, violets, bleeding hearts, and a few other forest herbs grew in them, in addition to a scattering of salal and seedling conifers. Near the northeast corner of the hectare was a dense, moderately large patch of thimbleberries, while another plot nearby contained a mixture of caneberries—salmonberries, thimbleberries, and wild blackberries.

Many kinds of plants grew in the two major openings. Fireweed was beginning to bloom. It stood higher than a person's head and bracken was so rank that we had difficulty moving through it. Beneath that vegetation small sword ferns, salal, and Oregon grape plants persisted, as well as several kinds of herbs. Wood sorrel and vanilla leaf survived in the shade at the edges of the conifer thickets and, in areas not crowded with bracken, thicket lotus, "dandelions," pearly everlasting, native thistles, and grasses thrived along with various other recent arrivals.

Butterflies, bronze flea beetles, and other insects we had never seen there before, as well as some familiar insects, were busy on the blossoms or leaves of the plants. A large thistle was almost in bloom, berries were forming on salal, huckleberries were turning red, salmonberries were beginning to ripen, and lotus plants were still blooming, though past their prime.

This young forest not only looked different, it felt different and it smelled different. Fragrances of the abundant flowers contrasted with the resinous aroma of conifer boughs. The forest also sounded different—new bird songs regaled us and some familiar songs were missing.

I wondered, *Could this thriving young community ever replace the ancient forest I knew and loved? Could it be the beginning of a new Eden?* Only time, a great deal of time, would tell.

After we had a general picture of the young forest community, we returned to our chosen activity center and settled down to work, following a

The author stands between Professor Victor Shelford and fellow University of Illinois graduate student Eugene Odum during a 1938 research trip to Reelfoot Lake, Tennessee. *Courtesy of Eugene Odum.*

All photographs used in this book are courtesy of the author, unless otherwise noted.

The hemlock ladder tree at the Saddleback research site is shown above in 1935; lower left in 1941, one year after logging; and with regrowth evident in 1954, fourteen years after logging.

The fire shelter area at Saddleback: above in 1935; lower left in 1941, one year after logging; lower right in 1954, fourteen years after logging.

Above: The author on her first trip to Saddleback, December 30, 1933.
Below: Dorothy McKey (Fender) in 1935. *Photo by Charles Sanford.*

Above: The author and husband Ray on site at the soil moisture sampling station during the National Science Foundation study, 1960. *Below:* Frances Daniels working a beating square, 1960.

Opposite: The research site as it appeared in 1985-86, showing vigorous regrowth of the forest. *Above:* Saddleback Mountain in 1995, after clear-cutting. *Photo courtesy Lyle Hubbard.*

Jane Claire Dirks-Edmunds at the Saddleback Mountain research site in 1995. *Photo courtesy Lyle Hubbard.*

routine we had learned from Professor Macnab. Frances and Wanda gathered weather data and collected insects while Howard and I tried to locate more of the landmarks I had sketched for the map I made during my student days. We all kept alert for signs of animal activities and plant growth.

At about six o'clock the breeze freshened. Soon a few clouds scudded overhead and we could see a bank of clouds near the western horizon. Not wanting to be caught in a summer thunderstorm we packed our gear and left through the south side of the hectare, following the route over which the salvaged logs had been removed.

As we neared the car we heard a pileated woodpecker hammering on a snag, a nostalgic ending for our first day of research under the NSF grant and our celebration of Independence Day 1959.

The next week, Nancy Myron was with us. She became a very capable and dedicated student assistant who made collections and worked on special projects for more than a year. Even after she left Linfield to continue her education at the University of Oregon School of Nursing, Nancy returned off and on to help.

This time as we climbed upward from the bridge, we made such careful notes along the trail that it was nearly two o'clock by the time we reached our destination. Immediately, Howard and I resumed the surveying we had begun the week before, while Frances and Nancy recorded weather data and collected insects. Each of us also watched for signs of animal activity and whether plants were blooming, fruiting, or fading. This soon became our weekly routine.

I aimed to parallel Prof's study as closely as we could, but differences were inevitable. All of Prof's field notes, from beginning to end of the project, were entered in his little 4 by 6H inch notebook, and most of the notes were made by him. The field notes for my study were made by many helpers, not solely by me, and for each trip we used three different cards designed by Ray: one for notes at the station, one for trail notes, and a third for travel notes. As a result, often on any one day several workers recorded on their individual cards what she or he saw, heard, or did. Though helpful in some ways, the three-card system lacked the uniformity of Prof's records, making it more difficult, sometimes, for me to get a clear picture of any one day or to make comparisons.

Also, instead of having free access to the entire research area as in Prof's study, we were restricted to about one-third of the hectare by thickets of young conifers, patches of salal, huckleberries, and caneberries, tangles of head-high bracken and fireweed, and log barriers. We spent most of our time in the larger, better lighted, airier openings, filled with herbs, ferns, and scattered shrubs, and we made most of our conifer insect collections from trees at the edges of the thickets. Those of us who knew the old forest missed the freedom to move about.

For Howard and me, locating landmarks, finding the boundaries of the research area, and making a map of the young forest demanded immediate attention. Without that information we could never be sure where we were in comparison with the old forest.

The young trees were so close together that we could see only a short distance into thickets, not through them, a major problem for surveyors. And the lower limbs of the trees, though now beginning to lose needles because of the lack of light, were so stiff and rigid that we needed an ax or machete to get through. A couple of years later, this changed. The dead limbs became brittle and broke off readily as part of the natural pruning process, but that didn't help us in 1959. We had to cope with the situation as it was. The dense thickets made the place very confusing. Where exactly was the southwest corner? Or the northwest one with the tree which had been struck by lightning? We had to find these, as well as other landmarks which would help in locating boundaries. It looked like an impossible undertaking, but we persevered.

We had located the broken remnant of the hemlock ladder tree on our first trip. By referring to it and using the map I had sketched as a student, we found various stumps and other landmarks. That map proved invaluable. We focused on hectare seventeen where Prof had concentrated his study and avoided the part of hectare sixteen that he used, for it was now an almost impenetrable mass of young trees.

Using the landmarks we had located as our base, we measured from stump to stump and from stumps to elevation levels. We sighted with the compass, checked, and sighted again, time after time. We kept measuring, and sighting, bit by bit, week after week.

Often, as the surveying progressed and I was out of sight working with Howard, little Timidity dog would work her way through the thickets hunting for me. Finding me, and evidently reassured that I was all right, she returned to her favorite perch on a fir stump near where Frances and Nancy or others were working.

That first year four inches of rain fell during the first week in September, an exceptionally early start for the rainy season, and by the end of that month a total of more than fifteen inches had fallen. Those rains forced Howard and me to shut down our surveying until spring, but by this time we were fairly sure of the location of most of the outer boundaries of the hectare and had some idea of the extent of thickets and open areas. The rains also greatly curtailed some of our other field activities.

However, to Nancy's delight and fascination, this soaking of the still-warm forest floor prompted the production of a fascinating number and variety of fruiting bodies of fungi—mushrooms, coral fungi, pore fungi, and others. She took upon herself the task of identifying as many of them as she could.

In April, we were back at the surveying. By the last of June, the end of the first year of the research project, we had established accurate outer boundaries, were locating contour lines, and had begun reconstructing the twenty-meter grid Prof had laid out.

Having a well-marked grid was imperative since the young trees restricted not only our moving around but also our view of the place so much that it was almost impossible to know exactly where we were in the hectare without grid lines, complete with tags at all intersections and corners of the grid. Putting up markers was a time-consuming undertaking, but by referring to them we always knew exactly where we were. Dorwin Lovell, one of my students who was now assisting every week, and Frank Collins, Nancy's friend, whom she later married, helped with this project, but we were well into the second year before the grid was complete with all the tags in place and we had reestablished the contour lines.

Then I began sketching a map of the young forest for comparison with the ancient forest. After putting in boundaries, grid, contour lines, and instrument locations, I added the conifer thickets, large open areas, craters, and the largest, longest logs. Working between other tasks bit by bit during many months, I completed the map by filling in the shrubs and other significant vegetation.

We had been collecting weather data from our very first trip because temperature, moisture, wind, light—all the elements that make up weather—are crucial parts of the physical environment of a natural community. Since I wanted this study to be as much like Prof's as possible, the instruments we used were similar to ones he'd used and we placed them in locations comparable to the ones he had chosen.

At the beginning of this study, on almost every trip we brought with us some new instrument until, by the middle of September, we had two twenty-inch capacity rain gauges and three maximum-minimum thermometers set up. The first thermometer was in a thicket of young trees; the second fastened to a stump in the central part of the large open area; and the third also in the open, but nearer the south end of the hectare close to the center of our activity. One of the rain gauges was near the thermometer in the conifer grove, and the other in the open near the thermometer attached to the stump. I had also purchased a Weston Illuminometer which we brought now and then for measurements of light intensity.

In October, Howard and Charlie Gnose, a student who had recently joined our crew, carried a hygrothermograph up the mountain—complete with the parts of a shelter which Howard had built in his spare time. They attached the shelter to a log in a conifer thicket near the center of the hectare, and that rounded out our battery of essential instruments.

I was eager to compare data from the two communities—the original forest and the young one—for weather is interesting but it is also capricious, varying from day to day, season to season, and year to year. My data from three years of records, compared with Prof's records from five years, show many interesting things.

The average annual temperatures for the two communities were not greatly different. For Prof's study, it was an overall 50°F. For mine, the average was 48.5°F for the thermometer in the thicket and almost 49.5°F for the three thermometers together, one in the thicket and two in the open, only a half degree lower than for the ancient forest.

Still, tall trees do make a difference. Immediately after the insulating canopy of boughs was removed when the giant trees were cut, the hot rays from the sun reached almost to the ground, drying winds had little to buffer them, and the rains beat with slight interference upon the scarred forest floor that had lost much of its ability to absorb and store winter's abundance of moisture.

In the young forest the physical environment was hotter and drier during the summer months and colder in the winter. These changes had a marked effect upon the creatures of the forest. On our very first visit after the trees were felled and before the logs had been removed, we had seen insects that had never been there before: grasshoppers, cucumber beetles, and others that live in dry, open habitats, not mature forests. (I wish I had weather data from those years.)

Gradually, as the groves of young trees formed and grew in height, the environment began shifting back toward the way it had been in the ancient forest, but even now, after twenty years, we noted significant differences in both the physical environment and in the community of life.

The huge, evenly spaced trees in the old forest created a basically uniform physical environment, with very little variation in light, temperature, or air movement from place to place on any given day. The young forest, however, was full of contrasts.

Precipitation comes in many forms. Fog is an important and rather frequent occurrence in the forests along our coast range. We had many experiences with fog, but only one stands out in my memory.

I think this was in the late fall of that first year. Out in the valley the sky was clear and the sun shone, but a bank of cloud hung low over the mountain. As I climbed toward the station, I was suddenly in the center of that cloud, completely engulfed in vapor. I could scarcely breathe. My hair, eyelashes, and clothing were drenched. I tried to shield my notepaper, but it became saturated. Snags, root masses, trees...all were veiled. Above me, below me, at my sides, fog was everywhere, inescapable. I felt completely isolated though Frances and Howard were nearby. Soon the fog lifted. The sun shone once more just as it had in the valley. That was a strangely haunting experience.

The spacious canopy of the old forest was a living framework hundreds of feet in thickness, where droplets of moisture condensed on needles and twigs whenever fog rolled in from the ocean or rain clouds covered the mountain. Moisture dripped from the trees for hours after the fog had cleared away or the clouds had passed. This "horizontal precipitation," recognized by scientists many years ago, increased the effective precipitation under the trees to nearly eleven inches more than that in the openings.

By contrast, in the young forest about twelve inches more moisture reached the ground in the openings than under the trees. The young trees were not tall enough to catch more than a small part of the condensed moisture and much of what they did catch evaporated before reaching the ground. Then too, they were so closely grouped that their twigs and needles caught much of the rain which fell in light showers and held it until it evaporated, often leaving the ground under them dry even after several days of light rain. As a result, the forest floor in the groves of young trees received some twenty inches less moisture each year than did the floor of the ancient forest. Small wonder the young forest seemed so dry. Actually, these differences were even greater in proportion to the total precipitation for the two studies because Prof's study, in the '30s, was made at a time when the entire United States and much of the rest of the northern hemisphere was unusually dry, while my study, in the early '60s, was made during a wet period. The average annual precipitation recorded by Prof for the five years of his study was eighty-nine inches, but for my study it was 136 inches, a surprising increase. However, weather has long been known to be cyclic. (Today we believe these wet-dry cycles may be, in part, aspects of the El Nino-El Nina climatic phenomenon.)

The ancient coniferous forests of the Northwest are well known as places of subdued light. Our majestic forest on Saddleback was such a place. On a clear summer day during Prof's study we had been able to get a reading of only slightly more than 10,000 foot-candles even in the most brightly lighted, widely scattered spots, while now we regularly had readings of nearly 12,000 foot-candles throughout all openings of the young forest. However, inside the thickets in the young forest it was quite the other way. There the maximum was seldom more than 30 foot-candles compared with regular readings of 300 foot-candles, or more, under the canopy of the mature trees—ten times the light that was available under the young trees.

On summer days it was cool in the thickets but hot and dry in the open where the sun beat down mercilessly. One July day, our hottest, it was 86°F in the thicket and 89° to 92° in the open. On those hot days of midsummer we had no relief from the relentless sun directly overhead. The only shade the entire research site now offered was in the dense thickets where light was dim, air circulation poor, movement nearly impossible, and the only place to sit a carpet of pitchy needles. Clearly, that shade was not useable. Occasionally, while eating lunch, recording notes, or doing some other task, one or two of us could find a partial reprieve in the shade of tall fireweed plants, bracken fern, or a young tree at the edge of a thicket, but this young community bore no resemblance to the spacious cathedral quality of the ancient forest.

Similarly on our coldest day in January 1962, it was 16°F in the thicket and as low as 11°F in the open. Breezes, blocked from the groves by the closeness of the trees, swept unimpeded through the passageways, bringing heat or cold from the valley below.

The trees of the ancient forest had kept the temperature fairly uniform, an effect known as thermal blanketing. Then in hot weather it was always cooler among the trees than outside. Temperatures above 70°F were rare. The highest recorded in Prof's five years was 89°F. Low temperatures were just as unusual, the lowest recorded being 11°F. In the winter when the temperature was very low outside the ancient forest and the soil there was frozen hard, only rarely could any sign of freezing be found within the forest, and the air would be noticeably warmer. Snow or a glaze of sleet usually covered the ground when the temperature was very low, helping to keep the soil beneath the trees from freezing, although, even in a heavy snowfall, the amount of snow reaching the ground was never great. Branches in the canopy caught most of it. There the snow rested until it evaporated, melted, or gradually sifted to the ground.

The mature forest also had a vertical layering of temperature. Though we could not climb to the tops of the huge firs, we learned from records obtained by instruments placed in the hemlock ladder tree that the temperature in the summer was several degrees warmer at 100 feet above the ground than it was at the ground level and even in the winter it was slightly warmer there. The average temperature for the entire year was seven degrees warmer 100 feet above the ground than it was at shrub level. We can only guess what kinds of differences we might have found 200 feet higher at the tops of the old giants.

The contrasts in temperature were mostly between the groves and the open places in the young forest, since the trees were not tall enough to produce much vertical layering. Among the shrubs, ferns, and herbs in the openings, it was always warmer on summer days and colder in winter than it was in the thickets—evidence that coniferous trees are efficient thermal blankets whether hundreds of feet tall or only thirty to forty feet. In the winter we often saw needles of ice pushing up the soil in exposed places along the trail, but even then the ground at the research site was not frozen except in completely bare spots near the center of the larger openings. Usually snow preceded this coldest weather.

During the NSF study light snowfalls happened every year and were usually no more than a slight inconvenience. One time, though, Charlie, Dorwin, Timidity, and I discovered when we began our trek from the car to the station that the foot or so of snow on the ground had a heavy crust which made the half-mile hike extremely difficult. The crust broke with every step, letting a foot sink nearly to the bottom of a ten-inch hole. Charlie and Dorwin took turns leading the way. It was much easier and less tiring for us to step where the leader had been than to break a new trail. I had to carry Timidity most of the way because she broke through the crust frequently and, having short legs, became bogged down in the snow. Ordinarily she enjoyed these outings but she wasn't very happy that day.

I recall another day. A wet snow had fallen a few days earlier but the weather had turned colder and the snow, now dry and powdery, still clung to the trees. All around us the young conifers, with their boughs pulled downward by the burden of snow, stood rigid and straight like slender white marble columns, while on the leafless twigs and shrubs nearby every twig was a white sparkling crystal. It was a fairyland.

Timidity had a fantastic time, bounding along through the seven-inch-deep snow. The snow was so dry and the temperature so low that she didn't get wet. The student helpers and I had a good time, too, except that the rain in the gauges was frozen and we got cold while waiting for our war-surplus stove to melt the ice. It seemed to take forever. Strong gusts of icy wind blowing from the northeast dropped the temperature to 16°F, and the sun dipped behind the mountain and was disappearing below the horizon as we finished our work. We lost no time in escaping to the relative comfort of the car, but we took with us the memory of a beautiful setting.

On a day in early March 1962, student assistants Bill Cotman and Bill Good were unprepared for the surprise they found when they arrived at Murphy Road. Sixteen to eighteen inches of snow filled the roadway. *Surely,* they thought, *this heavy utility GMC can make its way even in that snow.* So, they drove through the gate and proceeded along the logging road for about a mile. The snow got deeper, and they got stuck! They managed to turn the vehicle around, and at 3:30 p.m. they began hiking toward the research station. They had not gone far before the snow depth increased to nearly two feet. Then they realized that darkness would be falling before long. Wisely, they turned around, hiked back to their rig, and drove home. Total travel time that day, nine hours and fifteen minutes, a striking contrast with the usual two hours and thirty minutes for that time of year.

The following day the two young men started early, drove to Murphy Road, parked their car, and hiked to the research site and back, a round trip of ten miles through eighteen to twenty-four inches of snow. Total travel time that day, nine hours and forty minutes. But they accomplished their task.

That snowfall was the heaviest one we had in the years of the NSF study. However, Mr. Van Huyning, woods foreman for the Miami Corporation, told a student in the summer of 1969 that snow had been six-feet deep the previous winter at the bridge across Salmon River and it had even formed forty-foot drifts near the top of the mountain.

When storms blew in on winter weekends during our research, we spent only enough time at the station to take a sample of duff, service the recording instruments (usually a hygrothermograph and sometimes also a tempscribe), and record wind direction and data from the two rain gauges and three thermometers before hurrying back to the car, our only haven.

On such days we longed for the comfort of a fire shelter. We were cold and uncomfortable in spite of our waterproof rain gear. The young trees did not break the wind, nor could we take refuge under them like we had under the old trees. Besides, in heavy rain, these small trees were more of a problem than a refuge because moisture dripped from them constantly.

During much of the winter, especially on the stormiest days, I assigned the trip to a couple of my student assistants. They could do everything that I would do under those conditions and I could accomplish more by staying at home. At least a dozen students shared in these experiences during the three winters of the NSF research. Though the trips were rigorous, I think those who took part actually enjoyed them, as I did when helping with Prof's research in my student days.

Some of the most surprising things occurred in the wettest weather, as revealed by notes from student trips, such as: "Trail is a streambed today," and "Trail is almost a river." Clearly, the partially denuded forest floor and rocky, compacted logging road which served as our trail could not absorb a deluge but, instead, funneled the rain down the mountain, leaching out vital nutrients and eroding away the soil as it went—ultimately—to the river, burdening that body of water with silt. In the ancient forest, with its spongy moss and duff-filled floor, we had never experienced anything of that kind even during the most severe storms.

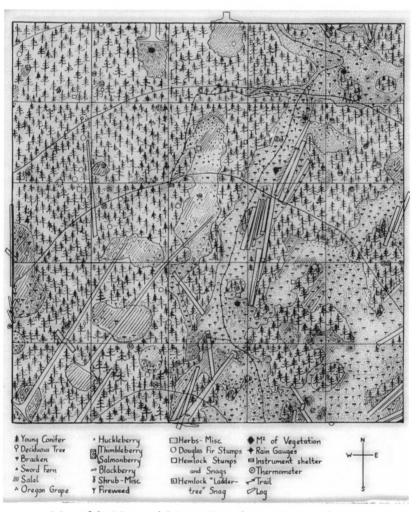

Map of the National Science Foundation grant study site.

Chapter Eighteen

The Community of Life

I WANTED TO KNOW whether the creatures Prof considered to be indicators of the various seasons had survived the havoc and destruction of logging. We looked especially for the tailed frog, *Ascaphus*, the large black millipede, *Harpaphe*, the black, banjo-shaped ground beetle, *Scaphinotus*, for a few other special insects, and for snails, slugs, and salamanders.

We occasionally saw one of these animals, but as time passed it became obvious that this community was a new combination, not a continuation of the mature forest. It was much like an ecotone, or forest edge community, some of which we had studied in Dr. Shelford's classes. This young forest was temporary and would change as the new trees grew and filled in the openings.

When a year had gone by and we hadn't seen even one *Scaphinotus*, I feared that frequent companion of ours had succumbed. Finally in July 1960, we saw two of the beetles in moist areas near the river, but we did not find any of them in the research area until June of the following year and that one was a loner. In the entire period of our study, we saw only one more *Scaphinotus*. It was near the river. Evidently a nucleus of these beetles had survived in a protected pocket of forest. Given time—many, many years—they might have recovered to their former importance in the forest community. But would this ever again be a forest? Or was it to be only a tree plantation?

Even though the annual rainfall was greater now than during Prof's study, the physical environment for the young forest community was much drier than it had been when the huge trees were present. Amphibians and mollusks were rare now. They need the moist conditions of the mature forest. We came across a single woodland salamander, heard one tree frog, saw one small brown hairy snail, chanced upon a partially eaten shell of a yellowish-green snail, and one spring found orange-bellied salamanders near a stream. Also, as time passed, we saw an occasional banana slug in a damp place.

One summer after the NSF project was finished, I was surprised to discover a large frog near a stream below the research site. It was probably the red-legged frog. (I had not seen this frog on Saddleback before then and Prof had not reported it in his notes.) But we never again found a tailed frog in our ventures onto the mountain.

Reptiles were unknown in the ancient forest. The environment was too damp and sunless. Now, we often surprised garter snakes and lizards in dry, sunny places along the trail and also at, or near, the station. Clearly, this young community provided a more favorable home for scaly-skinned, air-breathing reptiles than it did for scaleless, basically lungless amphibians and mollusks.

We saw lots of garter snakes of various sizes and color patterns. I am not a herpetologist. I am not even fond of snakes, but I had read that garter snakes give birth to living young. I was curious to find out if this is true. So when we found a large, dull-brown female that looked as though she might be pregnant, I took her to my office at the college where I could check her every day. In a few days, she gave birth to several slender babies, each about five or six inches long. The snake cage was improvised, small, and evidently inadequate, for the baby snakes lived only a few days. On our next trip we returned the female snake to her home on the mountain.

Garter snakes eat insects and all sorts of small creatures, but we were surprised when we found one a short distance above the river trying to swallow a smallish banana slug. We watched in fascination. After a long struggle—perhaps a half-hour—the snake finally managed to get the slimy slug down. I wish we had thought to keep an exact record of the time involved.

Little blue-tailed, brown-striped western skinks were common. We often caught glimpses of them as they darted into cover. Once we surprised one of them at rest in a sunny spot on a mass of upturned roots. Sensing our presence, it scurried for cover but not before we had a good look at it. We didn't try to catch the tiny creature because we didn't want it to cast off its tail, an escape mechanism they use.

The dull brown alligator lizards, which we encountered a few times on the trail or on the terrace not far from the station, were a marked contrast with the bright-colored, active little skinks. These short-legged reptiles, about five inches long, do look a lot like miniature alligators.

Insects were our major concern. Frances and Nancy accepted this challenge with enthusiasm. Both were interested in insects as well as in birds and mammals, and they made a good team to handle this work.

Summer was at its peak when we began our research on Saddleback Mountain. Tall fireweed plants with long slender tips flaming with purplish-red blossoms grew by the roadsides and in masses in open areas all over the mountainside.

Fireweed plants also flourished in the lower portion of the large open area below our chosen activity center in the research hectare and they attracted insect pests. On the evening of our first trip, Frances collected four slender, eighth-inch long, metallic bronze beetles from a fireweed plant by the trailside.

Frances and sharp-eyed Nancy soon observed that these beetles were chewing holes through the tender leaves at the tips of many fireweed plants, completely riddling some of them. Then they noticed coal black larvae, somewhat longer than the beetles, eating the soft tissues on the underside of some of the fireweed leaves. Often more than twenty of these larvae were on a single plant.

"Do you suppose those black creatures are larvae of the bronze beetles?" Nancy asked.

"I don't know," Frances said, "but I think it would be interesting to find out. I'll ask Kenny Fender if he knows the beetle. Maybe he can tell us if they are its larvae. If he doesn't know, we can try raising some. It would take a lot of our time, but it might pay off."

After studying the beetle a bit, Kenny said, "That's a chrysomelid, a flea beetle, in the genus *Altica*, but I don't know its species. Louis Gentner down in Corvallis can tell you that. He's a flea beetle specialist. The surest way to find out about the larvae would be to raise some."

Dr. Gentner identified our beetle as the bronze flea beetle, *Altica tombacina,* and said that not much was known about it. He also told us that he had never been able to recognize a male among the many beetles he had seen—suggesting that this species might be parthenogenetic (single parent reproduction)—and encouraged us to do a life history study.

Challenged by this information, Nancy brought a bunch of larvae to the college laboratory that fall, followed their development, and obtained thirty plus adult bronze flea beetles which established the identity of the larvae.

The next fall Nancy continued her study, concentrating on the metamorphosis of the pupae. Finally, in the summer of 1961, Frances recorded details of egg-laying and larval development from beetles she reared in the lab. Between May 16 and June 22, one female laid more than 453 yellow, cylindrical eggs, about the length of a printed comma and half as wide. She deposited the eggs in clusters of fifteen to forty-six on the undersurface of the leaves, arranged in rows end to end.

Since none of the adults showed the usual external characteristics for males of the genus *Altica*, and no mating pairs were observed, Kenny, our beetle specialist, used his expertise with microscopic dissection and found male genitalia in some of the beetles. He then demonstrated the procedure to Rose Gillette, who wanted to work on this problem for her senior thesis. She found fourteen males in a group of forty-four beetles. Kenny made drawings of the male genital organs and in 1965 we published the story of the life history of the bronze flea beetle in *Northwest Science*.

Bronze flea beetles had three relatives in the young forest: the common spotted cucumber beetle, green with black spots, and a brown one called the grape root worm. Both of these flea beetles fed on the leaves of almost every kind of green plant in our research area, while their larvae nibbled away at the plants' roots. The third flea beetle, a yellowish brown one, seemed to prefer pearly everlasting plants. We found the bronze flea beetle on nothing but fireweed. Flea beetles, along with all other leaf beetles, are notorious for chewing holes in the leaves, or even in the petals, of plants.

Every week during the seasons of insect activity we collected many hundreds of insects in sweepnets, amassing thousands of species in the course of the study. Frances, Nancy, and other helpers spent far more hours sorting, recording, pinning, and identifying insects than we spent in studying any other group of animals.

Though we tried to learn in the field as much as we could about insects, the great majority of them had to be sent as unknowns to systematists for identification. It was years later, after their identities were finally known, before I had time to work with that information.

The insects of this young community were an amazingly diverse mixture. Though certain ones characteristic of the mature forest were missing, many familiar ones were still present, and a generous sum of newcomers had been added from surrounding pastureland, fields, or meadows. Not yet a forest, this place with its inviting mixture of herbs, shrubs, grasses, caneberries, and young conifers served in all seasons as a smorgasbord for insects with a wide range of habits.

In the warm days of spring and summer, sunny, flower-filled spaces buzzed with activity. Many kinds of brightly colored flower flies darted from plant to plant, drinking nectar or gathering pollen from the blossoms, or they hovered above the plants like miniature aircraft, poised to dart, without warning, to a new spot.

Large, slender, longhorn beetles, honey bees, ten or more kinds of pudgy black and golden-yellow bumblebees, and several species of solitary wild bees, about half the size of a honey bee, visited the blossoms for pollen and nectar.

One of the larger wild bees looked like a bumblebee but was a false bumblebee with no worker caste. It is sometimes called a "cuckoo bee" because its queens lay their eggs in the nests of bumblebees, requiring those bees to raise the young. This wild bee is named *Psithyrus,* meaning "whisperer," because its hum is more subdued than the hum of a bumblebee, but the wild bees are stouter and can sting harder than their host.

Bee flies, which were new to me, were another kind of insect that visited flowers. Black, stout-bodied, and dusted with dense, colorful pile, these flies were easily mistaken for bees. The black, lance-like proboscis of one of our three species was nearly as long as her body. That long proboscis made the bee look like a tiny hummingbird when she hovered over flowers extracting nectar or pollen. That female bee fly lays her eggs in the soil near the nest of a solitary bee and, when the eggs hatch, the larvae find their way to the nest and parasitize the solitary bee's larvae.

Smallish, nondescript flies, relatives of the common house fly, also visited the plants for nectar or pollen and incidentally served as pollinators.

In sunny spots swarms of dark-colored miniature dance flies undulated in courtship maneuvers above patches of flowering herbs or shrubs during late afternoons and early evenings. When not dancing, most of these flies hunted other tiny insects which were visiting the flowers. Many kinds of dance flies lived in the young forest, but we had found only a few in the mature forest.

Tiny, soft-bodied, sap-sucking aphids flourished in this oasis. Yellow, green, or black, winged or wingless, these minuscule insects sucked the vital juices of all sorts of plants. Some, feeding on the undersurfaces of certain plants, caused leaves to curl. Different kinds of aphids fed on the stems, blossoms, and fruits of nearly every species of herb, shrub, or deciduous tree, and still others were on the needles, twigs, or bark of the conifers. Wherever they were, aphids occurred in great numbers.

Aphids were not lacking for enemies. Aphid lions, voracious, sickle-jawed larvae of golden-eyed green lacewings, and the larvae of flower flies searched the vegetation for them. Tiny wasplike braconids and even smaller chalcid wasps parasitized them for food for their young, and both the larvae and adults of predaceous ladybird beetles found and devoured them. In this way, the numbers of aphids were kept under control.

Small insects known as hoppers also fed on the sap of plants. Some of these, spittlebugs (or froghoppers), were easily noticed, for their nymphs surrounded themselves with frothy white "spittle" as they fed on succulent herbs and shrubs, such as fireweed, pearly everlasting, bracken, and huckleberries. Planthoppers, bumpy, humpbacked insects adept at flying and jumping, were often found on young conifers.

But leafhoppers were the most numerous of all the sap-feeding insects and were even more varied in species than aphids.

Green, yellow, or brown, these boat-shaped slender little creatures drew attention to themselves whenever disturbed by jumping from one plant and flying to another. Though they favored soft herbs and grasses, leafhoppers were so active that it was hard to see exactly where they were or what they were doing.

Many predaceous insects hunted all kinds of hoppers, but leafhoppers are an especial favorite of the tiny fast-flying big-headed fly, only slightly larger than its prey. The grotesque females, whose eyes are almost as large as the rest of their body (so large they can detect the slightest movement), fly swiftly, hover for long periods, and are frequently found on or above flowers or small plants. When a fly sees a leafhopper, she grabs it, and while hovering in the air lays an egg in it. Then she drops the parasitized leafhopper to the ground. Larvae hatch from the eggs, bore their way inside the leafhopper, and feed on the parasitized insect until they are full grown. Then they exit from the carcass.

More than two dozen kinds of true bugs, either as adults or nymphs, or both, feasted on the juices of plants, such as fireweed, pearly everlasting, lotus, bracken, caneberries, and needles of the young conifers. True bugs, though diverse in size, color, and other traits, all share one feature, a triangular-shaped pattern in the middle of their back.

Some of the bugs were green or brown stink bugs, broad of body and about a half-inch long. A brown species specialized on the drupelets of caneberries, leaving a very disagreeable odor on the berries and causing the fruit to wither and dry up. Another one, a plant bug, was a pretty little insect, resembling a tiny fleck of lace. Its nymphs, spiny and dark, lived on the underside of leaves, sucking the plant's juices and depositing blotchy specks of excrement.

Though most plant bugs suck the juices from plants, in this young forest three kinds were predators and hunted plant-eating insects for their food. Ambush bugs (phymatids), equipped with a long beak and front legs specialized for grasping prey, fed on aphids, leafhoppers, and small caterpillars; stilt bugs, slender, very long-legged, small brown bugs, hunted leafhoppers; and stout, medium-sized assassin bugs with long, narrow heads and three-segmented beaks, did not specialize in their selection of prey but attacked any living thing that they could overpower. Assassin bugs stalked their prey and then held it in their front legs while sucking its vital juices.

We occasionally heard the song of a katydid, a shrill but unmistakable sound because it often includes a distinct "Katy-she-did." These large, green, longhorned grasshopper-like insects blend in so well with the foliage where they feed that they are seldom seen but we found one on a salmonberry bush.

Sawflies rested in a sunny spot on the leaves of thimbleberries or salmonberries. These medium-sized wasplike relatives of bees and wasps do not sting but use the sawlike blades of their ovipositors for cutting plant tissues and inserting eggs into them. When the eggs hatch, the small caterpillar-like larvae feast on the leaves of the plants.

Snout nosed beetles, which we called weevils, chewed the margins of leaves, often producing a scalloped effect. One of the weevils we found is known to make saw-toothed edges on pine needles. I suspect that it also fed on the needles of our young conifers. Another of our weevils is said to feed on the margins of grasses, and a third one reputedly nibbles small round holes deep into rose hips and the buds of roses and thimbleberries. It then deposits eggs in these cavities and the larvae live and feed there. So far as we know, the larvae of the several other kinds of weevils we collected lived in the ground and fed on plant roots.

Shiny, dark-colored click beetles of assorted sizes clicked and flipped in an attempt to escape whenever we caught them from conifer boughs or from other plants. These acrobats fed on the buds, petals, and tender leaves of many herbaceous plants and the young needles of conifers. Their larvae, known as wireworms, nibbled away on new seedlings, roots, or stems of plants. Other click beetles lived under the bark of decaying logs and the larvae of some species preyed on other small insects.

We often gazed in wonder as butterflies flew about in the open space at the research station, a spirit-lifting experience those of us who had helped with Prof's study had not had previously. The only butterflies in the ancient forest were the little pine whites, which lived in the crowns of the firs, and a couple of smaller ones which we saw only rarely at the fringe of the forest.

The very first year after the beginning of the research in July, swallowtails came, and monarchs, several large white parnassian butterflies, and a mourning cloak. Then, in August, a colorful California sister passed overhead, half way to the tree tops.

After that, each year these colorful beauties appeared, some in the spring and others were with us all through the summer. On some days their flight seemed hurried. On others, it was a floating, graceful movement, with most of the butterflies skimming over plants close to the ground. There were the elegant monarchs, orange and black checker spots, many-colored tortoise shells, velvety purple mourning cloaks, admirals, painted ladies, several kinds of swallowtails, a small, pale blue azure, and a green hairstreak. Even others. We wished for Kenny. He could name these beauties at sight. We could identify only some of them, and many would not let us catch them, try as we might.

The adults of most butterflies feed on the nectar of flowers, serving as important pollinators. Their larvae, called caterpillars, are nearly all plant feeders. The butterflies that found the kinds of plants their larvae feed upon, stayed a while. The painted ladies had several kinds of thistles. Mourning cloaks had willows and poplars. Other butterflies had a wide variety of trees, shrubs, and herbs to choose from. Monarchs didn't tarry. No milkweed grew on that part of the mountain, so they moved on in their northward migration. Though the butterflies were often only a fluttering flash of color, we enjoyed them.

Moths, too, were there in abundance but we neither knew the names of most of them nor discovered their habits. Later I learned that the larvae of many of these moths are leaf miners or defoliators.

As we left the station to go down the mountain one day in mid-July, a troupe of little, multicolored, green-eyed flies caught our attention. They promenaded back and forth on bull thistle blossoms, slowly raising and lowering beautifully pictured wings.

"Peacock flies!" I exclaimed. "They remind me of male peacocks strutting about before their mates."

Fascinated by these little insects, Bill Good, a student helper, decided to study their life history. He checked week after week. First he found about two dozen tiny white eggs laid among the individual flowers of a thistle head. Two weeks later, he discovered that a large larva had chewed away pieces of a ring of ovaries about one-third of the way from the top of a thistle head and was now feeding inside an immature seed. Though Bill was not able to follow this larva through pupation, our peacock fly was identified as a fruit fly closely related to the currant or gooseberry fly and the highly destructive Mediterranean fruit fly.

Even though it was summer, the woods were dry, and we were far from any stream, mosquitoes tormented us from the very first day of our study. We wondered where they could be coming from. Then one day when Howard and I were running a grid line, we discovered a deep hole in the top of a Douglas-fir stump where a huge splinter had pulled free when the tree fell during logging. That hole was filled with water and swarmed with wriggling mosquito larvae with long white gills. Intrigued, Nancy took samples of the water to the laboratory and watched as these tiny straw-colored, dark-headed wrigglers completed their life cycle and revealed that they were larvae of *Aedes*, tree-hole mosquitoes which were with us during the entire study of the ancient forest without our ever discovering where they came from. Later, we found a similar pool in another stump.

Mosquitoes feed mostly on plant juices. It was only the females which were biting us. They had to have a meal of blood to assure the fertility of their eggs. In the damper seasons, other kinds of mosquitoes also pestered us.

Large dark horse flies and somewhat smaller deer flies bedeviled us on warm sunny summer and autumn days from the time we arrived at the station until we left the area. I don't recall that they actually bit any of us, but they flew around our heads and got into our hair and they did bite Timidity. These flies have the reputation for being one of the worst of many pests that suck blood from mammals. Again, the adult flies live on nectar and the juices of plants, except for the females' meal of blood for their eggs. Larvae of these flies are said to be predaceous or cannibalistic.

We collected a half-hundred kinds of muscids, relatives of the common house fly, from the abundant flowering plants or from decaying vegetation, dung, or dead and decaying animal matter. Many muscids were pollen or nectar feeders, some of which laid eggs on the plants they visited, and their larvae became cane borers or fed on the tissues of leaves or roots. Some others were predators of other flies. A great many were scavengers, like house flies and their distant relatives, the somewhat larger, metallic blue, green, or blue-green blow flies, some of which lay little maggots instead of eggs.

In 1969, several years after I had finished my field work, John Kerr, a biology major searching for a subject for his senior thesis, came across an article in *Ecology* which told of an experiment using fetal pigs in a study of the invertebrates which take part in decomposition of carrion. John decided to do a similar study on Saddleback. He wanted to learn how long it would take for the bodies of small animals, in this case fresh, unpreserved fetal pigs, to decompose and what invertebrates would be involved.

Blow flies played a major role in his experiment. These flies appeared within mere seconds after the pigs were exposed and settled on the carcasses, guided to them by their exceptionally keen sense of smell.

The flies were very active for three days, feeding on the sun-warmed body fluids and laying eggs around the eyes, noses, mouths, ears, and anuses of the piglets. After that, fewer flies came and carpenter ants and yellowjackets took over.

However, as the blow fly eggs hatched, the fly maggots crawled into the piglets' bodies through natural openings, and, during the next five days, the number of maggots gradually increased until, at the end of eight days from the time the pigs were placed in the forest, the carrion became too soft for the ants and wasps. Then fly maggots dominated the surfaces of the carcasses and vast numbers of maggots filled the body cavities.

On about the fifteenth day of the study, the carrion began to dry and most of the larvae disappeared into the ground to pupate.

Blow flies, scavengers of carrion, had accomplished this clean-up job in a remarkably short time, with only a little assistance from a few other insects and invertebrates.

John did not report seeing carrion beetles. Either they were under the carrion and out of sight or he did not recognize them. Unfortunately, he did not get any specific names for these insects because the material he sent to systematists was lost in shipping.

With the beginning of fall rains, many species of colorful mushrooms and fruiting bodies of other kinds of fungi sprang up everywhere, nourished by the plentiful debris from logging. Fungi were abundant in the ancient forest, but this young community was a veritable paradise for fungi and for many kinds of fungus-loving insects, fungus gnats in particular. About forty species of these small, delicate, mosquito-like flies, fed upon mushrooms, slime molds, and other fungal growths. Crane flies, long-legged, slow-flying insects which look much like overgrown mosquitoes but do not bite, were also diverse and abundant. Not much is known about the habits of crane flies but they are usually plentiful in coniferous forests. There were nearly fifty species of them here, at least half of which we had not found in the ancient forest.

Termites and ants—big, black carpenter ants and several kinds of smaller red or black ants—are important agents in the recycling of dead and decomposing wood. They were far more obvious and numerous in the young forest than they had been before the logging. Now, with food bountiful and lots of home sites, they apparently were in the middle of a population explosion.

The termites, which did not live in the ground but had their colonies in dead and decaying logs and stumps, were inconspicuous until their nuptial flights began in autumn. At first we saw only a few of the inch-long reddish-brown winged forms late in the day. However, as days passed, they began coming out in ever greater numbers and their flights began earlier, until in October they began emerging about noon. Then, for hours, the air would be full of termites, and one evening when we returned to the Daniels' car we found it plastered with the dead bodies of winged termites.

The giant black carpenter ants made their colonies under the rotten bark of old logs or in the wood of decomposing logs. Sawdust from their activities accumulated in piles beside or beneath unsalvaged logs. They did not eat the excavated wood but fed on dead and live insects and on nectar, honeydew, and any kind of sweets they could find and patiently attended honeydew-producing aphids. Once we saw carpenter ants fairly high in a young conifer, presumably attending aphids even higher in the tree. Carpenter ants seemed to be hungry for meat and gave us much trouble with our trapping studies. Almost as soon as a trap snapped on any creature, the ants would be there to begin chewing on it. Often, nothing was left of our catch but fragments of skin and bones. Nearly every mouse or other mammal I caught was damaged by these voracious creatures.

At least a dozen kinds of smaller ants lived in colonies in stumps or in other wood which was rotting in the ground. Roving workers were in all sorts of places—on bracken, on the leaves of berry canes and other shrubs, on herbaceous plants, on the boughs of conifers, in the samples of duff, and in rotten wood. Some were found attending aphids, others no doubt were predaceous, killing and eating insects and other small creatures, and some must also have fed on nectar and the sweet juices of plants. Many ants are known to be nearly omnivorous. Ones which visit flowers aid in pollination. Some are scavengers and have an indispensable role in the recycling process. Whenever an ant colony is in the soil, it aerates, enriches, and improves the texture and quality of that soil.

Tiny yellowish or brownish beetles known as short-winged mold beetles, or sometimes as ant-loving beetles, lived in such places as forest litter, rotting wood, and ant nests. These beetles may be found wherever there is mold. Some feed on mites. Others, which live with ants, emit secretions that are attractive to the ants—though sometimes the beetles feed on the larvae of their hosts.

Many of the insects living in the young community were predators, including certain small, cigar-shaped, dark-colored rove beetles which feed upon tiny animals; large, powerful, sun-loving robber flies which capture all sorts of big insects on the wing, pierce them with their stout beak, and drain them dry; and small, slender, square-shouldered soldier beetles which hunt small insects on many kinds of vegetation. The larvae of robber flies and soldier beetles are also hunters which live in soil or decaying wood.

Ground beetles too, both as adults and as larvae, are significant predators. They weren't plentiful in the young forest, but a small black one was taken from young hemlock boughs, and three kinds of rather large black ones of the genus *Pterostichus* were in many places. Some of these were under rotten wood or under logs, but all scurried about when they were discovered, presumably having been interrupted in their hunting activities.

Sometimes, a dragonfly would dart into our work area. A beautiful, bluish-green creature, it would hover motionless for a moment, its slender body supported by four long netlike wings, its enormous compound eyes searching for an insect-meal-on-wings. Swiftly as it appeared, it darted away, moving so rapidly that we could never tell whether it had caught an insect or had flown to a more promising site. On these forays, dragonflies pluck mosquitoes and myriad kinds of other insects out of the air.

Swift flying adult tachinids, somber black, gray, or brown flies which resemble house flies but are much spinier, visited flowers and fed on nectar, juices from plants, and honeydew secreted by aphids and other insects, but their robust larvae lived as internal parasites in host insects. Most tachinids parasitize the larvae or pupae of the host, some lay their eggs only in adults, while for still others the larvae are free-living for a time before finding a host. Certain tachinids were important enemies of butterflies and moths. The larvae of other tachinids parasitized plant-eating bugs, beetles, and sawflies.

Amazingly, though, it is the tiny, inconspicuous, parasitic wasps—ichneumonids, braconids, and chalcids—not the large hunters among the insects, which do the most in keeping insect populations in the forest under control. These masters of the art of parasitism are the most effective biological controls known. When we sorted through our weekly collections, we were astounded at the numbers of them that we had. Some of them were no larger than one of the commas on this page. Many were new, unnamed species, and some were not identified by the specialists to whom they were sent. Still, nearly 200 kinds of parasitic wasps were named from the young forest.

Bill Good, a senior student, worked on several projects, including one on insects associated with the thicket lotus. He concentrated on foliage-eaters, which were spinning webs over the growing tips of the plants and eating the young leaves, and on some other insects which were eating the seed pods.

The foliage-eaters were light green to greenish brown moth larvae, less than a half inch long and with five longitudinal white stripes. They spun threads over the young tips of the plants, pulling the leaves together and causing them to curl as the plant grew. In this way the larvae formed a house within which they fed. Some of these larvae pupated in the soil and two species of tiny gelichiid moths emerged.

Many of the foliage-eating moth larvae died in the rearing cages Bill made, but some lethargic and immobile larvae had external parasites on them. He collected fifteen parasitoids from the moth larvae, sent them to a systematist, and received identifications for one tachinid fly, two kinds of chalcid wasps, two kinds of braconid wasps, and one ichneumonid wasp.

Bill also made a study of lotus seed pods. When mature, each larva inside a pod made a small hole in the pod and escaped to pupate in the soil in the bottom of the cage. After most of the larvae had left the pods, Bill broke them open and found pupating parasites in some and, in a few, immobile larvae, apparently host to internal parasites. The parasitic wasps in this study were one chalcid, two species of braconids, and three kinds of ichneumons, a total of twelve parasitic species for the two studies. Unfortunately, the pod-eating insects all died during pupation, so their identity was not learned.

Bill made other discoveries, including a tiny female cynipid wasp under the carcass of an aphid that had been feeding on a green lotus pod. But the most interesting discovery in his entire lotus study was that an insect which developed in a dainty pupa case hanging by a slender thread from a lotus leaf was a black and amber braconid wasp, a species of *Meteorus*, many of which are internal parasites of moths. This one was less than one-eighth inch long.

Since more than half the moth larvae Bill collected were infested with parasitic wasps, he concluded "it is apparent that [the thicket lotus] is in little danger from an epidemic of the 'house-building' moth larvae for the reason that the parasites of this insect are numerous, varied, and effective." This project done by an undergraduate student demonstrated an excellent example of natural biological control.

As the insect collection from our weekly trips grew in volume, I became more and more aware that many of the species in this young forest were new and different from the ones in the ancient forest and that the number of insect species in the young forest community far exceeded the total for Prof's study. But by then I was teaching full time and had no opportunity to study the collections in detail.

It was years later, after I retired, before I was free to compare the lists of species from the two communities. Then I learned that nearly 60 percent of the insects we had found in the mature forest were no longer there. Also, I discovered that I had many species and even entire families (thirteen of them Diptera) from the young forest that had never before been found on Saddleback. Many of these species were new to science and most of them were still unnamed.

An insect's name alone tells little or nothing about its habits, the vital role each plays as part of the community of life. As we collected our insects we learned some details, but it has taken much searching to glean even bits of additional information. As a result, the material which I have given is often incomplete and sketchy, and I have learned a significant amount of it in the years since my retirement.

Chapter Nineteen

Birds

DOROTHY McKey-Fender and I had kept our friendship over the years, but she had never returned to the research site on Saddleback after that fateful day in 1940 when she, Kenny, and I had gazed in horror at the heart-breaking shambles logging had made of our treasured forest.

One day early in June 1957 she invited me to see their "new" home, a much larger historic house across the street from where they had been living. After a tour of the house, Dorothy said, "Kenny, the kids, and I are planning a research trip to eastern Oregon starting on Saturday. Could you take care of our finch and the family of Siamese cats?"

"I think I could manage that, but turnabout's fair play. Ray and I want to go to the research station on Friday. Why don't you come with us? You've never been back there to see how the young forest is developing."

"That sounds interesting. I'll give it a try."

The day dawned, overcast and blustery with frequent hard showers, but we made the trip anyway. Ray and I had not been there for two years and were eager to see the place again.

Our turnoff road beyond the Salmon River was blocked by limbs and trunks of young alders and Douglas-firs, shattered by the freezing rain, which with snow, ice, and severe cold, had nearly paralyzed the region for the entire last half of the previous January.

As we prepared to leave the car, Ray said, "Why don't we eat part of our lunch now and leave the rest here? It's almost eleven o'clock and I've always preferred to carry food in my stomach rather than on my back." After eating, we started toward the station afoot, with Dorothy carrying a notebook, me a camera, and Ray his small hand axe to clear the worst obstructions as we moved along.

The going wasn't too bad beyond the tree breakage, except for frequent, drenching showers. Where the trail divided, I suggested that we follow the low road that led to the spar tree below the station and then come down by the high road.

Ray led the way with his axe in hand, clearing the trail where necessary. That narrow pathway softly floored with mosses, skirted the north face of the mountain which was gently scalloped by low ridges and shallow clefts. Though overshadowed by young trees, the trail provided occasional glimpses to the north.

About halfway to the spar tree, Dorothy suddenly exclaimed, "Oh, look!"

There on the left side of one of the clefts was a sprawling patch of fine-leafed plant, forming an emerald curtain draped across the rocks and logs.

"Isn't that beautiful?" I said. "Can it be a club moss, Dorothy?"

"Yes, it's *Selaginella*, a lesser club moss. A very ancient plant which is sometimes called spike moss."

"I remember reading about club mosses in botany," I said. "I've also included them in my lectures, but this is the first time I've seen an actual plant. Have you noticed any of them here on the mountain before?"

"No, not here, but I've seen them near the coast."

"I can't recall ever seeing any of them either," Ray chimed in, "unless it was when I was a small boy living near Bandon. There were lots of interesting things there in the forest and around bogs. Have you any idea how this one got here?"

"No," Dorothy said. "Possibly just through traffic since parts of the plant are sticky. Or maybe it's been here forever. I haven't been in this area before, and you two haven't been here often. Perhaps it finally got large enough to grab attention."

As we walked along, we talked about the plant and Dorothy told us that this trailing evergreen is a survivor of the coal-producing forests of the Carboniferous Age, some 300 million years ago. Our pleasure at the sight was made more intense by that knowledge.

Not far beyond the club moss Ray remarked, "It looks to me like someone has been making hay here when the sun was shining." He had spied a mountain beaver colony in one of the fills. The rodents had laid out a number of clumps of bracken to dry near the opening into their home.

While we hiked along in the continuing showers, we saw a hairy woodpecker and two juncos, and frightened from its nest a bird which we guessed, from the sound it made in flight, was a band-tailed pigeon. We noticed old deer sign and what we thought were bear "diggins."

We ran into a series of slides which had carried trees—branches, roots, and all—into the trail. Ray used his trusty axe to clear some of the smaller branches and we were then able to weave our way over, under, and around those barricades.

A short distance farther along, the trail was full of nine-foot-tall bracken. When we had tunneled through that entanglement, we emerged within sight of the spar tree, but were face to face with a dense mixture of young conifers through which we must work our way. At the spar tree we ran into a thicket of brush and, failing to locate the lower part of the trail to the research area, had to fight our way through the shrubs and young trees much of the way up the steep slope. When we finally stumbled over the rim of the fire shelter crater we knew we had arrived.

We caught our breath and looked around. After a moment Dorothy exclaimed, "This doesn't even look like the same place. It's much too steep! It didn't seem that way before!"

We spent most of our time that afternoon inventorying plants in the fire shelter crater and measuring some of the young trees around its edge. Pigeon wheat (*Polytrichum*)—a common moss with large grainlike capsules—and other fern-like mosses carpeted the floor of the crater. Starflowers and clintonia blossomed in the basin where small false Solomon's seal plants were forming fruit. Pearly everlasting plants, sword ferns, bracken, and some baby hemlocks were scattered throughout. A log somewhat more than a foot in diameter lay diagonally across the crater and salmonberries and thimbleberries fringed its edges Tiny whiteflies, very much like the common greenhouse pest vaporaria, browsed on the salmonberry and Solomon seal plants, and a dense thicket of tall, dark-green conifers, tightly encircling the shrubby rim, seemed to be hovering protectively over this unique microcosm.

I tried to capture the scene with my camera, but the light was far too dim for the color film then available for my use.

After a brief interval of sunlight, another shower drenched us and we started our trek home by way of the high road. On the way we heard a flicker *wicker-wickering*, and when we reached the landing on that trail, a nighthawk flew up from a patch of wood chips left from the salvage logging.

"Why, that's a nighthawk!" I exclaimed. "I thought they were only birds of the open countryside, or towns. What's that one doing up here?" Neither Dorothy nor Ray offered any pertinent comment.

That event was my first real alert as to how different the birds of the young forest would be.

I had never thought of nighthawks as birds of forested areas, and yet when we visited the research site two weeks later, we discovered two baby nighthawks on a bit of ground that had been compacted and scraped bare of trees by salvage logging. The spot was a short distance inside the south side of the station and almost in the trail. The parent nighthawks had not made a nest. Nighthawks do not make nests. They had chosen a spot fringed by scattered chips of wood and fragments of bark. To them, it must have seemed an ideal place where the female could lay and incubate her eggs and raise her young. The site was isolated and relatively open. Food was ample—flying insects were plentiful. They needed nothing more. The young birds were well feathered fledglings about ready to test their wings. Evidently, in this instance, I was the only one who thought of this place as a forest in the making.

Later that day we discovered another nighthawk nest at the landing down the trail. The nestlings there were still downy and somewhat younger than the ones at the station.

Two years later, on the first day of the NSF study, we heard nighthawks and saw them flying nearby. A week or so after that one of the birds flew into the area where we were working in the afternoon and settled on a snag. It rested there quietly for a half-hour before being joined by another bird, probably its mate. They then flew around, above the station, until nearly seven o'clock when we left to go home. By that time, two more nighthawks had joined the pair, and the four birds were flying overhead, zooming and scooping insects out of the air. Every year of our study, nighthawks were with us throughout the summer, often catching insects in the morning or at midday, as well as at twilight. We also found other nests.

At that time, in the 1960s, these slim-winged, gray birds were common out in the valleys and often nested on the flat roofs of some of the stores in downtown McMinnville. I enjoyed hearing them on warm summer evenings as they flew overhead, scooping insects into their oversized mouths, but I haven't heard that *zooming* sound for more than twenty years. I wonder why. Is it insecticides? Or loss of habitat? There are still plenty of flat roofs! Whatever the cause for that silence, I miss the sound.

Nighthawks were only one of many surprises. This young, transitory stage of coniferous forest was home to an amazing mixture of birds.

On the first day of our study, Frances saw three fawn-colored cedar waxwings. These nomadic birds, which are a little smaller and more slender than robins, have a distinctive crest and a yellow band at the tip of their tails. The adults also usually have waxy red droplets accenting the tips of their secondary wing feathers, hence their common name. They live and travel in flocks, even nesting near one another but, being highly nomadic, they seldom nest in any area for more than a year at a time. All that summer until late in September, we saw these birds near where the trail turned to go down the mountain. Though we didn't see any nests, I think they nested there that year, but after that they were gone.

Cedar waxwings are extremely fond of fruits and berries. Many times flocks came to our yard in town. I often watched in amazement as the birds, flitting restlessly from place to place on the tree, stripped the entire crop of berries from our mountain ash in a couple of hours. There was much bird talk as they moved about gorging themselves.

Once I watched a flock of them darting about above a small pond, busily catching insects. Other birders have reported seeing them feed on a wide variety of insects, including carpenter ants.

During our Fourth of July trip, Frances had been puzzled by a bird song she heard—a loud-ringing, whistle-like melody. During the next two weeks she kept hearing the same song again and again throughout the day. She had never heard a wrentit but she had read about the birds and wondered if the songster could be one of them.

Finally, on our fourth trip while she and Nancy were busy collecting insects from the plants in the open area, one of the songsters came out of the brush nearby. Scolding all the while, it flew to a salmonberry bush and began pecking at a ripe berry. Then it disappeared into the brush. During the next hour, the bird returned from its brushy retreat three times and finally finished the berry. Each time it appeared, it scolded, and when it retired to the brush it sang three or four clear notes, followed by a trill. With all this display, the mystery was solved. The bird was a wrentit and obviously a male, for it behaved almost exactly like the description of a male wrentit I had read. The wrentit described had a nest nearby. So did this one.

According to John Terres in *The Audubon Society Encyclopedia of North American Birds*, the wrentit family is the only family of birds found solely in North America and this is the only species in the family. Male and female wrentits look alike. Both sing. Sometimes one of them picks up the song of the other and they sing antiphonally. These one-of-a-kind birds mate for life and are constantly together. They forage together, preen each other's feathers, and roost together—leaning against each other with their feathers interlaced and their inner legs drawn up, appearing as one ball of feathers. They feed on a wide variety of insects and eat berries and other small fruits whenever they can find them.

At least one pair of these interesting birds nested in the research area, perhaps more than one. They were with us constantly during the summers. In July 1960 we had the fun of seeing three fledglings perched on the upturned roots of the fire shelter tree.

Wherever wrentits are found along the Oregon coast or in California, they live the entire year in a home territory. However, the ones on Saddleback behaved differently. Evidently finding conditions too severe at that elevation, they left the research site by late November and retreated to a lower level for the winter, though they were always back with us by the middle of March.

At that time, wrentits in Oregon were known only as inhabitants of densely brushy areas along the coast. Consequently, these dark brown, sparrow size, wren-like birds were totally new to me.

Many of the birds we saw in the young community were newcomers to that part of the mountain. Some of them had lived in open meadow-like areas or brushy streamsides at much lower elevations and moved up as logging removed the ancient trees. Other birds, like the cedar waxwings, were species which frequent various kinds of sites far from the mountain.

One of these newcomers was the western tanager, a sparrow-size species the males of which have yellow bodies, bright orange or red heads and necks, and black backs, wings, and tail—a real eyecatcher. The colors of females and young birds are more subdued, mostly olive green tinged with gray. Male tanagers have a melodic song much like that of a robin.

A pair of tanagers nested for many years in the crown of a large oak in our yard in McMinnville, so I was surprised when I saw one of them in August in a wild cherry tree near the station. We'd been hearing them nearby during the summer, but I'd never seen one in all my years of working with Prof and he had recorded only one. It was not in the forest but at the edge.

Later, I learned that the normal habitat of tanagers is open conifer or mixed forest. They eat a wide variety of insects and small fruits. We heard their song at the station or nearby during the summer of every year of our study.

Bushtits traveled through our working areas in family flocks of a dozen or so, gleaning minuscule insects as they flitted from twig to twig and bush to bush, sometimes hanging upside down, constantly conversing in light, gentle notes. These tiny grayish or brownish-gray balls of fluff with absurdly long tails never seemed to pause to rest, but moved along quickly, staying but a few brief minutes. Prof had reported seeing them but only in the meadow at Boyer.

I enjoyed Pacific yellowthroats and Wilson's warblers as new summer residents in our young forest community. Both species live in the thickets of open areas along woodland streams. The male yellowthroat is an especially handsome fellow, with an olive-brown back, bright yellow throat and black mask. I had learned to enjoy his song, *witchity-witchity-witchity-witch*, whistled rapidly and clearly from a streamside tangle of briers near our garden in town. He was an interesting bird to watch as he darted about in wren-like fashion, gleaning caterpillars, insects, and spiders from the vegetation. Yellowthroats build a bulky nest of grasses and other plant materials on the ground or low on briers or bushes.

The male Wilson's warblers, slightly smaller than the yellowthroats, are also attractive bright yellow birds. They can be identified easily by their round black cap. Though their song, a rising wave of rich, full, loud fluty notes, is less easily described, I had learned to recognize these songsters while studying the ancient forest. We had heard and seen them frequently in the open area low on the mountain where our trail crossed the Little Salmon River. Wilson's warblers usually stay within ten feet of the ground when feeding. They are lively little fellows which jerk their tails while gleaning the leaves of the bushes and they frequently dart into the air to catch flying insects. Their bulky nest of mosses, dead leaves, grasses, twigs, and other materials is built on the ground.

Late in May 1961, Frances came upon a half-dozen "dumpy" birds, which she noted as "probably quail," working their way noisily through the brush just below the northeast corner of the hectare. Then, she recorded, "They flew." In July of the following year, a student reported seeing three quail at the "nighthawk-nest" landing, and in August of that same year she saw two adults and four young quail about two-thirds grown, near the river as she began her hike to the research site. We saw these mountain quail several times along the river road but they always scurried for cover. We felt a special affinity for them whenever we encountered a family of these modest birds.

The mountain quail is a plump gray and brown quail, the largest one in Oregon, and is recognized by its long, straight head plume. The smaller, grayish California, or valley quail, has a forward-curving, short black plume. Being secretive, mountain quails often burst from cover and dive again into the brush or weed patch after a short flight. Their flight is strong and swift and they are also rapid runners.

I have never seen one of their nests, but they are described as a well concealed, shallow depression at the base of a tree or bush, under a shrub, or beside a log, lined with dry leaves, needles, and grasses. Their coveys are small, varying from two to about twenty.

Mountain quail are shy and do not live in the deep forest but are found at forest edges or, especially, in brushy, logged-over areas, such as our research area on Saddleback Mountain. They feed on buds of legumes and other plants, wild berries, seeds, and insects. During the nesting season they may live at higher elevations on the mountains but move down to more sheltered areas for winter.

Loud-cawing crows showed up fairly often in or near our research area. Their loud call contrasted with the croaking *cr-r-ruck* of the ravens we had known in the old forest. Crows are one of the most adaptable of birds, having survived the disruption of many kinds of natural habitats and attempts of man to destroy them. Ecologically they are important, for they live in a wide variety of habitats and eat all sorts of insects, spiders, frogs, salamanders, and snakes, as well as the eggs and young of birds, corn and other grain crops, and wild and cultivated fruits. They also scavenge carrion.

Two species of chickadees provided us another surprise. The chestnut-backed chickadees probably were the only ones we encountered in the ancient forest, but in the young forest black-capped chickadees were by far the more common of the two. These are the chickadees usually found in mixed and deciduous woods and we saw many of them on Saddleback all summer and late into the autumn. We enjoyed their cheery *chick-a-dee-dee-dee* or their whistled *fee-bee* as they moved about, foraging over twigs and branches, peeping under bark scales and into crannies for caterpillars, insect eggs, spiders, and scale insects, or searching for conifer seeds and wild fruits. Though we did not discover any nests, which they usually make in abandoned woodpecker nests or knotholes, they probably did nest at the station.

Chestnut-backed chickadees were there, too, though we saw them rarely because they do much of their foraging high up on the trunks of trees. They do come down, however, to search for caterpillars, small insects, and spiders in crumbling logs or tangles of salal and they eat fruit pulp and seeds of conifers, as well. We never saw a nest, but I think from the way these chickadees behaved that at least one pair nested in the hectare. Normally, they nest in a natural cavity, though a pair may dig their own hole in a decaying fir.

The well-known robin and the less familiar Oregon junco are birds which are frequently seen in parks and gardens and in mixed or open forests. Though neither had been a summer resident in the ancient forest, they were among the birds we saw most frequently in this young developing community where they were present in large numbers every summer, building their nests on the mountainside or terrace and raising their young. The robins' nests, usually placed in a tree, are mud-walled, grasslined bowls, while juncos make their well-lined cups on the ground.

Robins need no description—almost everyone knows them. Juncos, snowbirds to some people, are smallish, gray sparrow-like birds and have conspicuous white outer tail feathers. The heads of male Oregon juncos are black. They have rusty backs, and buffy or rusty sides. The heads of females are grayer and the rust of the back not so well defined. Juncos eat weed seeds the year-round and add insects to their diet in the nesting season.

In June one year we found a robin nest about ten feet above the ground in a young Douglas-fir tree near the trail. On July 14 there was a young bird in the nest, but the nest was empty by July 21. Later, we saw several robins feeding on the fruit of a wild cherry tree not far from that nest site.

From the numbers of juncos we saw and their behavior, I am fairly certain that some of them nested on the terrace between the station and the trail down the mountain, though we didn't locate a nest. Frankly, we were too busy with many other things to spend much time searching for bird nests.

A few deep-forest species adapted to the young forest. One of these was the russet-backed thrush. These very furtive birds had moved about in the thickets of the mature forest like dark shadows. We heard them almost all day long, but seldom saw them. The same was true now in the young forest. Though we rarely saw them, we heard their rich-toned song throughout the nesting season.

Winter wrens were our constant companions in the developing community just as they had been in the ancient forest. All year long, even on the relatively pleasant days in the winter, we could hear their harsh *kip, kip* calls as they hopped about in the undergrowth searching for food, and in the spring we were delighted by the long, trilling songs of the males.

We heard, or saw, kinglets in almost every month of the year. Sometimes they came in flocks with chickadees and other birds, but more often they were in smaller family groups. These tiny birds have the habit of flicking their wings as they hop from twig to twig looking for aphids and other minute insects at the tips of branches, but because they moved about so rapidly, we weren't always certain whether they were golden-crowned or ruby-crowned. Both kinds visited but we are not sure that any of them nested.

Like silent ghosts, Oregon jays often slipped into a young tree near where one of us was working. Sometimes a bird would be alone, but more frequently with a mate or family. They were curious but seldom advertised their presence. Steller's jays visited, too, but they were never so quiet.

Both kinds of jays are so expert at hiding their nests that we found only one—a Steller's nest full of rambunctious nestlings whose raucous calls drew our attention and revealed the nest in a young Douglas-fir tree near the trail.

These fledglings soon joined their parents as they foraged about, seeking food for all.

We had seen both kinds of jays frequently in the mature forest.

Each year a pair of band-tailed pigeons nested near the middle of the hectare in a tall scraggly hemlock left topless by the 1940 logging. We couldn't see the nest, which was only a flimsy platform of twigs some forty or fifty feet above the ground, but we could see the parent birds moving about among the sparse foliage and often heard them cooing. They left the nest frequently. Sometimes one flew down into a patch of salal, perhaps to feed on the berries.

These pigeons are named for the large white band across the end of their tail. Traveling from their southerly wintering areas in large flocks, they arrive in northwestern Oregon in April. Mated pairs then leave the flocks and select their summer nesting territories. We saw them or heard them cooing at the station as early as May 13 and from then on until fall. Usually our pair had only one young, but one year we saw four pigeons near the nest site in early July, so it would seem that they had two offspring that year.

By early September, flocks of at least twenty-five pigeons began gathering as they prepared for their southward migration. Since they like berries, the pigeons may have congregated on the terrace to feed on the berries and many kinds of seeds so plentiful there. Then, shortly after the middle of September, the pigeons would all be gone until the following year.

Band-tailed pigeons were not new to me. We had seen them now and then during Prof's study, but the young forest gave me the chance to know them more intimately.

We learned that rufous hummingbirds time their arrival in the spring to coincide with the blooming of red flowering currants. Males arrived a couple of weeks before the females and their presence became known as we saw them, and heard them, darting from blossom to blossom and plant to plant.

Though attracted especially to flowering currants, hummingbirds feed, as well, on the blossoms of salmonberries, blackberries, columbine, tiger lilies, madrone trees, and many other flowers, preferably red ones. Their diet includes both nectar and insects, and sometimes tree sap.

The male hummingbird with his bright rufous upper parts and flaming orange-red throat, is the only North American hummingbird that has a rust-red back. His mate is less flamboyant. She has a green back and her sides and the base of her tail are dull rufous. Both sexes are very aggressive in defending their feeding and nesting territories and will attack birds or other creatures much larger than they, even people.

Their nest, which is usually placed on a low drooping branch of a conifer, is a tiny, delicate cup, no more than an inch and a half or two inches across. It is made of cottony plant down, mosses, and shreds of bark, decorated on the outside with lichens bound to the cup with spider silk. While hummingbirds seem to prefer to nest in conifers, they use other plants as well. We didn't discover any nests on Saddleback, but I've seen one at the coast on a branch of a hemlock tree and another in a tangle of blackberry plants. Two baby birds fill the tiny nest.

These delightful birds were with us in the young forest each year from late March or early April until August, but in the ancient forest we saw them only in springtime along well-lighted streamsides or in sunny spots in the deeper forest feeding at a favorite shrub.

Almost daily during the summer months we heard a new sound, a loud-ringing, challenging *whit-whee-oo, whee-oo*, shouted by a bird perched on a stubby branch near the lofty tip of a topless old hemlock, one of the dying remnants of the old forest. We discovered that the performer was a rather large, stout, bull-headed olive-sided flycatcher. From that vantage point he surveyed his domain and darted after passing insects or shouted a challenge to ward off other male flycatchers. They were new to me. We soon recognized their call and often watched as one darted after an insect.

Two of our earlier acquaintances, pileated woodpeckers and hairy woodpeckers, along with recently arrived red-shafted flickers, found the topless hemlocks which provided perches for the flycatchers to be well-stocked larders, teeming with carpenter ants and other wood-inhabiting insects. Cavities excavated by these wood-pecking birds served not only as nesting sites for them and for other birds, but also as homes for many other creatures.

These dying trees were also a source of nourishment for downy woodpeckers and red-headed sapsuckers, another newcomer. They drilled small holes into the trees for their sap.

When Joanne, a former student, and I camped near the river during a weekend in September 1961, each evening shortly after dusk we enjoyed hearing a pair of great horned owls *hoo, hoo-oo, hoo, hooing* to each other from the large trees near our tent. However, we never heard, or saw, great horned owls in any part of the logged-over area near the station. Nor did we see, or even hear, a screech owl, though we had heard them frequently during Prof's study and he had collected one.

Pygmy owls were a different matter. They seemed to be as active in the young forest as they had been in the old one. One day as I was hiking down the mountain from the study site, I paused and, glancing into the thicket beside the trail, looked directly into the eyes of one of these little owls perched on a branch of a small conifer a few feet away. I was thrilled and it did not seem the least bit disturbed.

Spotted owls, so much in the news in recent years, were never reported by any member of the research team in either study. Though reputed to be common residents in ancient Douglas-fir forests, spotted owls are strictly nocturnal and are seldom seen unless one knows how to call them. These owls may, or may not, have lived in the ancient forest on Saddleback. Actually, we didn't even know about them at the time.

Prof's research records refer to red-tailed hawks many times. We saw these rodent hunters, too, during the study of the young forest and heard them even more frequently.

One of our greatest surprises began late one afternoon shortly after we started our study when a very small, dark, swallow-like bird caught Frances's attention, darting about overhead in rapid, erratic flight, like that of a bat. She could hear a faint, rapid twitter whenever the bird was near. This unfamiliar bird was a Vaux swift, the smallest of North American swifts, and looked like a cigar with wings.

Vaux swifts, which normally live in mature Douglas-fir forests, are gregarious. They nest and sleep in groups in hollow trees and hunt insects far above trees or over rivers. If they were in our forest during Prof's study (as they probably were), we didn't know it for we couldn't have seen them through the dense crowns of the huge old trees. Whatever their history, these birds were now present in the young forest and we saw them from mid-May until about the middle of September, alone, in pairs, or in threes and fives, darting about, capturing insects above the mountainside or over the river.

John Terres says the Vaux swift is the counterpart of the eastern chimney swift, but this species seldom uses chimneys. As the forests disappear he expects this species will adapt more to chimneys. I wonder where the ones we saw on Saddleback went in September? Could they have found chimneys? Or hollow trees? A pair of swifts nested in the fireplace chimney of our house in McMinnville ten or fifteen years after this study on Saddleback ended.

As we worked in the young forest we often saw large, nearly eagle-sized turkey vultures, soaring nearby. We called them buzzards, though the buzzard is really a European hawk, a Buteo, like our red-tail or rough-legged hawks. Now and then one of the vultures flew very low and we could see its two-toned black wings and naked small red head. When one flew this close, we thought it might be zeroing in on some dead animal, for the food of vultures consists almost entirely of carrion. They also perched in the research area a few times. Prof did not mention these birds in his study. Perhaps they, like the Vaux swift, could not be seen through the canopy of the large trees.

Various birds, which we had looked for and listened to in the past, apparently now found homes only where some of the old conifers still survived near streams or in isolated pockets on the mountain. For them, the young trees offered neither conifer seeds for food, lofty trees for nesting and seclusion, nor the diversity of life they required. We never encountered even one raven, sooty grouse, hermit warbler, hermit thrush, brown creeper, nuthatch, wood pewee, western flycatcher, screech owl, or great horned owl in or near the research area during the three years of the NSF study.

Though we repeatedly heard crossbills near the river chirping as they flew from one group of trees to another far above us, they visited our research site in the young forest very few times during the entire study, and then only briefly. Once we did hear the call of a red-breasted nuthatch somewhere on the terrace, and one spring day a dozen pine siskins flew over us while we worked at the station. But we heard the plaintive vesper song of varied thrushes only when we were in the moist forest remnants near the river. Even then, the sound seemed to come from afar. We didn't see the songsters. The lone varied thrush Nick Simpson banded at the station in July 1964 was a great surprise. How he came to band birds at Saddleback grew out of a trip to eastern Oregon.

In the summer of 1963, one year after the NSF project officially ended, I made my first trip to Steens Mountain and the Malheur National Wildlife Refuge. I was so impressed with what I saw that I arranged for my ecology class to have a field trip there that fall.

When we visited the refuge, the biologist told us about the amazing number of birds they had added to their record through the use of Japanese mist nets made of such fine nylon fibers that they are nearly invisible to the birds and so flexible that, when a bird hits the net, the mesh forms a sort of pocket around it, making it possible for a person to take the bird out and band it without injury. However, these nets are tricky to work with. A person needs special training by an expert before beginning a project.

What a helpful tool mist nets would have been for our study on Saddleback, I thought, *but I don't have the time, myself, for that kind of project.*

To my surprise and pleasure, Nick Simpson, a sophomore, told me he'd like to do such a study for his senior thesis project. I obtained bird-banding permits and two government approved mist nets of one-and-a-half inch nylon mesh, each thirty feet long by seven feet wide, and we rounded up the other equipment he needed. Nick got his training, visited the research site, planned his lay-out, and began banding on July 2, 1964.

This was an ambitious undertaking for one student, especially since he had to carry all his equipment a quarter of a mile up a mountain trail. Friends helped sometimes.

Nick tried several locations, including the top of fallen logs, and always placed the nets in open or fairly open areas where he could extend them without too much difficulty. The nets had to be set up, taken down, and carefully stored each day they were used. Removing birds from the nets, placing bands on their legs, recording date, site, band number, and species of the bird was time-consuming. Most days Nick arrived at the station at about 6 or 7 a.m. and left at 11 or noon.

His last day of banding was August 20, 1964, though he visited the site about once each week until October 7 when he ended the project. Unfortunately, he couldn't do any banding in September because all his days were wet and the nets could not be used in wet or windy weather.

Even though he banded on only nine days, Nick's results were very interesting and contained some surprises. He banded twenty Oregon juncos, nineteen robins, eight olive-sided flycatchers, three Oregon jays, two red-shafted flickers, one Steller's jay, one varied thrush, four red-winged blackbirds, and ten violet-green swallows, a total of nine species and sixty-eight birds.

According to Prof's records only three species in Nick's list had lived in the ancient forest—the Oregon jays, the Steller's jay, and the varied thrush. The two jay species had adapted to the young forest, but we had not seen, or even heard, a varied thrush there.

Finding red-winged blackbirds and violet-green swallows as summer residents in the young community was a complete surprise.

Chapter Twenty
Mammals

ONE MORNING AS WE unloaded the car shortly after beginning the study, a pair of hounds rushed by and dashed up the mountain baying at the tops of their voices.

A few moments later a green Willys pick-up came by. "Hello there," the driver called. "Have you seen anything of my hounds? We've been trying since early morning to run down a couple of bear."

"A pair of hounds just ran by here," Howard replied. "They headed on up the mountain."

"Thanks," the man said, throwing his Willys into gear and driving across the bridge.

Four more hounds crossed the trail as we hiked toward the station. Then another hound, lagging behind, left the four and stayed with us the rest of the day. The dog had a name and address on its collar so we delivered him to his owner in Willamina when we left that evening.

"You'll find lots of bear on the mountain now," the Murphy woods foreman, McKinley, had told us when we first contacted him to get permission to do the NSF study. "At least 300, they say, and they're doing a lot of damage."

"How's that?" Ray asked.

"Well," McKinley continued, "in the spring when bears first come out of their winter's sleep, they often claw away the outer bark on the young fir trees. Foresters say that's to get to the juicy, nutritious cambium. But that damages the trees and if the bears girdle the trees, as they sometimes do, the trees die. Timber owners are up in the air about this and are promoting hunting of the bears."

"Do you think they'll be hunting where we're going to work?" I asked.

"Probably not right there. But you'll see lots of hunters and their hounds."

And we did.

We met hunters as we traveled the logging road to and from the research site, and we saw hounds or heard them from a distance even more often than we saw the hunters. One hunter told us that about 150 bears had been killed on Saddleback during the last three years.

We also met a bear trapper who said that he trapped only on the lower part of the mountain, not above the river where we would be, but he didn't say how many bears he had caught or for how long he had been trapping.

We saw little evidence of bears in our research area or on the trail to it. One time early in the study, as we came into the station from the lower trail, we heard a crashing noise as some large animal rushed through the brush, away from us toward the east. We thought that was probably a bear.

Another time when some of us came in by way of the lower trail, we noticed that some bark had been stripped off a young Douglas-fir tree beside the upper end of the walk-up log, leaving a bare place on the tree about eight inches long and four or five inches wide. The work was fresh, and when we examined it closely we could see streaks about four inches long and two inches wide in the cambium in the center of the stripped area. The streaks looked like tooth marks. We concluded that was the kind of damage about which we had been told.

Years later, in October 1968, some of the students who were checking a project at the station reported "fresh bear scat, copious, black, and seedy," in the upper trail to the station and discovered similar sign near the center of the hectare. Evidently this bear was fattening up on the available berries.

And in 1969 while John Kerr was doing his thesis research, he was told that only ten bears had been shot in the Saddleback area during the previous year. Evidently, by that time the bear population was declining. We hoped that bear hunting on the mountain would soon cease.

I had a fondness for the lower trail, the one which led to the spar tree below the station. I chose that route sometimes with one or two companions, letting others take the high road. I wanted to check the club moss, the mountain beaver colony, and a little white pine tree in the trail a short distance east of the spar tree.

The final section of that trail had become so heavily overgrown with the mixture of young conifers that Ray had used pruning shears to remove some of the limbs to make a tunnel-like passage through it. We dubbed that part of the trail "the bear trail," though we were never really concerned about meeting a bear there. It was just fun to use that name. Once in a while we referred to the entire lower trail as the bear trail.

Whenever I saw that little pine I recalled the mystic sunset experience I had in the pine forest above Ellis Barn that evening in the summer of 1937, just before I left for graduate school. Sadly, this little pine died before we finished our study.

By the end of November 1959 the club moss had sent its trailing stems over much more of the cleft bank and, during the summer of 1960, tiny, sporebearing cones formed at the tips of short, upright spikes on the club moss' many branches.

The mountain beavers, or sewellels, as the Indians knew them, are only remotely related to fur-bearing beavers and might more correctly be called mountain burrowers, for their heavy, compact bodies certainly were designed for burrowing. These rodents have no living relatives and all of them are in a single species, *Aplodontia rufa*, which is found nowhere in the world except in the Pacific Northwest and is the last of a line of rodents whose lineage can be traced back fifty million years to Eocene times.

These creatures somewhat resemble pocket gophers in habits and appearance, but they are much larger and have very tiny tails. The *Aplodontia's* color varies from dark brown to almost black and adults are about a foot long.

While surveying along the east side of the hectare, Howard and I located at least five groups of mountain beaver mounds. They were probably all part of one large colony, for students of the species say that burrows of a single colony may have a great many openings, some with mounds of earth, others without any. The burrows often go straight down for a foot or two and then enter the main tunnels which extend underground for long distances, frequently running through wet ground and springy places. They may even have streams of water running through their tunnels.

Years before, I had read that these rodents were haymakers. On the secluded trail that to the station I finally had an opportunity to observe their work. That first summer the ones in this colony were very busy and I often discovered freshly cut fronds of bracken or sword fern, or elderberry twigs lying near their burrows, drying in the sun.

Being strict vegetarians, these rodents feed on a wide variety of plants. Once we found leaf tops from many plants, so freshly cut that none had wilted, but the sweetest scents in all our experience came from a stack of vanilla leaf drying by one of the mounds.

They use some of the plants immediately as food but they cut and dry others before storing them for winter food or nest material. Though not true hibernators, mountain beavers are usually inactive above ground during the coldest part of winter and at that time they presumably use food from their underground stores. However, they may harvest plants even in winter. In early December one year we found freshly cut sword ferns stashed near the burrows in the southeast corner of the hectare.

Prof trapped a mountain beaver near our overnight shelter, Ellis Barn, in the summer of 1937. He had set that trap in a burrow which had fresh dirt and piles of false Solomon's seal, deer fern, lily of the valley, and skunk cabbage around its opening. He noted that the rodent, caught by one foot, "uttered grunting and small, squealing, complaining sounds" while in the trap but ate some wood fern and lily of the valley while waiting to be moved into a box. Though alive when captured, it lived only a few days. These creatures have the reputation for being difficult to keep in captivity.

Many kinds of mammals lived on the terrace, either near the research area, or inside it. But we had to do much sleuthing to learn about these animals because many of them were active only at night or hid themselves whenever we came around. Burrows, tracks in the snow or in rain-soaked ground, scat, evidence of browsing or of bucks polishing their antlers to remove the velvet from them—all of these were helpful clues. We also did some trapping of the smaller mammals.

Elusive, small, brown brush rabbits lived in the area. We noticed their tracks whenever there was snow on the ground, and, in all seasons, copious droppings lay in places wherever there was dense low cover. Being mainly nocturnal, these rabbits were seldom active during the hours when we were at the research site but remained hidden in their favorite runways. They cannot run rapidly and never venture far from thick cover. On one of her first trips Nancy noticed a baby rabbit in the brush beside the trail and later we saw an adult at the station.

We found no sure evidence of the somewhat larger and darker snowshoe, or varying, hare on the terrace though Prof encountered them occasionally. These hares are mainly forest dwellers and are rarely seen except as one of them hops out into a road or trail before dodging back into cover. Now and then we saw a lone hare on the river road or on the trail not far above the river.

Both the brush rabbit and the varying hare are herbivores—plant eaters—and favorite prey of bobcats.

Chipmunks, little squirrels with brown and yellow stripes on their cheeks and on the backs of their soft, dark coats, are gentle in their actions and so quiet that we often knew they were nearby only by their musical, whistled *chip* or their soft *chuck,chuck,chuck* from some far-away branch, stump, or log. Only rarely did we see them feeding in a huckleberry bush or scurrying out of sight into a thicket. Ours, known as Townsend's chipmunks, are large for chipmunks, being about ten inches from tip of nose to tip of tail, but their plumy tails make up about half that length. Busy little animals, they travel about a lot and eat a wide variety of foods, including berries, seeds, bulbs, roots, green vegetation, insects, and other small animal life as well as fungi. They are active most of the year but retreat to their warm, well-stocked underground nests in the coldest part of the winter.

The slightly longer, slender, orange-bellied chickarees—which we usually called pine squirrels—were a bit more visible as they ranged about harvesting cones from the branches of the conifers. They are bright little creatures which scold or chatter noisily when defending their territory or announcing possible danger. Sometimes a low, conversational *chirrr* told us that one of these small squirrels was nearby.

Normally, much of their food comes from the rich, oily seeds found in conifer cones. At the time of this study, tiny cones were abundant on young hemlock trees but few of the Douglas-firs were mature enough to produce cones, which are much larger. The squirrels worked industriously on whatever cones were available, harvesting them as soon as the seeds inside were half ripe. Carrying them to their regular feeding places, they clipped off the scales and ate the seeds that were beneath.

In the autumn when cones were fully ripe, they harvested and stored them for later use and supplemented the diet of cones with a wide variety of seeds, berries, and other fruits. They also made good use of mushrooms, one of their favorite foods, whenever those delicacies were in season.

Chickarees may nest in a hollow tree, but in this coastal region they more often construct a nest of twigs and leaves, line it with moss, and anchor it securely among the branches of some evergreen tree. Though they are active throughout the year, we saw or heard them only in the warmer months.

Once, in about the middle of our period of research, we saw a large gray squirrel on the south edge of the hectare. It was some distance away and we did not find a burrow, but from its size and behavior we concluded that it was a ground squirrel that is locally known as a gray digger. These squirrels (probably Beechey ground squirrels) are common in cultivated fields and pastureland and often move into previously forested areas after logging. They usually conceal the entrance to their burrows beneath stones, logs, or other materials and scurry to these burrows whenever alarmed. They eat a wide variety of green foliage, roots, flowers, seeds, berries, other fruits, and insects.

We learned about mice, voles, shrews, and moles—the smallest mammals of the forest—primarily through trapping. Most of them are nocturnal, live in shallow burrows which they make for themselves under the surface of the forest floor, or are just plain evasive.

White-footed deer mice were the most abundant. At least, we caught more of them. They are attractive little rodents with large dark eyes and white feet. A fully-grown one may measure nearly eight inches, including its tail, which usually is at least as long as its head and body combined. The undersides of both immatures and adults are white. They are dark gray when they're young but because the backs of our adults are a rich rusty brown, they are known as dusky or ruddy deer mice. This subspecies is restricted to wooded and brushy areas of the western part of Oregon and northern California, but deer mice are common throughout most of North America.

These mice can see in daylight but are most active at night. They eat many foods, including berries, nuts, insects and, especially, seeds of all kinds. We once discovered a mouse nest under a log and one January we found two young deer mice, about two-thirds grown, nesting in a towel in a can in one of our instrument shelters. Another January day one of my helpers saw one of these mice moving about in the grove of young conifers near the rain gauge. The many others which I have recorded, measured, and made into museum specimens were caught either during Prof's study or at some stage of my personal research.

Because deer mice breed throughout the year and have many young, they are an important source of food for predatory birds and mammals.

The Oregon creeping mouse is a vole, not a mouse, and is a burrower. Though mice and voles look much alike, they have some rather subtle, but significant, differences in their skulls—which only a specialist can recognize. The creeping vole is dusky brown and about three-fourths the size of a deer mouse. Its eyes are small. It has a short, dark tail and dark feet. It apparently travels almost exclusively underground in tunnels it creates and we learned that many of the "mole burrows" we had recorded in our trail notes for Prof's study were really passages made by this little species of vole. Its most common foods are herbs and grasses, but it also eats fungi. It, too, falls prey to birds and larger mammals.

The redbacked voles are very special little animals. I tell about them in a later chapter.

Shrews are insectivores, though they are often mistaken for mice. Their teeth are quite different and are specialized for capturing and holding insects and crunching their hard, chitinous exoskeletons, not like the teeth of rodents which are made for gnawing.

Trowbridge's shrews, the kind we found on Saddleback, are tiny, no more than five inches long—head, body, and tail. Having extremely small eyes, they cannot see well, but their senses of smell, touch, and hearing are acute. Because of their high rate of metabolism they must eat their own weight in food each day, so they are constantly on the go, poking around with their long, pointed noses seeking something to eat, sometimes on the surface, but more often beneath the surface in passageways made by other small creatures. Living around old stumps, under logs or slabs of loose bark, or among the surface roots of trees, shrews prey on a wide variety of animal life—centipedes, spiders, beetles, slugs, snails, young mice, or at times even other shrews.

Shrew-moles, specifically Gibbs's shrew-moles, lived in the young forest. This was a real surprise as I had seen only one of these moles before and it was not from a forest. They are insectivores, much smaller than most moles, their head and body being less than three inches long. Shrew-moles are shrew-like in that they live partly underground, but in their own little tunnels, not in the burrows of other creatures as shrews do. They also require more than their body weight in food each day and spend much time roving about on the surface, probing into the forest floor beside and under recently fallen trees, or digging into logs in the later stages of decay.

For digging, shrew-moles use their mole-like, broad front feet with stout claws which are ideally adapted for that purpose. The shrew-mole's ears, like those of its larger mole relatives, are mere holes near its shoulders, invisible through its dense fur coat. Its eyes, too, are nearly concealed by fur. Its nose is bare, with an extremely keen sense of touch, and the mole uses it when plowing under the surface to sniff out such favorite foods as earthworms, centipedes, and insects.

Shrew-moles are said to be active both day and night. Their blackish fur is dense and velvety, with a purple iridescence, much like that of their larger mole relative. Possibly some shrew-moles lived in the mature forest, but we didn't find any there. They may have migrated upward on the mountain as logging proceeded.

I was surprised to find the work of the larger moles very visible in the young forest community, for we had not often seen evidence of their presence in the ancient forest. At first, the only ones we were aware of were barely inside the hectare near the upper trail into the station through the southeast corner. But as the research progressed, the moles spread their activity, busily digging and moving about, and before 1962 ended, they had even burrowed into the grove of young trees south of the fire shelter crater.

These creatures, which dig for insects and other invertebrates, were especially numerous and active in patches of bracken and among the herbs and shrubs in the more open areas. A July 1960 notation reads, "Fresh mole mound [near our center of activity] and mole heaving it as we arrived." Another note in January 1961 states, "They [mounds] are in a straight line running north and south." Many of our field notes speak of fresh mole activity. We caught two in the young forest, and Prof has a record of one taken within the research area. He also referred to "mole activity" at times, especially in the trail notes, but we learned later that some of the burrowing activity along the trail was actually the work of voles.

These moles are rarely seen above ground and, according to naturalists who have studied their habits, spend most of their active lives underground. There they busy themselves in extending long tunnels just beneath the surface in search of insect food, or in digging deeper burrows, where their real life is lived. It is when they are working on these deeper burrows that they push out the loose earth into the mounds. Their food is mainly ground-inhabiting insects and insect larvae, earthworms, spiders, centipedes, and occasionally the roots of sprouting plants.

Chipmunks, chickarees, mice, voles, shrews, and moles had all been present in the mature forest, but our records seemed to indicate that they were much more numerous in the young forest community.

We knew skunks lived somewhere near. We smelled their scent and saw their tracks in the winter snow. One December we noticed freshly dug shallow holes in our trail inside the station. These we attributed to the pretty little spotted skunk, commonly, though incorrectly, called civet, which we knew to be resident on the mountain. It is smaller than the widely known striped skunk, black with a white spot on its forehead, a spot under each ear, and four broken stripes along its neck, back, and sides. Its tail has a white tip.

Exclusively forest creatures, spotted skunks nest in burrows among old logs and whatever the forest offers in the way of cover. They climb trees readily, and perhaps some even make their homes in them. Being strictly nocturnal, spotted skunks are seldom seen. They feed on mice, birds, eggs, insects, carrion, and some vegetable matter, such as mushrooms, berries, and other wild fruit. During Prof's study we caught one of them at Ellis Barn and I made a museum specimen of its skin.

I wonder why deer hold such an attraction for most people, bringing a thrill whenever one is seen. Is it because they are shy, or so graceful?

The deer on Saddleback were blacktails, a smaller, darker relative of mule deer. Unlike mule deer, which depend upon watchfulness and speed, blacktails use stealth and caution for their protection. They seldom feed during the day, but hide and rest in thick cover, coming out at evening to begin feeding. Being browsers, they really thrived on the forage provided by this rapidly changing community on Saddleback.

Though deer lived in the ancient forest, they were not plentiful. They needed more open areas to supply forage for a large population. Our field notes for the young forest, however, have more references to deer than to any other mammal.

Not long after we started the study we noticed deer tracks and droppings in the station. The following spring they bedded in a salal and huckleberry patch near the center of the east side of the hectare. Soon, fresh tracks and droppings began appearing in many places along that open, relatively tree-free side. In the fall we found another deer bed just outside the southeast corner and a trail through that area with lots of fresh droppings and much scarring of trees and shrubs where bucks had polished their antlers. A year or so after we had ended our weekly visits, the deer began using the trail through the station heavily, coming in through the south and making a veritable highway northerly through the hectare, leaving fresh droppings every few feet. These, as well as other signs, became much more abundant as time progressed. Obviously, the deer population was increasing.

They browsed on thimbleberry, alder, and fireweed and we saw where a buck had stripped bark from a young hemlock and from a much taller alder while polishing his antlers during the rutting season.

Various members of our group had the pleasure of seeing a deer on the trail now and then. But in July 1964 while doing his bird study, Nick Simpson had the most prized experience of any of us. Shortly after entering the research area, he came upon four does quietly resting under a tree beside the trail which wound through the middle of the site. Each of them was a beautiful tan, he said, and when they saw him they didn't seem at all scared but stood up and walked away unhurriedly.

The story about coyotes is different. Though apparently native in part of the Coast Range, they were not plentiful and were seldom encountered until extensive logging opened up the forest and made the mountainsides more attractive to them.

Close relatives of the wolf, coyotes are sometimes called brush wolves. They look much like a gray or reddish gray, medium-size dog with rusty legs, feet, and ears, but their nose is more pointed and their tail bushier than normal for a dog. Also, when a coyote runs it holds its tail down between its hind legs.

Coyotes are shy and elusive. However they are also bold and cunning, with little fear of man or dogs. They move about at any time, but chiefly at night. Though they hunt mainly small game, they are omnivorous and will eat almost anything animal or vegetable. Since coyotes are wanderers and adapt easily to different conditions and environments, they adjusted readily to life on Saddleback Mountain.

None of us ever saw any of them in the research site or anywhere on the terrace but we did see lots of evidence of their presence in scat on the foot trail and tracks in the snow almost all the way to the station.

John Kerr was the only one of us who actually saw coyotes anywhere on the mountain. Early in the summer of 1969 while he was doing his thesis study, he came upon a pair of "tawny color" coyotes running ahead of him down the Murphy road toward the bridge over Salmon River. Again, in mid-August, he surprised a group (probably a family) of four coyotes about five miles beyond the river, not far from the highway.

Unlike coyotes, bobcats were native to the ancient forest. They are large, richly colored reddish-brown cats with long legs, short tails, small feet, and erect, slightly tufted ears. Being both nocturnal and shy, they are very rarely seen. Prof made frequent reference to seeing tracks of bobcats, but, as far as I know, he never encountered one of the cats on Saddleback.

In our study of the young forest we knew we were in bobcat territory because we often found their scat along the trail. Some, near a group of varied thrush feathers, led us to suspect that a bobcat had caught and eaten the thrush. Other scat seen along the trail and also on the walk-up log below the station contained fur and claws, and one time when we arrived at the research site we found fresh bobcat tracks near our center of activity. Though we had lots of evidence of bobcat presence, the one Bill Good and I saw on Murphy road one hot, dry August evening was the only one any of our group ever glimpsed.

These cats are primarily hunters of small mammals and birds, but they seek a wide variety of prey and will even eat carrion. They make their dens in rock crevices, hollow logs, or beneath downfalls.

We also knew that cougars were in the vicinity. We had heard their deep-throated growls while working near the hygrothermograph, and we had seen their tracks in the snow along the east side of the hectare. But Nick Simpson had a personal encounter with one when he went to the research site on July 9, 1964 to work on his bird-banding project. This was the same day that he saw the four does.

Here is Nick's story as he recorded it in the field notes: "The mountain lion shook me. I had scared up the does and then walked in on the trail [through an open area] to...the thicket...there he was watching me. Probably took away his meal. He watched me, not moving except for tail and eyes. Large golden eyes. Real nice looking hide, real tan. Long tail. He was about 110-120 pounds, guessing. His paws were quite large and he had quite long whiskers. Beautiful animal, after he left.

"I sat down afterwards to think that one over. He was only around 10-12 feet from me when I came upon him."

Another comment in those notes: "Mountain lion looked me in the face, then left—thank God. Scared me bad. Sat down for a minute after he left."

Cougars, or mountain lions, have been common in Oregon since the earliest explorations and were mentioned many times by early naturalists. We had often noticed their tracks during Prof's study, but during that time none of us ever saw a live one in the forest.

These carnivores are reputed to be one of the most stealthy and secretive of hunters. So far as is known, they live only on meat and almost entirely on game that they kill. They are great wanderers and rarely remain long in one locality, except in the breeding season while their young are small.

One weekend Bill Good and another student stayed overnight on the mountain. At about ten o'clock the first night they saw a large porcupine walking near the bridge. The next day they came upon a mink swimming in the Salmon River about a mile below the bridge.

The porcupine was a surprise, for they are much more common in eastern Oregon and other dry areas than they are in the western part of the state. We had had no hint of its presence. Evidently it, too, was a newcomer.

Porcupines are next to the largest rodent in Oregon, second only to the beaver. They are short and broad, with short legs and a muscular tail which has heavy bristles on its underside. An adult's dark coat is partly hidden beneath a longer outer coat of coarse, yellowish hairs and long, sharp, barbed quills. In summer most of the black coat is lacking. Excellent climbers, porcupines spend much time in trees. They eat a wide variety of plants, including twigs and bark, especially in winter.

The mink was no special surprise as they are commonly found along streams, from which they get much of their food. They are said to show no preference for timber or open country but may be found wherever there is ample food—a combination of aquatic creatures, fish, frogs, crustaceans, and small land animals such as mice, chipmunks, and birds. Mink are dark brown weasel-like animals about two feet long with feet webbed for swimming, but they are heavier bodied than weasels.

On one of her winter trips Nancy saw a slender, dark creature, about fourteen inches long, moving rapidly through the brush in the part of the trail near the stream above the unnamed river. She thought it was a weasel. About a month later, when snow lay on the ground, she saw tracks in that area which matched those of a long-tailed weasel.

This gave a name to the animal she had seen earlier, for long-tailed weasels are dark brown, about twelve to sixteen inches long and live near water in forests and other places. Although they take some birds and other animals, they feed mostly on small mammals. They usually make their homes in old burrows of other animals.

The work of beavers caught Bill Good's attention on a chance trip to the research site in October 1963. He noticed that two wild cherry trees, each about four inches in diameter, had been cut down beside the trail. He knew there was a stream near the trail on the far side of that group of trees, and on his next trip he ventured to the creek and discovered "plentiful beaver work, both old and fresh." Most of the broadleaf trees nearest to the creek had been cut—vine maple and willow—as well as some hemlock. Some stripped limbs of trees were in the creek. Since Bill didn't say anything about a dam, probably these beavers had made burrows in the bank.

Throughout the entire NSF study period from July 4, 1959, to June 30, 1962, on almost every weekly trip we recorded some new, interesting experience, collected a new plant or animal, or made a new observation. In those few years both students and I saw many changes in the research area and I saw even more during the following ten years whenever I returned to the site with students or with Ray.

The diversity of life was greatly altered. One can only wonder, with a sense of foreboding, what effect logging, both intensive and extensive, is having and will have on the wealth of diversity once present in the ancient forest. Will it not cause a loss of overall diversity and diminished ecosystem vitality?

There was nothing static about this young forest community. It was a fascinating, dynamic period in the forest's journey forward from partial destruction toward a mature forest—a centuries' long journey that was not destined to be.

Chapter Twenty-one
Murphy Road

M URPHY ROAD, begun in the 1930s when the Murphy brothers owned much of the land on the north side of Saddleback Mountain, was a narrow, one-way, dirt and rock-surfaced road, often muddy, sometimes dusty, and occasionally icy or filled with snow. It was a regular roller coaster as it swung in tight curves around the numerous ridges or climbed up and dropped down in passing over them; still, the road had frequent turnouts within its four-mile ascent of 250 feet from the 793-foot elevation of its entrance at Salmon River Highway (State Highway 18) to a log bridge across Salmon River. Beyond that bridge, Murphy road began a steep, circuitous climb toward the top of the mountain, while our route turned to the right and continued for another mile along the nearly level "river road" to our parking site.

For Prof, the trail to the top of the mountain and for me Murphy road served the same basic purpose. They provided our means of access to the research site. Though the two differed in many ways, they both also furnished an overview of what was taking place in the mountain's ecosystem.

We had permission to use the road and to make our study at the research site, but permission did not immediately provide us with a key. We had been told we could arrange for access with the Crown Zellerbach woods foreman who lived on CZ property between Grand Ronde and the Murphy road. Though the Murphys still owned the research site and most of the land in that portion of the mountain, Miami Lumber Corporation owned a stretch of young forest along the west side of the road near the highway and Crown Zellerbach Corporation had extensive holdings near the top of the mountain. These companies, as well as the state fire warden, required access and had keys to the road.

The day of our second trip, as we had done the week before, we stopped at the CZ foreman's home for a key. He wasn't there, but the gate was open and Murphy workmen were "rocking" the road—placing crushed rock on soft or muddy places in preparation for more logging. On our way in we waited a half hour before we could pass the workmen. When we returned in the evening, the gate was locked. Hoping someone would come by, we waited nearly an hour. In desperation, Howard began hitchhiking to the CZ home. Soon a CZ workman came through in a pickup, unlocking the gate for us. After picking Howard up, we continued our journey home.

From that July day until mid-September we stopped at the CZ home twice a day—in the morning to get the key; in the evening to return it. Then, in September, the Murphy foreman gave us a key.

Even with a key in hand, we continued to have access problems. An "Area Closed" sign greeted Bill Good and me when we arrived at the gate one August morning of a particularly hot, dry summer. We needed to check some projects Bill was working on. We had a key but where could we get an entrance permit?

I don't remember all the details of that day, but as I recall, we first returned to the CZ foreman's home near Grand Ronde. From there we drove to the Grand Ronde Guard Station, then to the Cascade Head Experiment Station near Otis, and finally to the fire warden's station at Oceanlake. In getting that permit we had driven more than sixty miles and spent at least three hours.

In spite of all the discomfort and time spent, we had our reward. On our homeward journey that evening we saw a bobcat walking in the road a short distance ahead of us as we approached the ridge above Salmon River. It turned its head and gave us a regular photographic view of its face before vanishing into the brush beside the road. That picture still lingers in my memory. That was the first bobcat I had seen in the wild.

As the months rolled by and the research progressed, we had all sorts of access problems, ranging from sudden changes in locks as the result of vandalism to having our access rerouted temporarily to the Long Bell road a couple of miles farther toward the coast due to new fire protection laws.

The personnel of logging companies changed rapidly. During the ten years of our most frequent trips, we had keys from two CZ woods foremen, a Murphy foreman, and a Miami Corporation foreman. Later, in the 1980s when the Stimson Lumber Company owned much of the area, we got a key from them when we needed one.

The hauling of logs by Murphy workmen began in August of the first year of the research. We had to be prepared to use a turnout on short notice whenever we heard a truck roaring toward us from either direction. We were especially cautious at the Salmon River crossing. A log truck loaded with fifty-foot long logs carried a load of about 40,000 pounds. Those trucks commanded respect and had the right of way. Any sudden slowing, or stop, by a loaded truck could dump the load, wreck the truck, or do both and also injure or kill the driver.

Trucks roared down the mountain six days a week for the next sixteen or seventeen months, taking little time off except a day or two in the summers because of fire hazard or a few weeks in the winter when the road was impassable because of excessive rain or snow.

Hundreds of loads of logs were removed from that forest, which once covered the entire mountain. I have no official figures but in that period of time between two and three thousand loads must have passed over that road, based on the observations of our group. The trees they removed were majestic, not greatly different from the ones taken from our research area, with diameters averaging four feet at breast height and colossal trunks, straight and free of branches for at least 150 feet. In a single load, a truck might carry six such logs, the harvest from two of the monarchs of the ancient forest. We watched the forest steadily disappear from the north side of Saddleback. By the end of 1961 that barrenness had crept to the top of the mountain.

The scene along Murphy road varied. When Prof's research was under way, Miami Corporation had logged their land along the west side of the road near the highway. The Douglas-firs in that tree farm were now of good size and producing cones. Once, when we stopped to unlock and open the gate we noticed two signs. They declared, "No Cone Picking Without Permit, Miami Tree Farm." The only cone pickers we saw were sassy little pine squirrels. They paid no heed to the signs but kept right on harvesting their store of cones.

The river road, situated as it was on the north side of the mountain between Salmon River and one of its major tributaries, was quite different from Murphy road. It was at a slightly higher elevation, and a steep slope loomed above it as it wound its way in a large semicircle from Salmon River to the tributary. This part of the mountain had been logged earlier than the area nearer the highway—possibly at about the same time as the research site or perhaps even a little before that. It was much damper here and shadier. During the wetter months of the year, a short way beyond Salmon River, a small stream flowed across the road from the slope above and, during those damp periods, water often trickled, spilled, or cascaded down the mountain in other places, as well. Also, puddles and chuck holes full of water made the road somewhat hazardous.

The trees and other plants here contrasted with the ones which bordered Murphy road. They more closely resembled the vegetation of the ancient forest. From the roadway we could see a smattering of large firs, a few cedars, many hemlocks, clusters of young alders, a jumble of large and small logs and fallen trees, thickets of young conifers—hemlocks, Douglas-firs, spruces, and cedars—and remnant, towering ancient firs, standing like sentinels here and there.

When Ray, Timidity, and I visited the mountain during Thanksgiving vacation in 1959 we found the normally small stream beyond Salmon River overflowing, and a lot of mud, debris, shrubbery, and alder trees had slid down the mountainside from the slope above, blocking the road. The torrential rains, which began in early September, had now totaled more than thirty-four inches. That almost unbroken downpour had saturated the ground and a subsequent violent wind and rain storm had further loosened the soil from the underlying bedrock. The soil, having been disturbed and robbed of its spongy cover by the logging of earlier years, had lost its ability to retain the rain and, consequently, let that water rush down the mountain. Aided by earthquake-like jarring as load after load of logs plummeted down the mountainside to the Salmon River crossing nearby, gravity did the rest in producing this landslide. We worked for nearly two hours before we could move beyond the slide to continue on our way.

There were other times when uprooted alder trees partially blocked the road, and at Christmas in 1960, Howard and Frances recorded finding a broken cedar limb and several small alders in the road. That day Frances commented in her notes, "Quite a creek across road at parking area." This stream was one of the major cascades which, during rainy periods, plunged down the mountain from the steep ridge above. After many such rains, this torrent had now eroded a way into the river that we parked beside.

A new assault began on the forest ecosystem in April 1961, several months after the log-hauling over Murphy road had ceased. Two large caterpillar tractors began working just beyond the Salmon River bridge. Salvage logging had started along the river road. A log blocked our roadway, so we parked near Salmon River and hiked to the research station. When we returned later in the day, the cats were working below the road. The next week the road was clear to our usual stopping place, cat operators were busy, and logging was in full swing all along the river road. Trucks began hauling out logs by the first of June.

Much of this "salvage" was logs from windthrown trees or from the earlier logging, but a lot of it was standing trees, both ancient and young.

Whatever it was, removing all these trees and logs disturbed the life of the forest and depleted it of needed nutrients.

The salvaging went on until late in the summer. Then, with the first heavy rain, the burning of "slash" began. Debris from the logging—the limbs and tops of trees, unsalvageable logs, and old stumps—were all set on fire and left to smolder and burn. The burning continued for several more weeks. One of the stumps was still smoldering near the end of October. Though this salvage operation did not seem quite as devastating as a clear-cut, it disrupted the entire biotic community of that area and the burning destroyed untold numbers of forest floor species along with their sources of nourishment.

In late October the next year, Ray and I were surprised to find a mobile trailer parked in the middle of the river road a short way beyond the bridge, and a wire cable further obstructing the passageway. We left our car at Salmon River and started to the station afoot. Beyond the trailer, the roadway was filled for nearly a half mile with stack after stack of noble firs harvested for Christmas trees. Arranged in six rows across the road, they completely blocked the roadway. Even more of the trees lay heaped along the roadsides. Shocked, we could hardly believe our eyes. We had to go out into the brush to get by. "Tree strippers," as we were told they were called, were at work on Saddleback Mountain!

Most of the harvested trees had been hauled out by mid-December, but it was January before the strippers were gone and the river road reopened. Thousands of young trees, mostly noble firs but some Douglas-firs, were removed from the mountain that year. It was being robbed of its natural reforestation! Later on we had other chance encounters with tree strippers but nothing that compared with the 1962 harvest. Perhaps these trees would have had to go through the process of natural thinning if that stripping had not occurred. However, I cannot believe that much "thinning" was necessary!

Some of the most significant things we witnessed along these forest roads occurred after our regular weekly trips to the research site ended. They were seen entirely by chance, either by students working on individual projects or by Ray and me on one of our occasional visits to the research site.

In February 1964, Bill Good left his car near the Salmon River bridge because a cat was again operating along the river road. Several men were at work there. One of them told Bill they were getting ready to make cedar shakes from logs which had been left from the salvage operation. In making shakes, the cat operators move logs to places where they could be "bucked up" (sawed into blocks—usually eighteen or twenty-four inches long). These large blocks were then split in half or into quarters, depending upon the diameter of the log, and the smaller blocks were split into "shakes," slabs of wood about one-half inch thick and as wide as the size of the log permits. Those workmen had discovered a small gold mine, for cedar shakes, used in place of shingles, are highly prized by home builders and command a premium price.

On Bill's next trip he found five vehicles parked along the river road and noted, "Cedar cutters have messed up road just before the parking place." Several months later, all of the logs which had not been taken in the earlier salvaging were gone. These last ones had been used for shakes.

December 1964 was an extraordinarily wet month all through western Oregon and northern California. In McMinnville, 13.3 inches of rain fell that month compared with a norm of 7.6 inches. Severe cold in the middle of the month plummeted temperatures to a minimum of 9°F. This was followed by eight inches of snow and rapid warming and an additional six inches of rain on December 21-23, all of which resulted in a history-making Christmas flood throughout the Willamette Valley.

Our weekly trips had been discontinued long before this and the rain gauges had been removed, so I have no record of how much rain and snow fell on Saddleback Mountain at that time, but the roads and rivers gave mute evidence of devastating erosion and torrential flooding.

Nick Simpson was the first of our group to visit the area. In February he reported, "Salmon River bridge OK, but lots of logs and debris washed up along the banks." He also said, "Signs of beaver work right at the bridge over the river. No animals seen." And when he reached the river road, he noted that a stream, flowing down the mountainside and across the road, had eroded that roadbed down to bedrock in some places and that large boulders had rolled down into the road and trees and debris had fallen across it.

On my next trip to the mountain I was shocked at the size of the boulders which lay in both rivers and at the way erosion had changed the rivers' banks. It was obvious that tremendous force had brought about that havoc. No longer filled with overhanging ferns and shaded by maples and alders, the banks were now bare earth and rock, devoid of life, much like recently constructed canals into which huge boulders had been poured to strengthen the earthen walls. I wondered whether the flood had tugged these rocks from the banks and bottoms of the streams and hurled them along as the torrent plummeted down the mountain, or if men had hauled them in later and dumped them into the streams to help ward off further damage. With the big trees gone, much of the spongy forest floor removed, and the entire mountainside criss-crossed with gravel roads, there had been little to hold back the water and prevent erosion in the kind of weather which must have occurred that winter.

In 1961 Bill Good and Paul Danley followed the Salmon River up the mountain to the bog in Summit Prairie to study the river and the kinds of fish that were in it. They found small salmon and steelhead plentiful all the way up through the wide, relatively slow-flowing portion of the stream and on up through a narrow canyon, at the top of which the river plunges down the mountain through a series of falls. Beyond the base of the lowest falls the salmon ended. Above that point and in the small stream (the headwaters of Salmon River) which meanders through the meadow-like bog of the prairie, they found native cutthroat trout.

Because Salmon River had now been changed so much, I couldn't help wondering what had happened to the fish and to the future for fish in the river.

On one of his trips in the summer of 1969, John Kerr observed that Murphy road was being sprayed with herbicides to keep back the brush. On a later trip he learned that the old quarry above the station was to be re-opened and 80,000 cubic yards of rock taken out and a culvert was to be built in Salmon River because the bridge was too weak to support that kind of weight. Those plans for reopening the quarry indicated that more roads would soon be built on the mountain. *Why?* I wondered. *For what purpose?*

I now realized that everything that happened anywhere on the mountain had an impact on the mountain's ecosystem and affected its community of life. Logging; raiding the last pockets of ancient forest in order to salvage trees and logs; the making of cedar shakes; burning slash; gouging and scraping the forest floor; stripping young trees from the mountainsides; spraying with herbicides; building more roads; all of this was devastating. Even **our** work, to a lesser degree, was disruptive.

All these activities we had observed pointed toward the mountain's ultimate fate: *It would never again be home to a true forest but would be covered with tree farms which would be managed by humans, not by the forces of nature.*

Open area cleared by logging in 1940, as it appeared in 1960.

Part IV

Essence of the Forest

B EFORE HEAVEN AND EARTH had taken form all was vague and amorphous. Therefore, it was called the Great Beginning. The Great Beginning produced emptiness and emptiness produced the universe....The combined essences of heaven and earth became the yin and yang, the concentrated essences of yin and yang became the four seasons, and the scattered essences of the four seasons became the myriad creatures of the world.
—Huai-nan Tzu, 2nd Century BC

Whether we contemplate the whole or only some particular portion of the realm of living things...we are, indeed, obsessed by problems....It quite saddens me to think that when I cross the Styx, I may find myself among so many professional biologists, condemned to keep on trying to solve problems and that Plato, or whoever is in charge there now, may condemn me to sit forever trying to identify specimens from my own specific and generic diagnoses, while the amateur entomologists, who have not been damned professors, are permitted to roam at will among the fragrant asphodels of the Elysian meadows, netting gorgeous, ghostly butterflies until the end of time.
—"Entomologist in Hades," William Morton Wheeler
Author of *Ants: Their Structure, Development, and Behavior*

The same open area pictured on page 198, as it appeared in the 1980s, prior to clearcutting.

Chapter Twenty-two

Search for the Essence

N EARLY THIRTY YEARS had passed since I had studied the young forest. I retired from Linfield, my classroom teaching over. My husband Ray died. I left the never-quite-finished home we had loved and shared for almost forty years and moved into a retirement complex. There I began writing the story of the ancient forest, something I had never had time to do while teaching.

Prof died. Howard Daniels died. Kenny Fender died. One after another in close succession persons who had helped with the research were gone. Systematists we knew also died or retired.

The forest was gone. Not only the ancient forest on Saddleback, but also forest from nearly the whole Northwest. Less than 10 percent of the thousands of acres of primeval forest remained. Entire ranges of mountains revealed an ever-growing patchwork of clearcuts, single-species plantations, and forest fragments.

Now, in the late 1980s, I was trying to catch the essence of that magnificent forest I had known six decades before.

A forest is many things, plants, animals, weather, topography. It is people, too. All are part of it.

My immediate problem was insects.

I knew almost nothing about insects until my sophomore year at Linfield when I took a course in general zoology, learned the classification of insects, and studied the structure of a grasshopper. That was also the year I became involved in Prof's research.

He said insects were important, so we collected them, along with everything else. My personal introduction to insects was not exactly inspiring as I searched for all the creepy-crawlies I could find in samples of duff from the forest floor. Many of those bits of animal life were insects. As I learned more about them they became more interesting, but to this day I am not an entomologist.

Both Prof and I had been fairly systematic in our collecting. We amassed a lot of specimens and learned to recognize insects and other creatures which were common and some which were rare, and where and when we might find them. That in itself was quite an accomplishment. As far as I could learn no one in the entire Northwest had tackled a study which was that all-inclusive.

Our combined labors produced a list of nearly 1,400 species of insects, about 700 from the ancient forest and an equally long list from the young forest. I had their names, but I knew little about the lives of any of them.

Why, I wondered now, *had we collected all those insects? Were they really important? What roles did they play in the forest communities? What would happen to the forest if insects were not there?*

Clearly, if my questions about insects were to be answered, I must answer them myself. I now had to ferret out as much information as I could about the lives of those insects.

The millions of insects that live on the earth today have been divided into at least twenty distinct groups, but about three-fourths of them are in four groups, or orders, which are based mainly upon convenient characteristics of the wing, or "*pteron*." These orders are the Diptera, "two-winged" insects; the Hymenoptera, "membrane-winged" insects; Lepidoptera, "scaly-winged" insects; and Coleoptera, "sheath-winged" insects.

The mode of development of all four of these groups is complete metamorphosis, progressing from egg through larval and pupal stages into the adult form, which is usually a winged insect. The larva and the adult, the two active stages, almost without exception go separate ways in their life styles, living in places that are different and eating foods that are dissimilar. For instance, a larva that develops in the ground feeding on the roots of plants may become transformed into an adult that lives among herbs and feeds upon the pollen and juices of plants.

Early ecologists generally believed that insects were important in the natural communities they studied. After all, they reasoned, creatures so diverse and widely distributed as insects must fill many kinds of roles wherever they live. They discovered that insects did, indeed, often have key roles in their communities.

Ecology teaches that every kind of life has a position in its community—a role or niche—or, as I have just pointed out in the case of insects, even more than one niche because the habits of the immature and adult stages are often very different. Studying insects takes time, perseverance, and patience but the results are rewarding. However, not many people find insects particularly fascinating. As a result, the exact roles for most species are not known. As Peter Farb says in *The Insects:*

> Despite their abundance, insects are still largely an enigma, and ignorance has tended to clothe them in "wonders" and "marvels" that are not rightly theirs. Insects possess what appear to be many strange senses that are different from man's....What is remarkable is that with such crude senses the insects have survived for 300 million years the onslaughts of fellow-arthropods [and other creatures] to endure even in today's man-infested world.

I reviewed our records and field notes, reread correspondence, and searched through books, journals, and reprints, ever alert to material about the habits and life styles of our insects. Aside from what was in our field notes, pathetically little information surfaced about any of our insects except ones which were economically significant, such as wood borers. As a result, I usually had to depend not upon facts about our species, but upon sketchy information about species related to the ones we had found. Often not even that was available.

Some years ago, the Forest Service did a study in which it listed all Western forest insects reported as feeding on or "attacking" Douglas-fir trees. Beginning with the flowers, cones, and seeds in the tops of the trees, and moving downward through foliage, branches, bark, and wood, all the way to the roots, the researchers selected a total of twenty-five distinct sites in the trees. They identified 180 insect species associated with those sites, no two of which had exactly the same life style, which included such habits as leaf tying, web spinning, gall forming, needle or leaf mining, wood boring, encasing with scales, or eating the tissue of green seeds. We had a significant number of those insects. Further, we had many closely related species which were not on the Forest Service list.

We had no way to get into the crowns of the trees so our study was restricted to the insects we could reach from the ground, or from the two platforms in the trees, or the ones we could identify as we saw them flying in the crowns of the trees. Consequently, we had little more than a hint about numbers or kinds of insects in the treetops or their significance.*

Though the Forest Service study was helpful, it included only plant eaters (herbivores), the first step in a food chain. Since it did not tell anything about the other levels of consumers, the predators and decomposers. it gave an incomplete picture of the niches of insects. Moreover, because that study centered on Douglas-fir, it did not include the vast numbers of insects which have their niches with other forest vegetation: flowers, ferns, shrubs, and other trees.

Many insects prey upon the forest's plant eaters. Information about them is usually general, not explicit. I have learned that every species of plant-eating insect has insects, or spiders, or some other creatures which prey upon it and that even the smallest group of interactions may be quite involved.

In the pages that follow, I'll tell about some of the more common or more interesting insects my research companions and I met in the forest.

---

*Beginning in 1988, or thereabouts, forest ecologists in British Columbia, Washington, Oregon, and Northern California, using devices varying from simple climbing harnesses and long ropes to a 250-foot-high canopy crane in the Wind River forest near Carson, Washington, have "discovered" the canopy of our Western coniferous forest. While this work has been primarily by plant ecologists, others have found the treetop world teeming with unidentified insects and have learned that spiders and other predators make up about 40 percent of its arthropod population. Though a bit of pioneer canopy research was done in the 1970s, it was a decade or two later before the research really caught on.

Chapter Twenty-three

Mosquitoes and Their Ilk

To humans, mosquitoes are probably the most troublesome of the many kinds of dipterous insects in the forest. I recall one miserable day in early September 1936. I was with Prof and Bob Boyd, a junior who had been in the zoology class the year before. Everything was wet. Ferns and bushes were loaded with rainwater. The sky was sunless, the temperature a cool 56°F, a brisk breeze increased the chill factor, and mosquitoes were biting.

Though the little pests tormented us all day, they became really noxious late in the afternoon when we began surveying in the gully below the station. Swarms of tiny dark mosquitoes hovered around each of us, keeping up an incessant high-pitched hum. Now and then one of them would inflict a particularly painful bite.

After being the target several times, Bob exclaimed, "I'm sure glad that not all these pests are biting! But, Prof, why is it that they don't all bite?"

"Most of these are males," Prof explained. "Haven't you noticed how high-pitched their hum is? Females are the ones that bite and their voices have a lower pitch."

"Don't male mosquitoes have to eat?"

"Yes," Prof replied, seating himself on a log, obviously preparing to give a lecture, his voice lifting into its professorial tone, "but their mouth parts are different and not made for sucking blood. I understand they feed on the juices in fruits and the nectar of flowers. Females also probably feed that way most of the time, but I suspect they may need a blood meal in order to produce viable eggs." Later, when I was in graduate school, I heard an interesting account of the research that showed this to be true.

Well protected from the mosquitoes by his "tin" rain coat and clearly enjoying an excuse for a breather, while Bob and I continued to swat mosquitoes, Prof continued, "These dark little fellows with white-ringed legs have the scientific name *Aedes,* which comes from a Greek word meaning disagreeable. They're well named. They're commonly known as tree hole mosquitoes, but we haven't found any of their breeding places yet.

"Mosquitoes have been unusually bad this summer. Maybe the cool spring weather and rains that lasted into June were to blame. Now this early fall rain seems to have pepped them up."

"You told us in zoology that only one kind of mosquito carries malaria," I said. "Are there any of them up here?"

"Yes, we've collected a few. Their name's *Anopheles.* They're medium-sized and blackish with black-blotched wings. However, you don't have to worry about getting malaria from them unless the one biting you has bitten someone who has malaria. Do you remember what I told you about how to recognize an anopheline mosquito?"

"I think it was something about their standing on their head when they bite, wasn't it?"

Laughing, Prof said, "That's about it. When they bite, they stand so that their bodies form a triangle between themselves and their host. Other mosquitoes hold their bodies parallel to the surface. Even the different kinds of larvae can be distinguished by positions they assume when resting under water. Anopheline larvae rest horizontally while those of other species take an oblique position."

Not really eager to return to surveying, I asked, "Have you found out what those large dark mosquitoes we collected last spring are called? The ones with spotted wings?"

"Yes, they're *Theobaldia.* A mosquito man said they breed all year long and their larvae, which have frozen in sheets of ice, may yet live to produce normal adults. He said they don't attack people but prefer larger mammals; for instance, if a man is riding horseback, they will bite the horse, not the man. But we've had them bite us. Perhaps that was because there were no horses or deer nearby. They don't seem to bother much, though. Not like these little *Aedes.*

Then, chuckling at something he remembered, he continued, "We're fortunate that only *Aedes* are around today. You should've been here last week when Dorothy McKey was along. Mosquitoes were thick—biting, and mating. We collected a bunch of them, at least three species and there may have been four. For some reason they bit her more than anyone else. She really had a time—swatting right and left.

"When I accused her of killing scientific specimens, she retorted, 'I don't care if they are scientific specimens, when they bite *me* they're gonna git mashed.'

"I'll have to admit I was doing some swatting myself."

Then, rising from his seat on the log, he said, "We'd better get back to work now before it's so dark we can't see what we're doing."

When all the evidence was in and analyzed, we realized that our forest was predominately a dipterous community. It had in it more "two-winged" insects than any other kind. Dipterans ranked highest in number of families, number of species, and number of individuals, and also, quite possibly, in the greatest variety of roles, for their diversity was astounding. I cannot even guess how many species there were, probably thousands. Though more than 500 species were identified, entire families in our collections were untouched for lack of specialists. The systematists who did work on our Diptera told us that many of them were new to science, and unnamed.

We learned to expect many kinds of bloodsucking and biting flies and gnats to descend on us at fairly predictable times throughout the year.

Mosquitoes were there whenever the woods were damp and warm enough for insects to be active. *Aedes* were particularly bad on cloudy, humid days. *Theobaldia* might be around even when the weather was surprisingly cool, and other mosquitoes were there at other times.

Gnats known as midges and punkies were among the tiniest insects we encountered. Punkies are the infamous "no-see-ums" that almost anyone who has spent time camping or fishing in Northwestern forests has encountered. These tiny black or brown insects tormented us from May to early September but were most persistent on dull hot summer days, the "dog days" of June and July. Then they seemed to materialize out of nowhere to inflict their stinging bites. While rubbing the smarting wounds from these invisible tormentors, we were prone to grumble, "No-*see*-um but sure-*feel*-um." Their bite, one author says, "is all out of proportion to their size." They are so tiny that it was almost impossible for us to see the source of our distress.

Black flies, small, humpbacked gnats with short legs and broad wings, did their bloodletting during the warm, damp days of spring and early summer—and sometimes again in early fall when rains produced the right conditions. Though properly known as black flies, some of our species were yellow. They were larger than the no-see-ums and had stouter bodies with heads pointed down because of their humped backs. They were truly pestiferous but weren't necessarily interested in us; they were searching for a blood meal and we happened to come by instead of a deer or other mammal.

Bloodsucking snipe flies came on the scene in June and were with us through July and August, sometimes even later. Robust, long-legged flies, with bodies about the size of a large grain of rice or wheat, some velvety black, others gray, these incessant biters clustered around our faces, clinging to us at the edges of our hats, inflicting painful bites as they sucked our blood. Fortunately, not all snipe flies were bloodsucking; some preyed on insects. To us, those species were socially far more acceptable than the biting ones!

Inch-long, dark, broadbeamed tabanids, known as horse flies, dive-bombed us on clear, warm days from June through August. They have huge eyes and a wingspread of two inches or more. During the same season, deer flies, slightly smaller tabanids, got in our hair and bothered us even more than the horse flies.

Deer flies are pretty insects, with dark bodies, pictured wings with dark markings, and incredibly beautiful eyes. I had seen compound eyes of other insects but was unprepared for the captivating beauty of the eyes of a female deer fly viewed under a microscope: a brilliant golden-green mosaic of thousands of miniature six-sided facets with rainbow-hued zigzag stripes running through them. But as I watched, the eyes lost their fascination—the colors faded and the eyes became plain, colorless, compound eyes much like those of any other fly. I do not know whether that was due to death, or to time.

On hot summer days, we could expect both kinds of tabanids to hang around, pestering us from our arrival until dusk. Tabanids are notorious as the worst biting and bloodsucking pests of cattle, deer, horses, and other mammals, and in the years of the study of the young forest, often three or four of them at a time were plaguing and biting Timidity. We humans were suspicious of their intentions though I don't recall that they ever bit any of us.

The idea that these noxious pests could be useful to the forest community seemed almost absurd to me at first, but other experiences challenged me to learn more about them. I knew that the complex life cycles of insects made it possible for them to fit into several niches or roles.

Since the adult insects were present in the forest, the immature forms had to be there somewhere. Our study area teemed with larvae and pupae. They were in the duff. They were in the upper part of the moist soil beneath the duff. They were under the bark of recently fallen logs and in the spongy remains of ancient much-decayed logs. Every moist spot—and these were countless—was a potential home for larvae. As well, of course, as every kind of vegetation for the larvae which were plant eaters.

Often as we searched through the duff, we found maggots of assorted sizes, sometimes several in a single sample, and we recognized them as the larvae of flies or gnats. But we had no hint as to what kind of fly or gnat these maggots would be after metamorphosis or what their interrelationships were in the forest community.

Now, a half-century later, bits of information from scattered sources give a fragmentary picture.

Though these insects are often referred to as "biting" flies, actually they should be called "piercing," for they are unable to bite. Their mouth parts are modified into needle-like stylets that pierce the flesh of the host, and they siphon or suck blood from the wound. For mosquitoes, and probably for most of the others, the mouth parts are fully developed only in the female, and she alone possesses the blood-feeding habit.

Adults, both males and females, feed chiefly on the nectar or juices— and possibly pollen—of flowers. Apparently, for egg production, females of all biting and bloodsucking species must have a blood meal—which she gets from some forest bird or mammal or a transient human. Males, however, apparently live chiefly on nectar which has a high sugar content. Females also need sugar to sustain their extremely active lives, so probably both sexes visit flowers for nectar or feed upon other liquids oozing from plants. One authority says it is likely that wild hosts, especially birds, are the most impor- tant source of food for no-see-ums, but some of these tiny gnats are known to suck blood and body fluids from other insects.

Though we did not find larvae of the tree hole mosquito *Aedes* during Prof's study, after the research area was logged, students and I did find them in water-filled holes in the tops of some stumps. These larvae, known as wrigglers, feed on algae, minute particles of decaying materials, or on very small aquatic animals, even other mosquito larvae. They, in turn, are food for many aquatic insects and fish.

Larvae of both tabanids and snipe flies live in rotting logs and stumps, in damp decaying litter, or in wet soil. Tabanid larvae prey on soft-bodied invertebrates, such as snails and larvae of other insects. Some are cannibalis- tic. Snipe fly larvae eat minute insects and other small animals.

Many of the tiniest maggots we found while searching through duff, moist soil, or rotten wood could have been no-see-um larvae. They feed on newly hatched larvae of mosquitoes and other small insects, bits of decayed organic matter, or dead insects.

The black flies which troubled us probably had spent their early lives anchored to stones or other objects in the little stream below the station or in some other stream where tiny aquatic animals and algae provided food for them.

Though bloodsucking insects absorbed a lot of our attention when they were active, they actually made up only a minor portion of the forest's dipterous population. The forest was also an ideal environment for a great host of other gnats and flies.

There were thousands of long-legged, slow-flying, gauzy-winged insects called crane flies by some early naturalist who imagined that they resembled cranes. The larger ones, especially, attracted our attention as they flew around unhurriedly before finally settling on a fern frond, herb, or hemlock bough. Some of these big ones were about an inch long and had a wing span of two inches or more. Others, specifically the ones known as winter crane flies, were small, gnat-like, and very inconspicuous. All were fragile and we had trouble keeping them intact when we caught them. In spite of problems, we collected many kinds of crane flies.

A crane fly about three inches across is the largest native fly in North America. We did not find any of them on Saddleback, though they are seen frequently in McMinnville. An even larger fly is the European crane fly which has a "body-spread" of about five inches. It is a recent arrival in the Northwest and has become a terrible pest because its larvae chew away the roots of grasses, leaving lawns decorated with large round spots of brownish dead grass.

Sometimes we watched our largest crane flies depositing eggs in the ground of the research area and later found batches of inch-long larvae in the humus. We judged that those larvae fed on fungi or decaying plants. Worldwide, crane fly larvae are found in places where there is much decaying vegetation, and it is generally assumed that they have an important role in the recycling of woody materials. Some of the adults are said to feed on flowers.

In those days of our youth and innocence, we were so busy trying to learn what kinds of insects and other creatures lived in the ancient forest that it never occurred to us that perhaps no one knew *why* they were there. When Dr. C.P. Alexander and his wife, dear friends of Kenny and Dorothy Fender and the leading authority on crane flies, visited Prof while on a collecting trip, we were surprised to learn that even he was interested only in finding new species, not in their habits, the reason being that the thousands of species needing description worldwide gave him no time for biological work.

(Dr. Alexander named one of the Saddleback crane flies *Cladura (Cladura) macnabi* in honor of Prof.) Learning that the crane fly family has more species in it than any other family of Diptera makes me wonder why so little is known about them.

Fungus gnats, small gauzy-winged insects, often no longer than a sesame seed, seemed to be everywhere and with us always. Usually even in the winter months we could find some in the shelter of conifer boughs. They look much like mosquitoes, but fly rather quickly and are so delicate that many of those we collected lost legs or had their wings rumpled. Fungus gnats come in a variety of subdued body colors—gray, brown, tan, black, or rusty orange. Some have yellow legs.

The family names of fungus gnats, Mycetophilidae (*fungus lovers*, from Greek), and Fungivoridae (*fungus eaters*, from Latin), tell much about the habits of these insects, for we always found them near some kind of fungus, upon which they feed and where many species lay their eggs. Certain fungus gnats deposit their eggs in decaying wood and their larvae feed on the fungi growing on the wood; others lay eggs in damp soil where their larvae feed on fungi that are breaking down the tissues of dead plants; and still others feed upon mushrooms and lay their eggs on them.

The forest was also home to numerous species of tiny midges. Fragile and slender, many are no longer than the width of the lead in a pencil, others possibly twice that size. Though they look a bit like mosquitoes, midges do not bite, and they have the interesting habit of keeping their front legs raised and vibrating when they're at rest. Most midges, both larvae and adults, are scavengers, feeding in all sorts of places on decaying plant and animal matter. The larvae of many midge species are aquatic, and adult midges may be seen dancing above the water in immense swarms in early spring or in the autumn.

The diversity of Diptera was a constant surprise. One day in the '30s I met for the first time one of the most interesting and bizarre dipterans we discovered in our research. On our way to the station an assistant shot a little California pygmy owl. As we picked it up from the ground, several tiny flies fluttered about on it, obviously trying to find their way back under the bird's feathers. Each fly had a pancake-flat, leathery thorax, and a pair of miniature wings. They looked like nothing I had seen or heard of before.

Called featherflies, flatflies, louseflies, kedflies, or by some other names, they are known scientifically as Hippoboscidae, a name derived from the Greek: *hippos* for horse, and *boskein* to feed, in reference to an Old World species which feeds on the blood of horses. The adults of these flies have highly specialized mouth parts for sucking blood, and live permanently as parasites on the bodies of their hosts, some on birds, others on mammals.

Birdflies often carry hitchhiker insect parasites on the outside of their bodies, featherlice which feed on the bird's feathers. This pygmy owl was host to a number of such lice.

Years later when my assistants and I were studying the young forest, we captured another kind of hippoboscid in a sweepnet. Before that time I thought hippoboscids were never found anywhere except on a bird or mammal. These were deer keds—small flies, varying from about an eighth to a quarter inch long, flat, and dark with bristly black hairs, thick legs, and beaded antennae. They held their tiny wings above their abdomen.

Female deer keds do not lay eggs but carry the developing young inside their body, nourishing them with their bodily secretions until the larvae are fully-formed. She then drops the larvae, at that stage known as puparia, from her body into the vegetation. Winged adults hatch from these puparia and fly about searching for a deer. When a fly finds a deer, it attaches itself to the deer, sheds its wings, and spends the rest of its life feeding upon blood among the hairs of the deer. Dr. Joseph Bequaert, who identified our deer keds, said that at the season for hatching, the flies often swarm on low vegetation in such great numbers that they may light on any moving object, including people.

The flies of the forest varied from bizarre to beautiful. Brightly colored syrphids, also called flower flies or hover flies, are among the more attractive ones. Though rather small, no more than a half inch long, their mix of colors—metallic blue, blue-black, bronze, or green paired with bright yellow and brown stripes on the abdomen—more than compensates for any deficiency in size. Many with striped abdomens are near-perfect mimics of certain wasps.

Syrphids are remarkably quick in flight. I have often seen one poised above a patch of flowers in a sunny spot, hanging motionless, or darting without warning to a new place, there to resume hovering. I enjoy watching their aerial acrobatics. The hovering behavior may be a courtship display to attract a mate. They are important pollinators, visiting an even greater variety of plants than honey bees do. We collected many kinds of syrphids as they fed on nectar or rested on a sun-warmed blossom. Their active larvae specialize in hunting aphids and scale insects.

Hovering is rather common among flies. Dance flies, empidids, are named for their mating swarms and dances, which vary in pattern from species to species. We often saw swarms of these small, dark flies—a female surrounded by a swarm of males—dancing up and down in sunny spots in late afternoons or early evenings of spring and summer. Both sexes prey on small insects. Their larvae live in the soil, in decaying wood or other vegetable matter, or in water, and are believed to be predators or scavengers.

Big-headed flies, small-headed flies, long-legged flies, humpbacked flies, flat-footed flies, robber flies, and others live in the forest, each with its special niche, or role, in the community. Big-headed flies are an important natural control of leafhoppers.

A female big-headed fly seeing a leafhopper on a plant, grabs it, and while hovering in the air lays her eggs on it, and then drops it. Larvae hatch from the eggs, bore their way inside the leafhopper and feed on the parasitized insect until they are full grown. Then they exit from the carcass.

Robber flies are predators on all sorts of flying insects. Because they capture their prey on the wing, pierce the insect with their stout beaks, and then drain it dry, they are often called assassin flies. Their larvae live in the soil or in wood and, so far as is known, prey mostly on the larvae or pupae of beetles.

We found a surprising array of flies related to the common house fly. They are small to medium in size, some shade of gray or brown, yellowish or black, with plain wings and are called muscids for *Musca*, the Latin name of the house fly. Many are pollinators. Some of ours were closely related to species that have killed nursery Douglas-fir seedlings or to ones that destroy the seeds of hemlocks and true firs by boring into cones and feeding on the seeds. Certain muscids are predators that attack other flies, and some, like the house fly, are attracted to decaying plants for their food, or to dung or dead and decaying animal matter. There they lay their eggs and the larvae develop and feed. Muscids are very important as part of the clean-up crew in the forest.

Blow flies, too, are part of the forest's recycling squad. Their specialty is the removal of carrion and, as we learned from John Kerr's study with piglets in the young forest in the summer of 1969, they accomplish their tasks in remarkably short time.

Rather spiny flies resembling house flies, are known as tachinids, a name meaning "fast moving," which suits them well for they seem always to be in a hurry. They are robust, fairly large flies and are easily recognized as they walk rapidly over the ground or foliage or fly swiftly about. The adults visit flowers and feed on nectar and honeydew secreted by aphids and other insects. The larvae, however, are parasites which live inside the bodies of plant-attacking insects such as the western hemlock looper. Since these tachinid larvae are known to be important natural controls of insect pests of forest trees some of them are being used in biological control efforts.

In the forest these dipterous insects had an ideal physical environment in all seasons, with moderate temperature, adequate moisture, and shelter from strong winds and bright light. They also had an abundance of food: mosses, ferns, herbs, shrubs, and conifers of all ages, for the plant eaters; a vast array of large and small creatures for the parasites, predators, and flesh-eating scavengers; and an inexhaustible supply of fungi and decaying plant materials for the decomposers.

Diptera hold a prime position in the forest's recycling endeavors: blow flies are scavengers of carrion; muscids feed on decaying fruit; various species feed on dung or other decaying materials; and crane flies and fungus gnats specialize in mushrooms and wood-fungi, furthering the decomposition that other agents have begun. Some dipterans are important biological control agents as parasites and predators; and as pollinators they rank very high—either second or third among the major groups of insects. The involvement of these two-winged insects in the life of the forest would be difficult, if not impossible, to list in detail.

Chapter Twenty-four
Wasp-waisted Beauties

S OME OF THE MOST beautiful and interesting insects of the forests are slender-waisted wasps, bees, and ants, and their less common relatives, sawflies and horntails. These wasp waists are formed by one or two of the first abdominal segments of the insect's body being squeezed into a tiny stalk between the thorax and abdomen. This slender waist is most common in wasps, but bees and ants also have a slight constriction. Sawflies and horntails do not have wasp waists.

These insects are known as Hymenoptera. Their two pairs of wings are membranous, clear, and transparent. A row of tiny hooks on the hindwing, the smaller wing, clasps the forewing and holds the two together, almost as a single wing. This causes some hymenopterans to be mistaken for flies.

As we worked with the insects on Saddleback, we discovered that the order Hymenoptera (meaning *membrane wing*) ranked second in diversity in our forest and that much of this diversity was due to the presence of multitudes of minute parasitic wasps.

The story of such a wasp, told in the Portland newspaper *The Oregonian* a few years ago, caught my eye. This wasp, named *Epidinocarsis lopezi* and described as being "no larger than a comma...and too small to have been given a common name," had rescued millions of Africans from starvation.

That story unfolded from 1970 when a South American cassava plant infected with mealybugs—a kind of scale insect—was illegally taken into Africa. The dot-sized mealybugs reproduced so rapidly that they spread an estimated 100 miles a year, wiping out the major food source for millions of African people as they spread. Toxic sprays proved ineffective or too costly. With no native parasitic wasp or other insect in Africa to control it, the mealybug population exploded. With human starvation imminent, an international crisis had developed.

To avert a continental disaster, scientists of the International Institute of Tropical Agriculture decided to search the world for mealybug resistant cassavas. In desperation, they also gave some financial support to a young scientist who had a plan: find the mealybug's natural enemy, bring it to Africa, breed millions of the insects, and release them in affected areas. He began searching South America for the mealybug and its natural enemies. He found two tiny wasps, one of which was *E. lopezi*, which soon proved itself to be an effective biological control of the cassava mealybug, which by that time had spread into thirty countries, covering an area one-and-a-half times the size of the United States.

Before long the young scientist and his helpers set out, tiny wasp in hand, trailing the mealybug across Africa and dropping in affected areas all along the way 100 wasps per second from a plane flying 200 miles per hour. Soon that tiny parasitic wasp had saved the food supply for millions of people.

While we do not have any experiences to relate about parasitic wasps which are as dramatic as the story of *E. lopezi,* stories are hidden away in our forest. Parasitic wasps are such effective biological controls that one author calls them "specialists in population regulation." These wasps are constantly at work at that specialty. However, there are so many of them whose lives have never been studied that no one has even a hint of their full impact. These parasitic wasps are the unrivaled masters of the art of insect parasitism. I tend to think of them as the detective force of the forest which sleuths out troublemakers and brings them to terms.

I did not become aware of the great diversity of these wasps in our forest until late in our research. Near the end of the warm summer season we often brought from the study site a dozen or so kinds of wasps in assorted sizes, shapes, and descriptions. Most of them were very small and fascinating when viewed under a microscope, but they were a task to sort and even harder to classify.

Over the eons of time, parasitic wasps have become very different from their larger relatives, yellowjackets, hornets, bees, and ants, which are social insects and fashion homes for their young. Parasitic wasps lead solitary lives and never make homes for their young. These wasps encroach upon other insects for the welfare of their young by laying eggs inside or outside the body of an immature stage of their chosen host.

These guardians of the forest ecosystem come mostly in three large groups: ichneumons, braconids, and chalcids. A few of the ichneumons are comparative giants, while chalcids are the tiniest of all insects. *E. lopezi* is a chalcid.

Ichneumons, with thousands of species, are one of the largest families of insects. We had nearly ninety species named from the hundreds of ichneumons we collected from the two studies on Saddleback. Many others were new to science. Ichneumons vary in length from a few hundredths to about three-fourths of an inch and are slender, graceful, dark-colored insects with long antennae and transparent wings. Females are much larger than males and usually have a thread-like ovipositor that is often even longer than the insect's body. This ovipositor arises in front of the tip of the abdomen and is permanently pushed out, unlike the ovipositors of stinging wasps which issue from the tip of the abdomen and are withdrawn into the abdomen when not in use.

Adult ichneumons feed principally on nectar and the pollen of flowers or on honeydew and liquids that ooze from plants, as do many other hymenopterans. Some ichneumons, as well as other female parasitic wasps, require extra protein for the continued production of eggs. For this they suck up blood that oozes from the wound made by their ovipositor. Some wasps even puncture host insects solely for the purpose of feeding on their body juices.

When her eggs are mature, a female ichneumon finds a larva or pupa of her host insect, stings it with her ovipositor to paralyze or kill it, and deposits one egg—or many eggs, according to her species—in or on the host. Soon the eggs hatch and the wasp larvae feed on the immature insect, grow, and pass into the pupal stage within the cocoon that they weave either inside or outside of the cocoon of their host. During the time the immature wasps are inside their cocoon, their bodies are gradually transformed, and they finally emerge as adult ichneumons.

Details of the lives of most ichneumons are unknown. Sadly, I could find no precise information about any of the nearly ninety named species found.

Braconids, close relatives of the ichneumons, are similar in appearance and in many of their habits, though, in general, they are shorter and more stout-bodied, less strikingly wasp waisted, and have shorter ovipositors. Most of our braconids were small black wasps—rarely a half-inch long—with reddish or yellow legs. Braconids multiply very rapidly. The life cycle of many of them is short and they often have several generations, or broods, in one year. Also, some braconids produce an amazing number of eggs—as many as 2,000 from a single female.

Braconid larvae may feed internally or externally. Where feeding is external, the female usually paralyzes the host before ovipositing, keeping it from moving away from the egg before the larva hatches. Unlike ichneumons, many braconids pupate in silken cocoons on the outside of the body of the host. Others spin cocoons, often in a mass, near the host. Some hang their cocoons by a slender thread on a leaf or twig.

We collected lots of braconids in each of the forest communities and from that group specialists named more than sixty. But apparently nothing definite is known about the life histories of any except the *Meteorus* Bill Good obtained in his thicket lotus studies.

Chalcids, our third major group of parasitic wasps, are so widespread that they can be found almost anywhere. But most of them, being no more than a hundredth of an inch long, are so tiny that they are overlooked. Most chalcids are dark-colored, many are metallic blue or green, and a few, such as the golden chalcid, are yellow.

The name chalcid is used for a large group of species in a roster of many categories. They share a few distinctive characteristics but differ in so many ways that their classification is still chaotic. Most of our chalcids were so poorly known that they were incompletely identified. One systematist at the US National Museum commented that the American species in a certain subfamily of chalcids (referring to some we had sent) "are not classified even generically." Regrettably, the identification of one of our chalcids as a primary parasite of larvae and pupae of the green lacewing is the only specific information we have about the life habits of the myriad chalcids identified from our collections.

Typically chalcids have two pairs of clear wings which contain a distinctive pattern of veins but some have only tiny remnants of wings and others are wingless. Some chalcids have microscopic hairs on their wings, while the wings of fairyflies, the smallest of all known insects and less than 1/100th inch in size, are heavily fringed and lack veins.

The body shape of chalcids varies from long and linear, to short and stubby. Some are humpbacked, others have top-shaped abdomens, or abdomens triangular in cross section. The hind femurs of certain ones are greatly enlarged for jumping. A few chalcids are indescribably grotesque.

Most chalcids have several to numerous broods of huge numbers of individuals in a single season. Polyembryony, the production of ten to more than a thousand young from a single egg laid in the developing larva in a host's egg, is another interesting chalcid phenomenon.

Adult chalcids feed mostly on juices that exude from plants and on honeydew excreted by host insects. Females may also supplement their plant foods with the body fluids that ooze from the wounds made when they insert their ovipositors into the host insects. Certain chalcids puncture the host solely for feeding, and sometimes, when the host is out of reach of the adult parasite (as inside a seed, pod, or leaf roll), the wasp uses her ovipositor as a mold around which she secretes a viscous fluid that hardens, forming a tube in which the host's body fluid rises to a level where the chalcid can suck it up.

Numerous chalcids are egg parasites. Some attack insects which are parasites on other parasitic insects, sometimes even members of their own species. Others are primary parasites on the larvae or pupae of aphids, scale insects, mealybugs, whiteflies, true bugs, butterflies, moths, beetles, lacewings, and many other insects. A few attack gall insects or feed on seeds. One study lists ninety-seven hosts for a single chalcid species.

Big white-faced hornets were the largest wasps in our forest. The second in size were their short-tempered, yellowjacket cousins. All of these wasps are social insects, living in small colonies of three castes—queens, workers, and drones. Queens start the colony, but after the first brood of young workers is reared, the queens do nothing but produce eggs, while workers tend the queen, feed and care for the larvae, and do all the other housekeeping. Queens and workers are females. Drones, the males, contribute nothing to the colony except sperm to produce new queens at the proper time. Wasp colonies last only one season in our forests. In the fall young queens, fertilized by the drones, leave the nest and seek shelter in some protected place where they hibernate through the winter. All other members of the colony die as the weather grows colder.

Hornet queens who survive the winter begin a colony in the spring, fashioning their nests of pulp from chewed up wood or other plant material. These cone-shaped nests, made of many layers of hexagonal paper cells enclosed in a papery envelope, are often a foot or more in diameter, and being conspicuously placed, are usually easily avoided. Yellowjacket nests are a different matter. Smaller and usually underground, they are veritable traps. A person innocently blundering into one them (as some of us did now and then), can stir up the wrath of the whole colony.

Adults of all these large wasps feed mainly on nectar and ripe fruit but they are also predators, capturing all kinds of insects and chewing them partially before offering the fragments as food to the larvae. Adult wasps and larvae get most of their protein from bits of this food.

Few kinds of ants lived on Saddleback, besides the industrious, hard-biting, giant carpenter ants.* Though the carpenter ants we saw worked mostly on logs and stumps, they are also known to mine in the base of damaged standing trees or gnaw or girdle young conifers just above the roots while tending honeydew-producing aphids in the trees' canopies.

The other ants were smaller, dark reddish-brown members of several species. They were in all sorts of places—on bracken, on the leaves of berry canes and other shrubs, on herbaceous plants, on the boughs of conifers, in humus and soil samples, and in rotten wood—but because the ones we saw were workers, we did not observe nuptial flights or learn habits of the ants or where they lived. We learned a bit more about these small ants in the young forest where they were more conspicuous.

We found only three kinds of bees in the ancient forest, two species of bumble bees and a "short-tongued" solitary wild bee. Bees need flowers for food and some bees also require flowers as sites for mating or sleeping. But flowers were scarce among those mammoth trees and many of those which were there had long corollas through which only long tongues, such as the tongues of bumble bees or moths could reach.

The nutritional needs of adult bees are different from the needs of the larvae. Adults need energy. They feed chiefly on nectar, which is high in carbohydrates, and eat only a small amount of pollen, which is rich in protein. Larvae need food for growth. They are fed chiefly pollen mixed with a small amount of nectar.

Like honey bees and some wasps, bumble bees are social insects, with similar castes, but they do not have large colonies, usually about 200 individuals. The colonies break up in the fall with all of the bees perishing except the young queens which hibernate through the winter in a hollow tree or in some other shelter. In the spring each surviving queen starts a new colony, often in the ground.

The solitary wild bees nest in the soil and are considered to be beneficial, probably as pollinators.

Sawflies and horntails are the hymenopterans that do not have wasp waists. Each of these groups is named for the distinctive structure of its ovipositors, those of female sawflies being made up of two saw-like blades enclosed in two outer plates that act as guides for cutting and inserting

---

*Described in Chapter 28.

eggs into plant tissues, while those of horntails are long and sheathed for inserting eggs in wood, often an inch or more deep.

Sawflies are rather handsome, robust, smallish, wasp-like insects. We often saw them in sunny spots in the forest, resting on the broad leaves of a thimbleberry or salmonberry. Many had shiny black bodies and yellow or orange legs. An especially attractive one, *Tenthredo magnifica* (no common name), was a rich green with an orange-tipped abdomen and black eyes.

Sawfly larvae usually have dark heads and are some shade of green, dotted with white tubercles. A few secrete a covering of slime and look like little slugs. Most of them resemble butterfly caterpillars and, when feeding on a leaf, almost always have the posterior end of their long, cylindrical body coiled over the edge of the leaf. They are noted for waving back and forth together. All are free-living larvae, feeding on plants, forming galls, spinning webs, or mining or rolling leaves. The principal hosts for sawfly larvae are broad-leaved plants, including trees and shrubs. Gregarious sawflies occur in large, compact colonies, which oftentimes strip a tree branch of its leaves. Only a few feed on conifers.

Of the ten kinds of sawflies we collected in the ancient forest, at least two had not been named previously. Apparently little is known about the habits of Western sawflies.

We found only one species of horntail, the slender, dark metallic-blue, polished horntail which is about three-fourths of an inch long and has red or yellow legs. Its cylindrical larvae are yellowish white and, in profile, resemble a shallow letter "S." They are wood borers, mining out extensive galleries within the wood and packing them with fine wood dust. After the larvae complete their development, which may take more than one season, they construct pupal cells near the surface of the wood. Then, when they become adults, they bore round, emergence holes to the surface and escape. These horntails attack only dead or damaged conifers. We found them around ancient Douglas-firs which the wind had toppled over, but no horntails were seen in the young forest.

Hymenopterans, as a group, rank high among the most beneficial insects of the entire natural world.

Collecting insects from a sweep net during the National Science Foundation study.

Chapter Twenty-five
Insects in Armor

THIS IS ABOUT BEETLES. In the scientific world beetles are known as Coleoptera, sheath-winged insects, from the Greek words *coleo*, for sheath, and *pteron*, for wing, since they have hard and brittle or thick and leathery front wings that serve as a sheath to protect the thin, soft hind wings. Because of these protective sheaths, I tend to think of beetles as "insects in armor" or as "hard shelled insects." When they are not using their wings, most beetles fold the longer hindwings under this sheath, called the *elytra*, and then, for flight, they lift the elytra to their sides. Not all beetles are winged, however, and sometimes the elytra are even fused.

Worldwide, the number of beetle species is thought to exceed that of the three other major insect groups added together. On Saddleback, though, beetles were third. Still, with more than 200 species, we had lots of interesting ones to work with and learned a whole new lexicon of names and descriptive terms from these sheath-winged wonders.

People in ancient times were familiar with many of the beetles we know today, as shown by carvings, paintings, and manuscripts. An Egyptian hieroglyph dating earlier than 2100 BC depicted a scarab, a dung beetle. That specific beetle was a tumblebug which rolled up and buried a large ball of dung upon which the female had laid an egg. From that buried ball (with its egg) a new beetle emerged.

A mystical symbolism evolved from this rebirth. The Egyptians apparently equated the daily rebirth of the sun with that ball of dung. The scarab also became a symbol for them of the enduring human soul, for they placed dead scarabs in tombs with their dead, painted scarab pictures on their limestone coffins, and carved scarab images in stone and on precious gems.

Egyptians also adopted the belief that all of their sacred scarabs were males. To them, a race of males symbolized a race of warriors. Roman soldiers later picked up that superstition and wore rings bearing images of the scarab. Romans gave the beetle the name *scarabaeus.*

Two kinds of scarab beetles lived on Saddleback. One of them was a dung beetle, though not a tumblebug. By comparison with the remarkable Egyptian tumblebug, the habits of our little black dung beetles are dull and ordinary, but very important to the forest community. These beetles are attracted to the moist, soft excrement of bears, or of deer that have been browsing on fresh green foliage. Adult beetles come together in large numbers at the dung, feed around its edges, and mate. The females then deposit their eggs in the dung, which serves as the food supply for the developing larvae.

The other scarab is known as a June beetle, for these husky brown beetles with chalky white stripes are frequently attracted to street lights in large numbers on warm summer nights here in the Northwest. Larvae of June beetles chew into the roots of shrubs and trees (including conifers) and are sometimes very destructive.

In the first century AD, the Roman naturalist Pliny the Elder wrote about a beetle, *lucanus,* the males of which have large, heavy, branched jaws (mandibles). These beetles intrigued English naturalists. They called them stag beetles because, to them, the jaws resembled the horn of the stag of their red deer. Today, stag beetles are known scientifically as *Lucanidae,* from Pliny's reference to them.

After Dorothy and Kenny were married, Dorothy worked with Kenny in studying beetles. In one of their projects they began with the beaches, bogs, and forests at the coast and investigated sites all the way across the Coast Range, Willamette Valley, Cascade Range, and on to the extreme eastern part of the state. Stag beetles were one of Dorothy's special interests. She found them in many of the places they visited and in 1945 published a paper on her findings.

Stag beetles are rather flat, rectangular insects with a slightly convex back. While the jaws of the males of nearly all species of these beetles are enlarged and long, the jaws of some are elaborately branched and toothed and may be as long as the beetle itself.

Dorothy collected three kinds of stag beetle in the forest on Saddleback. The most common one, *Platycerus aeneus,* was shiny copper colored and a little over a half-inch long. A second, rarer one, *P. laticollis,* was about the same length but broader and dark brown, while the third, *Ceruchus striatus,* was an intense black, had the most massive mandibles and robust form and, at three-fourths inch, was the largest of the three. She found these beetles on boughs of conifers and on the leaves of shrubs such as salal and huckleberry. Stag beetle larvae were in rotten logs or in samples of duff which contained fragments of wood.

One day in the early years of Prof's study, Kenny was searching through the duff of the forest floor when he came across a beetle larva that glowed with a cold phosphorescent light. He recognized that long, flat, black grub as a glowworm, the larva of a firefly. He knew that the ancient Greeks had called the glowworm *lampyridos*, which scientists later modified into Lampyridae and used as the name for members of the firefly family of beetles. Kenny even then was fast becoming an authority in the identification of beetles and was Prof's indispensable helper with insects. He often turned up something new and interesting.

The fireflies of our Western forests do not have the "tail lights" for which the family is named and which distinguish many of the ones that live in the Eastern part of the country. Instead, in the West, females of many firefly species do not develop wings but, like glowworm larvae, retain a larva-like form, are phosphorescent, and live in the forest floor.

Adults of the glowworm Kenny found are rather flat black beetles, about three-quarters of an inch long. Their bodies are soft and the top of the front part of the body extends so far forward that it hides most of the beetle's head. Bright red "parentheses marks" on the sides of its long thorax make this beetle species easy to recognize. The adults were with us all the time from May through October, on the wing, or resting on conifers or other vegetation. Both the adults and the larvae of this beetle feed on smaller insects, but on different species and in different places.

Kenny continued to study beetles and gained international recognition as an authority on soldier beetles, whose family name, just as that of so many beetles, was derived from a name used for a beetle in the days of ancient Greece and Rome.

Soldier beetles (Cantharidae), closely related to fireflies, resemble them in many ways. A distinctive difference, though, is that the heads of soldier beetles are clearly visible, not hidden as they are in the firefly and, projecting forward from beneath the thorax, give to the insect a square-shouldered, military appearance, hence the name "soldier beetle."

Our soldier beetles were small and slender, with pliable, leather-like wing covers—the reason they are also known as leather-winged beetles. They have long antennae and bulging eyes. Our most common soldier beetles were black, others lighter. We saw these beetles so often on flowers that I thought of them as "flower beetles," though they were obviously hunters, seeking out aphids and other small insects, rather than feeding on pollen or nectar as true flower beetles do. Larval soldier beetles are predators.

Net-winged beetles are only distantly akin to fireflies though they have a similar general appearance and visit plants and hunt small insects, just as soldier beetles do. When I first learned to recognize one net-winged beetle, it bore the name of *Eros simplicipes*—*Eros*, for the God of Love in Greek mythology.

Eros simplicipes was a stunning little creature: scarlet above, black below, with the sculpture of its wings arranged in a netlike pattern. When at rest, it held those wings like a fan over its flattened body. Its name intrigued me. I wondered why anyone would assign the name *Eros* to an insect, even one as strikingly attractive as this. In recent years the beetle's name has been changed to *Dictyopterus* because someone discovered that name had been used for the beetle before it was called *Eros*. In scientific naming the name used first is the one that must be kept. Personally, I'm sorry this beetle lost its very special name.

We collected many representatives of a large group of brown or black beetles with short wing covers known as rove beetles, for they wander (or rove) purposefully into all sorts of places. Most rove beetles are small, uniformly long, and slender. They are principally scavengers in the duff or they feed on dung or carrion or other decomposing animal or vegetable matter or, more likely, they prey on small insects which are scavengers in those places. Some of our rove beetles seemed to be feeding on pollen in the blossoms of skunk cabbage or other flowers, though they may have been preying on tiny insects in those flowers. A few rove beetles are parasitic.

The wing covers of rove beetles are very short, but the soft hind wings of most of them are fully formed and are often longer than the insect's abdomen. When their wings are not in use, the beetles fold them under those wing covers. This procedure is interesting to watch, since the beetles often find it necessary to use the tip of the abdomen or one of their legs to help tuck the wing under the cover. In their roving, these little insects run swiftly about and, when disturbed, have the curious habit of raising the tip of the abdomen in a threatening manner, as though they might sting.

Click beetles are fun to watch. When a beetle which is on a plant is touched, it immediately tucks in its legs and drops to the ground as if shot. Often when the beetle falls, it will land on its back and lie there as if dead. After a time, it will bend its body sharply where it is loosely joined between the front and hind part of its thorax and, sliding a finger-like lobe into a socket, suddenly straighten out with a "click" and shoot itself several inches into the air—frequently only to land on its back once more. The beetle will try again and again until it finally succeeds in landing on its feet. Then it will scurry away.

Our most common click beetles were small or medium in size, dark brown or black, hard shelled, rather shiny, and had long, somewhat flattened bodies, tapered at both ends. Several kinds were common on the boughs of hemlock and Douglas-fir trees, and individuals of the same species were found on other plants as well. We found some click beetles in decaying wood and still others on the ground. M. C. Lane, an authority on click beetles, used to say, "A beetle has to sit somewhere."

The long, cylindrical larvae of click beetles, called wireworms, are usually reddish brown, very tough, and shiny. Many of them have horny hooks at their rear end. In the forest a few kinds of wireworms preyed on other insects, including wood borers and moth pupae in the soil, and some mined under the bark and in the rotten wood of dead trees, but the roles of many are unknown. Certain wireworms living in other places bore into and eat the roots of plants. We found these larvae rather often in our soil samples.

Weevils seemed the most hard-shelled of all the beetles I encountered. The weevil I remember best was a pretty, pinkish gray, boxy-bodied, extremely hard-shelled insect, a bit more than a half-inch long. Another weevil was a grayish little thing about half the size of the first and had a fat behind. It was so inconspicuous that it was known as the obscure root weevil. A third species, between the others in size, was similar to the second but was more robust, and darker, with rows of erect scale-like hairs covering it. This one is known to feed on Douglas-fir roots. All three of these beetles were often on the boughs of conifers. Now and then we found several other kinds.

Weevils are easily recognized because they have a downward-curved, snout-like extension from their heads, with bowed antennae attached to this snout and, as a result, they are often referred to as snout beetles. Most adult weevils chew away the edges of leaves, scalloping them, while the larvae, which live in the ground, feed on the roots of plants.

Loggers and other foresters know well the wood-boring larvae of long-horned beetles, while we knew the attractive adult beetles we saw busily feeding on the nectar and pollen of flowers. These slender, often brightly colored beetles have remarkably long antennae, occasionally even longer than the beetle's entire body. A dozen species of long-horns lived in the ancient forest. They varied in length from a fourth-inch to three inches, but most of them were in the larger part of the range.

Burying beetles, also known as sexton beetles because, like the sextons of earlier times, they bury the dead, are a fascinating portion of the clean-up squad of the forest. Most of these beetles feed on fecal matter or on the bodies of dead and decaying animals, transforming these materials into a state more readily available to the community of life.

The burying or carrion beetles on Saddleback were a little less than an inch long, smooth, shiny, and husky. Their heads were small, somewhat triangular, their shoulders squared and prominent, and their tails triangular. There were two kinds. One was black; the other black with orangish bands on the elytra. These beetles stink and carry many mites.

What burying beetles can accomplish is amazing. Being flat, with flexible body and wings, they can crawl under a dead animal and, by digging the ground out from under a carcass, bury it in a very short time, working around roots if necessary. Burying a mouse takes only a few minutes. Sexton beetles have been known to move an animal as large as a rat several feet to a spot where digging is easier.

After the carrion is buried, the beetles lay eggs on it. Soon long, flat larvae, with a triangular point at each tapering end, emerge from the eggs. For the first few days the parents feed the larvae by regurgitating carrion but, later, both adults and larvae can usually be found beneath the bodies of the dead animals feeding on the carrion.

We discovered burying beetles on a dead wood rat, on a bobcat carcass, and on a toadstool, indicating that either the adults or the larvae of these beetles feed on almost any kind of decaying organic matter.

We also found a few small, dark, and shiny dung-eating beetles in four very different families. Some of these were associated with soft dung, such as that of bears or deer which have been feeding on tender foliage or on fruit, though the larvae of one family of dung-eaters prey on the larval flies they find in dung.

There were many other beetles, including the familiar little, round, reddish or orange-colored spotted lady beetles whose larvae as well as the adults feed upon aphids, scale insects, mites, and other insects and which are very important biological controls of plant-eating insects.

There were small, brightly colored, short-legged leaf beetles which forage on various kinds of plants. Some of these, the flea beetles, are powerful jumpers.

There were also very small, slender, black or tan tumbling flower beetles with wedge-shaped bodies; clerids, also known as checkered beetles, most of which prey on other insects, including bark beetles; tiny brown scavenger beetles, banjo-shaped minute creatures which live in duff, debris, and mammal nests, or even on flowers; sap-feeding beetles which were found where plant fluids soured or fermented; and still others.

Kenny was able to identify many of the beetles, but whenever he was uncertain he did not hesitate to consult his friend, Dr. Melville Hatch, the Northwest's leading beetle authority, at the University of Washington.

These insects in armor have an amazing diversity of roles. They are plant-eaters, pollen-eaters, predators, parasites, and scavengers. Their role in the recycling of wood is crucial. Every kind of beetle, in its own individualized life style, helps to shape and preserve the forest, the home for all of them.

Kenny Fender sorting "bugs," NSF study, 1959.

Chapter Twenty-six
Scaly Wings

COLORFUL, FRAGILE BUTTERFLIES are among the most prized insects in the world, and exquisite pastel colors make certain moths close rivals to the butterflies in this pageant of artistry. The distinctive patterns of colors displayed by these insects are due to tiny, flat scales.

In the scientific world these scaly-winged insects are known as Lepidoptera from the Greek words *lepis,* for scale and *pteron,* for wing. The pattern of scales is different for every species and is important in identifying them, so we had to give special care to the moths and butterflies we caught.

One day in the summer of 1935 when Kenny and I were caring for the insects we had collected the day before, I noticed that he was placing moths on spreading boards and asked if he would mind my watching to learn the procedure.

"Nah," he said. "There's nothing to it."

"Sez you. It looks pretty complicated to me. You must've been doing it forever."

"Nah, not quite that long."

"Well, how old were you when you began?"

"About ten or twelve, I guess."

"How'd you happen to get started?"

"I saw an ad in a magazine by some man saying that he would pay for butterflies that were freshly emerged from their chrysalises. I thought I needed some money and that would be an easy way to get rich. So I sent for his instructions, read up on butterflies, learned what their caterpillars ate, and raised some. I also learned what the chrysalises of the different species looked like and where I might find them. I collected a bunch and waited for the butterflies to emerge. I was hooked when I saw them. They were so beautiful I couldn't give them up. I learned to spread them. You spread moths the same way."

"That's quite a story. How many butterflies do you have now?"

"I don't know. At least a thousand, and I keep adding more all the time."

"Where's your collection?"

"It's at home. My mother thinks I'm crazy, but she tolerates it," he said, picking up a pair of forceps and selecting a moth from the collection.

"Now, I'd better get busy. Let's see if this moth is still relaxed," he said, gently moving one of its wings.

"Yep, it's OK. See its wing is pliable. They usually are this soon after we catch them. It's better if you can spread the insects soon after catching them. They're still limp then, not stiff, and you won't have to use a relaxing chamber. But when we wait a day or so, I put them in the relaxing chamber overnight with some cotton dampened with a little hot water and some phenol added to keep them from getting moldy." (We used a large glass desiccating jar for this purpose, but other containers can be used as long as the insects are not allowed to get wet.)

"Now, we'll use the spreading board. I made this one, myself, as well as quite a few others for different size butterflies or moths."

Working as he talked and with me watching every move, Kenny demonstrated the procedure which today can easily be found described in such books as *Peterson's Field Guide to the Insects.*

After a while, he said, "Now there's your moth on its spreading board. The job's done."

"Why do moths have to be spread?"

"So you can see both sides of the wings. The patterns on both sides are important in identifying them. Have you ever seen the wings of a moth or butterfly under a microscope?"

"No, I haven't."

"They're really something else. The scales are tiny and flat and cover the insect's whole body in layers, like shingles on a roof. I've read that these scales are actually modified hairs which, instead of growing long and slender as most hairs do, remain short, but become very wide compared with their length. And they occur in every gradation from the ordinary hair-like form, which is most abundant on their bodies, to short, broad scales that strengthen the insects' thin membranous wings which have few supporting cross veins in them.

"The scales are slippery, too, and you've seen how easily moths shed their scales when we catch them and put them in a killing jar. The poison has to be really strong so that they're quieted quickly. Scales form a sort of armor which helps to protect the moths from their enemies. I've read that moths' scales are so thick that the moths can even escape from the webs of orb-weaving spiders, without being harmed except for losing a few scales. Something no other insects can do."

"That's fascinating. Thanks, Kenny. Now, I suppose I'd better get busy on some of the other stuff and let you do the other moths. Spreading them looks simple enough, but I don't know how well I'll do it when my time comes."

"You'll do OK. Just take your time. Everyone works out their own way. But once you get their wings spread on the boards, be sure to wait until they're really dry before trying to move them."

"I'll remember that, but I'll be content to let you do the job whenever possible."*

The ancient forest on Saddleback could hardly be called a lepidopterous community, for butterflies and moths were far less diverse there than the insects of any of the other three major orders. Still, these scaly-winged insects had important roles in the forest's network of interactions and made an impact on the community.

Almost all butterflies need sunshine and showy flowers that are fragrant or have sweet nectar. Since the ancient forest did not have these benefits, its only truly resident butterfly was the pine white, which found its niche on young branches in the well-lighted tops of the ancient firs. Two other species lived at the forest's edges. The niche of one, the western meadow fritillary, a small, orange-black butterfly, was on violets. Its adults drank nectar from the flowers and, in return, aided in their pollination, while its spiney-haired larvae fed on violet plants. The other butterfly was a tiny spring azure, a member of a group known as "blues." Its larvae feed on the flowers of shrubs.

The great expanse of branches, boughs, and twigs of the massive firs and the smaller hemlocks provided countless possibilities for insect niches, and a great host of moths were there, far more of them than were ever

---

*One day in 1930 while pursuing butterflies on the Macy farm west of McMinnville, Kenny captured a small blue butterfly he had never seen before. When he showed his find to his friend Ralph Macy, another avid lepidopterist, they discovered that this was a new, undescribed, species. Ralph named it *Icaricia icarioides fenderi*, in honor of Kenny. This butterfly has since become known as Fender's blue and is currently a candidate for listing as an endangered species and is also a target for research and conservation efforts. An interesting article, *Little Things*, by Alan D. St. John about the butterfly and the Fenders appeared in the October/November, 1993, issue of *Northwest Parks and Wildlife*.

identified for us. Some we observed resting on the boughs of young conifers, particularly in the thickets where the trees grew so close together that the light was dimmed. Others we found in more open areas. Some were active in the daytime, while others were active only at night, or in twilight hours, or on overcast days. We did not make a study of the night-flying species.

A fair number of moths fluttered about above shrubs and herbs or rested briefly on the plants. Most of those—more than twenty-five species— were geometrids, which far outnumbered any of the other kinds of moths in the ancient forest. These geometrids had slender bodies and a wingspread of about an inch or inch and a half. Their colors were subdued, often white or gray with black markings, pale gray or brown with darker bands, or mottled gray-brown. They were mostly a nondescript lot of moths. Adult geometrids do not feed. Their short life span is totally devoted to flying around, mating, and starting a new generation of larvae.

Geometrid larvae—literally, "earth measurers"—are smooth, nearly hairless caterpillars called inchworms or measuring worms. They are also known as loopers from their characteristic looping style of locomotion. While resting on prolegs (leg-like protrusions at their rear), they reach out with their forelegs. Then, grasping with their tiny claws, they bring the rear end forward by humping their back and walking forward on the hind pair of prolegs. These larvae have significant roles in the forest. A few feed in the cones, but a far greater number eat the needles of Douglas-firs, hemlocks, and other conifers.

The colors and markings of the geometrid larvae vary, and different species are active in different seasons and even at different levels in the trees. Most loopers do not form cocoons. Instead, when they are ready to pupate, they drop to the ground on silken threads, often for great distances, to pupate in the layer of duff. Others find their refuge in crevices in the bark of the trees.

We collected and preserved many looper larvae, but we learned little about their habits except where they were when we found them. Very few of the larvae were identified for us and we had no way of relating adult moths and loopers. The majority of our moths were so poorly known that they didn't have common names. So it was not unusual for us to call one by its scientific name as soon as we learned it.

Mesoleuca gratulata, for instance, is a geometrid for which we never did have a common name. It's a pretty little white moth with fine, well-patterned black spots on its front wings and white hind wings. Held in the hand, a faint pattern of chestnut and blue could be discerned. The moth's name, loosely translated into English from the Greek, is something like: the "half-white" moth "we welcome" or are "happy to see." And we *were* always happy to see it. As the first moth to appear in significant numbers each year, it was a sure sign of spring! It was important to us, even though we didn't learn its role in the forest. From what we observed we think its larvae feed on conifer needles.

One of the loopers interested us especially because it is an almost perfect mimic for a Douglas-fir needle when it's at rest on a twig of a fir tree. The looper is about an inch long and its smooth, lime green body has dark lines along the sides, making it almost impossible for one to distinguish it from a fir needle. We accidentally squashed more than one of those loopers because of this resemblance. We suspected then that it fed on Douglas-fir needles, and I have since learned that it is the phantom hemlock looper, a needle eater of both Douglas-fir and hemlock foliage. The adult is a pretty white or light gray moth with a yellow head and striking black markings on its wings.

I have read that two geometrid species we found have caused much damage in forests or city parks in Canada since the years of our research. I wonder whether the parks were too well manicured, with only Douglas-firs, a few ornamental shrubs and flowers, lawn, and paved or gravel walkways— nothing else for the geometrids to eat, and nothing to nourish parasitic wasps. Though the potential for devastation may have been present in our highly diversified forest, none of us ever saw a bit of destructive defoliation. I do not recall seeing silk threads by which larvae descended to the ground to begin pupation. Yet one writer, in telling of the habits of a similar defoliator species, says, "The larvae drop to the ground on silken threads, which are sometimes so numerous that 'the whole forest looks and feels like one big cobweb.'"

At least fifteen other moth families lived in our forest. Among them were the slightly larger tiger moths, or arctiids, with handsome striped or spotted wings. Their robust larvae are very hairy and are often called woolly bears. Some arctiid caterpillars band together and feed on the needles of conifers.

Some of the other moths were night-flying noctuids, owlet moths, commonly known as millers. Many of them are attracted to lights. They are dull-colored, heavy-bodied moths which fold their wings tent-fashion above their bodies when at rest. Because they cut off the stems of young succulent plants, some noctuid larvae are called cutworms. Noctuid pupae, like those of the geometrids and tiger moths, generally do not form cocoons but overwinter in the soil as naked chrysalids.

In 1964 noctuid larvae defoliated 8,000 acres of conifers in western Oregon. Those moths were members of a genus that lived in our forest. The outbreak occurred two years after the massive Columbus Day storm which blew down a lot of trees, especially large ones. Was there any connection between the fallen trees and the outbreak? I wonder what had happened to the ichneumons, braconids, and chalcids which were there. Was this outbreak of moths "managed" with insecticides, which killed the parasitic wasps as well as the noctuids? It would be interesting to know just what did happen.

The young caterpillars of this particular noctuid moth browse on the opening buds and tender new foliage of Douglas-firs. By mid- or late July, they have matured and have a large reddish-brown head and a translucent green body tinged with yellow and lavender. At that time they drop to the ground to pupate and overwinter in the soil.

The Saddleback Mountain forest was home to a great number of very small moths, sometimes known as Microlepidoptera; however, other names are often used since there are several distinct groups of these moths.

Tortricids are among the larger Microlepidoptera. Their larvae are leafrollers which forage on a great variety of plants. Some species are highly destructive in Western forests. The rolled leaves serve the larvae not only as homes but also as food, for they munch away on the enclosed portions of the leaves while being protected by the outer parts. Tortricid larvae usually feed individually, frequently in webbed shelters made of rolled leaves or needles tied together. Observers say these larvae often wriggle loose when disturbed and drop to the ground suspended by a thread.

Adult tortricids are between a quarter-inch and an inch in length and are usually brown, gray, or golden, rather than of brighter hues. We had only one tortricid that had been named. Though *Peronia brittania* had no common name and we did not learn its niche, it was seen so often that Prof used it as an indicator of the beginning of autumn.

Many other microlepidopterans are very beautiful, with scales of brilliant blue or green hues or ones that shine like silver or gold, but these insects and their scales are so small that a magnifying lens is required to fully appreciate their beauty. The colors of others are more subdued.

The wings of many of these tiny moths are narrow and bordered with wide fringes that are often marked with light or dark bands or distinctive patterns which show best when the wings are folded. Some of these moths are so minute that the larvae live until full grown inside the tissues of leaves.

Larvae of nearly all these little moths feed on plants, mostly upon or within leaves (or needles) as twig or leaf miners, leaf tiers, or leaf rollers, or as borers into twigs, buds, cones, seeds, and fruits.

The salal leaf miner is a little gray, or golden saffron moth with tiny white spots on its wings. The larvae work inside the leaves of salal plants and, by eating out the upper layer of cells at the top of the leaf, form round, clear blotches about the size of a dime.

Another of these small moths is the diamondback, a gray or brownish moth with white marks along the front of its forewings which form a white diamond when the wings are closed. Female diamondbacks, emerging from their cocoons in April, lay tiny disc-shaped, pale green or yellow eggs on the leaves of plants in the mustard family, an example of which is the spring beauty which flourishes in the drier, well-lighted areas of the forest. Diamondback larvae when young work as miners beneath the surface of the leaves, but when they are nearly full grown they move to the outside of the leaves where they either eat the outer layer of the epidermis or chew all the way through into the leaf. When they are ready to pupate they spin a delicate white cocoon on a leaf of the plant or on rubbish nearby. Some diamondback moths complete their entire life cycle in as little as two weeks; others may take as long as seven. Several generations are produced in one summer.

One of our tiny moths was identified only as a leaf cutter of the same genus as the maple leaf cutter. These moths have curious habits. Though leaf miners when young, they later become leaf cutters and eventually, as adults, become casebearers. These casebearers resemble tiny turtles moving about, with their bodies mostly hidden beneath a circular bit of leaf. Both vine maples and Oregon maples grew in our forest and vine maples were not far from the research area. Our leaf cutter moth may have been the maple leaf cutter.

Another small moth was one of a group which are thought to be conifer bud moths. The bud moth larvae that have been studied enter conifer buds when they start to open in the spring and feed on the tender new needles, webbing them together to form a shelter under the bud cap. As the twigs grow in length, the partly eaten needles die and the dead needles drop off by midseason, leaving little evidence of the feeding.

These few examples show some of the ways in which tiny moths are important in our forest. The lepidopterans had numerous niches, though all were in the general role of plant-eating primary consumer. However, these insects, in turn, provided food for many kinds of predators and also for other parasitic wasps. Like many other insects, these moths have not been well studied. Being so tiny, many of them are extremely difficult to spread; consequently there are few systematists who study them. Though we had lots of little moths, many we did not send away for identification because of this lack of systematists. Some moths we sent were not named.

Chapter Twenty-seven
Potpourri

Not all of the important insects fit into any one of the four more familiar major orders or groups. Some are very different from beetles, bees, flies, and moths, and many are strange looking. But many have significant roles in the forest community.

One, a snakefly, a rather small reddish-brown insect, no more than an inch long, is so distinctive that it was used for many years as the logo for the newsletter of the Oregon Entomological Society. It looks like a survivor from an earlier age, a miniature, winged serpent with short legs, large flattened head, long slender antennae that project forward, long camel-like neck, and clear, many veined wings which it holds roof-like over its back when at rest. The female has a long, slender, sickleshape ovipositor at the end of her abdomen. In spite of their small size, adult snakeflies are formidable looking creatures.

Their agile larvae, dark, slender and a half-inch long, live under the bark of trees where they move quickly either forward or backward as they seek out and capture caterpillars and bark beetles of various stages as well as other wood-boring insects for their food. The transition of these insects from larva to adult also takes place beneath the bark, where the rather active pupa is never enclosed in a cocoon.

The snakefly is a neuropteran, a "nerve-winged" insect, and has four membranous wings with many veins and cross-veins. The "nerve" part of the name is from the Greek word *neuron* and refers to the numerous strengthening veins with which the gauzy wings of neuropterans are supported.

Snakeflies are found only in forests west of the Rocky Mountains. We caught them occasionally in our sweeps on conifer boughs.

A green lacewing, sometimes called Golden-eyes for its large, golden or copper-colored eyes, also belongs to this order. It is strikingly attractive with transparent, dainty lace-like green wings about three quarters of an inch long and antennae that are long and of many segments. When at rest, lacewings fold their wings roof-like over their bodies.

Apparently, adult lacewings do not eat but they do bite! Their sturdy little spindle-shaped larvae make up for this deficiency. They run around on the leaves of herbs or shrubs or the bark of trees, capturing prey, puncturing it with a pair of sickle-like jaws, and extracting the juices from its body. Their enormous appetite is appeased only by consuming several hundred aphids or similar insects before reaching full development. Because of their especial fondness for aphids, these lacewing larvae are known as aphid lions. However, they also readily devour mites, leafhoppers, small caterpillars and, in fact, any insect, including their own kind.

Female Golden-eyes lay each egg on the top of a stiff stalk of silk about half an inch high. Groups of these eggs look a bit like a tiny forest of white stems bearing glistening little balls on their tops. As each larva hatches, it scrambles down to the surface of the leaf and runs off, hunting an aphid or other prey. In this way the larvae, hatching in close succession, avoid being devoured by their kin. When fully grown, a lacewing larva spins around itself an exquisite thin, white, globular cocoon, hidden away in a crack or in a crevice of bark, or in any sheltered place. At the end of pupation, the adult inside the cocoon cuts open a small lid at the top, and the adult lacewing emerges.

Slightly smaller lacewings of four species, with wings heavily clouded or mottled with brown, were more numerous in our forest though less spectacular than Golden-eyes. The brown ones were so active on the boughs of conifers throughout the summer season and into the fall that Prof considered them to be good indicators of those seasons. These brown lacewings have black eyes and their bodies and wings are covered with short hairs but otherwise they look much like their larger green relative.

The best studied species of brown lacewing lays oval white or pale amber eggs on the lower sides of leaves and in the cracks of bark. Immediately after hatching, the larvae are pale white but become darker and spindle-shaped. When fully developed, they spin a thin cocoon-like pupa case in which they undergo their transformation into the adult stage. Brown lacewing larvae feed chiefly on plant-eating mites and aphids, but they also eat other kinds of small insects.

Lacewings are very effective insect predators in their community. Their role also includes being food for other predaceous larvae and for some parasitic hymenopterans. If the details of the roles of these various lacewings were known, the differences might be quite surprising.

The forest was home to many sorts of homopterans. All of them are rather small insects which feed on the sap of plants in one way or another. Their name from *homo*, "alike," has been assigned to these mostly small insects whose two pairs of wings are membranous and alike and are held sloping at the sides in resting position. Many homopterans, however, do not have wings, at least under certain conditions. Unlike the metamorphosis of many other insects, the "coming of age" of homopterans is gradual. It involves a series of molts of the nymph. After each molt, the immature insect increasingly resembles the adult.

Spittlebugs, one kind of homopteran, are easily recognized by accumulation of frothy white "spittle" the nymphs produce as they feed. Adult spittlebugs are inconspicuous, mostly brownish insects, less than a half-inch long. They jump and fly when disturbed. We found spittlebugs on various herbs and other succulent plants, only occasionally on conifers.

Treehoppers are bizarre-looking little things whose enlarged prothorax projects above the head and back over the abdomen, creating a sort of humpbacked effect. Another homopteran, rather similar in appearance but not quite so bumpy, is the planthopper. Adults of both these insects are adept at flying and jumping, and the nymphs suck the sap of trees, shrubs, and herbs. Planthoppers feed on plant juices and also produce honeydew.

Whenever disturbed, little brown, green, or yellow boat-shaped leafhoppers jump from the boughs of conifers or from other vegetation. Unlike other hoppers, these adult insects have smooth, slick bodies. The nymphs are selective and those of any one species usually feed on only a few kinds of plants, while the adults seem to feed on many. Several kinds of leafhoppers lived in the forest. Some were abundant.

Aphids—plant lice—tiny, soft-bodied insects which suck plant juices, were the most numerous and diverse homopterans. They range from nearly colorless to green, yellow, or black and live on all kinds of plants: on leaves (or needles), buds, blossoms, twigs, bark, roots, and fruit. They occur in such huge colonies and reproduce so rapidly that they can be very harmful. Some cause leaves to curl, giving them protection, while others make galls or other deformities. Honeydew, a sweet, sticky anal excretion, attracts ants, which guard aphids from enemies. Some species are entirely wingless, though most aphid species have winged individuals. Certain entirely female species reproduce without the eggs being fertilized, a process known as parthenogenesis.

The life span of an individual aphid is about a month, and each female has from 80 to 100 offspring; thus numerous broods are produced in a season. Aphids were especially common on the needles and twigs of Douglas-firs.

Hemiptera are the true bugs. Though their name means "half-winged," it refers to the fact that the part of the forewing attached to the body is thickened, while the remaining part is membranous, like the hindwing. Two features in their appearance distinguish true bugs from all other insects: the membranous tips of their wings overlap when folded, forming a distinct "X," and the middle portion of their thorax, called the scutellum, is triangular in shape. Some hemipterans are tiny. Others are very large. The ones in our forest ranged from small to moderate size, the largest being a little over a half-inch long.

True bugs have incomplete metamorphosis. Though the nymphs resemble adults, they are wingless until almost mature when they begin forming wings. All true bugs have piercing-sucking mouths, but some get their nourishment from juices of plants, while the rest are predators on insects and other kinds of animal life. In our forest most hemipterans fed on plants. Only a few were predators.

Our true bugs were an interesting assortment. The largest ones were two kinds of stink bugs—long, broad insects which, when disturbed, give off a very unpleasant odor, hence their common name. Stink bugs could be recognized easily by the very large triangular scutellum in the middle of their back. We often found them resting on the boughs of firs in the wintertime. The larger, more common one, was brown and had a very bumpy back. The other was smooth and green. These stink bugs were plant feeders though we didn't learn their precise niche, or niches. However, the brown one was observed so consistently that Prof designated it as an indicator of the latter part of winter.

Smaller hemipterans included two species of lygaeids, commonly called plant bugs, and five species of leaf bugs (mirids). Lygaeids made their appearance so regularly during the last days of winter, just before the first promise of spring, that Prof also used them as indicators for this season of "farewell to winter." Though we did not learn their life style, we assume these bugs fed on plants as other members of their family do.

The leaf bugs (mirids) are small, fragile, elongate or oval bugs with variously colored bodies. Some, strikingly marked with red, orange, green, or white, run fast and fly freely. Though the majority of leaf bugs feed on the juices of plants and may be destructive pests, a rather large number prey on other insects.

The members of two families of true bugs are entirely predaceous and hunt other insects found on vegetation. A small brown stilt bug, slender and long-legged as its name implies, hunts and devours leafhoppers, while the common damsel bug, a small, slender, pale gray insect with long antennae and front legs designed for grasping its victims, preys extensively on aphids, leafhoppers, treehoppers, and small caterpillars.

The forest on Saddleback had a great mix of insects as well as other creatures, occupying almost every conceivable niche a community of life could offer.

In late summer and fall, at the time of harvest, daddy-long-legs appear. These spider-like harvestmen, as they are commonly known to scientists, usually roam about on the forest floor stalking their prey. They are not true spiders but phalangids, a term referring to the fact that their legs are stretched out in rows resembling the Roman *phalanx* or battleline. Harvestmen also climb onto herbs, shrubs, or the boughs of young hemlock trees, apparently searching for aphids, their preferred food. We even found a harvestman in a sweepnet collection taken from branches of the hemlock ladder-tree eighty feet above the ground. Sometimes we found these phalangids in forest floor litter or in rotten wood.

When they hunt, phalangids are said to pounce upon their prey like a cat pounces upon a mouse. After seizing the prey with their palpi, as if the palpi were hands, they proceed to chew and swallow the prey instead of merely sucking out (or slurping) the juices, as do spiders and most other arachnids.

Velvety pinhead-sized mites, red as a freshly-painted fire engine, were our constant companions in the forest during the warm dry summer months. Roaming the moss and litter or climbing herbs and shrubs, these "timid little ones," as their name *Trombidium* suggests, did us no harm though they were present in great numbers. Curious to learn just how many of them there were, I laid out a series of square meter plots near the fire shelter one June day and found that they averaged sixteen in each plot.

We usually began seeing these mites above ground in April, but they are known as harvest mites because they reach a peak in numbers in June or July when fruits and seeds ripen. The mites gradually became less abundant until the last ones retreated to protected areas beneath the surface in the cold wet days of October or November. I have read that a species of *Trombidium* which is common in fairly warm dry forests feeds on living or dead insects and often nibbles at insects trapped by resin that has oozed out of a tree.

Diptera held a prime position in the forest's recycling endeavors. They were also important biological control agents as parasites and predators, and as pollinators they ranked very high—either second or third among the major groups of insects.

Hymenopterans are most widely known to the general public for the activities of bees as pollinators and makers of honey and wax. However, in the forest the multitudes of parasitic wasps served as agents of biological control and their other roles in the forest were varied and complex.

If it were not for beetles the forest would soon be buried under tons of woody debris. Their role as recyclers of wood is crucial.

Potential defoliators were there, too—including many plant-eating moths, plant bugs, and stink bugs—but so were insect agents of control: parasitic wasps, predaceous flies, beetles, lacewings, stilt bugs, and damsel bugs. Spiders of many kinds were there as well as centipedes, amphibians, mice, and shrews. Insectivorous birds, too, were there on the ground and in the trees. Every one of these parasites and predators searched for food. Some found and fed on adult insects; others sought eggs, larvae, nymphs, or pupae.

Insects are choice tidbits for wrens, thrushes, flycatchers, and many other birds. Dragonflies feed upon mosquitoes and other insects near streams and in open areas. Bats scoop up night-flying mosquitoes, gnats, and moths, and predaceous insects also fatten their larder with all sorts of insects.

The marvelous network of interactions among forest creatures is slowly being revealed. A key factor in this complexity is insect metamorphosis. For me, the implications in the discovery that most insects are born with the capacity to have two (or in some cases more) modes of life—one following the other—was mind-boggling.

Thus, it is possible for an *Aedes* mosquito wriggler to live for a time in a tree hole, feeding on no-see-um larvae, and then become an adult feeding on the nectar of flowers. The mosquito may then be caught by a bat, a spider, or a bird, or die of old age—as some insects do.

A larva living in a well-rotted old log may feed on crane fly maggots before it changes into a deer fly which, as it moves from one flower to another siphoning up nectar, carries pollen which will insure development of the seeds of the plants. Eventually that deer fly may be caught in a spider's web or become a meal for a bird.

When a snipe fly larva which has wriggled about in the soil eating small creatures becomes an adult, it preys upon other flies. That snipe fly, in turn, may be eaten by some predator, or it may live out its life and eventually go back to the soil to enrich Mother Earth.

A female black fly larva feeding on algae in a streamlet, on becoming an adult, siphons nectar from flowers until she needs a blood meal to insure development of her eggs. Then she bites some mammal, or perhaps a bird, but when she flies away after her blood meal, she may be picked out of the air by a flycatcher to become a morsel for a nestling baby bird.

The scenario could go on and on. Even such plagues to humanity as mosquitoes and their ilk can give us a glimpse of the fascinating ways in which strands of life in the forest are interwoven—a complex sometimes referred to as a web of life.

This biodiversity—this tremendous variety in the kinds of life in the forest community, with all their roles or niches—protects the living things, the *biota*, in the forest, and provides the community with a high degree of stabilizing flexibility.

Wind-thrown trees in the old-growth forest, 1933.

Chapter Twenty-eight
Woodworkers

To us, as students of the ancient forest, the very old logs and stumps, well decomposed and ready to break apart, were a constant source of surprise. Some were nearly hidden by young trees they had nurtured for years, while others formed low mounds over which mats of delicate green moss trailed. Through the years, we learned much as we dug into many of these gifts from the past. Kenny Fender and Bob Rieder, our "beetleologists," investigated many of the logs in the old forest.

The age of a tree, its size, whether it is healthy, damaged, or diseased, and the kind of place in which it falls, all play a part in determining how long it will be before a fallen tree crumbles. Branches and small trees decay rapidly. Noble firs and hemlocks also disappear in a few decades, but an ancient Douglas-fir hundreds of feet tall, with a trunk three, four, or six feet in diameter, shows little sign of decay after thirty or forty years. Centuries pass before one of them disintegrates completely.

Usually the first creatures to chew their way into a fallen tree are small, cylindrical, dark-colored bark beetles of the scolytid family. The adults eat through the thick outer bark and chew galleries for their eggs in the softer, protein-rich inner bark and the cambium—the layer of cells which gives rise to new bark on its outer side and to sapwood on the side toward the center of the tree. As soon as the bark-beetle eggs hatch, larvae begin excavating feeding galleries which radiate out on the surface of the wood from the parent gallery. The patterns of these galleries, resembling intricate etchings, have earned the name of engraver beetle for these insects. Each engraver species has its own design.

Ambrosia beetles, a group of bark-boring beetles sometimes called timber beetles, are another kind of scolytid. They are so tiny that they look like a short piece of pencil lead. When these beetles bore through the bark to lay their eggs on the sapwood, they take a special kind of fungus with them which they cultivate in the galleries. As this fungus grows, it forms a sweet secretion called ambrosia, "food of the gods." After the eggs hatch, the larvae develop in small cells adjoining the main galleries and are usually fed by adult females until they are full grown and pupate. The females keep the larval burrows supplied with fresh fungus and the galleries clean by carrying away the feces of the larvae. Each species of ambrosia beetle usually feeds on one particular type of fungus, and when the young females emerge and fly to another tree, they carry spores of their natal fungus with them to be introduced into the gallery they excavate. Foresters call these little bark beetles pinhole or shothole borers because their galleries damage the wood so much that it looks as though it had been peppered with a blast of fine shot.

However, not all of the beetles that are found under dead bark work on the wood. One kind, a rhizophagid, is a very small, cylindrical, shiny brown beetle that travels in the tunnels of wood-boring beetles and feeds on the fungi in the beetles' fungus gardens, while colydiids, cylindrical bark beetles, prey on the larvae of the bark-boring beetles.

Both the adults and the larvae of the green ostomid hunt and eat wood-boring and bark beetles. An adult of this species is a little over one-half inch long, slender, flattened, and an iridescent metallic green. Adult green ostomids seek their prey in the outer bark, while their larvae hunt in the burrows. The adults bite fiercely when captured. Another ostomid is round, about one-fourth inch wide, and mottled brownish. It lives in and about woody fungi and bark where it presumably preys on tiny creatures.

The next beetles to attack naturally fallen trees are usually buprestids, or metallic wood borers as they're sometimes called, and cerambycids or longhorned beetles.

The golden buprestid is one of the most beautiful beetles in Northwestern forests. It is rather flat and broad, a little less than an inch long, and is a striking shade of iridescent green or blue with a copper strip down the middle of its back and along each side. There are also rustic buprestids, black ones with purplish iridescence, orange spotted and striped ones, and small plain black ones.

The sawyer, one of the longhorned beetles, is a cerambycid. Its body is arched, not conspicuously flattened, and its antennae are longer than its entire body. The sawyer's larvae become huge white grubs that tunnel about extensively all the way into the heartwood of logs. At least ten other species of longhorned beetles lived in the ancient forest.

Females of both buprestids and longhorns lay their eggs in crevices on the bark or in slits they cut. When the larvae emerge from the eggs, they bore through the bark and into the wood, often working through the outer sap-wood and into the inner, drier heartwood where they construct long irregular mines. Larvae of some species live in the wood for two years before becoming adults, and one species is known to take seven years or more.

The larvae of these two groups of beetles are very different, though to the casual observer the large grubs may look much alike. Most buprestid larvae are long, legless, and shaped like a horseshoe nail. Their heads are small and the first segment back of the head is much broader than the following body segments. That segment has horny plates on both the top and bottom. Buprestid larvae are called flathead borers.

The larvae of longhorns are also long and cylindrical, but they are usually plump at the head end. They are known as roundhead borers. The heads of some species are very much flattened; however, even these differ from the flathead borers because the horny plate is only on the top surface of the first segment behind the head. These big larvae aid tremendously in cycling wood back to the soil, not only through the great amount of wood they chew up and the quantities of frass they form, but because they also make ports of entry for wood-rotting fungi which thrive in the galleries inside the logs.

Shiny black carpenter ants about one-half inch long also are among the early insects to penetrate fallen trees. Young winged males and females leave their nests in early spring to find a partner and to mate. Shortly after mating, the males shed their wings and die and the females disappear.

Those who have studied carpenter ants say that the female selects a small cavity which she completely encloses for a tiny brood cell, leaving neither entrance nor exit. Then she sheds her wings and lays a few eggs. They hatch in about ten days. The only food this first small brood of larvae receives is a secretion from the young queen's salivary glands. In about thirty days the larvae complete their development, emerge as adults, and take over the work of the nest.

These workers cut galleries, principally where the wood is soft from decay, and chambers to make room for the enlarging colony. Unlike beetles, carpenter ants do not consume the wood but push it through windows cut to the outside where piles of extremely fine sawdust accumulate to be worked on by other creatures. When carpenter ant workers gather food they use the windows as access holes for leaving and returning to the colony. Workers feed the queen, care for the eggs she lays and, as the larvae hatch, feed them on secretions from their mouths.

Carpenter ants use a wide range of foods, varying from meats to sweets—from caterpillars (and trapped mice), to honeydew secreted by aphids, or to a sack of sugar in a forest cabin. We noticed few carpenter ants in the research area during Prof's study but after the ancient trees were felled, there was a population explosion.

When the bark beetles and others have opened the first holes through the bark and while other beetles and carpenter ants are constructing their galleries in the wood, bacteria and wood-rotting fungi which have been brought in by insects begin growing inside the log. These poorly known but highly significant forms of life soften wood fibers and make them more porous, create little passages, and generally alter conditions within the log.

At about this time two species of tiny brown or reddish rove beetles may be at work in the area between the bark and the thin layer of cambium which overlies the sapwood. Dorothy and Kenny found these beetles in both Douglas-fir and hemlock logs whenever the logs were moist and in a fairly early stage of decay. The bark of the logs they studied was mostly intact and the sapwood underlying the cambium unbroken—though in some logs it was punky for as much as a depth of three inches. These rove beetles were flat and less than a fourth inch long but, unlike most rove beetles, had a squarish body rather than an elongate one. They moved about rapidly and appeared to be preying upon other tiny creatures.

At this stage bright red, extremely flat bark beetles of moderate size known as cucujids may be found. Cucujids are usually found under the bark of intact logs where they prey on mites and small insects also living in those places.

While the wood of a log is still sound but has acquired a relatively high moisture content, damp-wood termites often move in and establish colonies which may grow for several years and eventually contain many individuals. Termite colonies are not visible externally, but we knew they were nearby when winged males and females swarmed out on their short nuptial flights in the evenings of warm, sultry days in late August or early September. At those times, the termites were soon everywhere—in the air, in our hair, on the surfaces of logs, and crawling on the ground.

Immediately after finding mates, paired insects fall to the ground and shed their wings. The couple then crawls about, seeking a log with some inconspicuous slit where they can find their way inside to establish a colony. The many galleries termites eat in the wood may completely honeycomb the interior of the log before the colonies run their course.

A mutually beneficial three-way relationship exists in termites. Cellulose-digesting flagellates (*Trichonympha* sp.) and nitrogen-fixing bacteria which live in their guts make it possible for termites to digest wood. The flagellates digest the cellulose in the wood and convert it into a form the termites can use as food. The termite's body provides a chamber full of food for the flagellates and for the nitrogen-fixing bacteria which supply the nitrogen required by the flagellates. This finely tuned relationship has been known for some time, and now there is increasing evidence that termites can digest other cellulose as well as wood fibers, though how they do that is not fully known.

Eventually, the bark of the tree loosens as the wood beneath it decomposes through the combined activities of many kinds of invertebrates. At this stage we found ten species of fungus-loving beetles from four very diverse families. All of them were either under the bark or in decaying wood. Some of them feed on the fungi and others probably are predators. It is also likely that some eat the spores of fungi and, as a result, help to spread the different sorts of fungi from one log to another.

All of these fungus-loving beetles were small or moderate in size. Five species were leiodids, or round fungus beetles. When alarmed, the colorful leiodids curl up by bending their head and thorax down under their bodies. Three fungus-lovers were derodontids, small beetles of subdued colors which are known as tooth-necked fungus beetles because some of them have notches on their thorax. Both the larvae and adults of derodontids may be found together with slime molds under bark. One, *Ditylus gracilis*, a slender, soft-bodied, shiny purple beetle about one-half inch long, was an oedemerid or false blister beetle. It resembles the so-called Spanish fly (considered by some to be an aphrodisiac but actually a highly dangerous mucosal irritant, including to the genitals). It is a meloid or blister beetle. The final fungus-loving species was in the helodid family, somber-colored beetles found under the bark. Their larvae, however, are aquatic and are known to frequent water in tree holes, like the larvae of the tree-hole mosquito.

Dorothy also discovered two kinds of stag beetle larvae in well-decomposed hemlock logs. They were large, fat, whitish or bluish, C-shaped grubs, about the size of the adult stag beetles described in Chapter Twenty-five. The larvae of one species were in moist, well decomposed hemlock logs while those of the other species were in humus and soil samples as well as in the hemlock logs. The duff where these larvae were found undoubtedly contained fragments of rotten wood. Stag beetle larvae feed on the juices of decaying wood. They do not bore into the wood or chew on it but are opportunists which incidentally aid the disintegration of the decaying wood as they drink the nutrient-rich juices it contains—juices formed by the fungi which are decomposing the tissues of the wood.

While all these things are going on inside the log, needles and litter accumulate on top of it, forming an ideal place for plants to germinate and grow. The log becomes covered with a blanket of mosses and ferns and, sometimes, with other plants. Frequently these decomposing logs serve as nurse logs for young hemlock trees, the rootlets of which penetrate deep inside the log, tapping the abundant nutrients that can be found there. The interior of the log becomes a reticulum of roots, fragments of wood, and the galleries of termites and other insects. Often in a mature forest, one may come across several fairly large hemlocks growing in a straight row atop an inconspicuous mound which was once one of these nurse logs.

Eventually the bark and decaying sapwood slip off the decomposing tree to accumulate at the sides of the log in large slabs and smaller pieces. These materials provide shelter for snails, slugs, salamanders, and small mammals, as well as for many insects and other invertebrates. Abandoned galleries make homes and convenient passageways for many small creatures.

Tenebrionids, known as darkling beetles, work on this kind of old stuff—dead or decaying vegetable matter, especially the smaller pieces of bark. Some darkling beetles are active in daytime, but more are active at night. All our darkling beetles were moderate in size, slow moving, and black or brown. Most of them were smooth and looked like ground beetles. One kind, though, was rough (and tough), resembling bits of bark. We described individuals of that species as "iron clad," because they were so hard we could barely pierce them with an insect pin. Darkling beetles also feed on bracket fungi. Their larvae are known as false wireworms because they look so much like the wireworm larvae of click beetles.

We also found two sorts of anobiids, death watch beetles, living in this decaying material. They make galleries in old wood, including houses, where their habit of clicking thorax and head together has led to superstitious beliefs that they portend death. Cylindrical, brown, and about one-eighth inch long, they are strange looking little creatures with their head bent down under their prothorax, not visible from above.

The logs continue to decompose and fragment as the years roll by until they are honeycombed with passages and tiny crevices. Slabs of bark and wood which sloughed off the fallen log become smaller and smaller until—hundreds of years later for large logs—fragments are finally scattered as part of the litter covering the surface of the forest floor. These wood-rich areas are microhabitats, little worlds of their own, within the sheltering forest. Dark and moist, they afford protection from extremes of temperature and offer a wide selection of food. Bacteria, fungus threads and secretions, fragments of wood, and other plant materials are there for creatures with a vegetarian diet, and a banquet of tiny animal life is there for predators.

Millipedes, whose name, literally translated, means a thousand feet, are popularly known as thousand-leggers. Their bodies are made up of many segments with two pairs of feet on each segment and they are typically cylindrical. Millipedes are slow-moving creatures which live in or beneath wood and other debris or in the humus and soil where they feed on wood or other decaying vegetation. This they break into tiny pieces for other sorts of organisms to work on in completing the job of recycling. With the exception of *Harpaphe*, a large black and yellow cyanide producing millipede, the ones we discovered in this forest were rather small and inconspicuous.

Chilopods are distant relatives of the millipedes. We found two sorts in the forest on Saddleback, centipedes and geophilids.

The centipedes, "hundred-footed" little creatures, have flattened bodies and fifteen or more pairs of legs—one pair on each segment of their body. Centipedes are mostly bright brown or reddish and rather broad in proportion to their length. When exposed they scurry about frantically to avoid light. They are predaceous, and as they capture their prey, they kill it with poison from an enlarged claw on the first pair of their legs, moisten the prey with digestive juices, and then suck in the liquefied body contents. Centipedes feed on insects, spiders, and other small invertebrates, the larger centipedes hunting larger prey and the small ones seeking out tiny creatures such as immature springtails.

On one April day I was surprised to find three large brown centipedes in an old log, each one curled around a group of tiny light-colored eggs. Excitedly, I showed my find to Prof. I had never dreamed that centipedes might protect their eggs or have any maternal instincts. I've learned since that females of this species not only coil around their eggs to protect them but are said to lick the eggs periodically to keep them clean. At a length of about two inches, these centipedes (*Scolopocryptops sexspinosa*) are believed to be the largest centipedes found in Douglas-fir logs. The adults overwinter in protected places and lay their eggs in the spring.

Geophilids, literally "earth-lovers," are thread-thin chilopods with bodies many segments in length. Being so slender, they are excellent exploiters of burrows and crevices. Some geophilids are short, others about two inches long. They feed on the abundant white worms, enchytraeids, and other small earthworms. One June day while searching through a small portion of partially rotted hemlock log we came across one of the larger geophilids protecting a clutch of eggs.

Several species of spiders live in well-decayed logs or other wood-rich areas of the forest floor. Though two of the common large kinds look a lot like tarantulas, they are trapdoor or folding-door spiders.

Dorothy discovered two grayish-brown folding-door spiders while digging in the forest floor on a day in July. One of the spiders was in a burrow four to five inches long immediately beneath the moss. The other was in a hole in decayed wood somewhat deeper in the humus. This species (*Antrodiaetus pacificus*) is believed to be the largest spider living in decaying fallen trees. Its home has been described as a horizontal tube lined with silk in the outer layer of a fallen tree with many cracks and crevices. To close this tube, the spider grasps the rim on opposite sides and pulls it in toward the middle. A female of this species seldom leaves her tube except to capture prey, but a male may wander in search of a mate.

In September one year, I found a slightly larger dark-brown folding-door spider (*Hexura picea*) and a nest full of tiny grayish immature spiderlings in rotten wood.

Another day at the same time of year, I searched through the top few inches of a mound of humus and decayed wood at the base of an old, collapsed snag. The mound was covered by hemlock needles and penetrated by hemlock, salal, and huckleberry roots. It smelled like mildewed hay. In this one-half square meter I found some twenty trapdoor spiders of two kinds. Some were just under the surface near web-lined burrows. Others were deeper, near larger honeycombed passageways. One silky tunnel, about ten millimeters in diameter and forty millimeters long, led from the surface to an animal burrow beneath, where a web curtain hung across the passage.

Trapdoor, or folding-door, spiders prey upon wood-digesting insects. In this microhabitat these spiders remove weak and unfit insects and help to assure that the wood-digesting insects have a healthy, vigorous population. Unfortunately, we never received identifications for these trapdoor spiders.

In this manner, even the giants of the forest, trees which have sheltered, protected, and sustained countless forms of life for eons of time, crumble and return to the soil the very elements which nourished them, a feat largely accomplished by the seldom-noticed and tremendously diverse woodworkers of the forest floor.

Chapter Twenty-nine
A Fine Day for Slugs

O CTOBER HAD ARRIVED, a month for colorful sunrises. As I hurried to the car at 6 a.m. I drank in the beauty of the new day. The sky along the eastern horizon blazed with a fiery glow which changed from burnished gold into shades of yellow as it spread upward toward the pale blue sky. *What a spectacular sunrise!* I thought. *I wonder what this day will bring?*

With daylight, the colors faded and the clouds in the western sky took on a somber hue. As we neared the mountains an ominous black curtain hung over them and rain began falling in huge widely spaced drops which turned into a steady downpour before we reached Boyer.

This was 1935. In recent weeks several brief storms had brought an end to the summer's drought.

Prof, Sody, and I took refuge in the cabin, hoping that the shower would end soon. When the sun finally peeked through the clouds three hours later, Prof and I started for the station, leaving our companion grading papers at the cabin since the clouds still looked threatening and Sody was not dressed for rain. I was lucky. I was wearing the old canvas jacket and pants Prof had discarded when he bought a new outfit for himself. He had warned me that this might be a wet day.

"I wonder what all we'll see today," Prof said as we trudged through the meadow toward the forest trail. "Rains like we've been having bring a lot of things out of hiding. It should be a fine day for slugs!"

"Do you think we'll see any of the little salamanders?" I asked.

"I think so. They usually come out of aestivation as soon as the woods get wet. *Scaphinotus* should be out, too, and maybe some earthworms. You count the ground beetles, slugs, and any other extras while I keep track of spider webs, mole burrows, chipmunks, and birds."

Inside the forest every bit of vegetation was loaded with water. We got an unwelcome shower whenever we brushed against a shrub or touched the branch of a tree. In the spongy forest floor many kinds of fungi, rejuvenated by the autumn rains, had renewed their growth and were hastening the decomposition of leaves, needles, twigs, and logs—anything awaiting recycling. The scent of decaying vegetation filled the humid atmosphere. Countless invisible spores, released from mushrooms and fruiting bodies of other fungi, heightened the musty odor.

We had barely begun our climb to the ridgetop when a *Scaphinotus* scurried across our trail. It was one of the inch-long, banjo-shaped black ground beetles we had seen many times before. I noticed two more beetles like it on the moss nearby.

A little farther along I exclaimed, "Look, Prof, here's one of the little salamanders." A tiny, smooth-skinned, red-bodied creature, not quite four inches long, moved ever-so-slowly over the ground near a rotting log. The bright yellow stripe on its back had caught my eye.

"Oh, yes! That one's known as the woodland salamander," Prof explained. "We haven't seen any of them since last spring. Doubtless this one spent the summer in some moist rotten log. Just as I expected, the rains brought it out of aestivation." (This one is now known as the western redback.)

As was our custom, from there on we did little talking. Eyes and ears had to be alert to observe plant and animal activity, and keeping a mental record of what we saw required concentration. Besides, climbing ridges, clambering over logs, and hiking at a brisk pace left little breath for conversation.

All sorts of creatures were afield including many we had not seen during the dry summer months. Soon we had to use care not to step on a large yellowish-green slug that was stretched out a full five inches across the trail, in no hurry to go anywhere. From then on we saw many of these large slugs, most of which were plain olive green though a few were spotted with black. Today these slugs are called banana slugs.

On the ridgetop we found a white-bodied snail (*Haplotrema*). Its thin, smooth, olive green shell stood out against the dark needles on the trail. We had often seen snails of this kind when the woods were damp but not cold.

Then as we climbed from Little Salmon River up to the main trail I spied a large millipede crawling laboriously over the trailside moss. About a fourth inch wide and fully two inches long, its shiny black back and yellow marginal spots made it conspicuous. "That's *Harpaphe*," Prof said. We saw another one nearby.

Just beyond Salmon River two orange-bellied salamanders were creeping beside the trail. These extremely toxic russet-backed amphibians, four to six inches long, are found in damp places throughout the Northwest, but we saw them only occasionally on Saddleback. They are noted for spectacular mass migrations which take place early in the spring when they return to their ancestral lakes or ponds for the annual breeding ritual. One morning years ago as I drove along the narrow paved coastal roadway near Tierra del Mar, a small community on the Oregon coast, hundreds, perhaps thousands, of these salamanders were struggling along on their laborious journey from a woodland to a small lake across the roadway. Males and females come together in tremendous numbers at these times but, once their eggs are deposited and fertilized, the parents depart, leaving their tiny offspring unattended in jelly-like egg masses in the shallow water near the shore for the whims of nature to determine their fate.

After we passed the salamanders we paused at our usual place for resting before starting the final climb up the ridge to the station. Prof seated himself on a medium-sized log and, assuming his characteristic note-taking posture with his right ankle resting on his left knee to form a table for his left-handed jotting, removed his small aluminum notebook from his coat pocket and said, "Now let's record what we've seen."

Our tally listed fourteen *Scaphinotus*, two *Harpaphe*, fifteen big green slugs, four spotted ones, four white-bodied snails, and two orange-bellied salamanders (now known as newts).

"Prof," I asked. "What do these big slugs eat? I've followed slime trails out onto the moss and seen them feeding on slime mold, but I haven't found any plants that looked as though slugs had been feeding on them."

"I can't say," he replied. "I saw one once feeding on a dead wood rat. I've discovered them up in salmonberry bushes and on ferns, and I've seen their ribbons of green excrement on plants. We know they feed some on vegetation. But I've never noticed much damage—nothing like there would be if this number of large garden slugs was in a yard. That subject needs more research.

"Now we'd better get going," he added, rising and tucking his notebook under his disabled arm.

We had gone only a short distance when he stopped abruptly, exclaiming, "Now see *this*! Let's find out what's going on here." Immediately in front of us a group of about twenty-five *Scaphinotus* were voraciously attacking a large white megascolecid earthworm which had become stranded, probably by the recent rain.

"I knew these big black beetles were snail eaters," Prof said. "That's their common name. They're also supposed to prey on slugs. But this is a new one. Now we can add earthworms to the list." After recording what we had seen, he closed his notebook, saying, "I wonder what we're going to find next."

What we found next was another group of the beetles clustered around a second large earthworm, all jockeying for the best positions for feeding on it. This time there were nineteen beetles, including a mating pair. Farther up the trail we came upon fourteen more beetles attacking a third, quite different earthworm, a small red one.

By the time we arrived at the station we had seen eleven more beetles, four more large green slugs, and a handsome, smaller gray-streaked slug with a yellowish mantle (*Prophysaon andersonii*).

Rain had begun again so we attended to the important task of starting a fire before we did anything else. Then I relaxed while Prof completed his meticulously kept trail notes, a record which has since proven to be indispensable.

As he finished his notations, the Professor commented, "It's interesting what the rains bring out of hiding, but we know so little about these animals. We don't really know anything about the *Scaphinotus* beetles except when they're active and a few things they eat. And we don't know a thing about that millipede except that its scientific name is *Harpaphe haydeniana* and that it moves about during the warm damp days of spring and again at this time of year.

"Also, at this point we know pathetically little about the habits of slugs and snails. However, I think what disturbs me more than anything else, though, is that we've collected only one of the large earthworms here at the station. Even on damp days like this we've seen them only rarely anywhere. Today, however, we found three of them in different places along the trail. We don't know their habits, where they may be found, or how common they are. It's frustrating."

Rising to get another stick of wood for the fire, he added with a sigh, "This place has a wealth of information to offer to those who have the time and patience to ferret it out. It's a shame so little is known. If only we had more time."

Noteworthy days such as this revealed to us many wonders of the forest floor waiting to be discovered by anyone with curiosity and an observant eye. Gradually we learned that the creatures the autumn rains had brought out were members of a troupe that patrol the surface. They hunt through mosses and litter, stalking unwary prey or sniffing and slurping decaying matter or, after exploring the surface, tunnel deep into the soil like mechanical roto-rooters cleaning the drainage pipes of a home. All of these creatures are active throughout the rainy seasons, except the coldest part of winter. Other members of the troupe enter the scene in the sunnier, hotter, drier seasons.

The head and thorax of the *Scaphinotus* are modified for getting into the whorls of snails and their long legs enable them to get around so well that they tackle not only snails, slugs, and earthworms, but also the larvae and pupae of insects and, in fact, almost anything that isn't too large for them to handle alone. Then, they may gang up in a free-for-all as they did with the worms. They may also resort to scavenging, sniffing out scraps of food from lunches, dead invertebrates, or small mammals that have been caught in traps. We never found them at rest, but these beetles are said to seek refuge in any place that is convenient. They are so conspicuous in the damp days of spring and fall that Prof used them in his thesis as an indicator for those seasons.

An interesting relative of the snaileater is a very smooth, very shiny, black beetle slightly less than an inch long. Its jaws project far forward from the rest of its head, giving it the name *Promecognathus*, meaning "prominent jaws." The rest of its name, *laevissimus*, means "very smooth." One observer has seen these beetles feeding upon the millipede *Harpaphe*. He says that the beetle sidles up to one of the millipedes and nips it behind the head, severing its nerve cord and immobilizing it. Then the beetle bites off the legs of its victim, cuts it into chunks, and eats the chunks at its leisure.

Because *Harpaphe* is a slow mover it is easy prey for *Promecognathus*. We found millipedes of this kind creeping about whenever weather conditions were favorable. Though we wondered about their habits, we were never able to learn what they ate, where they spent their time when not wandering, or what the young millipedes looked like. We assumed they were scavengers, feeding on decaying plant material as many other millipedes do. Though I have found no account of their habits, I have seen a published illustration of one of them curled up in a molting chamber made of organic debris under the loose bark of a fallen Douglas-fir.

We learned more about the slugs as the research progressed. Those detested, slandered, slimy, and yet fascinating creatures are always about on mild days when the forest is damp and clouds veil the sun.

The large olive green or dark spotted slug of our moist Northwestern forests, *Ariolimax columbianus*, is the giant slug of North America. The "ario" of its scientific name, meaning "very" and the "limax" meaning "slug," indicate that it is the "veriest slug" of slugs, while the "columbianus" says that it is found in the Northwest where the Columbia River flows. Adult slugs are commonly six to eight inches long and may measure as much as ten inches. In the entire world of land slugs, this one is second in size only to *Limax maximus,* the great gray slug of Europe. That one sometimes measures twelve inches. Our *Ariolimax* is drab in color throughout the northern part of its range. In California, however, it is often yellow with a greenish tinge and may even be pure yellow. That is where they were first called banana slugs.

Slugs and snails are closely related but a snail carries a little shell house on its back. The giant slug has no visible shell, but it does have a tiny vestige hidden beneath the mantle which covers its anterior end. On the right side of this mantle is the hole through which the animal breathes. Neither slugs nor snails have a true lung but both breathe air by using a large internal cavity that serves as a lung.

Slugs cannot control the loss of water through their thin skin, so they have to have a moist environment. They avoid dry weather and bright sunny days by retreating under logs and into holes and burrows. Once a slug finds a place which satisfies it, it may return to that place throughout the rest of its life.

Slugs are fascinating to watch in motion. Whenever one of them searches for food it extends two sets of tentacles. Functioning independently, the upper, longer tentacles swivel about like periscopes, stretching and rotating to gain a better view in all directions. Small black eyes at the tips of these tentacles do not form images but detect changes in light intensity and help the slug to avoid patches of bright sunlight. The lower, shorter tentacles are sensors for touch and smell. The slug uses them in feeling its way and in locating the sources of attractive odors. These "sniffers" are so keen that they can detect a suitable odor from a distance of several feet.

Gliding smoothly through the forest, this mild-mannered mammoth of the slug world skids over a carpet of thick, sticky slime secreted by a gland just under its head. Heavy slime protects its soft body from sharp objects while a thin watery slime, moving from the center toward the edges of its foot, helps the slug along, leaving a glistening slime trail behind it. A slug's footprint is a slime trail!

Sometimes slime can keep a slug from being eaten. When a slug is threatened, it retracts its tentacles, makes its body short and fat, folds its head and tail beneath its body, and emits a very thick mucus. The repugnant mucus, plus the contracted ball-like shape, keep some enemies from biting into the slug or from being able to swallow it if it is bitten. These defenses give protection from some enemies, but the giant slugs, as well as other slugs and snails, are an important food of shrews, shrew moles, and moles—all of which spend their days underground but come out at night to feed when the slugs are most active. Prof once saw a Pacific giant salamander feeding upon a giant slug. This wide range of predators keeps the populations of forest mollusks well in check.

Both slugs and snails use a toothed tongue known as a radula to take food into their mouths and tear it up. This unique scraper rasps food into a pulp and its tiny file-like teeth, pointing backward toward the throat, direct the food into the esophagus. Though the teeth break off constantly, they are replaced by new rows which form at the back of the radula.

With all their special equipment, slugs are indeed model sniffers and slurpers! Giant slugs eat living and decaying vegetation, fungi, lichens, algae, roots, fruit, seeds, bulbs, earthworms, centipedes, animal droppings, and carcasses. In fact, they apparently eat almost anything, even, as once observed, the epidermis from a sleeping small boy's dirty face. Mushrooms, though, are their favorite food.

I'm indebted to Alice Bryant Harper for much of my information about these interesting creatures which glide along "seeing," "smelling," or "tasting" their environment with their tentacles. For more than twenty years she devoted time to observing banana slugs in northern California. In her charming little book *The Banana Slug: A Close Look at a Giant Forest Slug of Western North America* she says, "For the most part, the banana slug keeps to its native habitat where it is in balance with other plants and animals. If all banana slugs were destroyed, the natural chain of life would be altered in these spectacular western forests."

The slender, three-inch-long gray-streaked or "humped" slugs (*Prophysaon*) are also fungus eaters. Once we saw two large humped slugs and four smaller ones nibbling at the underside of a shelf fungus. Humped slugs were less numerous than the giant slugs.

Snails were not abundant in our forest community but we encountered two kinds fairly often. One with a white body and pale olive green shell (*Haplotrema vancouverense*) we learned is a predator. It consumed completely the body of a smaller snail of its kind that we had placed in a container with it. That snail obviously is a hunter but it moves so slowly that it is more of a sniffer than stalker. It certainly can't pounce. Some observers say that these olive green snails specialize in enchytraeids and other small annelids. The other snail (*Vespericola columbiella*) which was relatively common is smaller, hairy, and brown. It feeds mostly on fungi which it finds in rotting wood or in the litter of the forest floor. This snail even leaves the ground to climb onto salal bushes, ferns, and vanilla leaf plants and other herbs, probably searching for decomposing fruit or leaves. A third snail, the handsome, heavy-shelled large brown snail (*Allogona townseniana*) that I have seen in other forest areas, was very rare on Saddleback. We learned nothing about its habits but it is said to feed on mushrooms.

A snail's shell "house" protects it in many ways. When the day becomes dry or too warm the owner of this house can retreat inside, close the door tightly, and wait until it is safe to venture forth again. The snail's shell is also a defense against some enemies, but not against the snaileater. With its narrow head and thorax this banjo-shaped beetle can reach into the shell for a satisfying meal.

Though neither slugs nor snails were abundant, they are part of the clean-up crew on the forest floor. They play a significant role in breaking down organic litter, and their ribbons of excrement are a nitrogen-rich fertilizer.

On a mild, not-too-dry day a watchful eye may also find one of the little plethodont salamanders or even one of the rare tailed frogs. Under such conditions both these amphibians wander about hunting spiders, small beetles, sowbugs, millipedes, springtails, or other tiny animals. However, during the dry months of summer, salamanders and frogs retreat to the cool, moist interiors of well-decayed logs to aestivate. Such spaces inside old logs or under slabs of bark and decaying wood are havens of safety for them at any time of year.

Native earthworms did not reveal their secrets easily. Prof had a special interest in them because he had studied earthworms for his master's degree at the University of Nebraska. He was puzzled because we never saw earthworms at or near the station except in wet weather when, with luck, we might find one crawling on the surface. Prof wondered where their burrows were and where the worms we saw on the trail came from.

He was familiar with nightcrawlers and other worms whose ancestors arrived in this country as imports. Many of them were in the soil which had been used as ships' ballast during early days of colonization and was then dumped near harbors to make room for American products to be exported to European markets. These worms had spread far and wide—some brought west by pioneers with their favorite plants—from those harbor areas until they are now found everywhere in settled rural and urban sites.

These European imports come to the surface to feed. There they break down soft-tissued plants and much of the litter layer, mixing it with underlying soil. Some species are easy to find because they deposit soft castings of undigested matter around the openings of their burrows.

Habits of the native worms are different. Learning those habits was a real challenge, taking time and much detective work. When the summer of 1937 arrived and Prof still had not found where the worms lived, he decided we had not been looking for them deep enough in the soil. He knew that the European nightcrawlers tunnel deeply into the ground particularly in dry and cold weather. Perhaps the native worms also did that. So in July and August we started digging deeper and taking larger samples than we had ever made before. During those months we found twenty-five earthworms in four samples. Most of those worms were down below ten inches, some were almost eighteen inches. Nearly all of them were immature and, unfortunately, several had deteriorated so much before we preserved them that they could not be identified. Prof concluded that the adult worms must be much farther down in the soil than we were able to dig.

From these samples, earlier observations, and especially from later research done by Dorothy McKey-Fender and her son William Fender, we learned many things. Our native worms usually do not have open burrows. That makes them difficult to find. As a rule, the worms are not seen when they come near the surface to feed because they move about under the moss and litter, grazing on those materials. Nor do they leave telltale piles of castings. Any castings these worms leave on the surface are inconspicuous, quite different from the rings of soft castings around the openings of burrows of nightcrawlers and some other imports. The native worms are, in a very real sense, the original roto-rooters. They literally chew their way into the soil, usually to a depth of several feet. In that way they increase the porosity of the soil and open channels into which plant roots can grow. Native worms do little or no mixing of litter with soil. Instead, they deposit granules of excrement far down in the soil in the tiny spaces which radiate out from their burrows.

Only in the wet weather of spring and fall when the soil was damp, the air humid, and the temperature mild did we occasionally see two different kinds of the large native earthworms moving about slowly on the surface. Some are much larger than even the largest nightcrawlers. When the weather is dry, as it is much of the summer, or cold, as it is in the middle of winter, these native worms go very deep into the soil where living conditions are more favorable.

These large native worms are unpigmented and white and smell like lilies, hence their name, *Driloleirus*, "worm lily." The smaller species is some twelve inches long and about the thickness of a little finger, the other, about the same thickness as the first, is fifteen to eighteen inches long. Neither had been described in scientific publications when Prof was doing this research.

Two other kinds of earthworms lived in the station area. One, an undescribed *Drilochaera*, is a slender white worm that grows to about six inches long. It was found a half-foot or so beneath the surface and seems to require the support provided by the soil of its burrow. The "chaera" part of that name means "happy," from Happy Valley where the worms were first collected. Two of these worms were in the samples taken in the summer of 1937.

The fourth sort of earthworm, *Arctiostrotus*, lives in rotten logs and in decaying vegetation near the surface of the soil. We discovered one worm of this kind in the upper soil in the summer of 1937. These worms are slender and up to about six inches long, but unlike the others, they are red and shiny and lash back and forth violently when picked up. Surprisingly, this kind of worm was described from the Queen Charlotte Islands in 1892. It is the most northerly of the North American native worms, hence the generic name which means "north spreader."

Due to their tunneling activities and the granules of excrement they deposit, our native earthworms are tremendously effective agents in returning nutrients to the soil. The work of the large worms is especially important because they penetrate deeply, opening and enriching the soil. It seems significant that nearly a century and a half has passed since Darwin wrote his book on the importance of European earthworms, yet the habits of native North American earthworms are still largely unexplored.

The casual visitor to the forest seldom notices the creatures of the forest floor. Even most people doing forest research pay little attention to them. And yet these animals are all part of the forest's clean-up and recycling crew. Each goes about its work in a different way. Some, as scavengers, chew up, break into bits, and partially digest many kinds of dead and dying plant materials, fungi, animal bodies and excrement. Others prey on sick, weak, old, or even overly abundant animals found on the lower vegetation or on the surface of the floor. And the large earthworms mix soil with bits of plants and other things and carry the residues deep into the soil in channels they create.

We learned the habits of some of these creatures before Prof's study of the Saddleback forest community ended. The work of many other observers in more recent years has added to that information. To this day, however, much is still unknown about the often overlooked stalkers, sniffers and slurpers, and roto-rooters of our Northwest forests.

Shelf fungus.

Chapter Thirty
Make Mine Truffles, Please

WHEN WE CAPTURED those little reddish-brown mice in 1937, we never dreamed that they were essential to the well-being and survival of Douglas-firs and other forest trees. To us they were merely pretty little mice with short legs and tail, a compact body, and fur partly concealing their ears.

We had no idea that they might be unusual, until Stanley G. Jewett told us that they were redbacked voles and that few of them had been found anywhere in Oregon and none had been taken before in the Oregon Coast Range. At his urging, Prof and I gathered the bits of information we could find, and wrote the paper which I gave at the meeting of the American Society of Mammalogists at Denver in June 1940. Nearly thirty years passed before wildlife biologist Chris Maser and co-workers began studying these voles and discovered that they had a gourmet taste: they ate nothing but truffles, fruiting bodies of mycorrhizal fungi, when given a choice.

Following that discovery, Maser and mycologist James Trappe made an intensive study of these voles. They uncovered a three-way support system shared by redbacked voles, mycorrhizae, and Douglas-firs. No one of these lives well without the others, at least in this region.

Mycorrhizae, meaning "fungus-roots," a term coined a little over a century ago, are webs of fungal threads which form among the tangle of tiny rootlets where they act as extensions of the plant's root system absorbing water and essential elements such as nitrogen and phosphorus from the soil. In return the plant supplies the fungal network with carbohydrates and vitamins. Thus a vital link is formed. The benign fungus takes carbon from the roots in exchange for the soil nutrients.

Woody plants, such as trees, have increased survival rates due to mycorrhizae. Further, it is now becoming clear that mycorrhizae probably control the successional development of a forest through the variable routing of nutrients, even between trees of other species. Many herbs also require this fungus-root association and grow far better with mycorrhizae than without.

When networks of mycorrhizal threads have grown enough to store an abundance of food they form truffles, fruiting bodies in the soil, not above the soil like mushrooms, to which they are related.

Truffles are fleshy and vaguely resemble small potatoes. Certain kinds are delicacies prized by gourmet cooks. Each species of truffle has a particular odor—fruity, cheesy, spicy, garlicky, fishy, or foul—which intensifies as the truffle matures. Truffle eaters have a keen sense of smell and are able to locate these fruiting bodies because of the odors they give off. Growing underground, truffles are better protected from frost and drying than are mushrooms. They mature slowly over a period of weeks or months so they ensure a more stable source of food than do mushrooms, which last only a few days after pushing through the soil's surface.

Each truffle contains millions of spores which can develop into mycorrhizae when they come into contact with plant rootlets, and these spores are still able to grow after passing through the digestive tract of a mammal. But unlike the mycelia, which fruit in the form of mushrooms, the spores of which may be scattered by the wind, mycorrhizae are completely dependent upon fungus-eating mammals, such as voles, for the scattering of their spores. Each species of the thousands of kinds of mycorrhizal fungi has evolved in partnership with a particular plant. One example of this is the fungus which forms mycorrhizae in the roots of Douglas-firs, enabling them to become healthy, vigorous trees.

The coniferous tree/mycorrhizal fungus relationship had been known for some time, but the mammalian link was unknown before the research of Maser and Trappe. This three-partner mutualism is to these men an example of the very essence of the interrelationships existing in an ancient Douglas-fir forest. The redbacked vole needs the truffle for food; the truffle depends on the vole for dispersal of spores and on a mycorrhizal tree host for energy; the tree requires this web of fungi for uptake of nutrients and eventually it provides the rotten wood needed by the vole for cover. Moreover, because both voles and truffles specialize in rotten wood as habitat, the vole disperses the truffle spores to the kinds of places in which the fungus will thrive.

The Coast Range mountains and the coastal areas of northwestern California and western Oregon are some of the few places in the world where climate permits year-round fruiting of truffles. Once scientists learned the habits of the redbacked vole, the vole was found to be common in the forests of this area. This vole makes its home in, or under, fallen trees in nearly all stages of decay, spending its time below ground, tunneling from one fruiting body to another, living on truffles. Rarely are truffles unavailable. When this does happen, the vole feeds on lichens.

Tragedy occurs when a forest is clearcut. Mycorrhizae cannot live without their host trees and so no truffles are formed. Within a year after the logging and burning of all the trees of an ancient forest, redbacked voles disappear. Both their food supply and natural habitat have been destroyed.

Besides this interdependency of vole, mycorrhizae, and Douglas-fir, many other surprising relationships have developed between widely diverse organisms in the natural world. Although often called *symbiosis, mutualism* is the more precise term for this relationship when both, or all, species are benefited as in the case of the vole, mycorrhizae, and Douglas-fir. It is even probable that Planet Earth (its biosphere [life], atmosphere [air], hydrosphere [water], and geosphere [rock and soil, "earth"]) form one great mutualistic system. Anything that happens to one affects all.

After the first heavy rains began in the fall, another striking example of mutualism appeared in our forest. Lichens resumed growth and developed fruiting bodies. The first lichens were encrustations on rocks along the trail and on the bark of old logs and stumps. Some were grayish-green filaments which looked a bit like moss, with which they are sometimes confused. The encrusting lichens appeared as a colorful bluish-green film on the rocks or on the logs and stumps. Their color caught our attention but their tiny shapes, granular or flaky and no larger than a pinhead, made them look more like bits of the rock than like plant life. Some encrusting lichens may be so deeply embedded in rock or other substrate that little is exposed but the fruiting bodies.

It seemed almost impossible that such mere flecks could be anything living, but under the microscope these tiny lichens, as well as the other forms of lichens, are revealed as a combination of two kinds of plants—great numbers of algal cells woven into a matrix of fungal filaments.

Lichens are one of nature's outstanding examples of mutualism. In this partnership, the relationship is so intimate that the species included form a single body. The "algae" (now known to be Cyanobacteria (Monera) and Chlorophyta (Protoctista), containing chlorophyll, provide the essential carbohydrates and other organic compounds, while the fungal filaments absorb water, supply anchorage when the lichens are attached, and perhaps also obtain minerals. Some lichens are leafy and form attractive rosettes or clusters on rocks and on tree trunks and branches. Others are filamentous, producing short moss-like plants or long streamers that drape from the branches of trees like Spanish moss. A third growth form is that of the tiny encrusting lichens. Though they contain algal elements, lichens are classified as fungi.

Lichens were plentiful and varied in both forest stages. Encrusting lichens were common in both, and moss-like filamentous lichens as well as leafy forms were widespread on the bark of ancient trees. However, we didn't have much chance to see the filamentous or leafy forms, for deer browsed them off in the wintertime whenever they were within reach.

In recent years (since the late 1980s) ecologists studying ancient forest canopies all along the Western mountains from British Columbia to California have been astounded by the size, weight, and diversity of leafy lichens they have found—around 130 species. These lichens are nitrogen-fixing and provide the trees with much of their supply of the essential nitrogen nutrients.

A few weeks after the lichens first appeared, usually by October, the woods were brightened with a colorful array of mushrooms and other fungal bodies of many shapes, sizes, and colors.

Fungi had flourished in the ancient forest but I had never seen an array equal to those in the young forest. Nourished by debris from logging, the area blossomed with mushrooms and other colorful fruiting bodies—the "flowers" of fungi which would provide the spores from which new fungi would develop.

The fungal body producing these fruiting structures was a mass of delicate, living threads, known as a mycelium. These threads, or hyphae, are so fine that they are invisible to the naked eye except when twisted or packed together in strands. A mycelium is not a structured body but an erratically shaped growth. When a spore germinates, a cylindrical, threadlike filament sprouts from it, divides, and grows into a mycelium on any suitable substrate, such as a twig, a log, or a mass of any kind of decaying organic matter. Few people, even those who collect mushrooms, have seen the mycelium from which the mushrooms grew.

This wealth of mushrooms, or toadstools as they are sometimes called, intrigued Nancy, my main student assistant at the time. She collected more than forty kinds of fungal fruiting bodies, took them to the lab, and tried to identify them. On a single day she found twelve different kinds in the station area alone (not all of them mushrooms) and several more along the trail. To her disappointment, only a few of those species were in the field guides available at that time.

Nearly three-fourths of these fungal growths were gill mushrooms, the kinds most familiar to collectors. Their spores form on gills, delicate leaf-like plates which hang down from the underside of the mushrooms' umbrella-like caps. Some of these gill mushrooms were five inches or more in diameter, and tall. Others were much smaller. Some were tiny. Many were solitary, the only fruiting body produced by a single mycelium. Sometimes several individuals grew from one mat of filaments, while still others occurred only in small clusters, or in dense, extensive clumps. Though the gill mushrooms were predominantly tan, brown, or yellow, we found some of every color of the rainbow except green, blue, or bright purple, though even such colorful kinds exist. Some were pure white. Some were black, others mottled, and many had colorful caps and white stalks.

Nancy discovered that a few of the mushrooms were pore fungi, which look much like the gill mushrooms but produce their spores in tubes instead of gills. One pore fungus was a bulky *Boletus*, five inches or more in diameter and with a heavy stalk. Two others were quite different in appearance. They were shelf or bracket fungi. One of them, growing on the ground in the fire shelter crater, was made up of small clumps of dark brown, woody-textured fungi bearing inverted caps with concentric lines on their tops and pores on their underside. The other species, a larger bracket fungus growing on the side of a log, had white pores and a pinkish top, which was brown near the base.

Inch-and-a-half wide, brownish-gray, pear-shaped puffballs, with a hole in the center of each cap through which spores had been released, thrived in thick clumps or clusters on the rocky soil of the trail.

Dainty tan and white (or brown and white), bell-shaped cups or "nests," about one-fourth inch across, grew on many kinds of dead twigs, each one holding a group of extremely tiny round "eggs" full of spores which are dispersed when raindrops strike. These birds' nests or fairy cups were, to me, the most interesting of all the kinds of fungus fruiting bodies we found. My notes report eighty-four cups on a single stick one inch wide and four inches long. Fairy cups were abundant all along the trail as well as in the research area. Often the twigs which held them were partly concealed by dead leaves.

Many-branched, fleshy coral fungi, bright orange shading into white at the base, closely resembled the colorful marine corals for which they are named. These beauties, several inches tall, grew in groups under the young hemlocks at the station. Other corals along the trail included a similarly formed but very different sort. It was tougher, white with a black base, and grew on the root of a decomposing log.

A bright orange fungus with thin, brittle flesh formed into amorphous shallow cups, varying from an inch to several inches in width, was abundant on rotten twigs beside the trail. This cup fungus, familiar to many people, often grows on woody mulch or chips by roadsides or in gardens.

A translucent white jelly, the individual caps of which were about one-half inch wide, rather lop-sided, and shaped like a spatula, we found only once.

This wealth of mushrooms displayed a wide range of odors, flavors, and edibility, as well as striking differences in appearance. Some of the mushrooms were ones prized by collectors for their delightful flavors, others were reputed to be less palatable, slightly poisonous, or even deadly. Our gill mushrooms included an *Amanita*, the genus containing some of the most deadly of all mushrooms. We decided not to test the edibility of our find.

Slime molds also had a resurgence of activity in the fall. One day we noted two rather small fan-shaped sheets of a jelly-like, semi-liquid living substance on decomposing wood in a cool, damp, shady place beside the trail. One of these was bright orange, the other, pale yellow.

These strange growths are not a kind of fungus but are classed as Myxomyceta in the Kingdom Protoctista. They are peculiar organisms which show both animal and plant characteristics in the course of their life cycle. Though we saw other slime molds later, we did not search especially for them in the young forest.

Since then I have learned that each of those jelly-like sheets was a slowly growing organism, feeding and expanding in size in the same way as an amoeba. These creeping, feeding, animal-like fans were the non-fruiting phase (the plasmodium) of the slime molds. Later in the year when the weather becomes drier and the slime molds mature, the plasmodium becomes dotted with fruiting bodies which look like pinhead-sized mushrooms. When touched, these release clouds of dust-fine spores. In this reproductive stage, the fruiting body (the sporangium) with its spores has characteristics of a lower plant, commonly known as a mold.

True slime molds are often found in the soil and among logs, twigs, and leaves decomposing on the forest floor. Slime molds, along with mushroom-producing fungi, are important agents in the decay of woody materials. If we had turned over old logs and searched for slime molds, we would have found them in abundance.

Though fungi are generally thought of as plants, they are in a kingdom by themselves. They are totally unlike common green plants which, with the aid of energy from the sun, manufacture their own foods (carbohydrates, fats, and proteins) from carbon dioxide and water through the process of photosynthesis. Hence, green plants are known as producers.

Fungi, on the other hand, having no chlorophyll, cannot build food from inorganic materials. They can only change compounds which have been built by other organisms. Fungi are decomposers. They get their nourishment by digesting organic compounds which are present in decaying plants—such as logs—or in other decomposing organic matter. Fungi are aided by slime molds in this process of decomposition and by some kinds of bacteria, tiny organisms in the Kingdom Monera.

As a mycelium develops from the fungal spore, its threads secrete enzymes which digest food material outside the body of the threads. This digested material, in solution, is absorbed by the threads and used in the life processes of the fungus. In time, the mycelium is so well nourished that some of its nutrients are used to produce fruiting bodies, the mushrooms.

The fall "blossoming" of mushrooms on Saddleback was brought about by a wonderful complex of materials and events. The autumnal rains, falling upon the warm floor of the forest, thoroughly dampened the logs and other vegetative debris, thus producing conditions which were ideal for the germination of fungal spores and rapid growth of mycelia. Under such ideal conditions, the mycelia grew rapidly and soon obtained food enough to produce their fruiting, or reproductive bodies, the mushrooms. In the spring when the temperature increased and warmed the cold, very wet forest floor, another series of mushrooms appeared, but this series was not as striking as the one in the fall.

A log decays, or decomposes, because fungi and/or slime molds digest the various elements of the wood. Usually many kinds of fungi are present, competing with one another, but not all of the fungi compete. There is a division of labor. Fungi are numerous and each has its own way of life, so the methods of this destructive process are many and varied. One kind of fungus may digest only cellulose and another only wood (lignin). After a succession of fungi have worked through a log, it is broken down to the point where it cannot be recognized any longer. In this way, through the action of fungi and slime molds, the dead wood in the forest is reduced to humus. At this point, ground-living fungi and bacteria take over the task of decomposition.

Another facet, another link, in the symbiotic interrelationships in this story of lichens, slime molds, and fungi involves the feeding activities of the horde of miscellaneous invertebrates, insects, molluscans, and mammals which depends upon them for nourishment. Some research on this subject has been done with small mammals. Little, for other organisms. More mutualistic relations are sure to be revealed with further study.

Several small mammals of the forest share in the gourmet appetite of the redbacked vole, preferring truffles even to mushrooms. Flying squirrels live almost entirely in the tops of trees, gliding from one tree to another as they move about through the forest crown. They are referred to as "moonlight trufflers" because they descend to the ground at night to dig out truffles, feeding on them exclusively as long as truffles are available. When there are no truffles the squirrels eat the moss-like lichens found on the trees. Flying squirrels are seldom caught and almost never seen because of their nocturnal habits.

Though we felt certain that flying squirrels must live in our forest, only once during Prof's entire study did he, or any of his students, catch even a glimpse of one of them. At about three o'clock one January afternoon Prof watched intently as a flying squirrel sailed from a hemlock to the base of a large fir, a distance of about forty feet. The squirrel was close enough for Prof to see that it was brownish gray with a light belly and was a little larger than a chipmunk. He said it resembled a robin fluttering down to the ground. As it climbed back up the tree, at about halfway (approximately seventy-five feet), he lost sight of the squirrel. He noted that a warbler accompanied the squirrel in its climb.

The Oregon creeping vole looks so much like the redbacked vole that at first we had trouble distinguishing between them. The food habits of the creeping vole are not very well known but it also digs out and eats the fruiting bodies of fungi. Researchers say that when creeping voles live side by side with redback voles in the old forests, they, too, feed heavily on fungi, especially truffles.

Though chickarees, the sassy little red squirrels which make their homes in coniferous trees, eat lots of conifer seeds, researchers have learned that truffles are one of their primary food sources. I've watched more than once as a chickaree dug a choice morsel out of the ground and rushed to the crown of a nearby Douglas-fir with it.

Deer mice forage over the forest floor using a wide variety of foods, but they are opportunistic and include great quantities of truffles whenever these delicacies are available.

Chipmunks also eat truffles. In one study truffles were present in the stomachs of 93 percent of the chipmunks caught and made up 77 percent of their diet.

Bushy-tailed woodrats are not generally thought of as fungus eaters, but sometimes truffles are a major food even for them. Woodrats are not tidy, but defecate in their bulky nests. Consequently, as roots of host trees grow into the decaying trash of the nests or as rains wash spores from the feces into the soil, new rootlets of the trees encounter concentrations of mycorrhizal spores whenever woodrats have been feeding on truffles.

Shrews, being insectivores, feed mostly on invertebrates and small mammals. But interestingly, even some of them, such as Trowbridge's shrews, the species we had on Saddleback, occasionally eat fruiting bodies of fungi, including truffles.

Pacific jumping mice, which we did not find at the station but did see on Summit Prairie, eat mainly fruit in summer and fall; but fungi, including truffles, made up 10 percent of the volume of the stomach contents of fourteen individuals examined by one researcher.

Another link between small mammals and forest trees has also been unraveled. C.Y. Li and others working with him discovered that, in addition to mycorrhizal spores, nitrogen-fixing bacteria and yeast survive passing through the digestive tracts of rodents. All these organisms—the mammals, the mycorrhizae, the nitrogen-fixing bacteria, and the yeast—are highly important agents in the recycling activities that go on in the forest floor.

The gourmet appetite of these little mammals adds a new and important chapter to the recycling of forest nutrients. The mammals get their nourishment by nibbling on truffles, or on mushrooms, or on rootlets of various plants. Then, by scattering nutrient-rich feces they inoculate rootlets of trees and other plants with the spores of mycorrhizal fungi, or with nitrogen-fixing bacteria, thus insuring the continuing life of the forest.

In replacing forests with tree plantations, this natural recycling is largely, or completely, ignored. The forest floor is disturbed or, even worse, denuded and compacted, and much, or all, of this multiplicity of life is destroyed. Manmade fertilizers, herbicides, and insecticides are no substitute for nature's diversity.

Winter thermometer reading at the research site, 1962.

Chapter Thirty-one

Miracle of the Seasons

Professor Macnab amassed a huge collection of plants and animals during his five-year study on Saddleback Mountain. He also observed the forest community closely through all its seeming whims and caprices and garnered from those observations a store of data showing plant and animal responses to weather's infinitude of changes.

When he scrutinized all this tabulated information, the one clear theme he noted running through it was the *seasonal rhythm of life*. As a result, he used that theme for his doctoral dissertation, "Biotic Aspection in the Coast Range Mountains of Northwestern Oregon," in which he described the changing aspect of the forest as it responded to seasonal influences. Basic material from that thesis is applicable to the cycle of seasons as they occur in much of the Pacific Northwest.

The passing of seasons is low-key and looks much the same the year-round where the forest floor is carpeted with evergreen ferns, shrubs, and mosses and is sheltered by a canopy from which needles constantly sift down. The differing seasons are not as evident as they are in a forest of broad-leaved, deciduous trees where cycles of falling leaves, dormancy, and reawakening are conspicuous and familiar. Yet seasons are just as real and vital in the coniferous forest as they are anywhere, for seasons are dictated not by figures on a calendar, but by that mysterious mixture of light, moisture, temperature, atmospheric pressure, and currents which we call *weather*.

Awakening

Out of the depths of winter, out of dormancy and apparent death, the first faint signs of awakening life appear in this coniferous forest community sometime between late January and early March when the temperature first rises above the annual mean of 50°F. The weather is generally cloudy and rainy with scattered snow showers at higher elevations. Humidity is high with prevailing light-to-moderate southwesterly winds.

Buds swell. Seeds which seemed lifeless crack their shells and begin to sprout. A lengthening of days and a slight warming of the air bring a greener tinge to the bark of deciduous trees. No flowers are yet in evidence.

A few insects become active. Fresh burrows of mice, shrews, and moles appear sporadically, and chipmunks may be seen now and then. Jays and juncos return to the forest from their wintering quarters. Varied thrushes establish pairs.

Prof named this period in which life awakened the *Emerginine Sector*. In his thesis it was the third and final part of winter, the *Hiemal Aspect*.

Spring, the Season of Renewal and Rebirth

Around the first of April, when the highest weekly temperatures jump from 50°F or below to about 60°F or above, this season, which Prof called the *Vernal Aspect*, reveals itself as a resurgence to life. Precipitation is much less than it has been earlier. Winds become boisterous, but vary throughout the season and from year to year.

During the first month or so the renewal is gradual. Buds of shrubs unfold, revealing brighter greens, and herbs spring up to carpet the forest floor with fresh leaves and flowers. Wet places boast bright yellow skunk cabbages, which bears—newly emerged from hibernation—seek for their first meal. Hummingbirds visit the red flowerets on currant bushes. Chipmunks, moles, and voles become consistently busy and deer may be seen more frequently. Salamanders, slugs, and snails come out of their winter hiding places. Fungus gnats, flower flies, moth-wing flies, and a few other kinds of insects make their first appearance.

About a month into this season the weather becomes fresh, warm, and mild. Seemingly almost overnight a great wealth of new flowers join the earlier ones. This explosion of blossoms brightens the woods and fills it with subtle fragrances.

Though spring is known as the season for pollen-eating insects, their food habits are really quite diverse. Over-wintering insect eggs hatch and larvae emerge to gorge on tender leaves, twigs, and blossoms. Hordes of pollen-eating, leaf-eating, or needle-eating insects pop their pupal pods or emerge from their winter hiding places to share in the banquet provided by the plants. Crane flies and fungus gnats prefer mushrooms and other fungal growths; blow flies feed on carrion; and still other insects are predators.

Beetles and flies top the list as the most varied and plentiful of all the insects, but geometrid moths, ants, bees, and wasps are also numerous. *Scaphinotus*, our familiar companion in all but the coldest and driest periods, emerges late in the season. Adult insects mate and produce eggs for a new generation of their kind. Nearly all the insects active at this time are unique to the season.

Summer resident birds, returning from their winter homes, add their voices to those of permanent residents, creating for the forest its own distinctive symphony, as the males advertise their chosen territories, and pairs court, mate, and set up housekeeping. They nest at all levels in the forest, from boughs in the tallest trees to nooks and crannies on the forest floor, usually near a good supply of their favored food. Many birds feast on the smorgasbord of insect eggs, larvae, pupae, and adults. Others prefer seeds, needles, leaves, petals or pollen, or the sap of trees. However, even the most confirmed vegetarians include some insects in their diet, either larvae or adults, as a source of protein. Some birds are predators, seeking birds, small mammals, or other creatures as their prey; a few are scavengers; and still others, known as omnivores, eat most anything.

It is also during this season that most mammals, large or small, give birth and begin displaying their young.

From the tips of the tallest trees to depths within the soil, warmth and light from the sun, gentle rains, cool breezes, and other inanimate forces stimulate growth and birth in all forms of life—green plants, animals, fungi, and bacteria. Sap moving upward in trees causes cambium cells to divide and increase the trees in diameter, in height, and—via the roots—in depth. Similar growth occurs in other plants. Conifer twigs wear bright green needles. Herbs and shrubs grow new leaves and produce flowers. All creatures, from those in the treetops to those in the soil find an abundance of food and bring forth young. Spring overflows with an exuberance of new life.

Summer, the Season of Maturity and Fruition.

In summer all sorts of living things mature. The busyness of spring ends. The last birds nest, the latest flowers bloom. Many fruits ripen, and expendable vegetative parts begin deteriorating. The tempo of life decreases slightly. Prof designated this period the *Aestival Aspect*. It covers roughly two months from late May or mid-June to mid- or late August. It begins when a long spell of sunny, cloudless days conjures up the hottest, driest, and brightest season of the year. Temperatures soar into the high 70s, precipitation drops to almost nil, and light intensity reaches its highest level. Winds are moderate or breezy, and relative humidity is usually comfortably low. The season almost always closes with an extremely hot, dry period when temperatures climb to or exceed 80°F and humidity descends to 40 percent or less.

By the beginning of summer, the newness of spring has faded from the flowers of most herbs and shrubs, but two new kinds of plants, coralroot and Indian pipes, add their colors to the display. Chlorophyll is lacking in both of them but they have formed close symbiotic or mutualistic relationships with other plants for their nourishment. Coralroots bear slender brownish or reddish purple stalks crowded with small, dark red orchids. The Indian pipes, by contrast, are entirely white and produce clusters of erect, fleshy stems, four to eight or ten inches high, each of which bears at its end a nodding, white, pipe-like blossom.

Though some flowers of spring linger, pea-sized, reddish, globose berries have formed on lily-of-the-valley plants and their leaves are becoming ragged. The flowers of most other herbs and shrubs begin developing their fruits. Salmonberries and red huckleberries have ripened. Green fruits are forming on Oregon grape plants, but pinkish floral bells still grace most bushes of the salal.

As summer progresses, the last blossoms become fruits: berries, seedpods, capsules, and grains. By season's end most fruits have ripened. Some are nearly gone. Leaves become ragged and yellow as their chlorophyll supply is used.

Summer is known for its biting and bloodsucking flies. At least a dozen sorts, ranging in size from barely visible no-see-ums to burly, inch-long horse flies, are abundant and annoying.

Early in the season, the insect population reaches a peak both in numbers and kinds. Some spring species remain. Aphids thrive. Flies and their kin dominate the scene in species and number of individuals and the variety of beetles drops but remains nearly 30 percent of the total insect diversity.

Summer has distinctive insects found in no other season, including a metallic blue, small-headed fly, skipper flies, some kinds of geometrid moths and parasitic wasps, spittlebugs, lacewings, scorpion flies, and cicadas.

As plants mature and summer progresses, the insect population decreases. Some insects live more than a single year, but those that have finished their duties of procreation die at this time or a little later, leaving the continuation of the species to larvae that are feeding and developing, to pupae in protective pupal cases, or to eggs deposited in carefully selected places to pass through the winter in a quiescent state.

Amphibia aestivate. Snails or slugs are seldom seen. The extreme dryness causes them to seek damper premises. About midseason *Scaphinotus* also disappears from the scene, awaiting the return of damp weather.

The woods are quieter, with less bird song. The frenzy of mating and establishing territories is over for the year. Parents are busy feeding and helping to rear their young, though some males leave that chore entirely to their mates. Young birds in rumpled-looking plumage sometimes appear with their adults.

Near the end of summer, birds tend to become very quiet. Adults with ragged, worn, plumage retreat to a secluded place until they grow new feathers. Most young birds, now fully grown and able to fend for themselves, shed their juvenile plumage and acquire their first adult feathers. Territorial boundaries disintegrate and, when the molt is finished, summer resident birds, adult and young alike, begin gathering in flocks as they feed and build a reserve of fat in preparation for their southward migration.

At this time creatures of all kinds grow from their childhood into early maturity. Deer fawns lose their spots, bear cubs go on hunting expeditions with their mothers, young chipmunks frisk in the bushes, and young chickarees work with their parents on immature conifer cones. Mice breed all year long, though they produce more young in the spring and summer than at any other time of the year. They mature so rapidly that those born in the spring often bear young of their own during the summer.

By the close of summer, the forest's biota, from green plants to insects, amphibians, birds, and mammals, achieves a recognizable state of maturity.

Autumn, the Season of Harvest and Storing

In Autumn, Prof's *Autumnal Aspect*, the bounty of the year is gathered and provisions made for another year, another generation.

Generally, as the dog days of August drag to a close, the first light rain of autumn cools the air, increasing the humidity and ending the summer's long dryness.

Early autumn is a time of a few light frosts and brief wind-and-rain storms, interspersed with glorious Indian summer weather. Haze in the atmosphere lowers the light intensity. Short, humid periods alternating with exceptionally dry ones lead into the later rainy part of the season.

The last fruits ripen. Herbs yellow with age. Plants commit their future to root, bulb, or seed.

With the first fall rains *Scaphinotus* becomes active again. Slugs and amphibians also reappear.

Spiders, both young and adult, are at the height of their predatory activity and far more abundant than at any other time of the year. Gossamer threads and many-patterned webs are everywhere. Laden with drops of dew or rain, they sparkle, jewel-like, in the morning sun. Long-legged harvestmen roam actively over the forest floor.

A drop in the insect population accompanies the ending of summer and the beginning of autumn. A full quarter of the insects are kinds present only in this season, hardy creatures able to be active even on the sunny days in the generally wet, cold weather of late autumn. Termites emerge in nuptial flights and the presence of adult leafhoppers also marks the beginning of autumn. Yellowjackets become irritable and inclined to sting. Mosquitoes swarm and are pestiferous. Beetles are less varied. Though many dipteran species change, they continue to be the most diverse order of insects.

The species of insects which live more than one season or year find secure places where they can overwinter, but a far greater number stash their future in the egg and die.

Nourished by the forest's plentiful supply of fruit, sap, and seed, and by insects, worms, and spiders, the summer resident birds depart about mid-September, while other birds begin forming flocks which pass over and through the forest in waves of intense activity, garnering their portion of the harvest.

Voles make ridges as they burrow through the humus, moles throw up fresh mounds, chipmunks are active, and chickarees harvest maturing cones. Larger mammals roam about restlessly, laying up a supply of fat from the forest's harvest to carry them through the rigors of winter. Deer of all ages are developing winter coats and bucks polish their antlers on shrubs and trees to remove the velvet.

The early part of autumn ends when the average minimum temperature falls to a point regularly below the annual mean of 50°F. Heavy rains and strong winds usher in this later portion of the season which is darker with more clouds and fog, and has few, if any, Indian summer days.

The annual destiny of plant life has now been fulfilled. Ragged leaves of herbs, attacked by mildew and fungi, become dark brown with decay and lose all vestiges of life. The leaves of deciduous shrubs and trees fall in steady showers and even conifers join in sprinkling the forest floor with worn-out needles. This litter becomes mulch, then humus for root and seed.

Beneath this cover, in the warm, moist, spongy floor of humus and woody decay, fungi of many sorts send out mycelial threads, and a wealth of mushrooms, coral fungi, and other fruiting bodies appear and reach a peak of abundance before the weather turns significantly colder.

Fungus-eating dipterans and beetles feed actively upon fungi, larvae of tiny leaf-mining moths gnaw tunnels in the tissues of salal leaves, and parasitic wasps are busy seeking hosts for their larvae.

Flocks of juncos drift through the mountains in their southward migration; otherwise, the bird population is rather stable with permanent resident birds feeding and moving quietly about.

Chipmunks and chickarees reach their peak in population as the young of the year help to store the winter food supply. Deer now have their winter coats of gray and adults are mating. Bears wander restlessly, completing their supply of fat before retiring into winter sleeping quarters.

When the weather turns colder, snails and slugs are rarely seen. *Scaphinotus* and amphibians disappear, marking the end of the season. Sometimes the first snow falls.

Cold-blooded creatures, whether insects, slugs, or salamanders, are always at the mercy of the sun, and as the sun sinks lower and lower, their clocks run down. The tempo for all life slows, the urgency of growth being over for another year. Life has been safely stored in root, bulb, pupa, embryo, and seed. In nature, survival of the species is important, not survival of the individual.

Autumn ends when the highest weekly temperatures fall to less than 55°F with a minimum of 40° or lower in late October or mid-November.

Winter, the Season of Quiet Rest

Winter, which Prof called the *Hiemal Aspect*, is dull, dark, and cold. It is a time of resting. Much of the forest is quiescent, asleep, or dormant and seemingly dead.

Extending from later October or mid-November to about the first of April, the season provides, at its beginning, nearly a month of transition from autumn into dormancy called the *Hiemine Sector* and, at its close, a month or more of gradual reawakening from quietude into full activity, the *Emerginine Sector*.

During this period the weather is usually cloudy with short clear periods punctuated by southwesterly gales. Precipitation (rainfall or snow) varies from an inch to more than five inches a week. Southwesterly winds predominate. Humidity is high. Minimum temperatures do not rise above 40°F, with highs near 50°F.

This transition sees the completion of processes begun earlier by plants and animals. Now that the leaves of deciduous trees and shrubs are gone, the evergreen character of the forest community reveals the many shades of green displayed by ferns, shrubs, and coniferous trees. Mosses and lichens, spurred by rain, brighten and form their distinctive reproductive bodies, adding to the display.

Only a few families of insects remain active consistently, chiefly fungus gnats, moth-wing flies, and winter crane flies. Whiteflies are present at first but soon decrease in numbers. Salal leaf-miner larvae end their season of work. A few small beetles are active for a while, then disappear. Adult spiders are busy on warm days only; otherwise they remain under leaves in a semidormant condition.

As the weather becomes colder, resident bird numbers diminish. Gray jays, juncos, and pileated woodpeckers commonly move to lower elevations, but reappear during warm periods. Transient winter visitors such as crossbills move about in the tree tops while bands of kinglets, chickadees, and other small birds flit through low-growing conifer thickets.

Winter's most severe weather usually begins about the middle of December when the temperature drops to between 50° and 30°F. This is the dead of winter, the period of deepest dormancy, Prof's *Hibernine Sector*. Everything seems dormant, even the conifers. An occasional insect may be found hanging quietly beneath a salal leaf. Tracks in the snow, however, disclose that life continues even in the depths of winter.

It is rainy and cold, with occasional heavy snows interspersed with clear, frosty days, and the lowest temperatures of the year. Humidity is high, light intensity is low, and precipitation usually averages two to three inches a week. These conditions last until about mid-February.

Like the pressing of a switch, the *Emerginine Sector* begins with a rise in temperature and light intensity.

Quietly, imperceptibly, during the seven or so weeks of the hibernine interval, clocks which have run down are being rewound in chrysalises or pupae, in gonads, wombs, rhizomes, bulbs, and seeds. The miracle of new life is beginning. One cycle of seasons ends; a new one begins.

Chapter Thirty-two
Bridging of Life in the Forest City

O N DOROTHY'S FIRST DAY at the research station, she and I sat near the fire searching through a few handfuls of duff spread out in a shallow pan. She was familiar with most aquatic organisms and knew many creatures from other kinds of habitats, but this was her introduction to the animals in the forest floor.

As we separated delicate strands of moss and searched through dead needles, bits of decaying wood, and particles of humus and soil, our first concern was to collect the collembolans. These tiny, wingless, gray or tan insects, commonly known as springtails, have phenomenal leaping powers—an ability which I learned later was due to a spring-like organ located on the underside of their abdomens. Stretched forward and held in place by an extremely small button-like catch, this spring snaps backward when the catch is released and launches the insect into the air for several inches, sometimes even for several feet. Snagging springtails required concentration and nimble fingers!

After a while, Dorothy asked, "Why does Prof want us to go through this stuff? It's awfully tiresome and boring."

Dimly remembered, our conversation continued something like this: "What we find here gives a pretty good idea of the kinds of creatures that live on and in the forest floor. Searching through this duff takes a lot of time, but Prof says it needs to be done, so like the soldiers in the *Charge of the Light Brigade*—'ours not to reason why, ours but to do or die!'"

Dorothy laughed, shrugged her shoulders, and said, "I guess if Prof wants it done, that's good enough for me."

We completed three samples, each about the size of a four-inch cube. In them were fifteen different kinds of animals, totaling ninety-two individuals, an average of thirty-one for each sample. Springtails made up more than a fourth of the total.

Dorothy looked thoughtful. In a little while she said, "These samples are ten-centimeter cubes, only slightly less than four cubic inches each. That means there are a hundred of them in a four-inch deep square meter, and a hundred times thirty-one equals 3,100, the number of these critters in each square meter of duff! I think I'm beginning to see why Prof thinks these samples are important. We step on a lot of critters every time we move around up here."

"We sure do and today we've collected only the ones we could see easily. There must be a lot of smaller creatures, and a bunch of springtails always get away. Probably many other things do, too."

"I wonder," Dorothy mused as though speaking to herself, "if loggers, hunters, and other people who pass through these forests *ever* think about the wealth of life hidden beneath their feet."

Sorting through litter and soil week after week was tiring and often boring, but it was interesting, too. Every sample was different. As time went by, we learned to recognize many kinds of creatures, and now and then we found one we had never seen or even heard of before.

Later, in graduate school, I learned about the Berlese funnel, a device Prof had not been aware of when he did his research. I found it to be a very effective method for separating tiny creatures from litter, and so, though I patterned my NSF study after Prof's research in most ways, I used a Berlese funnel for my litter samples.

The Berlese apparatus is simple. Ours was a galvanized metal funnel, some two feet long, with a top opening of about fourteen inches. The upper half did not taper, but the lower part tapered to a two-inch bottom opening. The metal lid had a receptacle for an electric light bulb. In use, a sample of duff was placed on a removable wire mesh fitted across the inside of the funnel where the taper began. There, under a bright light, the litter gradually dried out and the animals, seeking a dark, moist environment, moved downward until they fell into a collecting bottle below the funnel.

The results were amazing. We discovered that the forest floor literally swarmed with millions of tiny soil mites, many of them too small to be seen clearly without some magnification, and there were far more springtails and other creatures than we had dreamed. One of the first samples held 1,852 mites, 243 collembola, 10 false scorpions, 5 annelids, 4 geophilids, 2 spiders, 2 nematodes, 1 centipede, and 51 miscellaneous arthropods, a total of 2,170 microfauna in a sample of forest-floor litter that could have been cradled in a person's two cupped hands.

We took Berlese samples every week for a year and a half, usually several from different locations in the study area: under vegetation, in the open, near a crumbling log, where a fire had passed through, or from unburned spots. From ten samples, selected at random, we recovered 15,350 creatures. The numbers, per sample, varied from 2,318 to 638, with an average of 1,535. Translated into numbers of *visible* animals, that is 153,500 per square meter of duff, or 1,535,000,000 in a hectare (10,000 square meters or 2.47 acres). More than a billion and a half little creatures in the top four inches of an area slightly larger than two football fields! Yet many animals formerly recovered by handsorting were not retrieved by the funnel. Perhaps they dried out in the funnel and died before they could escape from the litter. Nor did those figures include the uncountable protozoans, bacteria, and fungi that live in the soil. Tread lightly. The ground is full of life!

We had hundreds of species of soil mites, but I was unable to find a systematist to identify mine.

Soil mites are wonderful converters of forest floor debris. Mostly they are oribatids, commonly called beetle mites because they have a hard outer covering and look a little like tiny beetles. Many of the oribatids in litter feed on mosses and algae, on mycelial threads of fungi, or on the decaying remains of higher plants. Some limit themselves to foods such as moss, while others, both young and adults, nibble deep passages in decaying wood. Still others bore into dead conifer needles and hollow them out. Certain ones are predators which feed on soft-skinned collembolans and on other small arthropods and their eggs.

This great host of mites nibbling away on plant and animal remains is tremendously important in the formation of soil. As they break down plant debris, they convert it into tiny balls of excrement (sometimes called "bug poop"), which are then acted upon by fungi or bacteria. Even in death, the empty exoskeletons of mites, collembolans, and other tiny creatures serve as incubators for the spores of some fungi.

Collembolans, the oldest known fossil insects (at least 400 million years old), have changed little in all that time. They are the most widespread of all soil insects, being found almost everywhere. Most of the collembolans in the Northwest forests are springtails that live in moss and surface litter, feeding on fungi, lichens, algae, and decaying vegetation. Ones that live deeper in the soil graze on microorganisms. All collembolans require pore space in the soil as well as moisture and food.

Springtails digest all sorts of organic wastes, an ability which makes them of great importance in the formation of soil. The mouths of some are built for chewing; others have long sharp stylets for sucking. Tiny live animals and carcasses, fecal pellets, bacteria, and an array of vegetable foods, including fungi, pollen grains, and bacteria are all common fare for them. Additionally, a bacterium in the intestine of collembolans can digest chitin, the horny covering of insects and mites, something many insects cannot do. Even when springtails do not chemically change the materials they eat, they break them into smaller bits, moisten, and make them available for use by even smaller organisms. They are also important agents in spreading fungi, another essential to soil formation, for fungal spores pass unharmed through the guts of springtails.

Our smallest collembolans were not springtails. They had very short legs and didn't jump. Most of them were immature. Though we had many kinds of collembolans, only forty-five species were identified, and all of those were springtails.

False scorpions—pseudoscorpions—are important predators in the forest floor. They resemble their much larger relative, the desert scorpion, but their habits are different. Ones that have been studied move in a slow walk. Instead of pursuing their food, they construct silken nests and wait for prey to come to them. When one is not spinning, it sits in its nest with its pinchers and front of its body projecting from the opening. It can snatch a passing mite or collembolan for a meal. Though there were many differences in the false scorpions we collected, I have no idea how many species there were, for the systematist who took mine never gave me any identifications. Prof had eight species named from his hand-sorted samples; four were new to science.

Sowbugs (woodlice or pillbugs) are more closely related to marine-dwelling crabs and shrimp than to insects. They are found worldwide in fairly moist places still wearing the gills and armor plates of their prehistoric marine ancestors. Their gills and lack of wax-coated skin make them sensitive to water loss and so they avoid dry sites. If they don't, they die! Since they feed mainly on moist, undecomposed leaf litter and bits of wood, sowbugs have an important role in the breakdown of litter and woody residues. Additionally, they mix fine grains of sand with their food, creating a desirable blend of organic and inorganic materials.

Great numbers of "white worms" lived in the litter and topmost portion of the soil. Like their larger relatives, the earthworms, these worms have bodies of many small segments and are true annelids, a name derived from the Latin, *annellus*, meaning little ring. As they move about feeding mostly on dead plant materials, these enchytraeids take in soil and mix it with plant and animal residues passing through their intestines. Consequently, they are important rapid formers of humus and soil. The few mature worms we found were about an inch long and from a new species which was named *Mesenchytraeus macnabi* in recognition of Prof.

We gathered scores of beetles: ground beetles, rove beetles, and click beetles, as well as lots of other tiny beetles that live in this hidden world. Most ground beetles are predatory; some are both predators and plant eaters; one species feeds almost entirely on springtails; another on Douglas-fir seeds; and several prey on other creatures in the litter. The rove beetles darting about in the humus were probably predators. Their larvae live in the top soil where some scavenge organic debris while others prey on an array of tiny creatures. Wireworms, click beetle larvae, feed on plant roots, but even they are helpful as they burrow about in the soil, leaving excrement and cast-off skins and opening channels which aid in aeration. A few wireworms are predators.

Larvae of craneflies, fungus gnats, midges, and some other dipterans spend their entire larval life in the forest floor feeding on rotting wood and other moist decaying plant materials. Students of some cranefly larvae report that they consume large amounts of litter which they break down into smaller pieces. They digest from this the soluble materials but leave the wood itself unchanged chemically. Fungus gnat larvae chew and quickly digest mushrooms and other fungi. Scavenging is the way of life for a huge assortment of dipterous larvae which aid in the decomposition of all sorts of things from animal excrement and bodies of dead creatures to decaying vegetation. Still other dipterous larvae are predators.

Tassel tails were entirely new to us. Wingless and fragile, they are tiny white insects with long antennae. Their name comes from a pair of slender feeler-like appendages at their tail end. Tassel tails are fast-moving and difficult to catch as they scurry about among fragments of litter or particles of soil. They are related to silver fish, a serious household pest in some places.

Another very small, delicate creature looked a lot like a tassel tail but was slightly larger and had a pair of forceps-like brown pincers at the tip of its abdomen. This insect is a japygid. Its name, *Japyx sp.* is apparently derived from Greek mythology, and refers to *iopys*, the northwest wind. The japygid has no common name.

Tassel tails and japygids are predators. Some tassel tails capture and eat midge larvae. Japygids prey on soil mites and other soil-dwelling insects, catching them and holding them with their pincers while they feed.

There were also fragile little symphilids which look like tiny, whitish centipedes, to which they are related. Unlike centipedes, they have no more than twelve pairs of legs. Some were mere white flecks, while the largest were only a little over an eighth-inch. Using cracks, crevices, and small tunnels formed by decaying plant roots, these tiny chilopods move freely and rapidly through the soil. They live entirely on plants and some can be serious pests in gardens. The ones in litter and humus feed on dead leaves and bits of moss, eating out the soft parts and leaving a skeleton of leaf veins.

Nematodes—delicate, tiny, unsegmented round worms which are generally considered to be among the most abundant of soil animals—were found in fair numbers in Berlese samples. Strangely, we have no record of their being in the hand-sorted samples of duff taken during Prof's study. We may have overlooked them since they are so small. In the summer of 1937, however, we did find nematodes in the larger samples taken from deeper soil. Certain nematodes graze on fungi or plant roots; some feed on bacteria; and still others prey on nematodes, white worms, protozoans, and other microorganisms. Under favorable conditions nematodes digest decaying plants and animals rapidly and do much toward enriching the soil with organic matter.

In our handsorting, we also encountered geophilids, centipedes, tiny snails, and small spiders. Many of the creatures we recovered were immature. Though we learned little about them, we know that every one of them had a role in the complex world of the forest floor.

In many ways an ancient forest resembles a city. Giant fir trees were the skyscrapers in our forest. Recent research has revealed that the canopies of such trees, which tower 250 to 300 feet (twenty to thirty stories) above the ground, overflow with a bounty of nitrogen-fixing lichens and myriad other kinds of life. These skyscrapers of the forest may be likened to the imposing edifices of corporate officials. However, in this analogy there is one supremely significant difference: the trees shower their wealth *on* the entire forest, continually enriching the whole community, while corporate officials plot to extract wealth *from* people. Also, marvel of marvels, hidden beneath the surface of the forest floor a great web of fungal filaments—mycorrhizae—entwine the roots of the trees, constantly supplying them with essential nutrients from the soil.

Beneath the skyscrapers, hemlocks (80 to 150 feet tall), scattered maples, and cedars form the forest's office buildings, apartments, and department stores.

Still closer to the ground are clusters of young hemlocks and patches of sword fern, salal, huckleberries, and Oregon grape—the suburban shops and residential areas. Each layer of plants with its distinctive animal life is a mini-community. The creatures in these layers interact somewhat as humans do in commuting from suburbs to the inner city.

The trees are the pillars, or primary support, providing food and shelter and creating an environment upon which the other kinds of life depend. The many-layered canopy captures sunlight and, through photosynthesis, transforms energy from the sun into food. Much of the sunlight is absorbed as it filters downward through the layers of trees. Some is reflected, and only a small percent of the full amount reaches the leaves on the plants of the lower layers. Virtually no sunlight makes it all the way to the forest floor.

The huge trees temper the weather, moderating wind force and extremes of temperature. Their needle-laden branches intercept winter snows and summer showers, keeping the ground beneath them relatively dry. When curtains of fog roll in from the ocean, those same towering crowns offer a place for moisture to condense and drip to the absorbent cushion of sponge-like forest floor.

Birds and mammals, amphibians, mollusks, and hordes of insects and other invertebrates make their homes and find their food in the forest, each with its own choice of level.

A visitor returning season after season to an undisturbed ancient forest will note little change in the appearance of the forest floor, though needles are constantly sifting down, twigs and branches break and tumble to the ground, lichens shower from the crowns high above, herbs wither and die, and birds, mammals, and other animals deposit excrement and leave their carcasses. Snags topple over or crumble, forming masses of decomposing wood. Giant trees, uprooted by windstorms, crash to the earth. Tons of plant and animal debris fall upon the forest floor each year. Why isn't the forest smothered under all this debris, this waste?

In the forest there is no such thing as waste: everything is recycled. A vast network of creatures breaks down, alters, and restructures, through countless steps, this "waste" from the forest. Those creatures are decomposers, the forest's recyclers.

Modern man with all his technology has only recently begun developing procedures for recycling the wastes he has created, but the forest's recycling system was perfected eons ago. Just as equipment which keeps a city functioning is stored in a series of levels beneath the buildings, so, too, is the life-sustaining support system of the forest found in a series of levels extending downward beneath the trees and forest floor, a Lilliputian world not readily seen by humans.

Decomposers in this microcosm remove from dead and decaying materials the nutrients on which new life builds. They keep the dynamos of the forest city charged and running.

At the top of this hidden world is a sponge-like mat of dead twigs, fir and hemlock needles, decaying leaves, and bits of wood. Mosses cover the forest floor in all but the most dense thickets of young trees. Tree limbs and logs of many sizes in all stages of decay lie on the moss or make up a layer of litter beneath the moss. This mat protects the forest floor inhabitants in many ways. It keeps them from drowning or being washed away by winter's rains. It also blankets them from the cold. By releasing moisture slowly, it acts as an air conditioning system in summer, regulating humidity and preventing sudden temperature changes.

Below the raw litter, or duff, is the humus layer, relatively shallow, but dark and rich and composed of bits of organic material.

Beneath those layers is the soil itself which has been changed, through eons of time, from the underlying primordial rock into material which will sustain the many kinds of life found in the forest city.

Once the forest's debris becomes litter, recyclers take over. They work constantly on the great mass of plant and animal material that reaches the forest floor. That debris provides the livelihood for myriad beings which attack the materials in a mind-boggling variety of ways. What they accomplish is amazing.

These recyclers fall rather naturally into four groups. One consists of slugs, snails, beetles, earthworms, and others which creep upon the mosses and litter, stalking unwary prey, or sniff and slurp decaying matter, or channel deep into the soil much like the roto-rooters that clean out drainage pipes for our homes.

A second group of recyclers, the woodworkers, are beetles, carpenter ants, termites, and fungus gnats which chew or bore their way into woody materials in various stages of decay.

A third group is made up of small mammals, many of which are highly selective in their choice of food.

Finally, there are untold millions (or billions) of tiny organisms living in darkness on, or in, the floor of the forest. This battalion of unseen

Lilliputians moves about in countless uncharted highways: in the mat of humus, in log fragments, or in the soil, stirring and restructuring the area in which they live. Many use channels left vacant when plant roots die, while others tunnel beneath the surface or dig burrows down into the soil or create passages in woody materials. Great numbers live in the microscopic spaces between particles of soil. They accomplish tremendous things as they explore the world beneath our feet.

The making of humus—the rich, dark, organic part of the soil—is the business of all these creatures. Each kind has its place in the process.

Animals that are nibblers or grazers—soil mites, symphilids, nematodes, springtails, wireworms, crane fly larvae, fungus gnat larvae, snails, slugs, weevils, and earthworms—chew off fragments of seeds, cones, dead mosses, tiny pieces of bark, cambium or wood, bits of fruiting bodies of woody fungi and mushrooms, and pieces of fungal filaments. Some also ingest bacteria or soil along with their food. These primary decomposers feeding on freshly-fallen plant debris or on fungi extract the digestible substances from the things they eat—proteins, carbohydrates, and fats (lipids)—but leave the materials from which the extractions were taken relatively unchanged. These animals produce large amounts of excrement with a high fiber content.

Then a host of different species, including springtails, soil mites, millipedes, and others go to work on that excrement. They chew up tough fibers, softening them and breaking them into lesser size for other smaller organisms to reduce even more. The decaying matter usually passes through a series of animals, accumulating at each step as droppings or "crumbs" made up of particles of ever lesser size but chemically altered very little if at all. Enchytraeids and earthworms hasten the decomposition by mixing soil with organic substances. Sowbugs blend microscopic grains of sand and bits of leaf litter and wood residue into a fine powder. This decomposition is very slow but eventually results in a dark mass—humus.

Lilliputian predators—insects, spiders, geophilids, false scorpions, and so on—are also busy throughout the recycling process. Their predation helps to regulate population levels and health.

As this long series of different beings feeds on bits of plants, scraps of dead insects, minute pellets of feces, snippets of organic matter, and one another, altering the organic substances, they gradually free life-sustaining nutrients from the litter and pass those nutrients from organism to organism until the vital nutrients reach mycorrhizal fungi or nitrogen-fixing bacteria.

Then, in the dark recesses of root channels and microscopic soil spaces, life in its beautifully integrated diversity completes the task. Mycorrhizal fungi and nitrifying bacteria remove the life-sustaining nutrients from the bodies of organisms and, forming associations with young roots of trees and other plants, transfer to them these vital organic and inorganic compounds which have passed through many recyclers' bodies.

From vole, or slug, or beetle to bacterium or mycorrhiza, the vital connection flows, transforming death—former life—into new life, creating a living bridge resembling the placenta which links a human mother to her unborn child.

That is the essence of the forest.

Epilogue

One Last Look:
I Never Thought it
Would be Like This!

Aﬀﬁﬂ RAY'S DEATH in May 1983, realizing that it would be unwise, and even unsafe, for me to remain alone in the large home under the oak trees, I moved into Hillside Manor, a newly constructed retirement complex on the west fringe of McMinnville. There, I began writing the story of the forest.

A year later, on October 26, I returned to Saddleback Mountain with Larry Whalon, a Linfield student who had learned of my research and wanted to visit the research site. On our way in, as we drove to our parking place beyond Salmon River, I became aware of change and disturbance.

Then, emerging from the trees on the far side of the river, I stopped, shocked with disbelief. Where I had expected to see a thriving young forest, a great swath of clearcut stretched before me. Mere days before, hemlocks, firs, and cedars had soared skyward in that place. Countless kinds of life, off-spring of the ancient forest I had known there fifty years earlier, had found home in that sheltering environment,

Now, only occasional battered stumps, shards of shrubs, and a few splintered saplings relieved a barrenness scraped free of everything organic. Every trace of the spongy forest floor with its untold abundance of life was gone. Woody debris mixed with soil lay pushed into long windrows many feet high, smothering acres of ground while awaiting the torch.

So this is modern clearcutting, I thought.

Presently, my companion asked, "When you were a student at Linfield, did it ever occur to you that Saddleback Mountain might be like this?"

"Oh, no!" I retorted. "I never thought it would be like *this*. How could I have imagined such an atrocity? Fifty years ago, I knew that the ancient forest might be logged someday. And it was logged, in 1940, but not stripped clear of all life, like this. The philosophy of logging was different then. At that time the monstrous machines used here hadn't even been invented. No way could I have anticipated this devastation.

"I've seen clearcutting from a distance, but even that has never remotely resembled this rape of the land! No, **no**, I never thought it would be like this!"

Why, I wondered, *is this area being logged? These trees seem far too small for this to be a profitable logging venture. There are new plantings nearby. They may be preparing the area for a tree farm, but how can anything thrive after this abuse of the land?*

From where we were, at the edge of the clearcut near the river, a gravel road toiled upward toward young forest and our destination, the research station, which had been the center of my ecological studies for more than fifty years. On that mountainside above us a straight, stark boundary of uncut young trees stood like a wall beside that road.

Threatening clouds urged us up the mountain. Hail began pelting down. Hurrying to shelter among the trees, we entered a different world. A heavy carpet of fresh-washed moss padded the rock road, making it a joy to walk upon. Huge stumps and moss-covered logs along both sides reminded me of that earlier forest.

Ten years had passed since I was here last. The whole appearance of the place had changed so much that I wondered if I would lose my way as we moved along the poorly defined trail. When we arrived at the research area, I needed a few minutes to get my bearings.

The forest was strikingly more open than it had been the last time I saw it. At my last visit the thickets were becoming more sparse as dead lower limbs of young trees dropped off and, in the years since then, countless smaller or less favorably placed trees had died, gradually opening the canopy. Great numbers of losers in this competition for light now lay strewn over the ground, while others leaned helter-skelter against the survivors.

This present forest was nearly as unobstructed as the ancient forest had been. In a way even more so, for, though the slender young trees were more plentiful, they did not block the view like the trunks of the old giants.

Strangely, where the terrain had seemed nearly level before, it now seemed slanted, sloping abruptly into the adjacent gullies. Those ancient trees had provided a feeling of stability which was lacking now since all that remained of them were masses of upturned roots and logs which had not been removed in that first selective logging.

Above the openings made by salvage logging the canopy had nearly closed, eliminating the lanes where, in summertime, head-high bracken fern had once made passage almost impossible. Now, only a few puny bracken plants lived on.

Beneath the dense canopy of the thickets, mushrooms of many kinds dotted the ground and grew lavishly on decaying logs and dead branches, but only a few highly shade tolerant plants survived—mosses, some ferns, tiny patches of oxalis, a bit of salal, and an occasional red huckleberry bush.

This forest which had sprung up—not from its own ashes, like the Phoenix, but from remnants of the virgin forest—seemed to speak to us. The tall young firs, some nearly two feet in diameter, pleaded for a longer period of growth. It was dark and very quiet. No bird sang. Not a sound was heard. It was a place of hushed reverie.

Sick at heart, I brooded, *So this young forest is to be sacrificed, too, destroying our research area. This is private land, and I know the owners can do whatever they wish with it. They will market only what is profitable and will replant that ravished soil with Douglas-fir seedlings, replacing this forest with a single species to be treated as a crop—a monoculture—which they will harvest at an early age. In such a plantation there will be no mixture of plants to serve as buffers against pests and disease or to provide the diversity needed by all ecosystems. I wonder if this is an example of the "new forestry"?*

Recurring showers nudged us homeward. Emerging from the mute young forest, I was touched to find several clumps of bleeding heart plants still feathery-leafed and full of blossoms on the forested side of the logging road.

We continued down the road to our vehicle parked near the clear, rushing stream at the edge of the clearcut.

As we stood gazing over the area, Larry said, "If logging progresses further, this stream will be choked with debris and loaded with silt during the rainy months. What will happen to its spawning beds?"

We wondered about the many kinds of life in the forest—all the webs of interacting plants, birds, mammals, insects, and other lowly creatures—many of which are still unknown to science.

We learned later that this clearcut was, indeed, preparation for a tree farm and that Stimson Lumber Company, which now owned the land, planned to cut the research area within a few years.

I thought this would be my last visit to the mountain. I didn't want to experience the pain of viewing the final devastation of that forest which had played such a significant role in my life.

Nevertheless, on a mild sunny day in September 1995, accompanied by two members of the press, a former student friend who had arranged the trip, and a young forester from Stimson Lumber Company who served as guide, I visited Saddleback Mountain again for one last look.

In my mind was a map, an indelible picture of what had been. I felt confident that I could relocate at least the general area of the research. But much had changed. We crossed Salmon River and the second stream. There the old logging road up the mountain was invisible, impassable, overgrown with weeds and brush, and planted with young firs. Even the gravel was gone from the roadway. No trace hinted of the trail we had used for nearly half a century.

Our guide took us much higher on the mountain to a site from which he thought I might be able to recognize the locale of the study area. There the ground was not scraped and compacted as in the earlier clearcut, but it was disturbed, rough, treacherous, and littered with woody fragments, scattered helter-skelter—a shambles of the young forest so callously felled. A pile of weather-bleached slash, like a heap of old bones, blocked the view down the mountain. However, the location did provide a hazy, distant view northward, framed by Mt. Hebo, other mountains of the Coast Range, and clearcut—area after area of clearcut denuded of all native flora. Within that bowl, below the band of most recent clearcut, dense plantings of Douglasfirs, regular as bristles in a scrub brush, grew at the edges of patches of older clearcut.

In this vast sameness of altered terrain, with the familiar trails and roads gone and new ones bulldozed to take their places, we could not recognize where the research station had been. Only a surveyor with rod, transit, and compass could relocate that site. No significant landmarks or relics of the old study area remained. It was as though the site had never existed.

On that December day six decades earlier when I looked out over a nearly uninterrupted expanse of ancient trees from a point near where I was now standing, I did not have an inkling that it would ever be like this. The cathedral-like forest I learned to know and love became my life's inspiration. It was gone. That forest was **not** just trees.

Appendix

A Note on Scientific Names

DURING THE YEARS since I began this study the terminology used in biological classification has changed significantly. Back then, scientists recognized two kingdoms: Plant and Animal. All living things were in one or the other. If they were mobile, they were placed in the Animal Kingdom. If they were immobile, they were called Plants. Most plants made their own food through photosynthesis.

Now, the tiny single-celled "animals" we called Protozoa are known as Protoctista and the single-celled Cyanophyta (blue-green "algae") we knew as algae are recognized as bacteria. Protozoa and algae seem to have disappeared from the formal scientific dictionary.

Taxonomists have revised their classifications reflecting new methods and insights. We now have a system consisting of two great divisions (super kingdoms) which include five lesser divisions (kingdoms).

These great divisions are separated on the basis of whether or not their cells have a membrane-bounded nucleus. The life forms that do not have nuclei are classified as Prokaryota. That division is made up of a single kingdom which consists exclusively of bacteria. All other cellular life forms are known as Eukaryota because they have nuclei. In that division there are four kingdoms.

Today, the five kingdoms listed below are generally recognized. Their names are in Latin in keeping with the system invented by Swedish scientist Linnaeus, who introduced his binomial system in 1735 using Latin names, the scholarly language of the day.

Modern Classification Summary

A. Prokaryota (non-nucleated single-celled organisms)
    1. Kingdom Monera: bacteria

B. Eukaryota (nucleated, single and multicellular organisms)

    I. *Protoctista:* single-celled organisms such as amoebas, diatoms and slime molds, and the multicellular seaweeds

    II. *Fungi:* non-motile, spore-forming organisms that lack chlorophyll: molds, mushrooms, cup fungi, and truffles

    III. *Plantae:* multicellular, chiefly photosynthetic, organisms, such as mosses, club mosses, and ferns, as well as herbs, shrubs, and trees

    IV. *Animalia:* animals of all kinds: insects, spiders, mites, worms, slugs, snails, frogs, salamanders, snakes, birds, mammals, and still others

Naming of Plants and Animals

Changes have also occurred in the naming of the plants and animals of the forest. By way of explanation, I'll give a few examples.

When Prof began his study, the common name of the Douglas-fir tree lacked the hyphen; the scientific name for the tree was *Pseudotsuga mucronata*. However, by the time Prof and I published our theses, that name had been changed to *Pseudotsuga taxifolia*. Now, the prescribed scientific name is *Pseudotsuga menziesii* and the common name is hyphenated. Also, we knew the Oregon grape as *Berberis nervosa*, but by the time Prof published his thesis its name had been changed to *Mahonia nervosa*.

At present the trend in classification of all vertebrate animals—amphibians, reptiles, birds, and mammals—is to combine all members of a species under the name, ignoring subspecies.

The story of Harris's woodpecker (a medium-sized, black woodpecker with a white back, a large bill, and a small red patch on the back of the head of males) is an interesting example of this.

When Prof was doing his research, we knew that bird as Harris's woodpecker, a clearly recognizable subspecies of the widely-distributed hairy woodpecker. Harris's woodpecker has less white on it and its underparts are smoky gray or light smoky brown.

Stanley Jewett identified our woodpecker as Harris's, and every bird book available to us at that time listed birds of that description living in the "humid coastal belt" from British Columbia to northern California as Harris's woodpecker, a distinct subspecies. Arthur Cleveland Bent says in

Life Histories of North American Woodpeckers, "...it was recognized, described, figured, and named by [Audubon] in honor of his friend Edward Harris."

That bird was still recognized as Harris's woodpecker in 1940 when Gabrielson's and Jewett's *Birds of Oregon* came out, but, sometime between then and 1961 when Peterson's *A Field Guide to Western Birds* was published, it became listed simply as a "Hairy Woodpecker" with no mention of its being a distinctive subspecies.

That woodpecker of our forest, whatever its accepted common name, Harris or Hairy, has been known by several different scientific names during these sixty years: P.A. Taverner, in *Birds of Canada,* published in 1934, says, "Harris's Woodpecker...*Dryobates villosus harrisi* is the Hairy Woodpecker of the Pacific Coast from Oregon north to Sitka. It is a very different looking bird from those before mentioned, having the whites of the breast decidedly tinged with smoky browns and the spots of the wing coverts almost absent." At that time the Hairy woodpecker was known as *Dryobates villosus villosus;* in 1961 it became *Dendrocopus villosus* in Peterson; and in 1980, *the Audubon Society Encyclopedia of North American Birds,* by John Terres, listed it as *Picoides villosus.* According to the American Ornithologists' Union that is still its name.

When Stanley Jewett identified our little redbacked voles, he said they were known as the California red-backed mouse, with the name *Clethrionomys californica californica.* Now, in the Peterson field guide *Mammals,* published in 1976, they are the western red-backed vole, *Clethrionomys occidentalis,* and are given no recognition as a subspecies.

The little weasel we called the Puget Sound weasel is now known as the long-tailed weasel, *Mustela frenata.*

The orange-bellied salamander is called the rough-skinned newt, *Taricha granulosa.*

The Oregon, or red, salamander is *Ensatina eschscholtzii.*

The woodland salamander, *Plethodon vehiculum,* is now the western red-backed salamander.

And so it goes. I have no inkling as to how many changes have been made in the names of insects.

Time marches on, and so does the changing of common and scientific names. As a result, I have chosen to retain in *Not Just Trees* the names we used during our studies and to cite in this appendix only a few of the changes.

The author, with Timmie, at the research site, 1959.

Glossary

Abiotic: All non-living elements of the environment, e.g. weather and soil.

Aestival Aspect: Summer, the season of maturity and fruition (chpt. 40).

Algae: Organisms that are photosynthetic, non-vascular, unicellular to multicellular. They are usually assigned to Kingdom Protoctista (or Protista).

Amphibian: Vertebrates usually possessing gills when immature, lungs as adults, e.g. frogs and salamanders.

Annelids: Organisms with true segmentation and a coelom belonging to the phylum Annelida, e.g. earthworms, enchytraeids ("White worms"), leeches, and clamworms.

Arthropods: Organisms characterized by having segmented bodies with jointed legs and bodies covered with a chitinous exoskeleton, e.g. insects, spiders, and mites.

Aspection: The seasonal rhythm in organisms produced by physical and biological changes they experience. Keyed particularly to appearance, growth, and reproduction of plants and animals. Also used to describe the passage of seasons in a community (chpt. 40).

Aspirator: An instrument used to remove fluids, gasses, or objects, e.g. insects, by suction from a cavity or surface such as a beating square.

Atmometer: An instrument used to measure rates of evaporation.

Autumnal Aspect: Autumn, the season of harvest and storage (chpt. 40).

Beating square: A one-meter canvas square, supported by two crossed sticks, from which insects and spiders can be collected when shaken from the boughs of trees or shrubs. A semi-quantitative sampling technique.

Biotic: All living organisms.

Chrysalis: Golden-colored, parchment-like case of some butterfly pupae; a type of cocoon.

Cocoon: Protective case for pupal stage of insects with complete metamorphosis, e.g. beetles, flies, wasps, and moths.

Coelom: A true body cavity found in insects, earthworms, and vertebrates.

Commensalism: A form of symbiosis where the host is neither harmed nor benefited by the presence of the guest species. The guest usually gains both "room and board."

Community: Refers, in an ecological sense, to all organisms living in a defined area.

Duff: Decaying organic litter constituting the upper layer of a forest floor, e.g. leaves, twigs, needles, and cones.

Dynamics: The study of the interrelationships within an ecosystem, both biotic and abiotic.

Ecology: The study of the interrelationships of organisms to one another and to their abiotic environment. This term comes from the Greek root *oikos* (house or home) and *logos* (discourse). Logos is now used frequently as indicating a science or scientific study. Though the term ecology is now used (or misused) in many ways, it was originally intended to be the study of living things at home in the natural world.

Ecosystem: Any specified area that includes both biotic and abiotic entities and their interactions, e.g. marine, terrestrial, and lacustrine (lakes).

Elytron (elytra, pl.): The hardened anterior (outer) wing sheath typically found in Coleoptera (beetles).

Emerginine Sector: Third subdivision of the Hiemal Aspect characterized by an awakening of organisms (chpt. 40).

Endoskeleton: An internal bony, cartilaginous, or chitinous supporting structure of vertebrates and some invertebrates.

Entomology: The study of insects.

Environment: The sum of biotic and abiotic influences acting on an organism, in part or whole.

Enzymes: Protein substances that function as catalysts to facilitate chemical reactions.

Eukaryote: A great division of cellular organisms comprising four Kingdoms: Protoctista, Fungi, Plantae, and Animalia. All possess membrane-bound organelles (nuclei, mitochondria, and chloroplasts). See also Prokaryotes.

Exoskeleton: Any hardened external supporting structure such as the chitinous coverings of insects and crustaceans or the shells of snails and clams.

Gills: In mushrooms, the plate-like structures that contain spore bearing elements and spores.

Habitat: The natural place of residence of plants and animals. Includes biotic and abiotic factors.

Hectare: Metric measure of an area equivalent to about two-and-a-half acres. A standard ecological measurement of area.

Hibernine Sector: Second subdivision of the Hiemal Aspect characterized by deep biotic dormancy (chpt. 40).

Hiemal Aspect: The winter season. Consists of three subdivisions, or sectors: hiemine, hibernine, and emerginine (chpt. 40).

Horizontal precipitation: Moisture which, after condensing on vegetation, such as trees in a forest, later falls to the ground.

Humus: Dark-colored upper soil layer, composed of partially decayed organic matter.

Hyperparasite (superparasite): A parasite that is parasitic within or upon another parasite.

Hypha (hyphae, pl.): A thread-like filament that is the vegetative component of a fungus. Many hyphae together form a mycelial mat of a fungus.

Lichen: A fungal/algal mutualistic symbiont.

Lignin (wood): An organic substance which acts as a binder for the wall materials in mechanical tissues in plants.

Metamorphosis: Process of going through a change in structure and form by an organism during its development. Insects may be divided on the basis of degrees of metamorphosis from none (collembolans) to complete, where the sequence is egg, larva, pupa, adult, as in coleopterans, dipterans, and lepidopterans.

Mushrooms: The fruiting bodies (reproductive structures) of most visible fungi (Ascomycota and Basidiomycota), e.g. gill and pore mushrooms.

Molting: The periodic shedding of external shell or skin. Allows for growth in insects and other arthropods.

Mycelium: A mass of intertwined hyphae that form a fungal vegetative body.

Mycorrhizae: A group of fungi that form a mutual relationship with the roots of plants. The mycorrihizal associations are crucial to the growth, development, and health of plants.

Naiads: Immature (nymphal) stage of aquatic insects which have an incomplete (hemimetabolic) metamorphosis growth pattern, e.g. dragonflies.

Nematodes: Any worms of the Phylum Nematoda with long, cylindrical, unsegmented bodies and a heavy cuticle. They are ubiquitous in occurrence and many are parasitic upon plants and animals.

Niche: Ecological term denoting the functional role of an organism in its community, e.g. aphids sucking juices from a rose.

Nymphs: Wingless, or incompletely winged, juvenile stage of insects having incomplete metamorphosis (hemimetabolic).

Ovipositor: In insects a specialized structure for depositing eggs.

Parasite: An organism that benefits in its relationship with a host that is negatively affected, e.g. parasitic wasps.

Parthenogenesis: The development of new individuals (female) from an unfertilized egg, e.g. aphids.

Photometer: A light meter which records the amount (intensity and fluctuation) of light striking a specific area.

Photosynthesis: The process whereby carbon dioxide and water are converted to natural sugars, and oxygen is emitted as a by-product. Energy from the sun is required to initiate this process.

Population: Within a species, an interbreeding group of organisms living in a specified area. Populations may also be subspecies.

Pre-oral digestion: Digestion outside the body by enzymes and other juices.

Prokaryote: One of two great divisions of cellular organisms. Prokaryotes are characterized by having no membrane-enclosed organelles (mitochondria, nuclei, or chloroplasts). Kingdom Monera. See also eukaryotes.

Protista: A Kingdom containing unicellular eukaryotes, such as amoebae, paramecia, euglena, and trypanosomes. Does not include multicellular macro-algal forms (seaweeds) or water molds.

Protoctista ("protokista"): A highly diverse Kingdom including all unicellular eukaryotes ("protists") plus the multicellular "algae" and water molds.

Pupa: A stage in insects with complete metamorphosis where the developing insect is enclosed in a case (cocoon) while its tissues are broken down and reorganized prior to its emergence as an adult.

Rhizome: A horizontal stem at or below the surface as in irises, some grasses, or strawberries.

Slime molds: Gymnomycota. A group of fungal-like organisms in the Kingdom Protoctista characterized by an aggregative stage (plasmodium), unicellular swarming cells, and spores.

Soil: Layer of weathered rock, lying above unweathered parent rock, containing organic material in various states of decay and life forms. Soil may, or may not, be covered by a layer of vegetation.

Spar tree: In a high-lead logging operation, a living tree that is limbed, topped, and used as a pole from which pulley blocks are hung. Used for moving downed trees to a central area for transport.

Species: A population of sexually reproducing organisms that are actually, or potentially, capable of producing viable offspring. Species are circumscribed by a reproductive barrier.

Succession: An ongoing process; a series of steps wherein one ecological community is replaced by another.

Symbiosis: Different species living together in some kind of defined relationship, e.g. mutualism, parasitism, and commensalism.

Vernal Aspect: Middle to late spring activities and appearances of vegetation in an area (chpt. 40).

Prof, the author, and crew at the site, 1937.

References
and Readings

Abrams, L. *Illustrated Flora of the Pacific States*, 4 vols. Palo Alto: Stanford University Press, 1940.

Ackerman, J. *Notes From the Shore*. New York: Viking, 1955.

Allen, T.B., ed. *Wild Animals of North America*. Washington, D.C.: The National Geographic Society, 1979.

Anderson, O.M. *Seeker at Cassandra Marsh*. New York: Christian Herald Books, 1978.

Anderson, R.M. "Methods of Collecting and Preserving Vertebrate Animals." *Bulletin of the National Museum of Canada*, Department of Mines and Resources, Ottawa, No. 69 (1948).

Arno, S.F. and R.P. Hammerly. *Northwest Trees*. Seattle: The Mountaineers, 1977.

Bailey, F.M. *Handbook of Birds of the Western United States*. Boston: Houghton Mifflin Co., 1902.

Bailey, V. *The Mammals and Life Zones of Oregon*. North American Fauna No. 55. Washington, D.C.: U. S. Department of Agriculture, Bureau of Biological Survey, 1936.

Baldwin, E.M. *Geology of Oregon*. Eugene: University of Oregon Cooperative Bookstore, 1959.

Becking, R.W. *Pocket Flora of the Redwood Forest*. Covelo, Ca.: Island Press, 1982.

Bent, A.C. *Life Histories of North American Birds*. Washington, D.C.: Smithsonian Institution; U.S. National Museum Bulletins, 1927.

Bever, D.N. *Northwest Conifers: A Photographic Key*. Portland: Binford and Mort, 1981.

Borrer, D.J. and D.M. DeLong. *An Introduction to the Study of Insects.* New York: Rinehart and Co., 1964.

Burt, W.H. and R.P. Grossenheider. *Mammals.* 3d ed. R.T. Peterson Field Guide. Norwalk: The Easton Press, 1976.

Bury, R.B. and M. Martin. "Comparative Studies on the Distribution and Foods of Plethodontid Salamanders in the Redwood Region of Northern California." *Journal of Herpetology* 7(1973; 4): 331-335.

Chief of Engineers. *Topographic Quadrangles, Oregon.* Denver: War Department, U.S. Army Corps of Engineers, 1941.

Clement, F.E. and V.E. Shelford. *Bio-ecology.* New York: John Wiley & Sons, 1939.

Croker, R.A. *Pioneer Ecologist: The Life and Work of Victor Ernest Shelford, 1877-1968.* Washington, D.C.: Smithsonian Institution Press, 1991.

Coombs, A.J. *Dictionary of Plant Names.* Portland: Timber Press, 1985.

Devine, R. "The Little Things That Run the World." *Sierra* 81(1996; 4): 32-37, 62-63.

Deyrum, M.A. *The Insect Community of Dead and Dying Douglas Fir, 1. The Hymenoptera.* Ecosystem Analytical Studies Bulletin 6. Coniferous Forest Biome. Seattle: University of Washington Press, 1975.

_____. "The Insect Community of Dead and Dying Douglas Fir: Diptera, Coleoptera and Neuroptera." Ph.D. diss., University of Washington, 1976.

Dirks-Edmunds, J.C. "A Comparison of Biotic Communities of the Cedar-Hemlock and Oak-Hickory Associations. *Ecological Monographs* 7(1947): 235-260.

_____. "Ecology of a Douglas Fir-Hemlock Forest Community." *Linfield College Bulletin* 59(1962; 8): 1-5, 16.

_____. "Habits and Life History of the Bronze Flea Beetle, *Altica tombacina* (Mannerheim) (Coleoptera-Chrysomelidae)." *Northwest Science* 39(1965; 4): 148-158.

Eastman, D.C. *Rare and Endangered Plants of Oregon.* Wilsonville, Or.: Beautiful America Publishing Co., 1990.

Elder, F. *Crisis in Eden.* Nashville: Abingdon Press, 1970.

Elliott, C., ed. *Fading Trails: The Story of Endangered American Wildlife.* New York: The Macmillan Co., 1942.

Essig, E.O. *Insects and Mites of Western North America.* New York: The Macmillan Co., 1958.

Evans, H.E. *Life on a Little-Known Planet.* Chicago: University of Chicago Press, 1984.

Farb, P. *Living Earth.* New York: Harper & Brothers, 1959.

_____. *The Insects.* New York: Life Nature Library, Time, Inc., 1962.

Fender, W.M. and D. McKey-Fender. "Oligochaeta: Megascolecidae and Other Earthworms from Western North America." In *Soil Biology Guide,* edited by D. Dindal. New York: John Wiley and Sons, 1990.

Forbes, S.A. "The Lake as a Microcosm." *Illinois Natural History Survey Bulletin* 15 (1925; 9): 537-550.

Franklin, J.F. and C.T. Dyrness. *Natural Vegetation of Oregon and Washington.* Corvallis: Oregon State University Press, 1973.

Furniss, R.L. and V.M. Carolin. *Western Forest Insects.* Washington, D.C.: U.S. Government Printing Office; U.S. Department of Agriculture, Forest Service, Miscellaneous Publication no. 1339, 1977.

Gabrielson, I.N. and S.G. Jewett. *Birds of Oregon.* Corvallis: Oregon State Monographs, Studies in Zoology 2, 1940.

Gilkey, H.M. *Weeds of the Pacific Northwest.* Corvallis: Oregon State College, 1957.

_____ and L.J. Dennis. *Handbook of Northwestern Plants.* Corvallis: Oregon State Bookstores, Inc., 1980.

Hall, E. and K.R. Kelson. *The Mammals of North America,* vol. 2. New York: Ronald Press, 1959.

Hall, E.R. *The Mammals of North America,* vols. 1 and 2. New York: John Wiley & Sons, 1981.

Harper, A.B. *The Banana Slug: A Close Look at a Giant Forest Slug of Western North America.* Aptos, Ca.: Bay Leaves Press, 1988.

Harrington, H.D. and L.W. Durrell. *How to Identify Plants.* Chicago: Swallow Press, 1957.

Hickman, J.C., ed. *The Jepson Manual: Higher Plants of California.* Berkeley: University of California Press, 1993.

Hitchcock, C.L., A. Cronquist, M. Owenby, and J.W. Thompson. *Vascular Plants of the Pacific Northwest,* 5 vols. Seattle: University of Washington Press, 1969.

Hitchcock, C.L. and A. Cronquist. *Flora of the Pacific Northwest.* Seattle: University of Washington Press, 1973.

Howard, A. *The Soil and Health-Farming and Gardening for Health or Disease.* New York: The Devin-Adair Co., 1947.

Hyman, L.H. *The Invertebrates,* vol. 6, Mollusca I. New York: McGraw-Hill Book Co., 1967.

Imms, A.D. *A General Textbook of Entomology.* London: Methuen, 1934.

Kelly, D. and G. Braasch. *Secrets of the Old Growth Forest.* Salt Lake City: Gibbs Smith Publisher, 1988.

Kendeigh, S.C. *Animal Ecology.* Englewood Cliffs: Prentice-Hall, 1961.

Kirk, D.R. *Wild and Edible Plants of Western North America.* Happy Camp, Ca.: Naturegraph Publishers, 1975.

Knapp, R.H. and H.B. Goodrich. *Origins of American Scientists.* Chicago: University of Chicago Press, 1952.

Kozloff, E.N. *Plants and Animals of the Pacific Northwest.* Seattle: University of Washington Press, 1976.

Krajick, K. "The Secret Life of Backyard Trees." *Discover* 16 (1995; 11): 92-101.

Krantz, G.W. *A Manual of Acarology.* Corvallis: Oregon State University Bookstore, Inc., 1978.

Kuhnelt, W. *Soil Biology, with Special Reference to the Animal Kingdom.* East Lansing: Michigan State University Press, 1976.

LaBonte, J.L. "Feeding Behavior in the Carabid Beetle, *Promecognathus.*" *Bulletin of the Oregon Entomological Society* 86 (1983): 681-682.

Lane, F.C. *The Story of Trees.* Garden City: Doubleday & Co., 1953.

Leopold, A. *A Sand County Almanac.* London: Oxford University Press, 1968.

Levi, H.W. and L.R. Levi. *Spiders and Their Kin.* New York: Golden Press, 1990.

Li, C.Y., C. Maser, Z. Maser, and B.A. Caldwell. "Role of Three Rodents in Forest Nitrogen Fixation in Western Oregon: Another Aspect of Animal-Mycorrhizal Fungus-Tree Mutualism." *Great Basin Naturalist* 46 (1986; 3): 411-414.

Macnab, J.A. "Biotic Aspection in the Coast Range Mountains of Northwestern Oregon." *Ecological Monographs* 28(1958): 21-54.

_____ and J.C. Dirks. "The California Red-Backed Vole in the Oregon Coast Range." *Journal of Mammalogy* 22(1941): 174-180.

Maser, C. *Forest Primeval.* San Francisco: Sierra Club Books, 1989.

_____ and E. Hooven. "Behavior and Food Habits of Captive Pacific Shrews." *Northwest Science* 48(1974): 81-95.

_____, J. Trappe, and R.A. Nussbaum. "Fungus Small-Mammal Interrelationships with Emphasis on Oregon Coniferous Forests." *Ecology* 59(1978; 4): 799-809.

_____ and J. Trappe, eds. *The Seen and Unseen World of the Fallen Tree.* U.S. Department of Agriculture, Forest Service, Pacific Northwest Forest and Range Experimental Station, General Technical Report PNW-164, 1984.

Margulis, L. and K.V. Schwartz. *Five Kingdoms: An Ilustrated Guide to the Phyla of Life on Earth.* San Francisco: W.H. Freeman and Co., 1982.

McArthur, L.A. *Oregon Geographic Names*. Portland: Oregon Historical Society, 1974.

McKey-Fender, D. "Distribution in Certain Lucanidae. *Coleopterists Bulletin* 2(1948): 5.

McMinn, H.E. and E. Maino. *An Illustrated Manual of Pacific Coast Trees*. Berkeley: University of California Press, 1946.

Moffett, M.W. "Tree Giants of North America." *National Geographic* 191(1997; 1): 44-61.

Murie, O.J. *A Field Guide to Animal Tracks*. R.T. Peterson Field Guide. Boston: Houghton Mifflin Co., 1954.

Neihaus, T.F. and C.L. Ripper. *Pacific States Wildflowers*. R.T. Peterson Field Guide. Boston: Houghton Mifflin Co., 1976.

Odum, E.P. *Fundamentals of Ecology*. Philadelphia: W.B. Saunders Co., 1971.

Orr, W.N. and E.L. Orr. *Geology of the Pacific Northwest*. New York: McGraw-Hill, 1996.

Paciuni, G. *Simon & Schuster's Guide to Mushrooms*. New York: Simon & Schuster, 1981.

Palmer, G. and M. Stuckey. *Western Tree Book: A Field Guide for Weekend Naturalists*. Beaverton, Or.: Touchstone Press, 1987.

Payne, J.A. "A Summer Carrion Study of the Baby Pig, *Sus scrofa*, Linnaeus." *Ecology* 46(1965): 492-602.

Peattie, D.C. *Flowering Earth*. New York: The Viking Press, 1939.

Peck, M.E. *A Manual of Higher Plants of Oregon*. Portland: Binford and Mort, 1941.

Peterson, R.T. *A Field Guide to Western Birds*. Cambridge: The Riverside Press, 1961.

Pojar, J. and A. MacKinnon. *Plants of the Pacific Northwest Coast*. Redmond, Wa.: Lone Pine Publishing, 1994.

Pyle, R.M. *Wintergreen*. New York: Houghton Mifflin, 1986.

Randall, W.R., R.F. Keniston, D.N. Bever, and E.C. Jensen. *Manual of Oregon Trees and Shrubs*. Corvallis: Oregon State Bookstores, 1981.

Read, D. "The Ties That Bind." *Nature* 388: 517-518.

Ross, C.R. *Trees to Know in Oregon*. Extension Bulletin 697. Corvallis: Cooperative Extension Service and Oregon State Forestry Department, 1967.

Ross, R.A. and H.L. Chambers. *Wildflowers of the Western Cascades*. Portland, Or.: Timber Press, 1988.

Saint John, A.D. "Little Things." *Northwest Parks & Wildlife* 3(1993; 1): 18-21.

Scott, L.M. "Military Beginnings of the Salmon River Highway." *Oregon Historical Quarterly*, 1935.

Sharnoff, S.D. "Lichens." *National Geographic* 191(1977; 2): 58-70.

Shelford, V.E., ed. *Naturalist Guide to the Americas.* Baltimore: The Williams & Wilkins Co., 1926.

————. *The Ecology of North America.* Urbana: University of Illinois Press, 1963.

Simard, S.W., D.A. Perry, M.D. Jones, D.D. Myrold, D.M. Durall, and R. Molina. "Net Transfer of Carbon Between Ectomycorrhizal Tree Species in the Field." *Nature* 388: 579-582.

Slater, J.R. and C.D.F. Brockman. "Amphibians of Mt. Rainier National Park." *Mt. Rainier National Park Nature Notes* 14(1936): 1-28.

Smith, A.H. *Mushrooms in Their Natural Habitats.* Portland: Sawyers, Inc., 1949.

————. *The Mushroom Hunters Field Guide*, rev. ed. Ann Arbor: University of Michigan Press, 1964.

Smith, J.P. *Vascular Plant Families.* Eureka, Ca.: Mad River Press, 1977.

Spellenberg, R. *The Audubon Society Field Guide to North American Wildflowers, Western Region.* New York: Alfred A. Knopf, 1979.

Stevens, J.E. "Scientist Successfully Deploys Wasps in War to Avert Famine." *The* [Portland] *Oregonian*, Sept. 8, 1993.

Strickler, D. *Forest Wild Flowers.* Columbia Falls, Mt.: The Flower Press, 1988.

Stuller, J. "Fight, Fight, Fight, Fight, Banana Slugs, Banana Slugs." *Audubon* 89(1987; 2): 128-130.

Sudworth, G.B. *Forest Trees of the Pacific Slope.* New York: Dover Publications, 1967.

Swan, L.A. and C.S. Papp. *The Common Insects of North America.* New York: Harper & Row, 1972.

Taverner, P.A. *Birds of Canada.* Bulletin no. 72. National Museum of Canada, Department of Mines, Ottawa, 1934.

Teale, E.W. *The Insect World of J. Henre Fabre.* New York: Dodd, Mead & Co., 1949.

Terres, J.K. *The Audubon Society Encyclopedia of North American Birds.* New York: Alfred A. Knopf, 1980.

Thoreau, H.D. *The Maine Woods.* New York: W.W. Norton, 1950.

Tilden, J.W. and A.C. Smith. *A Field Guide to Western Butterflies.* R.T. Petersen Field Guide. Norwalk: The Easton Press, 1986.

Trappe, J.M. and C. Maser. "Ectomycorrhizal Fungi: Interactions of Mushrooms and Truffles with Beasts and Trees. Mycorrhizae." In *Mushrooms and Man: An Interdisciplinary Approach to Mycology,* edited by T. Walters. Forest Service, U.S. Department of Agriculture, 1977.

Underhill, J.E. *Roadside Flowers of the Northwest.* Blaine, Wa.: Hancock House, 1981.

_____. *Upland Field and Forest Wildflowers.* Blaine, Wa.: Hancock House, 1986.

Wallwork, J.A. *The Distribution and Diversity of Soil Fauna.* New York: Academic Press, 1976.

Whitney, S. *A Sierra Club Naturalist Guide: The Pacific Northwest.* San Francisco: The Sierra Club, 1989.

Whittlesey, R. *Familiar Friends: Northwest Plants.* Portland: Rose Press, 1985.

Welty, C.J. *The Life of Birds.* Philadelphia: W.B. Saunders Co., 1962.

Wilson, E.O. *The Diversity of Life.* Cambridge: Harvard University Press, 1992.

_____. *Naturalist.* Washington, D.C.: Island Press, 1994.

Yocum, C. and R. Dasman. *The Pacific Coastal Wildlife Region.* Happy Camp, Ca.: Naturegraph Publishers, 1965.

Zimmer, C. "The Web Below." *Discover* 18 (1997; 11): 44.

Jane Claire Dirks-Edmunds. *Photo courtesy Olan Mills Portrait Studios.*

About the Author

J ANE CLAIRE DIRKS-EDMUNDS, Emerita Professor of Biology at Linfield College, McMinnville, Oregon, attained her doctorate in zoology at the University of Illinois in 1941 under the tutelage of the eminent ecologist, Dr. Victor E. Shelford. At that time few women held doctorates in science and even fewer in the little-known field of ecology. She was the first woman Ph.D. on the Linfield faculty, where she served for more than thirty years.

After a childhood on the open prairie, she had her first encounter with a forest at the age of twelve when her family moved from Kansas to the Puget Sound region of Washington. She loved it. After a few months, the Dirkses moved from that paradise to farm land in the Umpqua Valley near Roseburg, Oregon. There she attended high school, graduated, and worked as file clerk in a bank for two years before enrolling at Linfield College.

Halfway through her sophomore year, on a visit to the ecological research site of her mentor, Professor James A. Macnab, she was hooked. She hadn't seen anything like that magnificent forest since leaving Puget Sound. From that day, the forest on Saddleback Mountain in Oregon's Coast Range was never far from her mind. She had discovered the life-shaping love of her life.

Dr. Dirks-Edmunds's dedication to that forest persisted through her years of teaching; her retirement; on past the death of her husband and helpmate, Milton Ray Edmunds; and has culminated in *Not Just Trees*, a very personal account of the life of one forest, observed for six decades by one woman.

Index